Train

Recognition Guide

Jane's

Train
Recognition Guide

Howard Johnston & Ken Harris

Collins

First published in 2005 by **Collins**

HarperCollins Publishers
77-85 Fulham Palace Road
Hammersmith
London w6 8jb
UK
www.collins.co.uk

HarperCollins Publishers Inc
10 East 53rd Street
New York
NY 10022
USA
www.harpercollins.com

www.janes.com

ISBN: 0-00-718226-0
ISBN-10: 0-06-081895-6 (in the US)
ISBN-13: 978-0-06-081895-1 (in the US)

HarperCollins books may be purchased for
educational, business or sales promotional
use. For information in the United States,
please write to: Special Markets
Department, HarperCollins Publishers,
Inc., 10 East 53rd Street, New York, NTY
10022.

The name of the "Smithsonian",
"Smithsonian Institution", and the sunburst
logo are registered trademarks of the
Smithsonian Insitution.

Printed and bound by Imago in Thailand

05 06 07 08   10 9 8 7 6 5 4 3 2 1

Contents

Introduction

INTRODUCTION

It has been estimated there is 1.1 million kilometres (700,000 miles) of operational railway across the world, and the future of steel wheels on steel rails is promising. Contrary to popular opinion, traffic is rising is most countries. Developing nations recognise the value of railways as a convenient form of transport for bulk commodities and high volumes of passengers over both short and longer distances. North America and Europe, which witnessed a sharp decline in rail use over the last 50 years in the face of air and road competition, are reviving their interest in a big way to reflect the sea change in opinion in the face of pressure from environmentalists who argue that congestion and pollution will become major issues in the first quarter of the 21st century.

High levels of efficiency and reliability are crucial for the economic case for railway development, and the method of traction – the power that moves the train from A to B - has now settled firmly on diesel and electric power.

Although some of the early designs of locomotives that replaced steam were at best questionable, once the high capital cost is overcome, they can achieve a life of half a century with relative ease if regular maintenance is performed, and their modular nature often allows major component replacement to be carried out to improve their performance or carry out bespoke duties. Improving electronics technology is playing a useful part here, and more affluent railroads are reconditioning their locomotives for sale to other countries rather than consigning them to the scrapyard. The main frames of a locomotive, the fundamental bedrock, can theoretically last for ever, with expendables such as engines, traction equipment, electronics, wheels and superstructure relatively low cost items to replace.

As will be seen in this book, it is American thinking which dominates the world scene in supply of locomotives, ending an era of countries employing their own manufactured products. European designs, particularly from France and Germany, have made a significant impact in the high speed and commuter market, even in the Far East, traditionally tough markets for outsiders to crack.

WHAT IS A LOCOMOTIVE?

A locomotive is a vehicle that provides the motive power for a train, comprising passenger or freight vehicles. While it has traditionally been placed at the front of a train, this is now often not the case because it is a time-wasting exercise to have to change ends for a return journey. With passenger trains, the use of through wiring allows a cab in the last coach to be used as a remote-control driving area, with the locomotive staying at the other end, hence the description push-pull. For increased power, some trains have locomotives permanently placed at each end, while commuter trains often have their power equipment installed in a compartment of the passenger coach.

Note: The word 'locomotive' is used throughout this book to differentiate from the 'engine', which is regarded as the diesel power unit inside the box.

THE HISTORY OF LOCOMOTIVES

Steam propulsion reigned supreme from the early years of the 19th century until the 1930s, when it was recognised that it suffered serious disadvantages compared with diesel and electric power, and it was after the Second World War that American thinking inspired a worldwide takeover. Even so, steam is expected to survive on China's main lines into the middle of this decade, and some minor industrial lines in Australasia and Cuba use steam power because suitable fuel is in abundance, and the lives of the systems could be so short that it is not worth considering replacement.

The first-ever steam locomotive to run on rails was built by Richard Trevithick, and first ran in South Wales, UK, on February 21 1804. Named Penydarren, it was not a great success, and it would take another 20 years for the concept to be sufficient refined to be economically practical. George Stephenson, an engineer in the North East of Britain, persuaded the manager of a colliery to build a steam locomotive with flanged wheels, and this paved the way for today's railways to replace canals and waggonways for the movement of goods and labour needed for industrial growth.

The achievement of 126mph by British streamlined 'A4' 4-6-2 No. 4468 Mallard on 3 July 1938 was recognised as the zenith of steam, as well as the upper performance limit. Within another decade, steam development had virtually ceased worldwide. Although electric locomotives had been available since the 1890s, their use was always going to be limited because of the need to install overhead wires and land-based generating equipment and sub-stations.

Diesel-electric locomotives had first appeared in the modest volumes in the United States in the 1920s, but by the late 1930s, General Motors' Electromotive Division (EMD) had perfected the diesel-electric concept, first for passenger service, and later heavy freight.

By the 1960s, with world hostilities generally resolved and money and materials in greater supply, most Western countries had completely replaced steam in commercial service. Other propulsion methods such as gas turbines were experimented with without great success. Underground and inner-city railways with their unique 'clean air' atmospheric characteristics have relied on electric power since the 1890s, and this was followed by the development of electric tramways and eventually some main lines.

DEFINITIONS

Diesel

The diesel engine, a compression ignition unit, relies on fuel being ignited by the high temperature of a compressed gas, rather than a separate source of energy, such as a spark plug. It was invented and patented in 1892 by Dr Rudolf Diesel (born Paris 1858, died on the English Channel 1913) in 1892, and although intended to run on a variety of fuels including coal dust, it performed best on oil.

The prototype was built at the MAN factory at Augsburg, Germany, and in the railway application was found to work best with an attached gearbox (diesel-mechanical) or electric generator (diesel-electric). The first low-powered

Introduction

versions proved useful in switching (marshalling) yards where they were cleaner and unlike steam locomotives available for use 24 hours a day at the turn of a switch.

There are two classes of diesel engines: two-stroke and four-stroke, and many larger diesels operate on the latter cycle. Banks of cylinders are used in multiples of to 12.

While diesel engines create soot from their exhausts, there is less carbon dioxide released into the atmosphere. The addition of a turbocharger or supercharger greatly increases fuel economy and performance.

Diesel-mechanical

The simplest form of diesel locomotive has a mechanical gearbox, but this is normally only suitable for shunting (switching) or in passenger railcars because a 400hp (300kW) output is the recognised power limit.

Diesel-electric

The most common form of transmission for a diesel locomotive is electric. The power unit drives a generator or alternator, which transfers energy to the wheels via electric motors. In simple terms, the traction 'box on wheels' is an electric locomotive which carries its own generating station along with it.

Particularly in the United States, locomotives working in multiple are capable of hauling double-stacked freight trains a couple of miles long. High speeds are also possible, and in the United Kingdom High Speed Trains with a locomotive at each end have reached over 140mph (225 km/h) on test, and 125mph (200 km/h) in daily service since the mid-1970s.

Diesel-hydraulic

In the early 1950s, Germany actively pioneered pursued the diesel-hydraulic locomotive concept, which by definition uses hydraulic transmission to transmit the power from the diesel engine to the wheels. A torque converter, enclosed in an oil-filled bath, consists of three main parts, two of which rotate, and one fixed. In passenger units, a fluid flywheel also acts as a special gear for high speed operation.

Although attractive because of their high power output and low comparable weight, their higher maintenance cost has seen them lose favour. In the United Kingdom, the large fleet built under licence was eliminated after little over a decade in favour of diesel-electrics.

Gas Turbine

Jet-type engines widely used in aircraft have failed to find favour on railways because of their high fuel consumption which has not been economically possible since the late 1960s. Power reaches the wheels via an electrical transmission similar to a diesel-electric locomotive, with the turbines running at constant speed to drive the generator.

Electric

Electric locomotives are power transmission devices, collecting energy from an external source, overhead wires, or a third rail. Once the high cost of electrifying track has been met, electric trains are much cheaper to run than diesel ones, and capable of much greater acceleration and faster braking. This makes them ideal for intensive local passenger services as well as ultra-high speed main line trains where a suitably high-powered diesel engine would not be easily available. The world speed record for a wheeled train was set in 1990 by a French TGV which reached 320 mph (515 km/h).

Alternating current is now the normal installation although earlier systems are still commonplace, such as in South Africa, Spain, Switzerland, the Netherlands and Belgium (direct current, overhead or third-rail collection).

Magnetic Levitation

In the future, magnetic levitation (maglev) may gain favour. Electrically powered trains employ a motor which floats the train above the rail without the need for wheels, greatly reducing friction. The installation cost is very high, but an experimental Japanese magnetic train has reached 343mph (552 km/h).

Introduction

Major national networks

	Km	M
Algeria	3,973	2,469
Angola	2,761	1,716
Argentina	34,463	21,418
Armenia	852	529
Australia	41,588	25,846
Austria	6,024	3,744
Azerbaijan	2,122	1,319
Bangladesh	2,706	1,682
Belarus	5,523	3,432
Belgium	3,471	2,157
Bolivia	3,519	2,187
Bosnia and Herzegovina		
	1,021	635
Botswana	888	552
Brazil	31,543	19,603
Bulgaria	4,294	2,669
Burma	3,955	2,458
Canada	64,994	40,392
Chile	6,585	4,092
Colombia	3,304	2,053
Costa Rica	950	590
Croatia	2,296	1,427
Cuba	3,442	2,139
Czech Republic		
	9,462	5,880
Democratic Republic of Congo		
	4,772	2,966
Denmark	3,164	1,966
Dominican Republic		
	1,503	934
Ecuador	966	600
Egypt	5,105	3,173
Estonia	968	602
Finland	5,850	3,636
France	32,682	20,311
Gabon	814	506
Georgia	1,612	1,002
Germany	45,514	28,285
Ghana	953	592
Greece	2,571	1,598
Guatemala	886	551
Guinea	1,115	693
Hungary	7,875	4,894
India	63,518	39,474
Indonesia	6,458	4,013
Iran	7,201	4,475
Ireland	3,312	2,058
Italy	19,493	12,114
Japan	23,168	14,398
Kazakhstan	13,601	8,453
Kenya	2,778	1,726
Latvia	2,347	1,459
Lithuania	1,998	1,242
Madagascar		
	732	455
Mainland China		
	71,600	44,497
Malawi	797	495
Malaysia	2,418	1,503
Mexico	19,510	12125
Moldova	1,300	808
Morocco	1,907	1,185
Mozambique	3,123	1,941
Namibia	2,382	1,480
Netherlands	2,808	1,745
New Zealand		
	3,898	2,422
Nigeria	3,557	2,211
North Korea		
	5,214	3,240
Norway	4,178	2,596
Pakistan	8,163	5,073
Peru	1,829	1,137
Philippines	897	557
Poland	23,420	14,555
Portugal	2,850	1,771
Republic of China (Taiwan)		
	1,108	689

Republic of Congo		
	894	556
Romania	11,385	7,075
Russia	87,157	54,165
Saudi Arabia		
	1,392	865
Senegal	906	563
Serbia and Montenegro		
	4,059	2,522
Slovakia	3,668	2,280
Slovenia	1,201	746
South Africa		
	22,298	13,857
South Korea	3,125	1,942
Spain	14,189	8,818
Sri Lanka	1,508	937
Sudan	5,978	3,715
Sweden	11,481	7,135
Switzerland		
	4,511	2,803
Syria	2,743	1,705
Tanzania	3,690	2,293
Thailand	4,071	2,530
Tunisia	2,152	1,337
Turkey	8,607	5,349
Turkmenistan		
	2,440	1516
Uganda	1,241	771
Ukraine	22,473	13,966
United Kingdom		
	16,893	10,498
United States		
	194,731	121,018
Uruguay	2,073	1,288
Uzbekistan	3,950	2,455
Vietnam	3,142	1,952
Zambia	2,173	1,350
Zimbabwe	3,077	1,912
	Km	**M**
World total	1,122,650	697,688

Railway Companies

National railways are many and varied in structure, and the use of acronyms abound, not least because the bodysides of locomotives are often only large enough to carry the initials of their owner or operator.

This list details the major networks, and some no longer in existence have been included where they may concern the entries in this book.

Africa

Algeria	Algerian National Railways
	Société Nationale des Transports Ferroviaires (SNFT)
Angola	Benguela Railway Companhia do Caminho de ferro de Benguela
Benin	Benin Railways
	Organisation Commune Benin-Niger des Chemins de Fer et des Transports (OCBN)
Botswana	Botswana Railways (BR)
Burkina-Faso	
	SOPAFER-B
	Société de gestion du patrimoine ferroviaire du Burkina
Cameroon	Cameroon National Railways
Authority	Regie Nationale des Chemins de Fer du Cameroun (REGIFERCAM)
Egypt	Egyptian National Railways (ENR)
Eritrea	Eritrean Railways
Ethiopia	Djibouti-Addis-Ababa Railway
	Chemins de Fer Djibouti-Ethiopien (CDE)
Gabon	Gabon State Railways
	Office du Chemin de Fer Transgabonais (OCTRA)
Ghana	Ghana Railways Corporation (GRC)
	Hedjaz Railway
Ivory Coast	Ivory Coast Railway (SIPF)
Kenya	Kenya Railways Corporation (KR)

Introduction

Liberia	Bong Mining Co	Israel	Israel Railways (IR)
Madagascar	Madagascar Railways	Japan	Japan Railway Construction Public

Liberia   Bong Mining Co
Madagascar Madagascar Railways
              Société d'Etat Réseau National des
              Chemins de Fer Malagasy (RNCFM)
Malawi   Central East African Railways
Mauritania   Mauritania National Railways
              (TFM-SNIM)
Morocco   Moroccan Railways
              L'Office National des Chemins de Fer
              du Maroc (ONCFM)
Mozambique
              Mozambique State Railways (CFM)
Namibia   TransNamib Transport (Pty) Ltd
Nigeria   Nigerian Railway Corporation (NRC)
Republic of the Congo
              Congo-Ocean Railway
              Chemin de Fer Congo-Océan (CFCO)
Sudan   Sudan Railways (SRC)
Swaziland   Swaziland Railway (SR)
Syria   Syrian Railways
              Chemins de fer Syriens (CFS)
Tanzania   Tanzania-Zambia Railway Authority
              Tanzanian Railways Corporation (TRC)
Togo   Togo Railways
              Société nationale des Chemins de Fer
              Togolais (SNT)
Tunisia   Tunisian National Railways (SNCFT)
Zambia   Zambia Railways Ltd (ZR)
Zimbabwe   National Railways of Zimbabwe (NRZ)

Asia

Bangladesh Bangladesh Railway (BR)
Burma   Union of Burma Railways
China   Chinese Railways (CR)
              Kowloon-Canton Railway Corporation
              MTR Corporation
India   Indian Railway Board (IR)
Iran   Iranian National Railways Company
              Rahahane Djjomhouriye Eslami Iran
              (RAI)
Iraq   Iraqi Republic Railways (IRR)

Israel   Israel Railways (IR)
Japan   Japan Railway Construction Public
              Corporation (JRCC)
              JR – formerly Japanese National
              Railways - JR Hokkaido, JR East, JR
              Central, JR West, JR Shikoku, JR
              Kyushu, JR Freight
              Asa Kaigan Railway
              Chizu Express
              Eizan Electric Railway
              Hankyu Railway
              Hanshin Electric Railway
              Hojo Railway
              Hokuetsu Express
              Ihara Railway
              Ise Railway
              Keihan Electric Railway
              Keihin Electric Express Railway
              Keio Electric Railway
              Keisei Electric Railway
              Kinki Nippon Railway (Kintetsu)
              Kishu Railway
              Kita Kinki Tango Railway
              Kobe Electric Railway
              Kobe Rapid Railway
              Kurihara Den'en Railway
              Metropolitan Intercity Railway
              Company
              Miki Railway
              Mizuma Railway
              Nagoya Railroad (Meitetsu)
              Nankai Electric Railway
              Nishikigawa Railway
              Nishi-Nihon Railway
              Nose Electric Railway
              Noto Railway
              Odakyu Electric Railway
              Ohmi Railway
              Sagami Railway
              Sanyo Electric Railway
              Seibu Railway

	Shigaraki Kougen Railway		Pacific National
	Tobu Railway		Pilbara Rail
	Tokyo Kyuko Electric Railway		Queensland Rail (QR)
	Tosa Kuroshio Railway		V/Rail
	Wakasa Railway		VicRail (Victorian Railways)
	Yokohama MinatoMirai Railway		West Coast Railway
Jordan	Aquaba Railway Corporation (ARC)		Westrail (Western Australian
	Hedjaz Jordan Railway (HJR)		Government Railways)
Lebanon	Lebanon State Railways	New Zealand	
	Chemins de Fer l'Etat Libanais (CEL)		Connex Aukland
Malaysia	Express Rail Link		Toll Rail
	Keretapi Tanah Melayn		Tranz Scenic
	(Malayan Railway) (KTM)		

| Nepal | Janakpur Railway (JR) | **Europe** | |

Europe

	Nepal Government Railway (NR)	Albania	Albanian Railways/Hekurudhat
North Korea			Shqiperise (HSh)
	Korean State Railways (ZCi)	Austria	Austrian Federal
Pakistan	Pakistan Railways (PR)		Railways/Österreichische
Philippines	Philippine National Railways (PNR)		Bundesbahnen (ÖBB)
Saudi Arabia			Montafonerbahn Schruns (MBS)
	Saudi Railways Organisation (SRO)		Styrian Provincial
South Africa			Railways/Steiermärkische
	South African Railways (SAS/SAR)		Landesbahnen (STLB)
South Korea Korail		Belarus	Belarussian Railways/Belaruskaya
Sri Lanka	Sri Lanka Government Railway (SLR)		Chyhunka (BCh)
Taiwan	Taiwan Railway Administration (TRA)	Belgium	Belgian National Railways/Nationale
Thailand	State Railways of Thailand (SRT)		Maatschappij der Belgische
Turkey	Turkish State Railways/Turkiye		Spoorwegen/Société Nationale des
	Cumhuriyeti Devlet Demiryollari		Chemins de fer Belges (NMBS/SNCB)
	(TCDD)	Bosnia	Bosnia-Herzegovina Railways Public
Vietnam	Vietnam Railways		Corporation (BH)
	Duong Sat Viet Nam (DSVN)	Bulgaria	Bulgarian State Railways/Bâlgarski
			Dârzhavni Zheleznitsi (BDZh)
Australasia		Croatia	Croatian State Railway/Hrvatske
Australia	Australia Railroad Group (ARG)		Zeljeznice (HZ)
	Connex Melbourne	Czech Republic	
	Great Southern Railway (GSR)		Czech Railways/Zeské Dráhy (CD)
	Hamersley Iron Ore Railway	Denmark	Danish State Railways/Danske
	Interail		Statsbaner (DSB)
	National Rail Corporation Ltd (NR)		Arriva Danmark
	New South Wales State Rail Authority		Gribskovbanen/Hillerød-

Introduction

	Frederiksværk-Hundested Jernbane (GDS/HFHJ)		Organismós Sidiródromon Éllados (OSE)
	Odderbanen (Hads-Ning Herreders Jernbane (HHJ)	Hungary	Magyar Államvasutak Rt/Hungarian State Railways Co Ltd(MÁV)
	Capital City Local Railways/Hovedstadens Lokalbaner (HL)		Sopron-Ebenfurti Vasut/Györ-Sopron-Ebenfurth Railway (GySEV)
	Høng-Tølløse Jernbane/Odsherreds Jernbane (HTJ/OHJ)	Ireland	Iarnród Éireann/Irish Rail
		Italy	Ferrovie Italiane Dello Stato/Italian State Railways (FS)
	Lollandsbane (LJ)		North Milan Railway (FNME)
	LilleNord (LN)	Latvia	Latvian Railway/Latvijas Dzelzcels) (LDZ)
	Lyngby-Nærum Jernbane (LNJ)		
	North Jutland Railways/Nordjyske Jernbaner (NJ)	Lithuania	Lithuanian Railways/Lietuvos gelezinkeliai (LG)
	Eastern Railway - Østbanen Østsjællandske Jernbaneselskab (ØSJS)	Luxembourg	
	Lemvigbanen (Vemb-Lemvig-Thyborøn Jernbane (VLTJ)		Luxembourg Railways/Chemins de Fer Luxembourgeois (CFL)
	Western Railway – Vestbanen/Varde-Nørre Nebel Jernbane (VNJ)	Moldova	Moldovan Railway/Caile Ferate din Moldova (CFM)
Estonia	Raudteeamet/Estonian Railway Administration	Netherlands	
			ACTS Nederland
	Estonian Railways/Eesti Raudtee (EVR)		Netherlands Railways/Nederlandse Spoorwegen (NS)
	Edelaraudtee South-West Railway		NoordNed
	Elektriraudtee Electric Railway		Syntus
Finland	Valtionrautiet/Finnish Railways (VR)		Connexxion
France	Chemins de Fer de Provence (CFP)	Norway	CargoNet
	Eurotunnel		Flåm Railway
	Régie Autonome des Transports Parisiens/Paris Transport Authority (RATP)		Norwegian State Railways/Norges Statsbaner (NSB)
	Société Nationale des Chemins de fer Français/French National Railways (SNCF)	Poland	Polish State Railways/Polskie Koleje Panstwowe (PKP)
		Portugal	Portuguese Railways/Caminhos de Ferro Portugueses (CP)
Germany	Deutsche Bahn Gruppe/German Railways Group (DB)	Romania	Romanian National Railways/Cailor Ferate Romane (CFR)
	Deutsche Bundesbahn/German Federal Railways (DB)	Russia	Russian Railways/Rossiiskie Zhelezni Dorogi (RZhD)
	Deutsche Reichsbahn/East German Railways (DR)	Serbia and Montenegro	
Greece	Hellenic Railways Organization -		Montenegrin Railways/Zeleznice Crne Gore (ZCG)

	Railways of Republika Srpska/Zeljeznice Republika Srpske (RS)
Slovakia	Slovakian Republic Railways/Zeleznice Slovenskej Republiky (ZSR)
Slovenia	Slovenian Railways/Slovenske Zeleznice (SZ)
Spain	Catalan Railways/Ferrocarrils de la Generalitat de Catalunya (FGC)
	EuskoTren (Basque Railways/Eusko Trenbideak)
	Majorcan Railway Services/Serveis Ferroviaris de Mallorca (SFM)
	Narrow Gauge Railways/Ferrocarriles de Vía Estrecha (FEVE)
	Sóller Railway/Ferrocarril de Sóller (FS)
	Spanish National Railways Red Nacional de los Ferrocarriles Españoles (RENFE)
	Valencian Government Railways/Ferrocarrils de la Generalitat Valenciana (FGV)
Sweden	Arlanda Express
	Green Cargo
	Swedish State Railways/Statens Järnvägar (SJ)
	Tågkompaniet
	TGOT Trafik
Switzerland	Aare-Seeland Mobil (ASm)
	Aigle-Leysin Bahn (AL)
	Aigle-Ollon-Monthey-Champery (AOMC)
	Aigle-Sepey-Diablerets (ASD)
	Appenzeller Bahn (AB)
	Baselland Transport (BLT)
	Bergbahn Lauterbrunnen-Mürren (BLM)
	Berner Oberland Bahnen (BOB)
	Bex-Villars-Bretaye (BVB)
	Blonay-Chamby (BC)

BLS Löschbergbahn (BLS)
Bodensee Toggenburg Bahn (BT)
Bremgarten-Dietikon Bahn (BD)
Brienz Rothorn Bahn (BRB)
Chemin de fer Bière-Apples-Morges (BAM)
Chemin de Fer Montreux-Oberland Bernois (MOB)
Chemins de Fer du Jura (CJ)
Chemins de Fer Electriques Veveysans (CEV)
Chemins der fer Fribourgeois (GFM - Gruyére-Friburg-Morat)
Dampfbahn Furka-Bergstrecke (DFB)
Emmental-Burgdorf-Thun Bahn (EBT)
Ferrovia Lugano-Ponte Tresa (FLP)
Ferrovie Autolinee Regionali Ticinesi (FART)
Frauenfeld-Wil Bahn (FW)
Gornergrat-Monte Rosa Bahnen (GGB)
Jungfraubahn (JB)
Luzern-Stans-Engelberg Bahn (LSE)
Martigny-Châtelard (MC)
Matterhorn-Gotthard-Bahn (MGB - merger of FO and BVZ)
Meiringen-Innertkirchen Bahn (MIB)
Montreux-Glion-Rochers de Naye (MBG)
Montreux-Glion-Rochers de Naye (MVR)
Pilatusbahn (PB)
Regionalverkehr Bern-Solothurn (RBS)
Regionalverkehr Mittelland (RM)
Rhätische Bahn/Viafier Retica (RhB)
Rigi-Bahnen (RB)
Schweizerische Südostbahn (SOB)
Schynige Platte-Bahn (SPB)
Sihltal-Zürich-Uetliberg-Bahn (SZU)
Städtische Verkehrsbetriebe Bern (SVB)

Introduction

Swiss Federal Railways (SBB/CFF/FFS
Schweizerische
Bundesbahnen/Chemins de fer
Fédéraux/Ferrovie Federali Svizzere)
Transport Montreux-Vevey-Riviera
(MVR - merger of MGN and CEV)
Transports Publics du Chablais (TPC -
merger of AL, AOMC, ASD and BVB)
Trogenerbahn (TB)
Verkehrsbetriebe Zürich (VBZ)
Vitznau-Rigi Bahn (VRB)
Waldenburgerbahn (WB)
Wengneralpbahn (WAB)

Ukraine   UZ (Ukrainian National Rail Transport
               Administration - Ukrzalzalinytsya)
United Kingdom
               Arriva Trains Wales
               British Rail (1948-1996)
               c2c
               Central Trains
               Chiltern Railways
               Direct Rail Services (DRS)
               English Welsh & Scottish Railway
               (EWS)
               Eurostar (UK) Ltd
               Eurotunnel
               First Great Western
               First Great Western Link
               First ScotRail
               First Trans Pennine Express
               Freightliner
               Gatwick Express
               GB Railfreight (GBRf)
               Great North Eastern Railway (GNER)
               Heathrow Express
               Hull Trains
               Island Line
               Mendip Rail
               Merseyrail
               Midland Mainline
               Northern Rail

Northern Ireland Railways (NIR)
One
Silverlink
South Eastern Trains
South West Trains
Southern
Thameslink
Virgin CrossCountry
Virgin West Coast
Wessex Trains
West Anglia Great Northern (WAGN)

North America

Canada   Canadian National Railways (CN)
               Canadian Pacific Railway (CP)
               Government of Ontario Railway (GO)
               VIA Rail Canada
Mexico   Ferrocarriles Nacionales de Mexico
               (National Railways of Mexico)
               Ferromex
               Ferrosur
               Transpotación Ferroviaria Mexicana
United States
               Alaska Railroad
               Amtrak
               Atchison, Topeka & Santa Fe Railroad
               (AT&SF)
               Bay Area Rapid Transit (BART)
               Boston & Maine Corporation (B&M)
               Baltimore and Ohio Railroad (B&O)
               Burlington Northern Railroad (BN)
               Burlington Northern Santa Fe Railway
               (BNSF)
               Central Pacific Railroad
               Chessie System
               Chicago, Burlington and Quincy
               Railroad
               Chicago Great Western Railway
               Chicago, Milwaukee, St. Paul & Pacific
               Railroad (Milwaukee Road)
               Chicago, South Shore & South Bend

Railroad

Chicago, Rock Island & Pacific
Railroad

Conrail

CSX

Delaware & Hudson Railway

Denver & Pacific Railroad

Denver & Rio Grande Railroad

Denver & Rio Grande Western
Railroad (D&RGW)

Denver & Salt Lake Railroad

Denver, Northwestern & Pacific
Railroad

Detroit, Toledo & Ironton Railroad

Florida East Coast Railway

Great Northern Railroad

Illinois Central Gulf Railroad

Katy

Kansas City Southern Railway

Long Island Rail Road

Maine Central Railroad

Massachusetts Bay Transportation
Authority (MBTA)

Manitou and Pike's Peak Railway

Milwaukee Road

Missouri Pacific Railroad

Mount Washington Cog Railway

New York Central Railroad

New York, New Haven & Hartford
Railroad

New York & Atlantic Railway

Norfolk Southern Railroad

Northern Indiana Commuter
Transportation District (NICTD)

Northern Pacific Railroad

Pacific Electric Railway

Penn Central Railroad

Pennsylvania Railroad

Reading Railroad

Soo Line Railroad

Sounder Transit Board

Southeastern Pennsylvania Transit
Authority (SEPTA)

Southern Pacific Railroad (SP)

Union Pacific Railroad (UP)

Wabash Railroad

Western Pacific Railroad

Virginia Railway Express

South America & Central America

Argentina	Ferrocarriles Argentinos/Argentine Railways (FA)
	Rio Gallegos – Rio Turbino Industrial Railway (RFIRT)
Bolivia	Empresa Nacional de Ferrocarriles/Bolivia National Railways (ENFE)
Brazil	Carajás Railway (EFC)
	Central Atlantic Railway (FCA)
	Ferronorte
	Ferrovia Bandeirantes (Ferroban)
	MRS Logistica
	Rede Ferrovairia Federal/Brazilian Federal Railways (RFFSA)
	Vitoria A Minas Railway (EFVM)
Chile	Empresa de los Ferrocarriles del Estado/Chilean State Railways (EFE)
Colombia	Ferrocarriles Nacionales de Colombia/National Railways of Colombia
Costa Rica	National Atlantic Railroad
	Pacific Electric Railroad
Cuba	Ferrocarriles Nacionales de Cuba/Cuban National Railways (FdeC)
Ecuador	Empresa Nacional de los Ferrocarriles del Estado/State Railways of Ecuador (ENFE)
Guatemala	Ferrocarril de Guatemala/Guatemala Railway (FEGUA)
Guyana	Guyana Railways
Honduras	Honduras National Railway Ferrocarril Nacional de Honduras

Introduction

About this book

The world railway scene is an ever-changing one, and inevitably mirrors the volatile political and economic conditions that prevail in many countries. Over the last decade, the decision of governments to discharge financial responsibility to the private sector has resulted in wholesale upheaval and abandonment of tradition values. Locomotives and rolling stock are frequently interchanged between networks, resulting in a change of livery, branding and fleet numbering. Modifications are also often carried out to reflect changes in traffic patterns - the loss of a particular business stream, or the winning of a new contract.

Much of the technical information in this book has been supplied by national companies, information which has occasionally been proved not to be accurate. The reader's tolerance is requested in instances where judgements have been made to put this data in line with what is considered more reliable statistics from independent sources.

For more detailed reading, it is recommended that you refer to *Jane's World Railways* and *Jane's Urban Transport Systems*.

African Trains

CLASS 040 YDA DIESEL LOCOMOTIVE

Algerian National Railways (SNTF) Class 040 YDA

On the narrow gauge lines in the centre and west of Algeria, which account for more than one third of the national network's route mileage, SNTF operates two GM diesel types, Class 040 YDA forming the larger series.

SUB-TYPES

At the same time as the Class 040 YDA locomotives were supplied, GM delivered five standard gauge Co-Co versions of the GL18M model to SNTF. They are designated Class 060 WDK. Six examples of a more powerful turbocharged variant, Model GT18LC-2M (SNTF Class 060 YDD) were supplied by GM Canada in 1989.

SPECIAL FEATURES

A major operator of GM traction, SNTF is the only user of Model GL18M in its narrow gauge A1A-A1A configuration. That apart, this is a

SPECIFICATION

Number series: 040 YDA 1-040 YDA 25
Total built: 25
Builder: GM
Date introduced: 1977
Track gauge, ft/ins (mm): 3 ft 5.35 in (1,055)
Axle arrangement: A1A-A1A
Power unit type: GM 8-645E 8-cylinder 2-stroke
Transmission: Electric - GM - alternator, four nose-suspended DC traction motors
Weight, tonnes: 72
Power rating, hp (kW): 1,070 (800)
Design speed, mph (km/h): 50 (80)

conventional GM product employing the proven 645E3 engine. The class forms the principal motive power on the railway's three unconnected narrow gauge lines which run south from Blida, west of Algiers, to Djelfa, from Ighilizane to Mahdia and from Tizi southwest to Béchar. Class 040 YDA handles both freight and passenger traffic.

CLASS 6FE ELECTRIC LOCOMOTIVE

Algerian National Railways (SNTF) Class 6FE

Algeria

These six-axle electric locomotives were supplied to SNTF by GEC Alsthom in the mid-1990s to supplement and to some extent replace East German-built machines on heavy phosphate traffic in the east of Algeria.

SPECIAL FEATURES

Algeria's only electrified main line is the steeply graded route in the east from the Mediterranean port of Annaba south to Tébessa and Djebel Onk, providing access to the reserves of iron ore and phosphates that form SNTF's principal freight commodities. Designed to haul trailing loads of up to 2,700 tonnes, the 14 Class 6FE locomotives were ordered from GEC Alsthom to modernise the LEW/Skoda-built Class 6CE machines which in turn had replaced French-built traction dating from the 1930s. Traction equipment for Class 6FE was developed and supplied by ACEC, a Belgian company that now forms part of Alstom.

SPECIFICATION

Number series: 6FE 01-6FE 14
Total built: 14
Builder: GEC Alsthom
Date introduced: 1995
Track gauge, ft/ins (mm): 4 ft 8.5 in (1,435)
Axle arrangement: Co-Co
Power supply system: 3 kV DC
Electrical equipment: ACEC - chopper control, six nose-suspended DC traction motors
Weight, tonnes: 132
Power rating, hp (kW): 2,400
Design speed, mph (km/h): 50 (80)
Additional features: multiple working; rheostatic braking

CLASS BD 3 DIESEL LOCOMOTIVE

Botswana Railways (BR) Class BD 3

The 500 mile (888 km) 3 ft 6 in (1,067 mm) gauge BR system is served by both GM and GE types, the most recent of which are these U15C machines from the latter manufacturer.

PRINCIPAL MODIFICATIONS

The present power rating of Class BD 3 is the result of an upgrading which raised output from the original 1,500 (1,120 kW).

SPECIAL FEATURES

Meeting BR's requirement for reliable, rugged traction, the BD 3 locomotives joined 10 Krupp-built GE UM20C machines dating from 1982 and 20 GM Model GT22LC-2 units. Examples of GE's standard U15C design and built by the company's Brazilian subsidiary, the class handles both freight and the limited amount of passenger traffic operated by BR.

SPECIFICATION

Total built: 10
Builder: GE do Brasil
Date introduced: 1991
Track gauge, ft/ins (mm): 3 ft 6 in (1,067)
Axle arrangement: Co-Co
Power unit type: GE 7FDL8 8-cylinder 4-stroke
Transmission: Electric – GE – alternator, six nose-suspended DC traction motors
Weight, tonnes: 98
Power rating, hp (kW): 1,800 (1,340)
Design speed, mph (km/h): 65 (107)
Additional features: multiple working

TYPE JT22MC DIESEL LOCOMOTIVE

Egyptian National Railways (ENR) Type JT22MC

Among the earlier types in a fleet that with one exception is all GM-powered is this series of mixed traffic Co-Cos supplied to the Egyptian system by GM from the late 1970s.

SPECIAL FEATURES

These 45 locomotives were supplied in four batches over a six-year period from 1979, production being shared between GM's EMD plant in the USA and its London, Ontario, facility in Canada. The JT22MC model employs the 12-cylinder version of the GM 645E3 power unit in a full width body with a cab design similar to that fitted to contemporary deliveries to Ireland and Spain. ENR uses the fleet as general-purpose locomotives.

SPECIFICATION

Number series: 3222-3240; 3445-3470
Total built: 45
Builder: GM
Date introduced: 1979
Track gauge, ft/ins (mm): 4 ft 8.5 in (1,435)
Axle arrangement: Co-Co
Power unit type: GM 645E3 12-cylinder vee 2-stroke
Transmission: Electric - GM - generator, six nose-suspended DC traction motors
Weight, tonnes: 111
Power rating, hp (kW): 2,475 (1,845)
Design speed, mph (km/h): 87 (140)

OTHER COUNTRIES OPERATED

GM supplied examples of its JT22C model to Iraq, Ireland (IR Class 071/NIR Class 111); Sudan (Class 1900) and Yugoslavia (JZ Class 666).

TYPE AA22T DIESEL LOCOMOTIVE

Egyptian National Railways (ENR) Type AA22T

The most numerous ENR type is this large series of Henschel-built GM-powered locomotives, accounting for 40 per cent of Egypt's diesel locomotive fleet. Deliveries from the German manufacturer's Kassel plant extended from 1976 to 1993.

SUB-TYPES

A total of 99 examples of the basic AA22T version (75 mph/120 km/h gearing) were delivered (3016-3084, 3241-3270); the AA22T-DB (50 mph/80 km/h gearing for heavy freight work) totals 56 locomotives (3001-3015, 3189-3200 and 3271-3299); the AA22T-2, 125 of which were supplied between 1981 and 1990, features various improvements and is geared for 87 mph/140 km/h running for passenger work (3085-3188, 3201-3221).

SPECIAL FEATURES

Built by GM's German licensee, Henschel (later

SPECIFICATION

Number series: 3001-3221, 3241-3299
Total built: 280
Builder: Henschel
Date introduced: 1976
Track gauge, ft/ins (mm): 4 ft 8.5 in (1,435)
Axle arrangement: Co-Co
Power unit type: GM 645E3 12-cylinder vee 2-stroke
Transmission: Electric - GM - alternator, six nose-suspended DC traction motors
Weight, tonnes: 121-122
Power rating, hp (kW): 2,475 (1,845)
Design speed, mph (km/h): 87 (140), 75 (120) or 50 (80)
Additional features: multiple working

Thyssen-Henschel), the Egyptian AA22T machines have proved highly successful, handling both freight and passenger traffic on all parts of the network. Most remained in traffic in 2004, only six having been withdrawn.

TYPE DE2550 DIESEL LOCOMOTIVE

Egyptian National Railways (ENR) Type DE2550

Egypt

Delivered in both single- and dual-cab versions, the DE2550 machines perpetuated ENR's practice of purchasing GM-powered products of the German locomotive industry.

SUB-TYPES

The first 45 locomotives (2001-2045) feature a single cab and narrow hood; 2101-2123 are dual-cab machines with full-width bodies.

SPECIAL FEATURES

The first batch of these locomotives was originally ordered to provide traction for phosphates traffic between Abu Tartour and the Red Sea port of Safaga, conveyed in a dedicated fleet of 700 bottom-discharge wagons. They were followed in 1998 by 23 more for more general duties in the Nile Delta area. Manufacture of both series was undertaken at the former Henschel plant in Kassel, which had become part of Adtranz. They were among the last of a long line of GM-powered locomotives produced at this factory, now a Bombardier facility.

SPECIFICATION

Number series: 2001-2045, 2101-2123
Total built: 45, 23
Builder: Adtranz
Date introduced: 1995; 1998
Track gauge, ft/ins (mm): 4 ft 8.5 in (1,435)
Axle arrangement: Co-Co
Power unit type: GM 645E3 12-cylinder vee 2-stroke
Transmission: Electric - GM - alternator, six nose-suspended DC traction motors
Weight, tonnes: 132
Power rating, hp (kW): 2,475 (1,845)
Design speed, mph (km/h): 50 (80)
Additional features: multiple working, dynamic braking

CLASS BB 250 DIESEL LOCOMOTIVE

Madagascar National Railways (Madarail) Class BB 250

After years of neglect, the Madagascar metre-gauge network faces better times as a result of a rehabilitation programme that started in 2003. In recent years the railway has operated two types of French-built locomotives.

SPECIAL FEATURES

This small series of Alsthom-built SACM-engined locomotives joined examples of the earlier, less powerful BB 220 series of the same parentage in 1986. They serve the metre gauge 453 mile (730 km) northern part of the network that is operated as Madarail by a South African-led concession-holder. Typical of contemporary Alsthom export designs for lighter railways, the BB 250 machines feature dual-cabs and full-width bodies.

SPECIFICATION

Number series: BB 251-BB 255
Total built: 5
Builder: Alsthom
Date introduced: 1986
Track gauge, ft/ins (mm): 3 ft 3.375 in (1,000)
Axle arrangement: Bo-Bo
Power unit type: SACM UD30 V16 R5 16-cylinder vee 4-stroke
Transmission: Electric - Alsthom - alternator, four nose-suspended DC traction motors
Weight, tonnes: 64
Power rating, hp (kW): 2,145 (1,600)
Design speed, mph (km/h): 43 (70)

26

CLASS 500 DIESEL LOCOMOTIVE

Central East African Railways (CEAR) Class 500

Canadian-built Alco-engined machines have formed the core of the Malawi locomotive fleet for over 25 years. Surviving members of the class underwent refurbishment in the late 1990s.

PRINCIPAL MODIFICATIONS

Refurbishment under the USAID programme took place during the 1990s.

SPECIAL FEATURES

These locomotives were produced in batches of four and 16 in 1973 and 1979 respectively at the former Montreal Locomotive Works. Designated Model MX615 by its manufacturers, Class 500 features a boxy single cab and low short hood and is powered by an 8-cylinder version of Alco's 251 engine. In 1999, operation of the former Malawi Railways system was taken over by a consortium led by US-based Railroad Development Corporation under a 20-year concession.

SPECIFICATION

Number series: 500–519
Total built: 20
Builder: MLW (500–503); Bombardier (504–519)
Date introduced: 1973, 1979
Track gauge, ft/ins (mm): 3 ft 6 in (1,067)
Axle arrangement: Co-Co
Power unit type: Alco 8-251-E 8-cylinder vee 4-stroke
Transmission: Electric - GE Canada - generator, six nose-suspended DC traction motors
Weight, tonnes: 86
Power rating, hp (kW): 1,500 (1,120)
Design speed, mph (km/h): 72 (116)
Additional features: multiple working

OTHER COUNTRIES OPERATED

The only other significant operator of the Model MX615 is Nigerian Railways Corporation, which received 54 examples to become NRC Class 1700. The more powerful Models MX620 and MX626 are used by several African countries, some employing a 1-Co-Co-1 axle arrangement.

CLASS DF DIESEL LOCOMOTIVE

Moroccan Railways (ONCFM) Class DF

Among ONCFM's eclectic mix of diesel locomotive types are these 14 locomotives dating from the late 1960s and based on the French CC72000. Some have been earmarked for refurbishment to prolong their service lives.

SPECIAL FEATURES

Similar to the French National Railways (SNCF) Class 72000 introduced the previous year, the DFs were supplied to ONCFM from 1968. Like their French counterparts, they feature a single large traction motor powering all three axles of each bogie via gearing. This arrangement allows the selection of different gear ratios to suit freight or passenger operations, which they mainly operate on the Tangier line.

SPECIFICATION

Number series: DF-101 - DF-114
Total built: 14
Builder: Alsthom
Date introduced: 1968
Track gauge, ft/ins (mm): 4 ft 8.5 in (1,435)
Axle arrangement: C-C
Power unit type: SACM-AGO V16 ESHR 16-cylinder vee 4-stroke
Transmission: Electric - Alsthom - alternator, two fully suspended DC traction motors
Weight, tonnes: 108
Power rating, hp (kW): 3,015 (2,250)
Design speed, mph (km/h): 50/ 84 (80/135) (two gear ratios)
Additional features: monomotor bogies

CLASS E-1100 ELECTRIC LOCOMOTIVE

Moroccan Railway (ONCFM) Class E-1100

Having traditionally procured its electric traction from French builders, in the 1970s ONCFM turned to other sources for locomotives to modernise and strengthen its fleet. This led to the acquisition of machines from Poland and the Japanese-built E-1000 units featured here.

SPECIAL FEATURES

The E-1100s were significant at the time of their introduction, representing the first main line electric locomotives supplied by Japanese industry to an African railway. Acquired primarily for phosphates haulage, which represents around three-quarters of the ONCFM's freight tonnage, these six-axle machines are still mainly used on this traffic. They are conventional DC locomotives, with fine vernier control between main resistance notches to prevent power surges and so avoid wheel-slip. The success of this class led to the subsequent acquisition by ONCFM of further

SPECIFICATION

Number series: E-1101 - E-1122
Total built: 22
Builder: Hitachi
Date introduced: 1977
Track gauge, ft/ins (mm): 4 ft 8.5 in (1,435)
Axle arrangement: Co-Co
Power supply system: 3 kV DC
Electrical equipment: Hitachi - resistance control, six nose-suspended DC traction motors
Weight, tonnes: 120
Power rating, hp (kW): 3,820 (2,850) continuous
Design speed, mph (km/h): 77 (125)
Additional features: rheostatic braking

Japanese-built types in the shape of Classes 1200 and 1250 (see next entry).

29

CLASS E-1250 ELECTRIC LOCOMOTIVE

Moroccan Railways (ONCFM) Class E-1250

The last of three electric locomotive types supplied by Hitachi to ONCFM, the six-axle Class E-1250 is mainly employed on the railway's heaviest intercity passenger services.

SPECIAL FEATURES

Deployed mainly on ONCFM's passenger services between Marrakech and Fès, Class E-1250 followed two earlier electric freight locomotive types from Hitachi. The class was designed for 100 mph (160 km/h) operation but is now limited to 87 mph (140 km/h).

SPECIFICATION

Number series: E-1251-E-1262
Total built: 12
Builder: Hitachi
Date introduced: 1984
Track gauge, ft/ins (mm): 4 ft 8.5 in (1,435)
Axle arrangement: Co-Co
Power supply system: 3 kV DC
Electrical equipment: Hitachi - chopper control, six DC traction motors
Weight, tonnes: 120
Power rating, hp (kW): 5,225 (3,900)
Design speed, mph (km/h): 100 (160)
Additional features: rheostatic braking

CLASS E-1300/E-1350 ELECTRIC LOCOMOTIVES

Moroccan Railways (ONCFM) Classes E-1300 and E-1350

ONCFM's most recent electric locomotive acquisitions are these 3 kV DC derivatives of France's BB7200/BB/15000/BB22200 family. This is also the railway's most numerous and most powerful electric locomotive type, with the most recent deliveries dedicated to phosphates traffic.

SPECIAL FEATURES

Ordered in several batches between the late 1980s and the late 1990s, the E-1300 and E-1350 series together total 27 units, forming ONCFM's largest locomotive class. Based on the successful French BB7200/BB15000/BB22200 design and employing the same monomotor bogie configuration, the versatile Class E-1300s are multi-purpose machines, handling both freight and passengers on the Moroccan network, more than half of which is under the wires. The final batch of eight locomotives, designated Class E-1350, have lower gearing and were procured to replace now-retired Class E-900 machines on phosphates traffic.

SPECIFICATION

Number series: E-1301-E-1318, E-1351-E-1359
Total built: 18, 9
Builder: GEC Alsthom; Alstom
Date introduced: 1992; 1999
Track gauge, ft/ins (mm): 4 ft 8.5 in (1,435)
Axle arrangement: B-B
Power supply system: 3 kV DC
Electrical equipment: GEC Alsthom/Alstom - chopper control, two fully suspended DC traction motors
Weight, tonnes: 85.5
Power rating, hp (kW): 5,200 (4,000)
Design speed, mph (km/h): 100 (160), 62 (100)
Additional features: monomotor bogies, rheostatic braking, multiple working

OTHER COUNTRIES OPERATED

As well as operating in large numbers with SNCF in France, as detailed above, a 1.5 kV DC version of this design is in use in the Netherlands (Classes 1600 and 1700).

CLASS ZM EMU

Moroccan Railways (ONCFM) Class ZM

Currently ONCFM's only emu type, the ZM is a three-car version of Belgian National Railways (SNCB) Class AM80 'Break' units. They are mainly used on Casablanca-Rabat services.

SPECIAL FEATURES

The first eight of these units were ordered in 1982 for Casablanca-Rabat services. Based on SNCB's successful chopper-controlled 'Break' units, they were supplied by BN (now part of Bombardier) with traction equipment by ACEC (since absorbed into ALSTOM). A follow-on order for six more units was completed in 1995. Duties include shuttle services on the electrified line to Casablanca's Mohammed V international airport. From 2006, the supremacy of these units on the Casablanca-Rabat route and beyond to Fès will be challenged by new double-deck emus from Italian train-builder Ansaldobreda.

SPECIFICATION

Total built: 14
Builder: BN
Date introduced: 1984
Track gauge, ft/ins (mm): 4 ft 8.5 in (1,435)
Unit configuration: M-T-T
Power supply system: 3 kV DC
Electrical equipment: ACEC - chopper control, four nose-suspended DC traction motors
Power rating, hp (kW): 1,900 (1,415)
Design speed, mph (km/h): 100 (160)
Additional features: multiple working, electric braking, air-conditioning

OTHER COUNTRIES OPERATED

SNCB in Belgium operates the Class AM80 parent design.

CLASS 500 DIESEL LOCOMOTIVE

TransNamib Holdings Class 500

Morocco / Namibia

The backbone of the TransNamib fleet is formed of 1960s-built General Electric U20C locomotives mostly acquired from Spoornet (formerly South African Railways). In recent years, some examples have been sold to Brazil and Sudan.

SPECIAL FEATURES

Standard 'Cape gauge' U20Cs, TransNamib's Class 500 locomotives are mostly former South African Railways Class 33-200/33-400 machines, reflecting the fact that until 1989 the Namibian network was operated under contract by its large southern neighbour. The fleet once totalled more than 60 locomotives but in recent years this has been cut to around two-thirds of that size, some sold to the Ferrovia Centro-Atlántico system in Brazil, others to Sudan. As well as handling freight traffic in Namibia, these locomotives also work the country's limited passenger services. They were formerly numbered in the 4xx series.

SPECIFICATION

Number series: Locomotives numbered in 5xx series
Total fleet: 41
Builder: GE
Date introduced: 1966
Track gauge, ft/ins (mm): 3 ft 6 in (1,065)
Axle arrangement: Co-Co
Power unit type: GE 7 FDL-12 12-cylinder vee 4-stroke
Transmission: Electric - GE - generator and six nose-suspended DC traction motors
Weight, tonnes: 91
Power rating, hp (kW): 2,150 (1,605)
Design speed, mph (km/h): 62 (100)
Additional features: multiple working

OTHER COUNTRIES OPERATED

As one of GE's most versatile and popular export models, U20Cs are seen in many countries.

CLASS 34 DIESEL LOCOMOTIVE

Spoornet Class 34 (GE)

Together with their General Electric counterparts, also designated Class 34, these machines form a major part of the Spoornet diesel locomotive fleet. Some were manufactured by GM but most were produced in South Africa.

PRINCIPAL MODIFICATIONS

The three sub-series represent different batches of essentially the same locomotive type. The Class 34-200 machines were imported from GM, the remainder built domestically.

SPECIAL FEATURES

Seen on many parts of the Spoornet system, these versatile locomotives handle mainly freight traffic. Powered by a 16-cylinder turbocharged version of the GM 645E3 engine, the single-cab locomotives bear the manufacturers Model GT26MC designation. Confusingly, Spoornet's GE-built locomotives of the same general configuration

SPECIFICATION

Number series: 34-200-34-250, 34-601-34-700; 34-801-34-858
Total built: 209
Builder: GM, GM South Africa, GM South Africa
Date introduced: 1971, 1975, 1978
Track gauge, ft/ins (mm): 3 ft 6 in (1,065)
Axle arrangement: Co-Co
Power unit type: GM 16-645E3 16 cylinder vee 2-stroke
Transmission: Electric - GM - alternator, six nose-suspended DC traction motors
Weight, tonnes: 111
Power rating, hp (kW): 2,875 (2,145)
Design speed, mph (km/h): 62 (100)
Additional features: multiple working

and output are identified as Classes 34-000, 34-400, 34-500 and 34-900.

CLASS 35 DIESEL LOCOMOTIVE

Spoornet Class 35 (GE)

South Africa

Representing GE's contributions to the Spoornet diesel fleet is this family of medium-powered units dating from the 1970s.

SPECIAL FEATURES

Used on branch line and secondary duties in many parts of the South African network, these GE U15C locomotives were built in batches between 1972 and 1980. They are conventional single-cab machines, employed on both freight and passenger duties. Similar work is undertaken by their GM counterparts, Classes 35-200 and 35-600.

SPECIFICATION

Number series: 35-001-35-070, 35-401-35-500
Total built: 70; 100
Builder: GE
Date introduced: 1972, 1974
Track gauge, ft/ins (mm): 3 ft 6 in (1,065)
Axle arrangement: Co-Co
Power unit type: GE 7 FDL-8 8-cylinder vee 2-stroke
Transmission: Electric - GE - generator, six nose-suspended DC traction motors
Weight, tonnes: 82
Power rating, hp (kW): 1,650 (1,230)
Design speed, mph (km/h): 62 (100)
Additional features: multiple working

CLASS 6E AND 6E1 ELECTRIC LOCOMOTIVES

Spoornet Classes 6E and 6E1

Developed from the earlier Class 5E/5E1 designs, these 3 kV DC machines are Spoornet's most numerous type, mainly handling heavy freight but also providing power for some passenger services.

SUB-TYPES

The main difference between 6E and 6E1 is in the form of mass-transfer control adopted between bogies and locomotive body. 6E has an air bellows device between bogies and frames; 6E1 has low-level traction rods to control weight transfer.

SPECIAL FEATURES

Forming the core of the Spoornet 3 kV DC fleet, this numerous type is a development of the highly successful British-designed Class 5E/5E1, taking advantage of improvement in traction motor design to achieve an increase in output of over 70 per cent and a higher top speed. All were built between 1969 and 1982. They are mainly used on

SPECIFICATION

Number series: Class 6E - E1146-E1225; Class 6E1 - E1226-E2185
Total built: 80; 960
Builder: Union Carriage & Wagon
Date introduced: 1970, 1969
Track gauge, ft/ins (mm): 3 ft 6 in (1,065)
Axle arrangement: Bo-Bo
Power supply system: 3 kV DC
Electrical equipment: AEI (South Africa), English Electric (South Africa), GEC - resistance control, four nose-suspended DC traction motors
Weight, tonnes: 89
Power rating, hp (kW): 3,020 (2,252) continuous
Design speed, mph (km/h): 65 (105)
Additional features: multiple working, regenerative braking

freight traffic, although passenger duties include haulage of the prestigious 'Blue Train' over the Beaufort West-Cape Town section.

CLASS 7E, 7E1, 7E2 and 7E3 ELECTRIC LOCOMOTIVES

Spoornet Classes 7E, 7E1, 7E2 and 7E3

A 1970s decision to henceforth employ the 25 kV AC system in South Africa led to orders for large numbers of these six-axle freight machines, Spoornet's first series-built AC type.

SUB-TYPES

The major differences between the four sub-classes are a result of their manufacture by different suppliers. In Classes 7E2 and 7E3, detail differences occur on each type, creating Series 1 and Series 2 groups of locomotives.

SPECIAL FEATURES

Developed as a heavy hauler, the Class 7E machines were initially used on routes such as the Richards Bay coal line. The operator procured generally similar locomotives both from the 50 Cycles Group, with Union Carriage & Wagon responsible for the mechanical parts, and from a South African-Japanese partnership that included Hitachi and Dorman Long (later Dorbyl). A feature

SPECIFICATION

Total built: 100, 50, 65, 85
Builder: Class 7E and 7E2 - Union Carriage & Wagon, Class 7E1 - Dorman Long, Class 7E3 - Dorbyl
Date introduced: 7E - 1978; 7E1 - 1980; 7E2 - 1982; 7E3 - 1983
Track gauge, ft/ins (mm): 3 ft 6 in (1,065)
Axle arrangement: Co-Co
Power supply system: 25 kV AC 50 Hz
Electrical equipment: 7E and 7E2 - 50 Cycles Group; 7E1 and 7E3 - Hitachi - silicon rectifiers, six nose-suspended DC traction motors
Weight, tonnes: 7E - 123; 7E1 - 125; 7E2 - 126; 7E3 - 124
Power rating, hp (kW): 4,020 (3,000)
Design speed, mph (km/h): 62 (100) except Class 7E2 55 (88)
Additional features: multiple working, rheostatic braking

of these locomotives is their prominent traction rods linking the bogies to the body, controlling weight transfer when starting heavy trains.

CLASS 8E ELECTRIC LOCOMOTIVE

Spoornet Class 8E

Spoornet is of one of few railway systems in the world to employ electric traction for shunting. One hundred of these centre-cab machines were built by a Siemens-led consortium for this purpose in the 1980s.

SPECIAL FEATURES

Acquired for heavy yard work on the South African 3 kV DC network, Class 8E was the country's first design to employ chopper control. The locomotives were supplied by a Siemens-led consortium that included BBC as a partner in the supply of traction equipment and Union Carriage & Wagon, which undertook mechanical construction in South Africa at its Nigel plant. A further seven locomotives of the same type were supplied to an industrial user, Impala Mines.

SPECIFICATION

Number series: E8001–E8100
Total built: 100
Builder: Union Carriage & Wagon
Date introduced: 1983
Track gauge, ft/ins (mm): 3 ft 6 in (1,067)
Axle arrangement: Bo-Bo
Power supply system: 3 kV DC
Electrical equipment: Siemens; BBC - chopper control, four nose-suspended DC traction motors
Weight, tonnes: 82
Power rating, hp (kW): 920 (687) continuous
Design speed, mph (km/h): 47 (75)
Additional features: multiple working

CLASS 9E ELECTRIC LOCOMOTIVE

Spoornet Class 9E

Class 9E was introduced in 1978 to serve the 537 mile (864 km) Sishen–Saldanha Bay iron ore line, the world's first common user railway to employ a 50 kV AC power supply. In recent years the class has undergone complete refurbishment.

SPECIAL FEATURES

The heavy haul needs of the Sishen–Saldanha Bay iron ore line led the company that built it, the South African Iron and Steel Industrial Corporation (ISCOR), to select a 50 kV AC power supply, enabling three of these Class 9E machines to handle trains of up to 20,200 tonnes. A train of this weight calls for three of these powerful locomotives to provide traction. Supplied by GEC Traction, with mechanical manufacture sub-contracted to Union Carriage & Wagon, the single-cab Class 9E features the unusual configuration of a lowered section at No 2 end to accommodate the roof-mounted 50 kV current collection equipment. The former South African Railways ordered 25 of these locomotives; a further six were procured by ISCOR. All 31 are now owned by Spoornet.

SPECIFICATION

Number series: E9001–E9031
Total built: 31
Builder: Union Carriage & Wagon
Date introduced: 1978
Track gauge, ft/ins (mm): 3 ft 6 in (1,067)
Axle arrangement: Co-Co
Power supply system: 50 kV AC 50 Hz
Electrical equipment: GEC Traction - thyristor control, six nose-suspended DC traction motors
Weight, tonnes: 166
Power rating, hp (kW): 5,145 (3,840) continuous
Design speed, mph (km/h): 56 (90)
Additional features: multiple working, rheostatic braking

CLASS 10E, 10E1 AND 10E2 ELECTRIC LOCOMOTIVES

Spoornet Classes 10E, 10E1 and 10E2

Spoornet's only six-axle DC locomotive design is this type built by Union Carriage & Wagon in the 1980s and 1990s to provide a more powerful solution to the railway's heaviest freight needs, especially for mineral traffic.

SUB-TYPES

Classes 10E and 10E2 feature Toshiba traction equipment; Class 10E1 has GEC equipment.

SPECIAL FEATURES

Spoornet's switch to Co-Co designs for most new main line electric locomotive orders started with the 25 kV AC Class 7E series in the late 1970s. The Class 10E 3 kV DC family is of similar mechanical design. Early duties for the class included heavy hauls over the DC section from the Transvaal coalfields to Ermelo, the first leg of the journey to the Indian Ocean export coal terminal at Richards Bay. All three batches of these locomotives were

SPECIFICATION

Number series: From E10001
Total built: 50, 100, 25
Builder: Union Carriage & Wagon
Date introduced: 1986, 1987, 1989
Track gauge, ft/ins (mm): 3 ft 6 in (1,065)
Axle arrangement: Co-Co
Power supply system: 3 kV DC
Electrical equipment: GEC, Toshiba, GEC – GTO chopper control, six nose-suspended traction motors
Weight, tonnes: 125; 126; 126
Power rating, hp (kW): 4,140 (3,090) continuous
Design speed, mph (km/h): 56 (90), Class 10E2 62 (100)
Additional features: multiple working, regenerative and rheostatic braking

assembled at the Nigel plant of Union Carriage & Wagon.

CLASS 14E AND 14E1 ELECTRIC LOCOMOTIVE

Spoornet Classes 14E and 14E1

South Africa

The use of two overhead power supply systems on the South African rail network created a limited requirement for locomotives capable of operating from both 3 kV DC and 25 kV AC. This resulted in the procurement of these two small series of three-phase locomotives, mainly for long-distance intermodal transport.

SPECIAL FEATURES

These are Spoornet's most powerful and most modern electric locomotives, introducing three-phase technology to the railway. The first three were supplied by the 50 Cycles Group, led by Siemens, and assembled in Switzerland by SLM. The second series, Class 14E1, which has a lower gear ratio, was ordered directly from Siemens and built in South Africa. They are mainly used on intermodal services on Cape Town-Johannesburg and Durban-Johannesburg routes.

SPECIFICATION

Number series: 14-001-14-003, 14-101-14-110
Total built: 3, 10
Builder: SLM; Union Carriage & Wagon
Date introduced: 1990, 1994
Track gauge, ft/ins (mm): 3 ft 6 in (1,065)
Axle arrangement: Bo-Bo
Power supply system: 3 kV DC/25 kV AC 50 Hz
Electrical equipment: 50 Cycles Group - three-phase traction motors
Weight, tonnes: 93, 98
Power rating, hp (kW): 5,360 (4,000)
Design speed, mph (km/h): 100 (160), 80 (130)
Additional features: multiple working; rheostatic braking

CLASS 5M EMU

South African Rail Commuter Corporation (SARCC) Class 5M

Large numbers of these ageing emus serve the heavy commuter flows in the metropolitan areas around six major South African cities. A limited programme to modernise the fleet has been started. A contract to operate these services is held by Metrorail.

PRINCIPAL MODIFICATIONS

A refurbishment programme was started based on prototypes produced in the late 1990s and designated Classes 10M and 10M1. This includes provision of new bodies and an upgrade of electrical equipment. Contracts covering 44 motor cars and 132 trailers were shared equally by Transwerk/Bombardier and Union Carriage & Wagon/Siemens. Modernised trains are designated Classes 10M2 and 10M3 respectively.

SPECIAL FEATURES

These rugged but now dated trains have for nearly 50 years characterised commuter

SPECIFICATION

Total built: 379 sets/4,635 cars in service in 2003
Builder: Union Carriage & Wagon
Date introduced: 1957
Track gauge, ft/ins (mm): 3 ft 6 in (1,065)
Unit configuration: 11- to 14-car sets, 3-4 motor cars per set
Power supply system: 3 kV DC
Electrical equipment: GEC - resistance control, four DC traction motors per motor car
Power rating, hp (kW): 1,180 (880) per motor car
Design speed, mph (km/h): 62 (100)

operations in six South African conurbations: Cape Town, Durban, East London, Johannesburg, Port Elizabeth, and Pretoria. Based on British traction equipment and local mechanical construction, they provide the high capacity needed to handle the large passenger flows experienced by SARCC.

CLASS DE1000 DIESEL LOCOMOTIVE

Tanzania-Zambia Railway Authority (TAZARA) Class DE1000

South Africa / Tanzania

These GE U30C machines are interlopers in an otherwise all-Chinese TAZARA locomotive fleet, handling both freight and passenger traffic on the line.

SPECIAL FEATURES

Commissioned in 1975, the 1,155 mile (1,860 km) TAZARA line was built and equipped by Chinese industry and provides land-locked Zambia with rail access to the Tanzanian Indian Ocean port of Dar-es-Salaam. An initial fleet of Chinese-built locomotives was joined in the 1980s by these GE U30C machines. The first 14 were built by the US company's German licensee, Krupp, in 1982-83. GE added 17 more from its Erie plant, completing deliveries in 1991. Well adapted to the arduous operating conditions found in sub-Saharan Africa, they handle both passenger and freight traffic on the line.

SPECIFICATION

Number series: DE1001-DE1031
Total built: 31
Builder: DE1001-DE1014 - Krupp (GE licence), remainder - GE
Date introduced: 1983
Track gauge, ft/ins (mm): 3 ft 6 in (1,067)
Axle arrangement: Co-Co
Power unit type: GE 7 FDL-12 12-cylinder vee 4-stroke
Transmission: Electric - GE - generator, six nose-suspended traction motors
Weight, tonnes: 120
Power rating, hp (kW): 3,200 (2,350)
Design speed, mph (km/h): 62 (100)
Additional features: multiple working

OTHER COUNTRIES OPERATED

GE also supplied U30Cs to Iran and Mexico.

CLASS 040-DO DIESEL LOCOMOTIVE

Tunisian National Railways (SNCFT) Class 040-DO

Built in Hungary by Ganz-Mávag and developed from that country's Class M41.2/M41.23 designs, the 040-DO locomotives are active on mainly passenger services on both standard and metre gauge sections of the Tunisian network.

SUB-TYPES

Delivery of the Class 040-DO locomotives was preceded in 1981 by 10 similar but less powerful Class 040-DL diesel-hydraulics from the same builder.

SPECIAL FEATURES

Delivered to SNCFT by Ganz-Mávag in the mid-1980s, these four-axle diesel-hydraulics operate in both standard and metre gauge versions. The former is concentrated on the Tunis-Ghardimaou line. Reduced passenger requirements for metre gauge machines has led to the reported fitting of one example with standard gauge bogies.

SPECIFICATION

Number series: 040-DO-281-040-DO-285 (standard gauge); 040-DO-321-040-DO-335 (metre gauge)
Total built: 5, 15
Builder: Ganz-Mávag
Date introduced: 1983
Track gauge, ft/ins (mm): 4 ft 8.5 in (1,435), 3 ft 3.375 in (1,000)
Axle arrangement: B-B
Power unit type: Ganz-Pielstick 16PA4-185VG 16-cylinder vee 4-stroke
Transmission: Hydraulic - Voith
Weight, tonnes: 68, 64
Power rating, hp (kW): 2,365 (1,766)
Design speed, mph (km/h): 87 (140), 80 (130)

CLASS 060-DP DIESEL LOCOMOTIVE

Tunisian National Railways (SNCFT) Class 060-DP

Tunisia

The most modern of three Alco-engined types operated by the railway, the 060-DP machines also enjoy the distinction of being the final locomotives employing this type of power unit to be produced by Bombardier at the former MLW plant in Montreal. As with some other SNCFT types, examples were supplied for use on both standard and metre gauge lines.

SUB-TYPES

Of the 22 locomotives built, 18 were equipped with metre gauge bogies and four were for standard gauge. At least one of the metre gauge machines has since been re-bogied.

SPECIAL FEATURES

Built originally mainly for passenger work, in the case of the metre gauge machines for work on lines south of Tunis, Class 060-DP marked the end of Alco-engined production at the former MLW plant in Montreal. Designated Model MXS624 by

SPECIFICATION

Number series: 060-DP-131-060-DP-152
Total built: 22
Builder: Bombardier
Date introduced: 1984
Track gauge, ft/ins (mm): 4 ft 8.5 in (1,435), 3 ft 3.375 in (1,000)
Axle arrangement: Co-Co
Power unit type: Alco 251 12-cylinder vee 4-stroke
Transmission: Electric - GE Canada - alternator, six nose-suspended DC traction motors
Weight, tonnes: 91
Power rating, hp (kW): 2,365 (1,764)
Design speed, mph (km/h): standard gauge - 80 (130), metre gauge - 62 (100)

Bombardier, these boxy twin-cab locomotives feature full-width bodies. By 2004 some were reported to be unserviceable, while most of the metre gauge examples were concentrated on freight work.

CLASS 040-GT DIESEL LOCOMOTIVE

Tunisian National Railways (SNCFT) Class 040-GT

The most recent locomotive type to enter service on the SNCFT system is this series of 21 metre gauge machines supplied by General Motors of Canada. Duties include push-pull passenger services south of Tunis.

SPECIAL FEATURES

Acquired to modernise traction on passenger services on metre gauge lines running south of Tunis, these Model GT18B locomotives were acquired by SNCFT in 1999. As well as covering long-distance trains to Sfax and Gabès, they also work push-pull suburban services. In addition to their three-digit fleet numbers, the 040-GT locomotives carry a UIC-type computer-friendly identification.

OTHER COUNTRIES OPERATED

While General Motors GT18 is one of the company's standard export models, most examples are Co-Co machines. Other users are national operators in Algeria, Bangladesh, Ghana, Malaysia and South Africa.

SPECIFICATION

Number series: 551-571
Total built: 21
Builder: GM, Canada
Date introduced: 1999
Track gauge, ft/ins (mm): 3 ft 3.375 in (1,000)
Axle arrangement: Bo-Bo
Power unit type: GM 645E3C 8-cylinder vee 2-stroke
Transmission: Electric - GM - alternator, four nose-suspended DC traction motors
Power rating, hp (kW): 1,800 (1,340)
Design speed, mph (km/h): 80 (130)
Additional features: push-pull operation

CLASS YZ-E EMU

Tunisian National Railways (SNCFT) Class YZ-E

This small fleet of metre-gauge three-car emus was supplied by Ganz-Mávag in 1984 to serve the Tunisian network's sole electrified route, the Metro du Sahel line.

SPECIAL FEATURES

These thyristor-controlled emus were supplied by Ganz-Mávag to provide services on the metre gauge Metro du Sahel line from Sousse, southeast of Tunis, to Monastir, Moknine and Mahdia, on the Mediterranean coast, electrification of which was completed in 1987. Train formation consists of a central motor car flanked by two driving trailers. Seating capacity in each three-car unit is for 300.

OTHER COUNTRIES OPERATED

50 examples of a standard gauge version of this type were supplied to the former Yugoslav Railways (JZ).

SPECIFICATION

Total built: 6
Builder: Ganz-Mávag
Date introduced: 1984
Track gauge, ft/ins (mm): 3 ft 3.375 in (1,000)
Unit configuration: T-M-T
Power supply system: 25 kV AC 50 Hz
Electrical equipment: Ganz Electric - thyristor control, four DC traction motors
Power rating, hp (kW): 1,610 (1,200) continuous
Design speed, mph (km/h): 75 (120)
Additional features: multiple working, rheostatic braking

CLASS 01 DIESEL LOCOMOTIVE

Railway Systems of Zambia Class 01

The most modern locomotives on the Zambian national network are these GM Model GT36CU-MP machines introduced in the mid-1990s.

SPECIAL FEATURES

Since 2003 operations of the former Zambia Railways have been undertaken under a concession as Railway Systems of Zambia. Assets taken over include this fleet of modern high-powered locomotives built at GM's London, Ontario, plant in 1992. They joined a mostly GE fleet and now handle the system's heaviest services.

SPECIFICATION

Number series: 01-601-01-615
Total built: 15
Builder: GM (Canada)
Date introduced: 1993
Track gauge, ft/ins (mm): 3 ft 6 in (1,067)
Axle arrangement: Co-Co
Power unit type: GM 16-645E3 16-cylinder vee 2-stroke
Transmission: Electric - GM - alternator, six nose-suspended DC traction motors
Power rating, hp (kW): 3,500 (2,610)
Design speed, mph (km/h): 62 (100)
Additional features: multiple working

Asian Trains

CLASS DF4, DF4A and DF4B DIESEL LOCOMOTIVES

Chinese Railways (CR) Classes DF4, DF4A and DF4B

By far CR's most numerous diesel locomotive type, with over 5,000 examples produced, these versatile machines operate in both freight and passenger versions throughout the country.

SUB-TYPES

Classes DF4 and DF4B were produced in versions with 62 or 75 mph gearing for freight or passenger work. While most of the class carries green livery, some examples used for passenger traffic are painted in an orange colour scheme. Others have been turned out in blue and cream.

SPECIAL FEATURES

The first domestically designed high-powered main line diesel-electric locomotive to enter large volume series production in China was this six-axle type, which was eventually built at four plants. The three sub-series represent progressive improvement of the design, with the DF4B, introduced in 1984, by far the most numerous. Production has been undertaken at four of China's locomotive-building plants, Dalian, Datong, Sifang and Ziyang. The introduction of this type played a key role in the elimination of steam traction in China, while development of the design continued with the more powerful DF4C and the DF4D family. Introduction of newer locomotives and continuing electrification have led to some withdrawals of older examples of the class. The type is also used by the many local and joint-venture railways that exist in China, with output continuing for such operators into the present millennium.

SPECIFICATION

Total built: DF4 – 330, DF4A – 360, DF4B –
4,250 (total approximate)
Builder: DF4 – Dalian, Ziyang, DF4A – Dalian,
DF4B – Dalian, Datong, Sifang, Ziyang
Date introduced: 1969, 1976, 1984
Track gauge, ft/ins (mm): 4 ft 8.5 in (1,435)
Axle arrangement: Co-Co
Power unit type: Dalian 16V240ZJB 16-
cylinder four-stroke
Transmission: Electric Yong Ji – AC/DC with six
DC traction motors
Weight, tonnes: 138
Power rating, hp (kW): 3,255 (2,430)
Design speed, mph (km/h): DF4 and DF4B –
62 or 75 (100 or 120), DF4A – 62 (100)

CLASS DF5 DIESEL LOCOMOTIVE

Chinese Railways (CR) Class DF5

This single-cab six-axle type dating from the 1980s is seen throughout the CR network performing trip and secondary duties.

SUB-TYPES

Some locomotives built to 5 ft 0 in (1,520 mm) gauge for exchange traffic at Chinese-Russian border crossings. A more powerful 1,970 hp (1,470 kW) Class DF5D variant was introduced in 1999, entering series production in 2002.

SPECIAL FEATURES

Initially locomotives of this basic type were built at Tangshan, before the large-scale production of this present type commenced at Sifang. With more than 900 examples built since 1984, this versatile diesel-electric type subsequently became a standard CR design, replacing Class JS 2-8-2 steam locomotives on local and yard work. The

SPECIFICATION

Total built: 930 approximately
Builder: Dalian, Sifang, Tangshan
Date introduced: 1984
Track gauge, ft/ins (mm): 4 ft 8.5 in (1,435)
Axle arrangement: Co-Co
Power unit type: Dalian 8V240ZJ eight-cylinder four-stroke
Transmission: Electric AC/DC, with six nose-suspended traction motors
Weight, tonnes: 138
Power rating, hp (kW): 1,620 (1,210)
Design speed, mph (km/h): 50 or 62 (80 or 100)

full 23 tonne standard CR axle-load is at the DF5's disposal for optimum adhesion. Locomotives of this type are seen throughout China.

CLASS DF7 DIESEL LOCOMOTIVE

Chinese Railways (CR) Class DF7

The Beijing 7 February plant in China's capital introduced the first of the DF7 family in 1982. Like the DF5, this type is intended for secondary and shunting work but is more powerful. Development of the design was continuing in the new millennium.

SUB-TYPES

Some DF7B equipped for multiple working, intended for the Beijing-Guangzhou main line before its electrification. The DF7D features full width bodywork and is usually employed using two locomotives in multiple coupled back-to-back. Construction of an updated version, the DF7C3, commenced at the Beijing plant in 2002. Class DF7F is a twin-section variant of the design. Class DF7G is an AC-motored version, introduced in prototype form in 2002.

SPECIAL FEATURES

The general-purpose DF7 (except the DF7D) is a

SPECIFICATION

Total built: DF7 – 250, DF7B – 190, DF7C – 480, DF7D – 220 (figures approximate)
Builder: Beijing 7 February
Date introduced: 1982, 1990, 1991, 1995
Track gauge, ft/ins (mm): 4 ft 8.5 in (1,435)
Axle arrangement: Co-Co
Power unit type: Dalian 12V240ZJ 12-cylinder four-stroke
Transmission: Electric AC/DC with six nose-suspended traction motors
Weight, tonnes: 138
Power rating, hp (kW): DF7, some DF7C – 1,970 (1,470), remainder 2,465 (1,840)
Design speed, mph (km/h): 62 (100)

single-cab machine with a high main hood. Construction of the original series was undertaken at the Beijing plant until the improved and more powerful DF7B and DF7C models superseded it from about 1993. By 2003 more than 1,100 of various versions were in service

CLASS DF8B DIESEL LOCOMOTIVE

Chinese Railways (CR) Class DF8B

CR's most powerful domestically built diesel locomotive is the 4,930 hp (3,680 kW) DF8B freight design, which remained in production in 2004.

SUB-TYPES

Uprated Class DF8BJ and DF8CJs variant with AC traction motors has been produced by Ziyang and Qishuyan respectively. The DF8CJs were initially intended for work on the QingZang Railway between Qinghai and Tibet and feature modifications for high-altitude operation.

SPECIAL FEATURES

Continuing demand from CR to increase the trailing loads of freight services while maintaining speeds that enable track capacity to be optimised contributed to the introduction in 1997 of the DF8B, itself a significantly improved development of the 4,435 hp (3,310 kW) DF8 produced by the

SPECIFICATION

Total built: 380 approximately (still in production in 2003)
Builder: Qishuyan
Date introduced: 1997
Track gauge, ft/ins (mm): 4 ft 8.5 in (1,435)
Axle arrangement: Co-Co
Power unit type: Qishuyan 16V280ZJ 16-cylinder four-stroke
Transmission: Electric AC/DC, with six nose-suspended DC traction motors
Weight, tonnes: 138 or 150
Power rating, hp (kW): 4,930 (3,680)
Design speed, mph (km/h): 62 (100)

Qishuyan plant from 1984. Some examples of the class are ballasted to 150 tonnes, the first CR locomotives with a 25 tonne axle-load in place of the standard 23 tonnes.

CLASS DF11 DIESEL LOCOMOTIVE

Chinese Railways (CR) Class DF11

Introduced in 1992 for express passenger work, this six-axle Qishuyan-built design now numbers some 400, with production continuing in 2004.

SUB-TYPES

Two examples of a Class DF11Z twin-section version of this type were produced by Qishuyan in 2002; the Dalian plant is reported to have equipped a DF11 with a new 12-cylinder 5,120 hp (3,820 kW) engine.

SPECIAL FEATURES

Developed exclusively as an express passenger type, the DF11s are used primarily on CR's growing network of quasi-high-speed intercity services. Distinguishable by their semi-streamlined appearance, they are powerful but fairly conventional machines apart from featuring fully suspended traction motors with hollow shaft drives.

SPECIFICATION

Total built: 400+ approximately (still in production in 2003)
Builder: Qishuyan
Date introduced: 1992
Track gauge, ft/ins (mm): 4 ft 8.5 in (1,435)
Axle arrangement: Co-Co
Power unit type: Dalian 12V280ZJ 12-cylinder four-stroke
Transmission: Electric AC/DC, with six fully suspended DC traction motors
Weight, tonnes: 138
Power rating, hp (kW): 4,835 (3,610)
Design speed, mph (km/h): 100 (160)

CLASS NY7 DIESEL LOCOMOTIVE

Chinese Railways (CR) Class NY7

In the 1970s CR procured several diesel-hydraulic types, mostly from domestic sources but two small batches of high-powered machines were obtained from Henschel in Germany, including 10 examples of Class NY7.

SPECIAL FEATURES

The 10 Class NY7 locomotives were supplied in 1972 to CR by German industry, along with five slightly less powerful but broadly similar Class NY6 machines. They formed part of China's strategy at the time of exploring Western technology before its own industry switched to production of diesel and electric traction. The powerful NY7s reflect German practice at the time, with two high-speed engines and Voith hydraulic transmission. The class was reported as intact in 2003.

SPECIFICATION

Total built: 10
Builder: Henschel
Date introduced: 1972
Track gauge, ft/ins (mm): 4 ft 8.5 in (1,435)
Axle arrangement: C-C
Power unit type: two MTU MA12V956 12-cylinder four-stroke
Transmission: Voith - hydraulic
Weight, tonnes: 138
Power rating, hp (kW): 4,930 (3,680)
Design speed, mph (km/h): 68 (110)

CLASS BJ DIESEL LOCOMOTIVE

Chinese Railways (CR) Class BJ

Now in their final years, the BJs are four-axle diesel-hydraulic passenger locomotives. With demands for increased speeds and heavier trailing loads, their work is being taken over by more powerful types and by electrification.

SPECIAL FEATURES

Class BJ was one of several diesel-hydraulic types constructed in China between the 1970s and the early 1990s, when production mostly switched to diesel-electrics. The four-axle design employs a 12-cylinder version of the Dalian '240' series power unit with a hydraulic converter and cardan shaft drives. The BJs have been primarily employed in passenger service but their numbers were diminishing rapidly in 2003-04 as more contemporary traction took over.

SPECIFICATION

Total built: 350
Date introduced: Beijing, 7 February 1970
Track gauge, ft/ins (mm): 4 ft 8.5 in (1,435)
Axle arrangement: B-B
Power unit type: Dalian 12V240 12-cylinder four-stroke
Transmission: hydraulic
Weight, tonnes: 92
Power rating, hp (kW): 2,660 (1,985)
Design speed, mph (km/h): 75 (120)

CLASS NZJ2 INTERCITY TRAINSET

Chinese Railways (CR) Class NZJ2

Introduced in 2000, the double-deck NZJ2 provides CR with a solution to the need for a high-speed, high-capacity diesel trainset for its busiest intercity routes.

SPECIAL FEATURES

CR requirements for a high-capacity train for the fastest services over its most densely used short-distance intercity routes led to the adoption of a double-deck configuration for this diesel-powered trainset, which was developed from the earlier NZJ1 design. The train configuration employs two streamlined six-axle power cars and 10 double-deck trailers. Axle-load of the power cars is 22.5 tonnes. In 2003 the type was mainly used on the Beijing-Tianjin route.

SPECIFICATION

Builder: Dalian
Date introduced: 2000
Track gauge, ft/ins (mm): 4 ft 8.5 in (1,435)
Unit configuration: two power cars and 10 trailers
Power unit type: Dalian 16V240ZJE
Transmission: electric – main alternator and six fully suspended DC traction motors per power car
Power rating, hp (kW): 2 x 3,670 (2 x 2,740)
Design speed, mph (km/h): 112 (180)
Additional features: double-deck trailers

CLASS SS1 ELECTRIC LOCOMOTIVE

Chinese Railways (CR) Class SS1

China

China's first electric locomotive to be series-produced, the six-axle SS1 remains in service in large numbers despite deliveries of more powerful modern types.

SUB-TYPES

A thyristor-controlled Class SS2 prototype based on the SS1 was produced in 1969, yielding valuable data for the SS3 which followed.

SPECIAL FEATURES

Derived from French-built Class 6Y2 machines supplied in the early 1960s, the SS1 was China's first main line electric locomotive type to be series-produced. Intended mainly for freight traffic, the SS1 initially operated in the Baoji-Chengdu line through the Qinling mountains. The class remained the only electric locomotive type in production in China until the SS3 was produced in numbers in the 1980s.

SPECIFICATION

Number series: From 1001
Total built: approximately 810 in service in 2002
Builder: Zhuzhou
Date introduced: 1968
Track gauge, ft/ins (mm): 4 ft 8.5 in (1,435)
Axle arrangement: Co-Co
Power supply system: 25 kV AC 50 Hz
Electrical equipment: Zhuzhou – tap-changer control, silicon rectifiers and six nose-suspended DC traction motors
Weight, tonnes: 138
Power rating, hp (kW): 5,065 (3,780) continuous
Design speed, mph (km/h): 93 (58)
Additional features: rheostatic braking

CLASS SS3 and SS3B ELECTRIC LOCOMOTIVES

Chinese Railways (CR) Classes SS3 and SS3B

The more powerful successor to the SS1 was the SS3, which with the generally similar SS3B is now China's most numerous electric locomotive type, production totalling nearly 1,600 examples.

SPECIAL FEATURES

From the early 1980s until 2002, this remained the standard electric locomotive type produced for CR. Initially manufactured at the Zhuzhou plant, these machines were also built at Datong after steam locomotive construction finished there in 1988. Similar in many respects to the less powerful SS1, the SS3 design was further improved with the introduction of the SS3B in 1992. This version featured control system improvements, notably to the traction control system to provide enhanced adhesion. A third factory, Ziyang, was also equipped to produce the SS3B, which remained in production in 2002.

SPECIFICATION

Total built: approximately 725 and 850 respectively in service in 2002
Builder: SS3 – Zhuzhou, Datong, SS3B – Zhuzhou, Datong, Ziyang
Date introduced: 1978, 1992
Track gauge, ft/ins (mm): 4 ft 8.5 in (1,435)
Axle arrangement: Co-Co
Power supply system: 25 kV AC 50 Hz
Electrical equipment: Zhuzhou – tap-changer control, silicon rectifiers, six nose-suspended DC traction motors
Weight, tonnes: 138
Power rating, hp (kW): 5,830 (4,350) continuous
Design speed, mph (km/h): 62 (100)
Additional features: rheostatic braking

CLASS SS4/SS4G AND SS4B ELECTRIC LOCOMOTIVES

Chinese Railways (CR) Classes SS4/SS4G and SS4B

This twin-section electric locomotive design from the mid-1980s has been built in large numbers as a standard heavy freight design. Examples are seen in most parts of the CR electrified network.

SUB-TYPES

Class SS4C was produced in prototype form to test and evaluate three-phase AC transmission. This variant also has a 25 tonne axle load rather than the 23 tonnes of the rest of the class.

SPECIAL FEATURES

Although the twin-section SS4 design was developed in the mid-1980s, it was some time before the type entered volume production. This occurred from around 1991, with Zhuzhou and Datong undertaking construction. Subsequently, the Dalian and Ziyang plants joined the manufacturing programme for this highly successful freight type, which was still in production in 2003. The availability of growing

SPECIFICATION

Total built: approximately 950 in service in 2002
Builder: Zhuzhou, Dalian, Datong, Ziyang
Date introduced: 1985, 1999
Track gauge, ft/ins (mm): 4 ft 8.5 in (1,435)
Axle arrangement: Bo-Bo+Bo-Bo
Power supply system: 25 kV AC 50 Hz
Electrical equipment: Zhuzhou, Hitachi – DC traction motors
Weight, tonnes: 184
Power rating, hp (kW): 8,575 (6,400)
Design speed, mph (km/h): 62 (100)
Additional features: rheostatic braking

numbers of these locomotives has enabled CR to increase capacity by lifting maximum trailing loads on some key routes from 3,500 to 5,000 tonnes.

CLASS SS7, SS7C and SS7D ELECTRIC LOCOMOTIVES

Chinese Railways (CR) Classes SS7, SS7C and SS7D

The first Datong-designed electric locomotive type to enter series production was the SS7 Bo-Bo-Bo, which has since been built in versions geared for both freight and passenger traffic.

SUB-TYPES

An SS7B freight version with a 25-tonne axle-load has been developed. A Co-Co passenger development of the type, the SS7E was also produced in 2001 by Datong.

SPECIAL FEATURES

Developed as a flexible 'tri-bo' design for heavy haulage on steeply graded and sharply curved routes, the SS7 initially appeared as a 62 mph (100 km/h) freight machine. Subsequent evolution saw increases in speed and a reduction in weight to produce the SS7C multi-purpose and SS7D 100 mph (160 km/h) express versions. Introduced in 1999, the SS7D features a more modern

SPECIFICATION

Number series: From SS7.0001
Total built: SS7 – 100, SS7C – 100, SS7D – 50 (approximate numbers in service in 2002)
Builder: Datong
Date introduced: 1992, 1998, 1999
Track gauge, ft/ins (mm): 4 ft 8.5 in (1,435)
Axle arrangement: Bo-Bo-Bo
Power supply system: 25 kV AC 50 Hz
Electrical equipment: Datong – DC traction motors
Weight, tonnes: 138, 132, 126
Power rating, hp (kW): 6,430 (4,800)
Design speed, mph (km/h): 62 (100), 75 (120), 100 (160)

exterior styling. Its area of operations includes the mountainous Zhenzhou-Lanzhou line.

CLASS SS8 ELECTRIC LOCOMOTIVE

Chinese Railways (CR) Class SS8

China

This four-axle type, introduced in 1996, is a Zhuzhou product developed as a standard design for CR's quasi-high-speed passenger services. It was the first Chinese electric locomotive built for 100 mph (160 km/h) running.

SPECIAL FEATURES

At least 240 examples of this four-axle design for fast passenger services have been placed in service on CR's electrified routes. One member of the class established a Chinese rail speed record in June 1998, when it achieved 149 mph (240 km/h) on the Beijing-Guangzhou line south of Zhengzhou.

SPECIFICATION

Number series: From SS8.0001
Total built: approximately 240 in service in 2002
Builder: Zhuzhou
Date introduced: 1996
Track gauge, ft/ins (mm): 4 ft 8.5 in (1,435)
Axle arrangement: Bo-Bo
Power supply system: 25 Kv AC 50 Hz
Electrical equipment: Zhuzhou – DC traction motors
Weight, tonnes: 88
Power rating, hp (kW): 4,825 (3,600)
Design speed, mph (km/h): 100 (160)
Additional features: rheostatic braking

CLASS SS9/SS9G ELECTRIC LOCOMOTIVE

Chinese Railways (CR) Class SS9/SS9G

One of the most modern designs and the fastest Chinese passenger electric locomotive type is this powerful Co-Co machine developed by Zhuzhou. The SS9 looks likely to be the last significant electric locomotive to feature DC traction motors as Chinese industry moves towards AC propulsion.

SUB-TYPES

Machines designated Class SS9G feature regenerative brakes.

SPECIAL FEATURES

A need to increase progressively both the speed and weight of CR's fastest passenger services led to the development of the SS9. Designed for 105 mph (170 km/h), the type was initially deployed on the newly electrified Harbin-Dalian line but has subsequently appeared on other CR routes. Early examples feature a flat, 'shovel-nosed' front-end but the majority have semi-streamlined

SPECIFICATION

Number series: From SS9.0001
Total built: at least 80 in service in 2003
Builder: Zhuzhou
Date introduced: 1998
Track gauge, ft/ins (mm): 4 ft 8.5 in (1,435)
Axle arrangement: Co-Co
Power supply system: 25 kV AC 50 Hz
Electrical equipment: Zhuzhou – DC traction motors
Weight, tonnes: 126
Power rating, hp (kW): 6,430 (4,800)
Design speed, mph (km/h): 105 (170)
Additional features: regenerative braking on SS9G

cabs, giving an appearance reminiscent of contemporary German practice.

CLASS DJ1 ELECTRIC LOCOMOTIVE

Chinese Railways (CR) Class DJ1

China

While Chinese industry has been able to meet most of the traction needs generated by increasing electrification of the CR network, some 'Western' technology has been applied to the development of three-phase propulsion locomotives. The powerful twin-section DJ1 is the result of a joint venture established between Zhuzhou and Siemens Transportation Systems.

SPECIAL FEATURES

The Class DJ1 three-phase electric locomotives are the first product of STEZ, a joint venture set up by Siemens Transportation Systems, Works and Zhuzhou Electric Locomotive Research Institute. The first three machines were built by Siemens in Austria, deliveries commencing in 2001, leaving the remainder to be constructed at Zhuzhou. Initial deployment of the class was on the Chengdu-Baoji line. Annual output of 70-100 locomotives of this type is planned at Zhuzhou, with export orders anticipated.

SPECIFICATION

Number series: DJ1.0001-DJ1.0020
Total built: 20
Builder: STEZ (Siemens, Zhuzhou)
Date introduced: 2001
Track gauge, ft/ins (mm): 4 ft 8.5 in (1,435)
Axle arrangement: Bo-Bo+Bo-Bo
Power supply system: 25 kV AC 50 Hz
Electrical equipment: STEZ (Siemens, Zhuzhou) – three-phase propulsion system
Weight, tonnes: 184
Power rating, hp (kW): 8,575 (6,400)
Design speed, mph (km/h): 75 (120)

EAST RAIL/WEST RAIL CLASS SP-1900/SP-1950 EMU

Kowloon–Canton Railway Corporation (KCRC)) Class SP-1900/SP-1950 emus

These high-capacity suburban emus were first introduced in 2001 to meet growing demand on KCRC's East Rail network in Hong Kong. They formed part of an order placed with a Japanese consortium for 250 cars that also included vehicles to serve the West Rail system, which opened in 2003.

SUB-TYPES

East Rail (Class SP-1900) – 12-car sets, West Rail (Class SP-1900) – 7-car sets, Ma On Shan Rail (Class SP-1950) – 4-car sets

SPECIAL FEATURES

Eight 12-car and 22 7-car sets of these units were originally ordered by KCRC for its existing East Rail and new West Rail systems in Hong Kong. Later four 4-car units were added to equip the new 7 mile (11.4 km) Ma On Shan Rail line. As well as incorporating the latest inverter control and Variable Voltage Variable Frequency (VVVF)

traction technology, these vehicles have also been designed to give low life-cycle costs. Other features include skirts along the lower bodyside to shroud the running gear as a means of minimising noise emissions and five pairs of externally hung doors per side on each car to optimise passenger handling at stations.

SPECIFICATION

Total built: East Rail – 8, West Rail - 22
Builder: IKK Consortium (Itochu, Kawasaki, Kinki Sharyo)
Date introduced: 2001
Track gauge, ft/ins (mm): 4 ft 8.5 in (1,435)
Unit configuration: East Rail – T-M-M-T-T-T-M-M-T-M-M-T, West Rail – T-M-M-T-M-M-T, Ma On Shan Rail – T-M-M-T
Power supply system: 25 kV AC 50 Hz
Electrical equipment: IKK Consortium – IGBT VVVF inverters, AC traction motors
Power rating, hp (kW):
Design speed, mph (km/h): 80 (130)
Additional features: regenerative braking, automatic train protection, automatic train operation, air-conditioning

AIRPORT EXPRESS/TUNG CHUNG EMU

MTR Corporation(MTRC) Airport Express/Tung Chung emu

Two versions of this European emu design were supplied to equip the new railway commissioned in 1998 to serve Hong Kong's new airport at Chek Lap Kok. Of essentially similar technical design, trains with different interior accommodation were supplied for airport express and suburban services.

SPECIAL FEATURES

A consortium formed by Adtranz and Spanish train-builder CAF supplied MTR Corporation with these 23 emus to provide services over the line constructed in the 1990s to link Hong Kong with its new airport at Chek Lap Lok, on Lantau Island. Essentially a common fleet, the trains were supplied two versions: 11 with a high standard of interior accommodation for airport services and 12 high-density suburban sets with more basic provision for passengers. Body construction is of extruded aluminium profiles. Reflecting their more intense passenger-handling requirements, the Tung Chung units have five pairs of doors per

side on each car, compared with two for the Airport Express sets. The two variants are recognisable by their brown and blue liveries respectively.

SPECIFICATION

Number series:
Total built: 11 for Airport Express services, 12 for Tung Chung services
Builder: CAF
Date introduced: 1998
Track gauge, ft/ins (mm): 4 ft 8.5 in (1,435)
Unit configuration: M-M-T-M-M-T-M-M
Power supply system: 1.5 kV DC
Electrical equipment: Adtranz – GTO thyristor inverters and three-phase traction motors
Power rating, hp (kW): 8,520 (6,360)
Design speed, mph (km/h): 84 (135)
Additional features: rheostatic and regenerative braking, multiple operation, air-conditioning

CLASS WCG-2 ELECTRIC LOCOMOTIVE

Indian Railways (IR) Class WCG-2

SUB-TYPES

Some locomotives are designated Class WCG-2A and have lower gearing for banking work.

SPECIAL FEATURES

These six-axle freight locomotives were built for the Mumbai Division IR's Central Railway, where they remain, primarily working between Mumbai and Igatpuri or Pune. Other duties include banking on ghat (mountain) sections of the Central network. To compensate for their relatively low power, the class often works in pairs or in threes.

SPECIFICATION

Number series: 20104–20160
Total built: 57
Builder: CLW
Date introduced: 1970
Track gauge, ft/ins (mm): 5 ft 6 in (1,676)
Axle arrangement: Co-Co
Power supply system: 1.5 kV DC
Electrical equipment: CLW – rheostatic control, with six nose-suspended DC traction motors
Weight, tonnes: 132
Power rating, hp (kW): 2,165 (1,640) continuous
Design speed, mph (km/h): 50 (80) or 56 (90)
Additional features: regenerative braking, multiple working

CLASS WAM-4 ELECTRIC LOCOMOTIVE

Indian Railways (IR) Class WAM-4

The first Indian electric locomotive type to be designed and built indigenously, the highly successful WAM-4 now forms a complex family of variants and also served as the basis for significant DC and dual-voltage types.

SUB-TYPES

As well as the lower-geared WAM-4A, several other sub-types have resulted from subsequent modifications. Locomotives numbered 21101-21138 were regeared for freight traffic, initially becoming Class WAM-4B and now designated Class WAG 5B. Within the main series variants include: Class WAM-4P, regeared and electrically modified for passenger work and Class WAM-4PD a dual-braked version of this sub-class; Class WAM-4E has air brakes only; Class WAM-4G is a freight-only version; Class WAM-4H has Hitachi rather than Alsthom traction motors; other variants have also been reported, mainly adaptations for various types of passenger work.

SPECIFICATION

Number series: Class WAM-4/WAM-4A – 20400-20699, 21200-21399
Total built: 500
Builder: CLW
Date introduced: 1970
Track gauge, ft/ins (mm): 5 ft 6 in (1,676)
Axle arrangement: Co-Co
Power supply system: 25 kV AC 50 Hz
Electrical equipment: CLW- silicon rectifiers, six nose-suspended DC traction motors
Weight, tonnes: WAM-4 – 113, WAM-4A - 120
Power rating, hp (kW): 3,640 (2,715) continuous
Design speed, mph (km/h): WAM-4 – 68 or 75 (110 or 120), WAM-4A – 50 (80)
Additional features: rheostatic braking, multiple working

Other CLW-built types sharing mechanical and in some instances electrical features with the WAM-1 are Class WAG-5 (an AC freight design); Class WCAM-1 (dual-voltage, mixed-traffic) and Class WCG-2 (DC, freight).

CLASS WAG-5 ELECTRIC LOCOMOTIVE

Indian Railways (IR) Class WAG-5

India'a most numerous electric locomotive type was introduced in 1978 is used throughout the IR network. Over 1,100 examples have been built at two plants specialising in electric locomotives.

SUB-TYPES

Various versions introduced either during production or as a result of subsequent modifications include: Class WAG-5A, equipped with Alsthom traction motors; Class WAG-5H, Hitachi traction motors; Class WAG-5E is a version adapted for passenger use; variants with a '-5H' suffix are fitted with high-adhesion bogies. Class WAG-5B was converted from Class WAG-4. There is also a Class WAP-5PA, created by modifying WAG-5 machines for passenger services.

SPECIAL FEATURES

Chittaranjan and the BHEL plant in Bhopal took part in the Class WAG-5 production programme, undertaken from 1983 to 1998. With over 1,100

SPECIFICATION

Number series: 21139-21153 (Class WAG-5B), 23000-23999, From 24000
Total built: approximately 1,100
Builder: CLW, BHEL
Date introduced: 1983 (Class WAG-5B sub-series 1978)
Track gauge, ft/ins (mm): 5 ft 6 in (1,676)
Axle arrangement: Co-Co
Power supply system: 25 kV AC 50 Hz
Electrical equipment: CLW, BHEL – silicon rectifiers, six non-suspended DC traction motors
Weight, tonnes: 119
Power rating, hp (kW): 3,850 (2,870) continuous
Design speed, mph (km/h): 50 or 62 (80 or 100)
Additional features: rheostatic braking, multiple working

examples delivered, the class is a common sight on IR's AC lines, mostly on freight, although deliveries of the more powerful WAG-7 and WAG-9 types have seem some employed on secondary passenger services.

CLASS WAG-7 ELECTRIC LOCOMOTIVE

Indian Railways (IR) Class WAG-7

Dating from the early 1990s, this significant and numerous 25 kV AC electric freight design was a more powerful successor to the WAG-5 on the CLW production line.

SUB-TYPES

Two locomotives (27002 and 27061) experimentally ballasted to 132 tonnes and designated Class WAG-7H.

SPECIAL FEATURES

Developed as a more powerful successor to the WAG-5, the WAG-7 takes advantage of the superior qualities of the Hitachi traction motor to produce a 5,000 hp machine which is further enhanced by the use of high-adhesion bogies. Its capabilities include starting a 4,500 tonne freight on a 1 in 200 gradient. The class is widely used on freight services across the IR 25 kV network.

SPECIFICATION

Number series: 27001-27635
Total built: 635
Builder: CLW
Date introduced: 1992
Track gauge, ft/ins (mm): 5 ft 6 in (1,676)
Axle arrangement: Co-Co
Power supply system: 25 kV AC 50 Hz
Electrical equipment: CLW, BHEL – silicon rectifiers and six nose-suspended DC traction motors
Weight, tonnes: 123
Power rating, hp (kW): 5,000 (3,730) continuous
Design speed, mph (km/h): 62 (100)
Additional features: rheostatic braking, multiple operation, air-conditioned cabs

CLASS WAG-9 AND WAP-7 ELECTRIC LOCOMOTIVES

Indian Railways (IR) Classes WAG-9 and WAP-7

Freight and passenger versions of the same basic design, these two classes are among the more recent 25 kV AC electric locomotive types to enter service in India. They are IR's most powerful electric locomotive type.

SUB-TYPES

Locomotive 31030 was experimentally ballasted to increase its axle-load from 20.5 to 22.5 tonnes and re-designated Class WAG-9H. It was later restored to its original state.

SPECIAL FEATURES

These locomotives are the result of a 'technology transfer' arrangement which enabled the Indian locomotive industry to capture the three-phase technology developed by ABB (now Bombardier). The first six Class WAG-9 machines were supplied fully assembled by ABB, followed by 16 more in kit form to be completed by CLW. Subsequent

SPECIFICATION

Number series: WAG-9 – 31000-31059, WAP-7 – 30201-30215
Total built: 60, 15
Builder: ABB, CLW
Date introduced: 1996, 2000
Track gauge, ft/ins (mm): 5 ft 6 in (1,676)
Axle arrangement: Co-Co
Power supply system: 25 kV AC 50 Hz
Electrical equipment: ABB (subsequently Adtranz, now Bombardier) CLW – GTO thyristor converters, six nose-suspended three-phase asynchronous traction motors
Weight, tonnes: 123
Power rating, hp (kW): 6,030 (4,500)
Design speed, mph (km/h): 100, 140
Additional features: multiple operation

examples and all of Class WAP-7 were built domestically. These latter machines handle the heaviest IR passenger services, consisting of up to 26 coaches.

CLASS WAP-4 AND WAP-6 ELECTRIC LOCOMOTIVES

Indian Railways (IR) Classes WAP-4 and WAP-6

These two related classes were produced by CLW in the 1990s for passenger work on IR's 25 kV AC network and are capable of hauling 24-coach formations at up to 87 mph (140 km/h).

SUB-TYPES

Class WAP-6 locomotives are former WAP-1 machines converted effectively to become higher-geared variants of Class WAP-4. Initially intended for 100 mph (160 km/h) operation, the class was subsequently restricted to 65 mph (105 km/h). Some examples are reported since to have been equipped with improved running gear to restore their 100 mph capability.

SPECIAL FEATURES

Class WAP-4 is a more powerful development of the WAP-1 passenger design. Like the contemporary Class WAG-7 freight locomotive, it employs well-proven Hitachi traction motors.

SPECIFICATION

Number series: WAP-4 – 22200-22399, 22500-225xx, WAP-6 – 22400-22416
Total built: approximately 250, 16
Builder: CLW
Date introduced: 1994, 1997
Track gauge, ft/ins (mm): 5 ft 6 in (1,676)
Axle arrangement: Co-Co
Power supply system: 25 kV AC 50 hz
Electrical equipment: CLW – silicon rectifiers, six nose-suspended DC traction motors
Weight, tonnes: 113
Power rating, hp (kW): 5,000 (3,730)
Design speed, mph (km/h): 87 (140), 65 (105) or 100 (160)
Additional features: multiple operation

Flexicoil bogies are used and weight-reduction measures at the design stage enabled CLW to deliver a 5,000 hp machine within virtually the same axle-load as the 3,760 hp Class WAP-1 that it succeeded.

CLASS WAP-5 ELECTRIC LOCOMOTIVE

Indian Railways (IR) Class WAP-5

This 100 mph (160 km/h) four-axle passenger electric locomotive employs three-phase technology and is used on IR's heaviest and fastest passenger services.

SUB-TYPES

CLW-built locomotives feature cabs of different appearance.

SPECIAL FEATURES

These powerful high-speed passenger electric locomotives are mainly based in northern India, where they handle principal express services. Ten examples of 11 built (one was damaged in transit) were imported from ABB (Adtranz) in 1995. Delivery of the small batch of five units from CLW began in 2000. The WAP-5 design features Henschel Flexifloat bogies and fully suspended traction motors. One example has run at 114 mph (184 km/h) during tests.

SPECIFICATION

Number series: 30000-30014
Total built: 15
Builder: ABB (Adtranz), CLW
Date introduced: 1995
Track gauge, ft/ins (mm): 5 ft 6 in (1,676)
Axle arrangement: Bo-Bo
Power supply system: 25 kV AC 50 Hz
Electrical equipment: ABB (Adtranz), CLW - GTO thyristor converters, four fully suspended three-phase asynchronous traction motors
Weight, tonnes: 79
Power rating, hp (kW): 5,440 (4,060) continuous
Design speed, mph (km/h): 100 (160)
Additional features: head-end power for train onboard equipment

CLASS WDP-2 DIESEL LOCOMOTIVE

Indian Railways (IR) Class WDP-2

The streamlined external appearance of the WDP-2 defines it as a passenger locomotive. And with IR having acquired access to General Motors technology via the agreement that resulted in the WDG-4 and WDP-4 designs, this may prove to be one of the last Indian types to employ the Alco 251 series engine that has been the cornerstone of the country's diesel locomotive fleet since its creation.

SUB-TYPES

Some locomotives are designated Class WDP-2A to signify dual (air and vacuum) brakes.

SPECIAL FEATURES

Examples of this passenger type are found on the Konkan Railway and the Southern Railway. Based around a 16-cylinder Alco 251 series engine, these AC/DC machines are unusual in Indian diesel locomotive practice in featuring a full-width body. Bogies employ Flexicoil suspension.

SPECIFICATION

Number series: 15501-15569
Total built: 69
Builder: DLW
Date introduced: 1998
Track gauge, ft/ins (mm): 5 ft 6 in (1,676)
Axle arrangement: Co-Co
Power unit type: Alco 251C 16-cylinder vee four-stroke turbocharged
Transmission: BHEL – alternator, six nose-suspended DC traction motors
Weight, tonnes: 117
Power rating, hp (kW): 3,100 (2,300)
Design speed, mph (km/h): 87 (140)

CLASS WDM-2 DIESEL LOCOMOTIVE

Indian Railways (IR) Class WDM-2

With over 2,700 examples built, the Alco-engined Class WDM-2 is the diesel workhorse of the Indian network. Locomotives of this type played a key role in the elimination of steam traction from many parts of the Indian network. The class's development has seen an uprated version produced as well many earlier examples modernised or modified.

SUB-TYPES

Several variations exist within the main series: Class WDM-2A have retrofitted air brakes in addition to vacuum equipment; Class WDM-2B mostly have air brakes only; some Class WDM-2s have been refurbished and uprated to become part of Class WDM-2C (see below); some locomotives assigned to shunting work only are designated Class WDM-2S; a batch of around 100 locomotives were built with full-width short hoods and are know among IR staff as 'Jumbos';

and a few examples have been modified with full-width cabs, necessitating relocation of the equipment located in the short hood. Class WDM-2C is a more powerful AC-DC version of the type introduced by DLW in 1994. Variants of this model include Class WDM-2CA, believed to signify dual brakes, and Class WDM-2D, used for push-pull passenger work on the Eastern Railway. Class WDP-1 is a four-axle AC-DC adaptation of the WDM-2C.

PRINCIPAL MODIFICATIONS

Some WDM-2s are reported to have been refurbished with AC-DC transmission.

SPECIAL FEATURES

IR's standard diesel locomotive type, the WDM-2 is Alco's DL560C design, one of a series of models developed by the now defunct US company for world markets. Deliveries from Alco started in

1962 but from 1964 production was undertaken at the DLW plant set up in collaboration with Alco at Varanasi, Uttar Pradesh. This facility enabled IR progressively to produce these rugged and reliable locomotives to eliminate steam traction. As a mixed traffic type, WDM-2s operate both freight and passenger traffic, although their use on the heaviest trains has been reduced with progressive electrification and the introduction of more powerful designs.

OTHER COUNTRIES OPERATED

Locomotives of this type have been built by DLW for the national railways of Bangladesh and Sri Lanka (above).

SPECIFICATION

Number series: WDM-2 - 16000-16887, 17100-17999, 18040-18999, WDM-2C – 14001-141xx
Total built: approximately 2,700, approximately 115
Builder: Alco, DLW (Class WDM-2C – DLW only)
Date introduced: 1962, 1994
Track gauge, ft/ins (mm): 5 ft 6 in (1,676)
Axle arrangement: Co-Co
Power unit type: WDM-2 – Alco 251B 16-cylinder four-stroke turbocharged, WDM-2C – Alco 251C 16-cylinder four-stroke turbocharged
Transmission: GE, BHEL, DC generator (AC alternator on Class WDM-2C) and six nose-suspended traction motors
Weight, tonnes: 112.8
Power rating, hp (kW): 2,600 (1,940), 3,100 (2,310)
Design speed, mph (km/h): 75 (120)
Additional features: rheostatic braking, multiple operation

CLASS WDG-4 AND WDP-4 DIESEL LOCOMOTIVES

Indian Railways (IR) Classes WDG-4 and WDP-4

This Indian version of General Motors GT46MAC model is the result of a technology transfer agreement signed in 1995 between the company and DLW, which is producing the locomotive.

SUB-TYPES

Class WDG-4 is the freight version, Class WDP-4 is intended for passenger services

SPECIAL FEATURES

The WDG-4 introduced three-phase AC traction to India's main line diesel fleet. Powered by a Series 710 engine, the locomotives feature three-phase AC traction motors and SIBAS microprocessor traction control equipment. GM supplied the first 13 machines complete and eight more in kit form. Production then switched to the DLW plant at Varanasi. Initial examples were allocated to the South Central Railway. The first examples of the WDP-4 passenger version were supplied by

SPECIFICATION

Number series: WDG-4 – 12001-12050, WDP-4 – 20000-20009
Total built: 50 (including examples in production in 2003), 10
Builder: General Motors, DLW
Date introduced: 1999, 2001
Track gauge, ft/ins (mm): 5 ft 6 in (1,676)
Axle arrangement: Co-Co, Bo1-1Bo
Power unit type: GM-EMD 16-710 G3B 16-cylinder two-stroke turbocharged
Transmission: GM-EMD – alternator with six or four nose-suspended three-phase AC traction motors
Weight, tonnes: 126, 119
Power rating, hp (kW): 4,000 (2,985)
Design speed, mph (km/h):
Additional features: rheostatic braking, multiple working

General Motors in 2001. Their lower weight of 119 tonnes has been achieved by the simple expedient having two fewer traction motors to give an unusual Bo1-1Bo axle arrangement.

CLASS YDM-4/YDM-4A DIESEL LOCOMOTIVE

Indian Railways (IR) Classes YDM-4 and YDM-4A

India

IR still operates an extensive metre-gauge network totalling over 9,000 miles despite a continuing programme to convert more important routes to broad gauge. The most numerous metre-gauge diesel locomotive type is this Alco-designed six-axle design initially built in the USA and Canada and subsequently domestically by DLW.

SUB-TYPES

Class YDM-4A signifies MLW-built locomotives (6130-6198, 6259-6288).

SPECIAL FEATURES

This example of Alco's DL-535A model forms the main motive power on IR's metre-gauge lines. Initial orders were fulfilled by Alco in the USA (55) and Canadian manufacturer MLW (99) before domestic production was undertaken at the DLW facility at Varanasi. Deliveries from here continued until 1990. Sisters of the broad-gauge WDM-2 family, the YDM-4/YDM-4A is a rugged single-cab

machine well suited to Indian conditions.

OTHER COUNTRIES OPERATED

DLW has exported this type to the national railway systems of Bangladesh (dual-cab variants), Tanzania and Vietnam. In addition, 39 YDM-4s were transferred from IR to Malayan Railway (KTM) in 1996 under a hire arrangement.

SPECIFICATION

Number series: 6020-6049, 6105-6769
Total built: 695
Builder: Alco, MLW, DLW
Date introduced: 1961
Track gauge, ft/ins (mm): 3 ft 3.375 in (1,000)
Axle arrangement: Co-Co
Power unit type: Alco 251B-6 six-cylinder four-stroke
Transmission: GE, BHEL
Weight, tonnes: 72
Power rating, hp (kW): 1,400 (1,045)
Design speed, mph (km/h): 60 (96)
Additional features: rheostatic braking, multiple operation

CLASS 60 DIESEL LOCOMOTIVE

Islamic Iranian Republic Railways (RAI) Class 60

The most numerous type in the RAI fleet consists of examples of the GT26-CW and GT26-CW2 models, a General Motors standard export design dating from the 1970s. Forming the backbone of the railway's fleet, the class has been the subject of recent refurbishment, leading to some examples being modified and upgraded for higher speeds.

PRINCIPLE MODIFICATIONS

Some Class 60 locomotives have received substantial modifications to equip them for express passenger work. These include replacing the six original traction motors with four more powerful units (altering their axle arrangement to A1A-A1A), changing the gear ratio and providing a full-width cab. Taken from the later series delivered in the mid-1980s, these locomotives are re-designated Class 62.

SPECIAL FEATURES

RAI proved to be the biggest customer for General Motors GT26-CW and later GT26-CW2 models, procuring 263 examples of the type. Construction was shared between GM's US and Canadian sites, with Korean licensee Hyundai contributing 20 of the improved GT26-CW2 model, delivered from 1984. The Class 60 is the most powerful of several GM types owned by the railway and is used on both passenger and freight traffic. Demands from RAI's passenger subsidiary, Raja Passenger Trains, for improved performance has led to some examples being modified and upgraded for 100 mph (160 km/h) operation (see above) while others are the subject of a general refurbishment programme.

OTHER COUNTRIES OPERATED

With just over 500 built, General Motors' GT26-CW and GT26-CW2 designs have proved a very successful element in the motive power fleets of many railway operators worldwide. Users include: Algeria (SNTF, 95 examples), Australia (25), Israel (IR, 1), Korea (South) (Korail, 167), Morocco (ONCFM, 22, above), Pakistan (PR, 36), Peru (Enafer, 7), and the former Yugoslavia (JZ, 14), these units now in Croatia as HZ Class 2.063.

SPECIFICATION

Number series: 60.501-60.569, 60.801-60.914. 60.915-60.994
Total built: 141 (in service 2003)
Builder: General Motors, EMD, General Motors, Canada, Hyundai
Date introduced: 1971
Track gauge, ft/ins (mm): 4 ft 8.5 in (1,435)
Axle arrangement: Co-Co
Power unit type: GM 16-645-E3 16-cylinder two-stroke turbocharged
Transmission: GM – DC generator and six nose-suspended DC traction motors
Weight, tonnes: 119.6
Power rating, hp (kW): 3,000 (2,235)
Design speed, mph (km/h): 75 or 100 (120 or 160)
Additional features: rheostatic braking, multiple operation

81

CLASS TM1 ELECTRIC LOCOMOTIVE

Tehran Urban & Suburban Railway Co (TUSRC) Class TM1

This rare example of a Chinese-built electric locomotive for the export market operates on a recently built line serving Tehran's western suburbs.

SPECIAL FEATURES

These locomotives were supplied under a major contract that saw Chinese industry responsible for equipping both the 42.5 km suburban railway on which they operate and the Iranian capital's new metro system. The TM1 locomotives, designated Type SS5 by their builders, operate at each end of eight-coach double-deck coaching stock formations also sourced from China. Further extensions are planned to the Tehran suburban network.

SPECIFICATION

Number series: TM1001-TM1012
Total built: 12
Builder: Zhuzhou
Date introduced: 1999
Track gauge, ft/ins (mm): 4 ft 8.5 in (1,435)
Axle arrangement: Bo-Bo
Power supply system: 25 kV AC 50 Hz
Electrical equipment: Zhuzhou – DC traction motors
Weight, tonnes: 88
Power rating, hp (kW): 4,290 (3,200)
Design speed, mph (km/h): 87 (140)
Additional features: rheostatic braking, equipped for TVM300 automatic train control, push-pull operation

CLASS IC3 DMU

Israel Railways (IR) Class IC3

The Danish-designed IC3 dmus have played a key role in the rapid development of IR's railway system. These Israeli examples of the type feature some local content.

SPECIAL FEATURES

IR has been progressively building its fleet of IC3 dmus since 1992, adding follow-on orders as upgrading and extension of its network progressed. Assembly work and provision of components for some of the units have been undertaken in Israel by local builder Haargaz. These vehicles are frequently used in combinations of up to 12 cars.

OTHER COUNTRIES OPERATED

These Israeli units are in most respects similar to the Danish parent design – see under Denmark.

SPECIFICATION

Number series: 7001/7101/7201-7035/7135/7235
Total built: 35
Builder: ABB-Scania (Adtranz, Bombardier)
Date introduced: 1992
Track gauge, ft/ins (mm): 4 ft 8.5 in
Unit configuration: M-T-M
Power unit type: KHD-Deutz BFBL-513-cp
Transmission: ZF - hydromechanical gearbox, Kaeble-Gmeinder - final drive
Power rating, hp (kW): 1,575 (1,175)
Design speed, mph (km/h): 100 (160)
Additional features: articulated configuration, multiple-unit operation of up to five units

SERIES 200 HIGH-SPEED TRAINSET

East Japan Railway (JR East) Series 200

The Series 200 units present the classic image of Japanese shinkansen trainsets. Dating from the 1980s, survivors of a fleet that originally numbered some 700 cars remain in use on JR East services and some have undergone recent refurbishment.

SUB-TYPES

Since their introduction for Joetsu and Tohuku Shinkansen services, the Series 200 units have undergone many changes and reconfigurations. Survivors now fall into two sub-series: the 12-car 'F' sets and the 10-car 'K' sets. One set (F80) is additionally equipped to operated from a 60 Hz frequency supply.

PRINCIPAL MODIFICATIONS

Since 1999 some 'K' sets have undergone refurbishment.

SPECIAL FEATURES

Series 200 was the last shinkansen design to

SPECIFICATION

Number series: F8, F19, F80, F91, F93, K21-K31, K41-K51
Total in service: 'F' sets – 5, 'K' sets – 22
Builder: Hitachi, Kawasaki, Nippon Sharyo Seizo, Toshiba
Date introduced: 1980
Track gauge, ft/ins (mm): 4 ft 8.5 in (1,435)
Unit configuration: 'F' sets – 12 cars, all motored, 'K' sets – 10 cars, all motored
Power supply system: 25 kV AC 50 Hz
Electrical equipment: Fuji Electric, Hitachi, Mitsubishi, Shinko Electric, Toshiba, Toyo Denki Seizo – thyristor control, DC traction motors
Power rating, hp (kW): 'F' sets – 14,740 (11,000), 'K' sets – 12,290 (9,170)
Design speed, mph (km/h): 150 (240)
Additional features: rheostatic braking, aluminium alloy bodyshell

employ DC traction motors. Features also include a weather-resistant body design that prevents the ingress of snow into underfloor equipment. These trains are now mostly used on the Joetsu Shinkansen.

SERIES 300 HIGH-SPEED TRAINSET

Central Japan Railway (JR Central) and West Japan Railway (JR West) Series 300

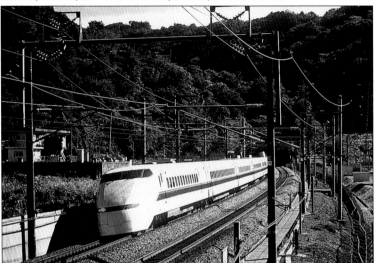

Introduced in the early 1990s, the Series 300 trainsets enabled JR Central and JR West to phase out the original Tokaido and Sanyo Shinkansen Series 0 vehicles that pioneered Japanese high-speed operations in the 1960s. Production continued until 1998, by which time the improved Series 500 and 700 trainsets were being delivered.

SUB-TYPES

Set J1 subsequently removed from revenue service to be adapted as a test unit.

SPECIAL FEATURES

Now mainly used on JR Central and JR West 'Nozomi' limited stop services between Tokyo and Shin-Osaka, the Series 300 16-car trainsets entered traffic on Tokaido and Sanyo Shinkansen services in 1992 after a two-year trial period with a pre-production unit that became set J1. They represented a step-change in Japanese high-speed traction, combining the use of aluminium construction with VVVF traction technology and

SPECIFICATION

Number series: JR Central 'J' sets – J1–J61, JR West 'F'sets – F1–F9
Total built: 70
Builder: Kawasaki, Kinki Sharyo, Nippon Sharyo Seizo, Tokyu Haryo
Date introduced: 1992
Track gauge, ft/ins (mm): 4 ft 8.5 in (1,435)
Unit configuration: T-M-T-M-M-T-M-M-T-M-M-T-M-M-T-M
Power supply system: 25 kV AC 60 Hz
Electrical equipment: Nippon Sharyo Seizo, Tokyu Haryo, Toshiba – VVVF inverter control, three-phase traction motors
Power rating, hp (kW): 16,080 (12,000)
Design speed, mph (km/h): 168 (270)
Additional features: regenerative braking, aluminium bodyshell, bolsterless bogies, eddy current braking on trailer wheelsets

three-phase AC motors to enable service speeds to be raised from the 150 mph (240 km/h) of the Series 200 to 168 mph (270 km/h). The styling of the Series 300 also signifies a departure from the classic Japanese 'bullet train' concept.

85

SERIES 700 HIGH-SPEED TRAINSET

Central Japan Railway (JR Central) and West Japan Railway (JR West) Series 700

Introduced from 1999 by JR Central and JR West to replace older vehicles on the Tokaido and Sanyo Shinkansen lines respectively, Series 700 has been produced in both 16- and 8-car versions. The design also forms the basis for trainsets for Taiwan's new high-speed railway.

SUB-TYPES

'C' sets are JR Central vehicles for Tokaido Shinkansen services, Series 700-7000 ('E') and 700-3000 ('B') sets are used by JR West on 'Hikari Rail Star' services, the latter forming through trains from Tokyo.

SPECIAL FEATURES

Representing the latest generation of Japanese high-speed trains, the Series 700 entered service in 1999 after a two-year trial period with a pre-production set that later became unit C1. Both 16- and 8-car versions feature refined design characteristics intended to minimise weight, optimise passenger comfort and control external

SPECIFICATION

Number series: JR Central 'C' sets – C1-C54 (plus C55-C60 on order/under delivery 2004), JR West 'E' sets (Series 700-7000) – E1-E15, JR West 'B's sets (Series 700-3000) – B1-B12
Total built: 54 (+ 6 on order/under delivery 2004), 15, 12
Builder: Hitachi, Kawasaki, Kinki Sharyo, Nippon Sharyo
Date introduced: 1999, 2000, 2001
Track gauge, ft/ins (mm): 4 ft 8.5 in (1,435)
Unit configuration: 'C' and 'B' sets – T-M-M-M-M-M-M-T-T-M-M-M-M-M-M-T, 'E' sets – T-M-M-M-M-M-M-T
Power supply system: 25 kV AC 60 Hz
Electrical equipment: VVVF inverter control, three-phase asynchronous traction motors
Power rating, hp (kW): 'C' and 'B' sets – 17,700 (13,200), 'E' sets – 8,850 (6,600)
Design speed, mph (km/h): 177 (285)
Additional features: regenerative braking, 'E' sets equipped for multiple operation, aluminium alloy 'double-skin' construction, semi-active suspension, bolsterless bogies

noise. The Series 700-3000 vehicles are the latest to be delivered, working JR West services throughout from Tokyo.

SERIES E1 HIGH-SPEED TRAINSET

East Japan Railway (JR East) Series E1

Japan's first all-double-deck high-speed trainsets, the 12-car Series E1 was introduced in 1994 by JR East on its Joetsu and Tohoku Shinkansen lines to provide high-capacity 'Max' (Multi-Amenity Express) commuter services in a bid to ease overcrowding.

PRINCIPAL MODIFICATIONS

A three-year refurbishment programme for the class began in 2003.

SPECIAL FEATURES

These six trains were introduced on the Joetsu and Tohoku Shinkansen lines in 1994-95. High-density 3 + 3 seating is provided in the upper decks of four of the 12 cars. Onboard catering provision is minimal, confined to a service counter and vending machines. Bodyshell construction is of steel. Six of the 12 cars have all axles motored. Axle-load is 17 tonnes.

SPECIFICATION

Number series: M1-M6
Total built: 6
Builder: Hitachi, Kawasaki
Date introduced: 1994
Track gauge, ft/ins (mm): 4 ft 8.5 in (1,435)
Unit configuration: T-M-M-T-T-M-M-T-T-M-M-T
Power supply system: 25 kV AC 50 Hz
Electrical equipment: Hitachi, Mitsubishi, Toshiba, Toyo Denki Seizo – VVVF inverter control, three-phase traction motors
Power rating, hp (kW): 13,185 (9,840)
Design speed, mph (km/h): 150 (240)
Additional features: regenerative braking

SERIES E2, E2ı and E2-1000 HIGH-SPEED TRAINSETS

East Japan Railway (JR East) Series E2, E2ı and E2-1000

Although operating on several JR East high-speed routes, the E2 was initially developed for use on the steeply graded Hokuriku (now Nagano) Shinkansen.

SUB-TYPES

Series E2ı ('J' sets) is the first batch, 10 originally supplied as 8-car sets, subsequently strengthened to 10 cars to match four delivered later, and is equipped for multiple operation, with retractable couplers at one end only. Series E2 ('N' sets) delivered as 8-car sets. Series E2-1000 ('J50' sets) is a 10-car improved version of the design introduced in 2000.

SPECIAL FEATURES

The first Series E2ı trainsets were delivered for Akita Shinkansen and subsequently also worked on the Joetsu Shinkansen between Tokyo and Niigata. Both these sub-classes are dual-frequency units, reflecting geographical

SPECIFICATION

Number series: N1-N13, N21, J2-J15, J51-J64
Total built: E2 – 14, E2ı – 14, E2-1000 – 14
Builder: Hitachi, Kawasaki, Nippon Sharyo, Tokyu Car
Date introduced: 1997, 1995, 2000
Track gauge, ft/ins (mm): 4 ft 8.5 in (1,435)
Unit configuration: E2 - T-M-M-M-M-M-M-T, E2ı and E2-1000 - T-M-M-M-M-M-M-M-M-T
Power supply system: 25 kV AC 50 Hz/60 Hz (E2-1000 25 kV AC 50 Hz only)
Electrical equipment: Hitachi, Mitsubishi, Toshiba, Toyo Denki Seizo – VVVF inverters, three-phase asynchronous traction motors
Power rating, hp (kW): 9,650 (7,200)
Design speed, mph (km/h): 170 (275)
Additional features: regenerative braking, multiple operation (Series E2ı)

differences in the Japanese national grid supply, which affects the Nagano line. The later E2-1000 units are equipped for 50 Hz only, restricting their operation to Joetsu and Tohoku Shinkansen lines. All feature bodyshells of aluminium extrusions and have an axle-load of just 13 tonnes.

SERIES E3 AND E3-1000 HIGH-SPEED TRAINSETS

East Japan Railway (JR East) Series E3 and E3-1000

The E3/E3-1000 trainsets are 'mini-shinkansen' units design to operate at maximum speed over Shinkansen lines, continuing at conventional speeds over classic routes. Deliveries of this type were still in progress in 2004.

SUB-TYPES

Series E3 (also known as 'R' sets) comprises 16 sets originally delivered as five-car sets and subsequently strengthened to six cars together with seven six-car units delivered from new. Series E3-1000 ('L50' sets) were delivered new as seven-car sets.

SPECIAL FEATURES

The first batch of these trainsets was deployed on Akita Shinkansen services after conversion of the Morioka-Akita section from 3 ft 6 in (1,067 mm) to standard gauge in 1997. Provision of an automatic coupler at the Tokyo end of each unit facilitates multiple working with E2 trainsets over

SPECIFICATION

Number series: E3 – R1-R23, E3-1000 – L51-L52
Total built: 25
Builder: Kawasaki, Tokyu Sharyo
Date introduced: 1995, 1999
Track gauge, ft/ins (mm): 4 ft 8.5 in (1,435)
Unit configuration: E3 – M-M-T-T-M-M, E3-1000 – M-M-T-M-T-M-M
Power supply system: 20/25 kV AC 50 Hz
Electrical equipment: Hitachi, Mitsubishi, Toshiba, Toyo Denki Seizo – VVVF inverter control, three-phase asynchronous traction motors
Power rating, hp (kW): E3 – 6,430 (4,800), E3-1000 – 8,040 (6,000)
Design speed, mph (km/h): 170 (275) in high-speed lines, 80 (130) on conventional lines
Additional features: regenerative braking, auto-couplers at Tokyo end to enable multiple operation with Series E3 and Series 200

the high-speed lines. The two E3-1000 units were procured for Shinjo line services. As with most recent Japanese high-speed vehicles, construction is of aluminium extrusions.

SERIES E4 HIGH-SPEED TRAINSET

East Japan Railway (JR East) Series E4

Developed initially for the Tohoku Shinkansen line to move large numbers of passengers on 'Max' services, this eight-car double-deck emu offers seating for more than 800. Two recently delivered sets are dual-frequency units for Nagano line services.

SUB-TYPES

Two sets delivered from 2003 and also designated Series P80 are equipped for both 50 Hz and 60 Hz, enabling them to operate Nagano Shinkansen services beyond Karuizawa, where the power supply frequency changes.

SPECIAL FEATURES

A development of the Series E1 Shinkansen design, the E4 employs aluminium alloy construction rather than steel and by using a double-deck configuration provides more capacity in its eight cars than the E1 in 12. The train's design enables JR East to operate two sets in

SPECIFICATION

Number series: P1-P22, P51, P52, P81, P82
Total built: 26
Builder: Hitachi, Kawasaki
Date introduced: 1997
Track gauge, ft/ins (mm): 4 ft 8.5 in (1,435)
Unit configuration: T-M-M-T-T-M-M-T
Power supply system: 25 kV AC 50 Hz ('P80' sets also 60 Hz)
Electrical equipment: Hitachi, Mitsubishi, Toshiba, Toyo Denki Seizo – VVVF inverters, three-phase asynchronous traction motors, cardan shaft drive
Power rating, hp (kW): 9,000 (6,720)
Design speed, mph (km/h): 150 (240)
Additional features: regenerative braking, multiple operation, air-conditioning, automatic train protection, onboard passenger information and seat reservation displays, wheelchair lift

multiple, providing capacity for 1,634 passengers. The canopy-style driver's cab of the E4 is designed to reduce air resistance and noise and a maximum axle-load of 15 tonnes has been achieved.

CLASS E653 EMU

East Japan Railway (JR East) Series E653

Typical of contemporary Japanese emu designs for intercity services on the 3 ft 6 in (1,067 mm) gauge network is this Hitachi-built train introduced in 1997 on JR East's Joban Line.

SPECIAL FEATURES

These seven-car emus were introduced by JR East in 1997 to replace life-expired Series 485 units to provide limited-stop 'Hitachi Express' services on its Joban Line between Mito and Ueno, on Honshu's Pacific coast. Bodyshell construction is of double-skin large extruded aluminium sections and the train runs on bolsterless bogies. A high standard of saloon interior is provided, with air-conditioning, reclining seats and at-seat radio.

SPECIFICATION

Number series: K301–K304
Total built: 4
Builder: Hitachi
Date introduced: 1997
Track gauge, ft/ins (mm): 3 ft 6 in (1,067)
Unit configuration: T-M-M-T-M-M-T
Power supply system: 1.5 kV DC/20 kV AC 50 Hz
Electrical equipment: Hitachi – VVVF inverter control, four three-phase asynchronous traction motors in each motor car
Power rating, hp (kW): 3,110 (2,320)
Design speed, mph (km/h): 80 (130)
Additional features: multiple working, regenerative braking

CLASS 885 EMU

Kyushu Railway (JR Kyushu) Series 885

This award-winning narrow gauge tilting train was introduced in 2000 by JR Kyushu to upgrade services on its principal Hakata-Nagasaki route.

SPECIAL FEATURES

An example of Hitachi's 'A-Train' concept employing double-skin aluminium bodyshell construction, the Series 885 units are a development of the earlier steel-bodied Series 883, also supplied to JR Kyushu. Like those vehicles, they employ an active-control tilt system that has enabled the operator to cut the Hakata-Nagasaki limited-stop journey time by 15 mins to 1 hr 47 min. The high-quality passenger interior of the Series 885, including leather seats and wooden flooring, contributed to the train winning the Grand Prix in the 2001 Brunel railway design awards. With their distinctive white livery, the trains are branded Kamome (Seagull) units.

SPECIFICATION

Total built: 10
Builder: Hitachi
Date introduced: 2000
Track gauge, ft/ins (mm): 3 ft 6 in (1,067)
Unit configuration: 3M3T
Power supply system: 20 kV AC 60 Hz
Electrical equipment: Hitachi – VVVF inverter control, three-phase asynchronous traction motors with cardan shaft drive
Power rating, hp (kW): 3,055 (2,280)
Design speed, mph (km/h): 80 (130)
Additional features: active tilting system, regenerative braking, air suspension, air-conditioning

CLASS DD51 DIESEL LOCOMOTIVE

Japan Freight Railway (JR Freight) Class DD51

An unusual B-2-B axle arrangement is used in these Japanese diesel-hydraulics dating from the 60s and 70s. Once numbering over 700 examples, the class is now much depleted. The majority of survivors operate secondary freight services.

SUB-TYPES

The first 53 locomotives featured control equipment differences, DD51-500, DD51-800 and DD51-1000 series were built with steam-heating equipment, variants also include locomotives equipped to operate in cold-climate areas.

SPECIAL FEATURES

This twin-engined diesel-hydraulic design has been the principal diesel power for the former Japanese National Railways companies since the 1960s, although electrification, changing operational needs and shrinking freight traffic have resulted in a big decrease in numbers. The DD51 was originally conceived as a mixed traffic

SPECIFICATION

Number series: DD51-1 – DD51-53, DD51-501 – DD51 – 799, DD51-801 – DD51-899, DD51-1001 – DD51-1186, DD51-1801 – DD51-1805
Total built: 642
Builder: Hitachi, Kawasaki, Mitsubishi
Date introduced: 1962
Track gauge, ft/ins (mm): 3 ft 6 in (1,067)
Axle arrangement: B-2-B
Power unit type: 2 x DML61Z or 2 x SA12V170
Transmission: hydraulic
Weight, tonnes: 84
Power rating, hp (kW): 2,210 (1,650)
Design speed, mph (km/h): 60 (95)
Additional features: multiple operation, variable axle-load system

main line type and many were originally fitted with steam generators for train-heating. A feature of the class is the centre carrying bogie, which can be adjusted pneumatically to bear more or less of the locomotive's weight, varying this from a 14 to 15 tonne axle-load according to adhesion requirements.

CLASS EF65 ELECTRIC LOCOMOTIVE

Japan Freight Railway (JR Freight) Class EF65

Once Japan's most numerous DC electric locomotive design, the EF65 remains in service with JR Freight. A few examples also survive with passenger operators.

SUB-TYPES

EF65-500 series are members of the original series modified with increased braking capacity for express passenger work. EF65-1000 series are intended for mixed-traffic work and equipped with increased braking capacity. Class EF64, designed for more steeply graded routes, is broadly similar to the EF65, while the EF81 is essentially a three-voltage version of the design.

SPECIAL FEATURES

Originally developed by Japanese National Railways for freight services over its DC lines, the EF65 employs the Bo-Bo-Bo axle arrangement that has proved successful on the country's narrow gauge lines. Features to maximise

SPECIFICATION

Number series: EF65-01 – EF65-135, EF65-501 – EF65-501 – EF65-542, EF65-1001 – EF65-139
Total built: 274
Builder: Kawasaki, Nippon Sharyo Seizo, Toshiba,
Date introduced: 1964
Track gauge, ft/ins (mm): 3 ft 6 in (1,067)
Axle arrangement: Bo-Bo-Bo
Power supply system: 1.5 kV DC
Electrical equipment: Kawasaki, Toshiba, Toyo – resistance control, six nose-suspended DC traction motors
Weight, tonnes: 96
Power rating, hp (kW): 3,415 (2,550) one-hour
Design speed, mph (km/h): 62 (100) or 68 (110)
Additional features: multiple working (EF65-1000 series)

adhesion include automatic wheelslip control and axle-load compensation. The EF65-1000 series, which are fitted for multiple-unit operation, are distinguishable by cab-front doors which enable crews to pass between coupled locomotives.

CLASS EF66 ELECTRIC LOCOMOTIVE

Japan Freight Railway (JR Freight) Class EF66

For many years, Class EF66 was Japan's most powerful electric locomotive type and is still in use on DC lines on some of the heaviest JR Freight services, as well as some passenger services. It also formed the basis of Spain's Class 251 locomotives.

SPECIAL FEATURES

Series production of this former Japanese National Railways type followed the introduction of a prototype, No EF66-901, in 1966. Deliveries of the first batch continued until 1975. After a 14-year gap, production resumed in 1989 with machines numbered in the EF66-1xx series. These later locomotives feature updated front-ends. The class was initially developed for express freight haulage on the Tokaido and Sanyo main lines. Subsequently the type was also used for passenger work, although the later batch was ordered only for freight. Its design features a Bo-Bo-Bo axle arrangement with a system of air suspension and swing-levers to provide lateral

SPECIFICATION

Number series: EF66-1 – EF66-55, EF66-101 - EF66-101-EF66.133, EF66-901
Total built: 89
Builder: Kawasaki, KSK
Date introduced: 1966
Track gauge, ft/ins (mm): 3 ft 6 in (1,067)
Axle arrangement: Bo-Bo-Bo
Power supply system: 1.5 kV DC
Electrical equipment: Kawasaki, Toyo Denki - rheostatic control, six fully suspended DC traction motors
Weight, tonnes: 101
Power rating, hp (kW): 5,225 (3,900) one-hour
Design speed, mph (km/h): 68 (110)
Additional features: rheostatic braking

displacement of the middle bogie when the locomotive negotiates curves. Traction motors are fully suspended, with hollow shaft drive. In 2004 JR Freight was operating 75 of the type. JR West also retained a few examples for passenger traffic.

OTHER COUNTRIES OPERATED

Spanish National Railways Class 251 is in some ways derived from the design of the EF66.

CLASS EF81 ELECTRIC LOCOMOTIVE

East Japan Railway (JR East)/West Japan Railway (JR West)/Japan Freight Railway (JR Freight) Class EF81

Developed from earlier designs, including the ED75 and EF65, this dual-voltage 'Tri-Bo' type has been a standard design in Japan since the late 1960s. While the class's passenger role has declined, examples remain active both in this capacity and for freight traffic.

SUB-TYPES

EF81-300 series built with stainless steel bodies for services via the Kanmon Tunnel linking Honshu and Kyushu, EF81-400 series built to operate at the 60 Hz frequency prevalent in the Kyushu area, EF81-500 series equipped with thyristor control.

SPECIAL FEATURES

Development of the EF81 was a response to Japanese National Railways requirement for locomotives capable of working from older DC-equipped electrified lines to a growing number of routes employing the AC system. It was first used on the Hokuriku main line. The Bo-Bo-Bo axle

SPECIFICATION

Number series: EF81-1 – EF81-152, EF81-301 – EF81-304, EF81-401 – EF81-414, EF81-451 – EF81-455, EF81-501 – EF81-503
Total built: 178
Builder: Hitachi, Mitsubishi
Date introduced: 1968
Track gauge, ft/ins (mm): 3 ft 6 in (1,067)
Axle arrangement: Bo-Bo-Bo
Power supply system: 1.5kV DC/20 kV AC 50 Hz (Sub-class EF81-300 – 60 Hz)
Electrical equipment: Hitachi, Mitsubishi, Toshiba – silicon rectifiers (EF81-500 thyristor), resistance control, six nose-suspended DC traction motors
Weight, tonnes: 101
Power rating, hp (kW): 3,175 (2,370) one-hour
Design speed, mph (km/h): 68 (110)
Additional features: multiple working

arrangement provides a solution to their use on lines featuring numerous curves, the centre bogie incorporating lateral displacement. Production extended from 1968 to 1992. Principal users in 2004 were JR East and JR Freight, both with around 60 examples in their fleet, but a few were also owned by JR West.

CLASS EF200 ELECTRIC LOCOMOTIVE

Japan Freight Railway (JR Freight) Class EF200

Japan's most powerful electric locomotive type is this 8,040 hp (6,000 kW) design introduced in 1990 for heavy freight services on the country's DC lines.

SPECIAL FEATURES

Designed to haul fast container trains at up to 75 mph (120 km/h), the EF200 was a response to JR Freight's need for a much more powerful locomotive than the ex-Japanese National Railways types it acquired on privatisation, and features state-of-the-art traction equipment. The class is mainly employed on the Sanyo and Tokaido lines. Series production commenced in 1992 after trials with a prototype, EF200-901.

SPECIFICATION

Number series: EF200-1 – EF200-20, EF200-901
Total built: 21
Builder: Hitachi
Date introduced: 1990
Track gauge, ft/ins (mm): 3 ft 6 in (1,067)
Axle arrangement: Bo-Bo-Bo
Power supply system: 1.5 kV DC
Electrical equipment: Hitachi – inverter control, three-phase induction traction motors
Weight, tonnes: 101
Power rating, hp (kW): 8,040 (6,000) one-hour
Design speed, mph (km/h): 75 (120)

CLASS EH500 ELECTRIC LOCOMOTIVE

Japan Freight Railway (JR Freight) Class EH500

As part of JR Freight's fleet modernisation, the multi-system Class EH500 twin-section electric locomotives were introduced from 1997 primarily to haul trains between Tokyo and Hokkaido via the undersea Seikan Tunnel.

SUB-TYPES

Class EH200 is a DC-only version of this design. Two examples were supplied to JR Freight in 2001.

SPECIAL FEATURES

Representing a departure from recent Japanese electric locomotive practice in adopting a twin-section eight-axle configuration rather than the more widely used Bo-Bo-Bo arrangement, the EH500 was built mainly to operate freight services northwards from Tokyo to the island of Hokkaido, entailing use of the Seikan Tunnel. The locomotives' dual-frequency capability when drawing AC power reflects the variations in

SPECIFICATION

Number series: EH500-1 – EH500-22
Total built: 22
Builder: Toshiba, Kawasaki
Date introduced: 1997
Track gauge, ft/ins (mm): 3 ft 6 in (1,067)
Axle arrangement: Bo-Bo+Bo-Bo
Power supply system: 1.5 kV DC, 20 kV AC 50 or 60 Hz
Electrical equipment: Toshiba – VVVF inverter control, three-phase asynchronous traction motors
Weight, tonnes: 134.4
Power rating, hp (kW): 5,360 (4,000)
Design speed, mph (km/h): 68 (110)

Japan's national grid supply. JR Freight designates these machines the 'Kintaro' type.

'RED FLAG' CLASS ELECTRIC LOCOMOTIVE

Korean State Railway (Zci) 'Red Flag' Class

One of several electric locomotive designs to operate on North Korea's network is this eight-axle, twin-section design derived from Czechoslovakian 1950s technology.

SPECIAL FEATURES

Few details are known of these twin-section DC electric locomotives built domestically in North Korea. Their design is believed to have been developed from that of locomotives imported from Czechoslovakia and based on that country's Class E499.0. The Red Flag machines were built mainly for work on more mountainous routes in central North Korea.

SPECIFICATION

Number series: not known
Total built: 60 approximately (estimated)
Builder: Kim Jong Tae plant, Pyongyang
Date introduced: early 1980s
Track gauge, ft/ins (mm): 4 ft 8.5 in (1,435)
Axle arrangement: Bo-Bo+Bo-Bo
Power supply system: 3 kV DC
Electrical equipment: Kim Jong Tae plant – resistance control, eight nose-suspended DC traction motors
Weight, tonnes: 160 approximately
Power rating, hp (kW): 5,360 (4,000) approximately
Design speed, mph (km/h): 62 (100) (estimated)
Additional features: rheostatic or regenerative braking

CLASS 7000 DIESEL LOCOMOTIVE

Korean Railways (Korail) Class 7000

The Korail diesel locomotive fleet is all General Motors-based, mostly produced by local licensee Hyundai (now Rotem). The Class 7000 is an interesting localised adaptation for passenger service featuring a full-width semi-streamlined body.

SPECIAL FEATURES

Designated Model FT36CHW by General Motors, Class 7000 was created for the former KNR by Hyundai as a power car for express passenger services. Designed to operate with conventional hauled stock, the single-cab locomotive features a semi-streamlined body built around otherwise conventional GM running gear and the proven 16-645E3 power unit and based on the GT26CW. The locomotive incorporates a power supply for onboard services such as air-conditioning and lighting.

SPECIFICATION

Number series: 7001-7015
Total built: 15
Builder: Hyundai
Date introduced: 1986
Track gauge, ft/ins (mm): 4 ft 8.5 in (1,435)
Axle arrangement: Co-Co
Power unit type: GM 16-645E3 16-cylinder vee two-stroke
Transmission: GM – electric, alternator, six nose-suspended DC traction motors
Weight, tonnes: 113
Power rating, hp (kW): 3,000 (2,240)
Design speed, mph (km/h): 93 (150)
Additional features: head-end power supply

CLASS 8100 ELECTRIC LOCOMOTIVE

Korean Railways (Korail) Class 8100

Korea, South

Built as a collaborative venture between the German and Korean locomotive industries, this type is a version of Siemens second-generation EuroSprinter design and is used on electrified lines in the north of South Korea.

SPECIAL FEATURES

Delivery of two prototypes of this class was the result of a 1995 contract between Siemens and Daewoo Heavy Industries which included a technology transfer element covering local mechanical manufacture. They were the first locomotives in South Korea to employ three-phase transmission. After tests with the first two locomotives, an option for 10 more machines of this type was taken up to create the present class. In common with other Korail traction, they are equipped with AAR-type automatic centre couplers. Their duties cover both freight and passenger traffic on the steeply graded electrified mountain routes in the north of South Korea.

SPECIFICATION

Number series: 8101-8112
Total built: 12
Builder: Daewoo Heavy Industries (subsequently Koros, now Rotem)
Date introduced: 1998
Track gauge, ft/ins (mm): 4 ft 8.5 in (1,435)
Axle arrangement: Bo-Bo
Power supply system: 25 kV AC 60 Hz
Electrical equipment: Siemens – three-phase asynchronous traction motors
Weight, tonnes: 88
Power rating, hp (kW): 6,970 (5,200) continuous
Design speed, mph (km/h): 93 (150)

OTHER COUNTRIES OPERATED

See also entry for German Rail (DB) Class 152.

CLASS 24 DIESEL LOCOMOTIVE

Malayan Railway (KTM) Class 24

Until the arrival in 2003 of the Class 26 'Blue Tiger' locomotives and two Chinese-built units, these Japanese-built machines were KTM's most powerful diesels.

SPECIAL FEATURES

These 2,400 hp machines are the most powerful and most recent of several Japanese-built diesel locomotive types operated by KTM. They are also the railway's most numerous class. Employed on both freight and passenger traffic, they are conventional AC/DC machines powered by an uprated version of the French-designed SEMT Pielstick engine fitted to the earlier Hitachi-built Class 23 series.

SPECIFICATION

Number series: 24101-24126
Total built: 26
Builder: Toshiba, Kawasaki
Date introduced: 1987
Track gauge, ft/ins (mm): 3 ft 3.375 in (1,000)
Axle arrangement: Co-Co
Power unit type: SEMT Pielstick 16V-PA4
Transmission: Toshiba – electric, alternator with six nose-suspended DC traction motors
Weight, tonnes: 90
Power rating, hp (kW): 2,400 (1,790)
Design speed, mph (km/h): 75 (120)

CLASS 26 DIESEL LOCOMOTIVE

Malayan Railway (KTM) Class 26

KTM's most powerful locomotive type, Class 26 is a metre-gauge version of the 'Blue Tiger' AC-motored design produced as a collaborative venture between Bombardier Transportation and General Electric.

SPECIAL FEATURES

The Blue Tiger concept was developed as a joint venture by the former Adtranz (now Bombardier Transportation) and GE Transportation to bring the latest in diesel locomotive technology to European and world markets. Designated Model DE-AC33C by its builders, Class 26 is a metre-gauge 'low profile' adaptation of the design, featuring twin cabs. Construction was undertaken at Bombardier's Kassel plant in Germany, with delivery to Malaysia completed in early 2004. KTM's main requirement for these more powerful locomotives was to handle heavier freight trains, but as mixed traffic units they are also expected to see passenger service.

SPECIFICATION

Number series: 26101-26120
Total built: 20
Builder: Bombardier Transportation
Date introduced: 2003
Track gauge, ft/ins (mm): 3 ft 3.375 in (1,000)
Axle arrangement: Co-Co
Power unit type: GE 7FDL12 12-cylinder vee
Transmission: General Electric – AC/AC, IGBT inverters with six three-phase asynchronous traction motors
Weight, tonnes: 116.4
Power rating, hp (kW): 3,300 (2,460)
Design speed, mph (km/h): 75 (120)

OTHER COUNTRIES OPERATED

Other users of Blue Tiger locomotives include private operators in Germany and Pakistan Railways (30 examples).

TYPE CKD8C DIESEL LOCOMOTIVE

Malayan Railway (KTM) Type CKD8C

Signalling a possible change in KTM locomotive purchasing trends, these two machines are examples of the Chinese traction industry's growing penetration of export markets.

SPECIAL FEATURES

China's growing role as a global traction and rolling stock supplier is exemplified by these two locomotives, the first to be supplied by the country's industry to Malaysia. These CKD8C units (manufacturers' designation) are conventional AC/DC machines employing technology well proven in locomotives produced for China's domestic market. Their 110 mph (180 km/h) capability is unlikely to be exploited on KTM's metre gauge network but is an indication of a suitability for express passenger work. While it seems unlikely that KTM will order more locomotives of this type, in 2003 the railway signed a contract with China to procure 20 3,500 hp (2,610 kW) AC-motored locomotives.

SPECIFICATION

Number series: not confirmed
Total built: 2
Builder: Dalian Locomotive and Rolling Stock Works
Date introduced: 2001
Track gauge, ft/ins (mm): 3 ft 3.375 in (1,000)
Axle arrangement: Co-Co
Power unit type: 12V240ZJD-2 12-cylinder vee
Transmission: Dalian – electric, alternator with six nose-suspended DC traction motors
Weight, tonnes: 120
Power rating, hp (kW): 2,465 (1,840)
Design speed, mph (km/h): 110 (180)

OTHER COUNTRIES OPERATED

Variants of the CKD8 family have been supplied to: Nigeria (Class 2100, single-cab, narrow hood), Tanzania-Zambia Railway (TAZARA Class DE2000), and Iraq (50 locomotives).

CLASS ERL/CRS EMUs

Express Rail Link Classes ERL and CRS

These Siemens-built emus were supplied in 2001 to equip a 35 mile (57 km) electrified standard gauge line built to provide a fast link between Kuala Lumpur's new airport (KLIA) and the city centre.

SPECIAL FEATURES

Members of Siemens' Desiro vehicle family, these four-car emus were supplied as part of a turnkey contract to equip a new railway linking the Malaysian capital to its new airport. Eight of the trains, designated Type ERL, are used on dedicated premium services for airport passengers and are provided with a higher grade interior and a stowage area for baggage containers. The remaining four Type CRS trains are used for high-density commuter services over the line.

OTHER COUNTRIES OPERATED

The design of these trains is based on that of the German Rail Class 425 emus (see entry).

SPECIFICATION

Total built: ERL – 8, CRS - 4
Builder: Siemens
Date introduced: 2001
Track gauge, ft/ins (mm): 4 ft 8.5 in (1,435)
Unit configuration: M-T-T-M
Power supply system: 25 kV AC 50 Hz
Electrical equipment: Siemens – IGBT converters, three-phase asynchronous traction motors
Power rating, hp (kW): 2,410 (1,800)
Design speed, mph (km/h): 100 (160)
Additional features: aluminium bodyshell, articulated, air-conditioned

CLASS DD.914 DIESEL LOCOMOTIVE

Myanmar Railways (MR) Class DD.914

These versatile metre-gauge diesel-electrics dating from the 1970s are a standard Alsthom export design used for both freight and passenger traffic.

SPECIAL FEATURES

For many years Alsthom was a major supplier of diesel locomotive to the railways of Myanmar, formerly Burma. The single-cab DD 914 series is not the most powerful of the types supplied by the French builder but it remains a versatile unit for lighter duties. A basic DC/DC machine, it is well suited to the rather arduous MR operating environment.

SPECIFICATION

Number series: DD.914 – DD.942
Total built: 29
Builder: Alsthom
Date introduced: 1977
Track gauge, ft/ins (mm): 3 ft 3.375 in (1,000)
Axle arrangement: Bo-Bo
Power unit type: MGO V12 vee four-stroke
Transmission: Alsthom – electric, DC generator and four nose-suspended DC traction motors
Power rating, hp (kW): 900 (670)
Design speed, mph (km/h): 50 (80)

CLASS DF.2016 DIESEL LOCOMOTIVE

Myanmar Railways (MR) Class DF.2016

In the mid-1990s MR turned to China for its locomotive requirements, procuring these Bo-Bo-Bo machine that mechanically bear many similarities with Alsthom-built machines introduced a few years earlier.

SPECIAL FEATURES

Designated Model CKD7 by Dalian, these modern Chinese-built diesel-electric locomotives were supplied to MR in three batches, the first six introduced in 1993. Their configuration and general appearance resembles the Alsthom-built DF.2000 series supplied in 1987. However, unlike many other recent Chinese locomotive exports, these feature imported power units supplied by Caterpillar. Among MR's most powerful types, they are used on both freight and passenger traffic.

SPECIFICATION

Number series: DF.2016 – DF.2036
Total built: 21
Builder: Dalian Locomotive and Rolling Stock Works
Date introduced: 1993
Track gauge, ft/ins (mm): 3 ft 3.375 in (1,000)
Axle arrangement: Bo-Bo-Bo
Power unit type: Caterpillar 3516 6-cylinder vee four-stroke
Transmission: Dalian – electric, alternator, six nose-suspended DC traction motors
Weight, tonnes: 76
Power rating, hp (kW): 1,675 (1,250)
Design speed, mph (km/h): 56 (90)

CLASS 3500 DIESEL LOCOMOTIVE

Saudi Railways Organisation (SRO) Class 3500

The desert rail system in Saudi Arabia employs mostly General Motors power, including these examples of the US builder's SDL50 model, the most powerful in the SRO fleet.

SPECIAL FEATURES

Specially adapted from General Motors standard SD50 model to operate in the demanding climatic and environmental conditions found in Saudi Arabia, the 3500s are SRO's most powerful and most numerous locomotives. Delivery of the present class was made in three batches over a long period extending from 1981 to 1998. Ten of the class are equipped with dynamic braking. The locomotives operate both freight and passenger traffic over SRO's main line linking the Gulf port of Dammam with Riyadh.

SPECIFICATION

Number series: 3500-3522
Total built: 23
Builder: General Motors
Date introduced: 1981
Track gauge, ft/ins (mm): 4 ft 8.5 in (1,435)
Axle arrangement: Co-Co
Power unit type: General Motors 16-645F3 16-cylinder vee two-stroke
Transmission: General Motors – electric, alternator, six nose-suspended DC traction motors
Weight, tonnes: 120-125
Power rating, hp (kW): 3,500 (2,610)
Design speed, mph (km/h): 100 (160)
Additional features: multiple operation, 3506-3515 have dynamic braking

CLASS M5 DIESEL LOCOMOTIVE

Sri Lanka Railway (SLR) Class M5

Saudi Arabia/Sri Lanka

These medium-powered lightweight Hitachi-built diesel-electrics dating from the mid-1970s handle many lighter duties on the SLR network. Some have undergone re-engining to extend their service lives.

SUB-TYPES

Re-engining as detailed in the table has created sub-classes M5A (1993) and M5B (1997).

SPECIAL FEATURES

With an axle-load of just 16.5 tonnes, these ageing locomotives have proved sufficiently useful on lightly laid lines for SLR to undertake re-engining of several members of the class to give them a new lease of life. This work has been carried out in the railway's own workshops at Ratmalana. Originally built in Japan in the 1970s, these are conventional AC/DC machines and are found on most parts of the SLR system.

SPECIFICATION

Number series: 770-785
Total built: 16
Builder: Hitachi
Date introduced: 1975
Track gauge, ft/ins (mm): 5 ft 6 in (1,676)
Axle arrangement: Bo-Bo
Power unit type: M5 – MTU-Ikegai 12V652TD11, M5A – MTU396, M5B – Caterpillar 3516
Transmission: Hitachi – electric, alternator, four nose-suspended DC traction motors
Weight, tonnes: 66
Power rating, hp (kW): 1,575 (1,175)
Design speed, mph (km/h): 50 (80)

CLASS M7 DIESEL LOCOMOTIVE

Sri Lanka Railway (SLR) Class M7

SLR's M7 diesel-electrics combine a British mechanical design with a General Motors power plant to provide a four-axle machine for lighter main line duties.

SPECIAL FEATURES

UK builder Brush Traction pioneered the use of main line diesel traction in Sri Lanka (then Ceylon) with the classic M1 locomotives in the 1950s. These Class M7 single-cab units were acquired from the same builder by SLR in 1981 mainly for passenger work. While of conventional design, they are unusual for a British-built diesel locomotive in employing a General Motors power unit. By 2004 some withdrawals had taken place, although some limited modernisation of survivors had also occured.

SPECIFICATION

Number series: 800-819
Total built: 20
Builder: Brush
Date introduced: 1981
Track gauge, ft/ins (mm): 5 ft 6 in (1,676)
Axle arrangement: Bo-Bo
Power unit type: General Motors 8-645E 8-cylinder two-stroke
Transmission: Brush – electric alternator, four nose-suspended DC traction motors
Weight, tonnes: 67
Power rating, hp (kW): 1,000 (745)
Design speed, mph (km/h): 50 (80)

CLASS S9 DMU

Sri Lanka Railway (SLR) Class S9

Sri Lanka

These Chinese-built MTU-powered dmus were procured by SLR in 1999 to modernise its commuter services.

SPECIAL FEATURES

Fifteen of these five-car broad gauge dmus were supplied to SLR in 1999, enabling the railway to raise standards of passenger accommodation on some of its longer distance commuter routes. They employ the less common configuration of a single power car with an above floor engine and four trailers. Transmission is electric, a necessity as the trains are designed to be converted to emus should SLR ever realise its long-term ambition to electrify sections of its network.

SPECIFICATION

Number series:
Total built: 15
Builder: Sifang Locomotive and Rolling Stock Works
Date introduced: 1999
Track gauge, ft/ins (mm): 5 ft 6 in (1,676)
Unit configuration: M-T-T-T-T
Power unit type: MTU 12V396E
Transmission: Sifang - electric
Power rating, hp (kW): 1,360 (1,015)
Design speed, mph (km/h): 62 (100)
Additional features: multiple working

CLASS LDE-1800 DIESEL LOCOMOTIVE

Syrian Railways (CFS) Class LDE-1800

These 1970s-built medium-powered General Electric locomotives have long formed the backbone of the CFS fleet, with versions geared for freight and passenger work. Despite the arrival of modern ALSTOM machines, they still play a key role in the railway's operations.

SPECIAL FEATURES

An example of GE's successful U17C export design, the LDE-1800s have proved a good investment for CFS. For nearly 30 years they have handled a large share of the railway's freight and passenger traffic in the face of the unreliability of the Soviet-built LDE 2800 locomotives. The U17C is a rugged single-cab hood design, well adapted to the harsh operating conditions encountered in Syria.

SPECIFICATION

Number series: 301-315, 351-365
Total built: 30
Builder: General Electric
Date introduced: 1976
Track gauge, ft/ins (mm): 4 ft 8.5 in (1,435)
Axle arrangement: Co-Co
Power unit type: GE 7FDL-8 8-cylinder four-stroke
Transmission: GE – electric, alternator, six nose-suspended DC traction motors
Weight, tonnes: 90
Power rating, hp (kW): 1,800 (1,340)
Design speed, mph (km/h): 15 locomotives – 68 (110), 15 locomotives 84 (135)

OTHER COUNTRIES OPERATED

As one of GE most successful export designs, examples of the U17C and the slightly more powerful U18C can be found in many countries.

CLASS LDE-2800 DIESEL LOCOMOTIVE

Syrian Railways (CFS) Class LDE-2800

Syria

The former Soviet Union's locomotive industry supplied these locomotives to CFS in two batches in the 1970s and 1980s. Unreliability has seen some examples re-engined.

PRINCIPAL MODIFICATIONS

In recent years the class has been dogged by reliability problems, leading CFS to initiate a re-engining programme using General Electric power units. At least 20 examples are reported to have undergone conversion.

SPECIAL FEATURES

These are the most powerful locomotives operating on the CFS network. Designated Model TE114 by its builders, Class LDE-2800 is an export version of the TE109 (German Rail Class 232 and derivatives) specially developed to operate in desert or tropical climates. It employs the well-proven Kolomna 1A-5D49 power unit, with AC/DC transmission. Mechanical design features a full width cab and narrow main hood. There is no

SPECIFICATION

Total built: 110
Builder: Voroshilovgrad
Date introduced: 1974
Track gauge, ft/ins (mm): 4 ft 8.5 in (1,435)
Axle arrangement: Co-Co
Power unit type: Kolomna 1A-5D49 16-cylinder vee 4-stroke (some locomotives modernised with General Electric FDL-12 power units)
Transmission: Jaricov – electric, alternator and six nose-suspended DC traction motors
Weight, tonnes: 120
Power rating, hp (kW): 2,800 (2,090)
Design speed, mph (km/h): 80 locomotives – 62 (100, 30 locomotives – 75 (120)

front hood. The first tranche of 80 units supplied from 1974 was followed by a further batch of 30 from 1984.

OTHER COUNTRIES OPERATED

Voroshilovgrad also built over 100 examples of this design for Cuban Railways (UFC Class TE114K).

113

CLASS E200/E300/E400 ELECTRIC LOCOMOTIVES

Taiwan Railway Administration Classes E200, E300 and E400

Supplied from the late 1970s by General Electric in the USA to work services over TRA's newly electrified West Trunk line, these thyristor-controlled locomotives continue to play a key role for the railway.

SPECIAL FEATURES

This family of locomotives was supplied by GE to meet the heavier traction needs created by progressive electrification of TRA's West Trunk line. Designated Model E42C by their builders, they are thyristor-controlled machines incorporating automatic regulation of tractive effort and wheel-slip. The E300s were notionally supplied for freight traffic but they also operate passenger services, using a generator car to provide an onboard power supply. Class E400 is generally similar but is geared for a slightly higher top speed of 75 mph (120 km/h). While some of their duties have been taken over by

SPECIFICATION

Number series: E201-E240, E301-E339, E401-E418
Total built: 40, 39, 18
Builder: General Electric
Date introduced: 1976, 1976, 1980
Track gauge, ft/ins (mm): 3 ft 6 in (1,067)
Axle arrangement: Co-Co
Power supply system: 25 kV AC 60 Hz
Electrical equipment: General Electric – thyristor control, six nose-suspended DC traction motors
Weight, tonnes: 96, 96, 92
Power rating, hp (kW): 3,750 (2,800) continuous
Design speed, mph (km/h): 68, 68, 75
Additional features: multiple working, Class E200 equipped to provide train heating/power

Class E1000, these locomotives continue to handle many West Trunk duties, which they share with the lighter British-built E1000 machines.

CLASS E1000 ELECTRIC LOCOMOTIVE

Taiwan Railway Administration (TRA) Class E1000

These stylish South African-built single-cab locomotives provide traction for push-pull express passenger services on TRA's electrified narrow gauge trunk routes.

SPECIAL FEATURES

Unique to Taiwan, these 64 electric locomotives – effectively power cars – were supplied to TRA to operate principal intercity services on electrified sections of its 3 ft 6 in (1,067) gauge network on the east coast. They are used in pairs, formed at each end of rakes of conventional coaching stock that is through wired to enable the trailing locomotive to be remotely controlled. Formations are of up to 15 trailers. A gangway is provided at each 'blunt' end of the locomotive to provide through access for staff. Although supplied under a contract placed with GEC Alsthom, construction of the class was undertaken in South Africa by Union Carriage & Wagon at its Nigel facility.

SPECIFICATION

Number series: E1001-E1064
Total built: 64
Builder: Union Carriage & Wagon
Track gauge, ft/ins (mm): 3 ft 6 in (1,067)
Axle arrangement: Bo-Bo
Power supply system: 25 kV AC 60 Hz
Electrical equipment: GEC Alsthom
Weight, tonnes: 58
Design speed, mph (km/h): 80 (130)
Additional features: push-pull working, rheostatic braking

CLASS DHL 100 DIESEL LOCOMOTIVE

Taiwan Railway Administration Class DHL 100

The latest locomotives an otherwise all GM TRA diesel fleet are these diesel-hydraulic machines supplied by Japanese builders in 2002.

SUB-TYPES

Class R100 (39 supplied from 1969) is an A1A-A1A version of this type, designated Model G22AU by General Motors.

SPECIAL FEATURES

TRA acquired this fleet of 16 diesel-hydraulic locomotives from Japanese builders. Intended as trip and shunting machines to replace the GM Class S300 units dating from the 1960s and other older types, they are now widely distributed around the network. Introducing hydraulic transmission to a previously all diesel-electric fleet, the DHL 100 units feature an off-centre single cab with low hoods. The first example,

SPECIFICATION

Number series: DHL 101 – DHL 116
Total built: 16
Builder: Niigata Engineering (now Niigata Transys)
Date introduced: 2002
Track gauge, ft/ins (mm): 3 ft 6 in (1,067)
Axle arrangement: B-B
Power unit type: Cummins KTA38-L 12-cylinder four-stroke
Transmission: Hydraulic - NICO
Weight, tonnes: 75
Power rating, hp (kW): 1,200 (900)
Design speed, mph (km/h): 75 (46)

DHL 101, was delivered with the upper headlight group positioned on the front of the short hood. On subsequent deliveries, the lights were located on the cab-front as depicted in the illustration.

CLASS DR1000 RAILCAR

Taiwan Railway Administration (TRA) Class DR1000

These modern Japanese-designed single-unit railcars were procured by TRA to improve service levels of non-electrified branch lines. They share design characteristics with Class DR3100 three-car dmus also obtained from Japan.

SPECIAL FEATURES

TRA ordered these aluminium-bodied diesel-hydraulic railcars to upgrade services on its Chi-chi, Neiwan and Pingshi branches, awarding a contract to Nippon Sharyo that also covered the supply of 10 three-car DR3100 units of similar general design. The first two vehicles were built in Japan, the remainder were supplied as 'knocked-down' kits for local assembly in Taiwan.

SPECIFICATION

Total built: 36
Builder: Nippon Sharyo (with some local assembly in Taiwan)
Date introduced: 1998
Track gauge, ft/ins (mm): 3 ft 6 in (1,067)
Unit configuration: M
Power unit type: Cummins NTA855-R1
Transmission: Nico - hydraulic
Power rating, hp (kW): 350 (260)
Design speed, mph (km/h): 68 (110)
Additional features: multiple working within type and with other TRA dmu types, air-conditioning, toilet and other facilities for disabled passengers in DRC-B variant.

CLASS 'ALSTHOM'/AHK/ALD/ADD DIESEL

State Railway of Thailand (SRT) Classes 'Alsthom', AHK, ALD and ADD

This group of essentially similar French-designed classes is the most numerous main line type operating in Thailand, with over 100 examples in traffic, handling both freight and passenger traffic.

SPECIAL FEATURES

These versatile mixed traffic locomotives were supplied to an Alsthom design between 1975 and 1985. Most were built in France but the German manufacturers Henschel and Krupp assisted with construction of the 30 Class AHK machines. Accounting for over one third of the SRT main line fleet, these locomotives are seen over the entire system.

SPECIFICATION

Number series: 4101-4149, 4201-4230, 4301-4309, 4401-4420
Total built: 49, 30, 9, 20
Builder: Alsthom (Class AHK – Alsthom, Henschel, Krupp)
Date introduced: 1975, 1980, 1983, 1985
Track gauge, ft/ins (mm): 3 ft 3.375 in (1,000)
Axle arrangement: Co-Co
Power unit type: SEMT-Pielstick 16PA4 V183 or 16PA4 185VG 16-cylinder vee 4-stroke
Transmission: Alsthom – electric, alternator, six nose-suspended DC traction motors
Weight, tonnes: 82.5
Power rating, hp (kW): 2,400 (1,790)
Design speed, mph (km/h): 62 (100) ('Alsthom' locomotives - 59 (95))

CLASS GE (4000 SERIES) DIESEL LOCOMOTIVE

State Railway of Thailand (SRT) Class GE (4000 Series)

Thailand

Still an essential component of the SRT fleet but now largely confined to secondary and shunting duties, these General Electric veterans are the oldest units of the railway's eclectic mix of main line diesel types.

SPECIAL FEATURES

SRT traffic demands have seen this veteran class remain in use, with some examples re-powered to prolong their service lives. Like several types added later to the SRT fleet, these are twin-engined machines with conventional DC/DC transmission. They are designated Model UM12C by GE. Duties of the class are now mainly limited to secondary passenger and shunting/pilot duties.

SPECIFICATION

Number series: 4001–4050
Total built: 50
Builder: General Electric
Date introduced: 1964
Track gauge, ft/ins (mm): 3 ft 3.375 in (1,067)
Axle arrangement: Co-Co
Power unit type: 2 x Cummins KT36L or 2 x KT2300L
Transmission: General Electric – electric, generator, six nose-suspended DC traction motors
Weight, tonnes: 75
Power rating, hp (kW): 1,320 (985)
Design speed, mph (km/h): 62 (100)
Additional features: multiple working

CLASS HID (4500 SERIES) DIESEL LOCOMOTIVE

State Railway of Thailand (SRT) Class HID (4500 Series)

The most powerful locomotive type in the SRT fleet is this twin-engined Hitachi-built design dating from the early 1990s. These machines share principal main line duties with the Class GEA units from the same period.

SPECIAL FEATURES

The Class HID machines highlight the suitability of a twin-engined design, with its weight distribution benefits, for higher power requirements on narrow gauge lines. Hitachi's design for SRT couples two Cummins KTA50-L power units with an AC/DC transmission to produce this powerful locomotive that is at the limit of the SRT's axle-load tolerance. While essentially a mixed traffic type, the class is particularly evident on the railway's heaviest passenger services.

SPECIFICATION

Number series: 4501-4522
Total built: 22
Builder: Hitachi
Date introduced: 1993
Track gauge, ft/ins (mm): 3 ft 3.375 in (1,000)
Axle arrangement: Co-Co
Power unit type: 2 x Cummins KTA50-L 16-cyliner vee four-stroke
Transmission: Hitachi – electric, alternators, six nose-suspended DC traction motors
Weight, tonnes: 90
Power rating, hp (kW): 2,860 (2,135)
Design speed, mph (km/h): 62 (10)
Additional features: multiple working

CLASS GEA (4550 SERIES) DIESEL LOCOMOTIVE

State Railway of Thailand (SRT) Class GEA (4550 Series)

Thailand

The most recent additions to the SRT main line locomotive fleet are these General Electric machines that continue the railway's practice of adopting a twin-engined traction configuration.

SPECIAL FEATURES

For its latest main line locomotive acquisitions SRT again adopted a six-axle mixed traffic design powered by two Cummins KTA50-L engines, as fitted to the Hitachi-built Class HID machines. On this occasion, General Electric was selected as the builder, designating the type Model CM22-7i and supplying 38 examples from 1995.

SPECIFICATION

Number series: 4551–4588
Total built: 38
Builder: General Electric
Date introduced: 1995
Track gauge, ft/ins (mm): 3 ft 6 in (1,067)
Axle arrangement: Co-Co
Power unit type: 2 x Cummins KTA50-L 16-cyliner vee four-stroke
Transmission: General Electric – electric, alternator, six nose-suspended DC traction motors
Weight, tonnes: 86.5
Power rating, hp (kW): 2,500 (1,865)
Design speed, mph (km/h): 62 (100)
Additional features: multiple working, dynamic braking

CLASS DE 11000 DIESEL LOCOMOTIVE

Turkish State Railways (TCDD) Class DE 11000

Among the more recent main line types to enter TCDD service is this German-designed four-axle diesel-electric for secondary duties. Later examples employ AC traction motors.

SPECIAL FEATURES

Mainly used for lighter passenger work, these single-cab Bo-Bos were a collaborative venture between Krauss-Maffei, leading European transmission equipment suppliers and Turkish domestic manufacturer Tülomsas. The first 15 are provided with DC traction motors, but subsequent examples have three-phase AC motors, the first TCDD diesel locomotive type to be so equipped.

SPECIFICATION

Number series: DE 11001–DE 11085
Total built: 85
Builder: Krauss-Maffei, Tülomsas
Date introduced: 1985
Track gauge, ft/ins (mm): 4 ft 8.5 in (1,435)
Axle arrangement: Bo-Bo
Power unit type: MTU 8V396 TC13
Transmission: GEC, BBC, ABB – electric, alternator and four nose-suspended DC (DE 11001–DE 11015) or AC (remainder) traction motors
Weight, tonnes: 68
Power rating, hp (kW): 1,065 (785)
Design speed, mph (km/h): 50 (80)
Additional features: some equipped for electric train-heating

CLASS DE 24000 DIESEL LOCOMOTIVE

Turkish State Railways (TCDD) Class DE 24000

By far TCDD's most numerous diesel type, the single-cab DE 24000s are versatile mixed traffic machines.

SUB-TYPES

Lower-powered Bo-Bo and A1A-A1A versions of this design, Classes DE 18 000 (5 units) and DE 18100 (20), are also in service and were produced under the same technology transfer contract.

SPECIAL FEATURES

Introduced in the 1970s to eliminate steam traction, the Class DE 24000s form the principal part of the TCDD diesel locomotive fleet. They are the result of a technology transfer agreement between Turkish industry and a group of French companies led by MTE and subsequently all becoming part of ALSTOM. The agreement provided for manufacture at the Tülomsas plant at Eskisehir with increasing amounts of equipment and manufacturing sourced in Turkey.

SPECIFICATION

Number series: DE 24001-DE 24418
Total built: 418
Builder: Tülomsas
Date introduced: 1970
Track gauge, ft/ins (mm): 4 ft 8.5 in (1,435)
Axle arrangement: Co-Co
Power unit type: SEMT-Pielstick 16PA4-185
Transmission: Alsthom – electric, alternator, with six nose-suspended DC traction motors
Weight, tonnes: 112.8
Power rating, hp (kW): 2,400 (1,790)
Design speed, mph (km/h): 75 (120)
Additional features: multiple working (some locomotives), dynamic braking (some locomotives)

The design is built around the SEMT-Pielstick 16PA4-185 power unit that was already well proven in France but adops a single-cab 'hood' configuration considered more suited to TCDD conditions. By 2003 over 130 examples had been withdrawn but the class remains in the front line of TCDD freight and passenger traffic.

CLASS E 43000 ELECTRIC LOCOMOTIVE

Turkish State Railways (TCDD) Class E 43000

These Japanese-designed 'Tri-Bos' are TCDD's most numerous and most powerful electric locomotives. They are employed on both freight and passenger traffic on TCDD's unconnected electrified sections west of Ankara and in central Turkey.

SPECIAL FEATURES

These boxy thyristor-controlled electric locomotives were initially procured by TCDD to operate freight and passenger services over the newly electrified mountainous line from the Mediterranean port of Iskenderun to Diyrigi, in the centre of Turkey. Subsequently they were also deployed on the line west from Ankara to the Bosphorus. Construction was a collaborative effort between Toshiba in Japan and the Eskisehir plant of Tülomsas. Features defining these locomotives as mountain machines include the adoption of a Bo-Bo-Bo axle arrangement, well-proven in Japan, and provision to employ

SPECIFICATION

Number series: E 43001-E 43045
Total built: 45
Builder: Toshiba, Tülomsas
Date introduced: 1987
Track gauge, ft/ins (mm): 4 ft 8.5 in (1,435)
Axle arrangement: Bo-Bo-Bo
Power supply system: 25 kV AC 50 Hz
Electrical equipment: Toshiba – thyristor control, six nose-suspended DC traction motors
Weight, tonnes: 120
Power rating, hp (kW): 4,260 (3,180)
Design speed, mph (km/h): 56 (90) / 75 (120) (two gear ratios)
Additional features: rheostatic braking

different gear ratios according to the haulage task being undertaken.

Australasian Trains

CLASS FQ DIESEL LOCOMOTIVE

Asia Pacific Transport (APT)/FreightLink Class FQ

Among the newest locomotives supplied to an Australian operator, these powerful Co-Cos were delivered in 2003 to operate services over the newly built Alice Springs-Darwin standard gauge line from its opening in 2004. Their design is similar to machines operated by Australian Railroad Group (ARG) in Western Australia.

SPECIAL FEATURES

Designated Model GT46C by their manufacturers, these four GM-engined machines were built for services over the 880 mile (1,420 km) line from Alice Springs to Darwin, commissioned in early 2004. Contiguous with the line from Adelaide to Alice Springs, the new railway offers an important route for freight, especially container traffic, between South Australia and east and southeast Asia. It is also used by 'The Ghan' transcontinental passenger service.

Locomotives FQ01 Kurru Kurraka and FQ02 Purna were employed on the inaugural Adelaide-Alice Springs-Darwin service, which reached the Northern Territories port on 17 January 2004. Trains are operated by FreightLink, the operating subsidiary of Asia Pacific Transport, which supervised construction of the new line and holds a concession to operate it for 50 years.

The FQ locomotives are conventional single-cab AC/DC machines employing the 16-cylinder GM 710 series engine. A fleet of 19 similar locomotives (Class Q, Nos 301-319, above right) is operated by ARG, which took over the freight operations of Westrail on its partial privatisation. These were built at the former Clyde Engineering's Forrestfield plant in Western Australia in 1997-98.

SPECIFICATION

Number series: FQ01-FQ04
Total built: 4
Builder: Evans Deakin Industries
Date introduced: 2003
Track gauge, ft/ins (mm): 4 ft 8.5 in (1,435)
Axle arrangement: Co-Co
Power unit type: GM 16-710G3B-ES
16-cylinder vee 2-stroke
Transmission: GM - alternator, six nose-
suspended DC traction motors
Weight, tonnes: 134
Power rating, hp (kW): 4,155 (3,100)
Design speed, mph (km/h): 70 (115)
Additional features: multiple working

CLASS P DIESEL LOCOMOTIVE

Class P Australian Railroad Group

The sole GE model in the former Westrail fleet is this series of 17 narrow gauge six-axle machines dating from the late 1980s and bearing the manufacturers' Model CM25-8 designation. Their duties include grain traffic.

SPECIAL FEATURES

Successful GE interlopers in an otherwise all-GM-powered fleet, the Class P locomotives were Westrail's most powerful units on its narrow gauge system until the arrival of the Class S machines. The locomotives are of a single-cab, narrow hood configuration employing GE's proven 7FDL power unit in its 12-cylinder version. Production was undertaken by Goninan (now United Goninan) at Bassendean, Perth. All 7 subsequently passed to Australian Railroad Group on privatisation of the state operator's freight business and now handle a range of traffic in which grain haulage predominates.

SPECIFICATION

Number series: 2001-2017
Total built: 17
Builder: Goninan
Date introduced: 1989
Track gauge, ft/ins (mm): 3 ft 6 in (1,067)
Axle arrangement: Co-Co
Power unit type: GE 7FDL-12 12-cylinder vee 4-stroke
Transmission: GE - alternator, six nose-suspended DC traction motors
Weight, tonnes: 101
Power rating, hp (kW): 2,680 (2,000)
Design speed, mph (km/h): 56 (90)
Additional features: multiple working

CLASS S DIESEL LOCOMOTIVE

Class S Australia Railroad Group

These are the most powerful locomotives on the narrow gauge lines of the former Westrail system in Western Australia. Displacing less powerful types from the 1960s and 1970s, they are used for both heavy haul and general freight services.

SPECIAL FEATURES

Westrail's final locomotive acquisitions before its freight operations were privatised and taken over by Australian Railroad Group, the twin-cab Class S machines are among the world's most powerful narrow gauge locomotives. Final assembly of the class was undertaken locally by Clyde Engineering (now Evans Deakin Industries) at Forrestfield, Perth. Designated Model JT42C, the locomotives' features also include microprocessor control, Super Series adhesion control and integrated cab electronics.

SPECIFICATION

Number series: 2101-2111
Total built: 11
Builder: Clyde Engineering
Date introduced: 1998
Track gauge, ft/ins (mm): 3 ft 6 in (1,067)
Axle arrangement: Co-Co
Power unit type: GM 12N-710G3B-ES 12-cylinder vee 2-stroke
Transmission: GM - alternator, six nose-suspended DC traction motors
Weight, tonnes: 118.5
Power rating, hp (kW): 3,250 (2,425)
Design speed, mph (km/h): 62 (100)
Additional features: multiple working, radial steering bogies, dynamic braking

TYPE CM40-8/CM40-8M (DASH 8) DIESEL LOCOMOTI'

bhpbilliton Iron Ore Railroad CM40-8/CM40-8M (Dash 8)

Together with eight GE AC6000 locomotives, these 36 GE Dash 8 derivatives handle heavy haul iron ore traffic on two commonly operated lines from Mount Goldsworthy and Mount Newman to Port Headland, on Australia's northwest coast. Most are rebuilds of Alco-engined C-636 machines.

SUB-TYPES

Nos 5646 and 5647 (Model CM40-8) built new. The remainder are rebuilds of the railway's former C-636 locomotives. Three of the class ran as cabless units for a while as mid-train helpers but were subsequently restored to standard configuration with cabs.

SPECIAL FEATURES

These locomotives and their more powerful GE-built AC6000 cousins handle over 70 million tonnes of iron ore annually on the isolated 435 mile (700 km) bhpbilliton system in northwest Australia. Most of the fleet was formed by a comprehensive rebuilding by Goninan of the railway's former Alco C-636 locomotives. Axle-load is 36 tonnes. A fleet of 12 similar locomotives operates on the Robe River iron ore system (right), now operated as part of Pilbara Rail.

SPECIFICATION

Number series: 5634-5669
Total built: 36
Builder: Goninan
Date introduced: 1991
Track gauge, ft/ins (mm): 4 ft 8.5 in (1,435)
Axle arrangement: Co-Co
Power unit type: GE FDL-16 16-cylinder vee 4-stroke
Transmission: GE - alternator, six nose-suspended DC traction motors
Weight, tonnes: 195
Power rating, hp (kW): 4,200 (3,135)
Design speed, mph (km/h): 70 (112)
Additional features: multiple working, dynamic braking, Locotrol radio remote control

TANGARA EMU

CityRail Tangara class

Most of Sydney's commuter services are provided by different generations of double-deck emus. The distinctive flat-fronted Tangara sets were introduced in the late 1980s and operate in both inner and outer suburban versions.

SUB-TYPES

Outer suburban G Sets, distinguishable by a yellow warning panel below the cab front window, feature higher grade seating and are provided with a toilet in one of the driving trailers.

SPECIAL FEATURES

With their characteristic front ends, the Tangara emus are a familiar sight on CityRail's Sydney electrified suburban network, sharing duties with older stainless steel-bodied units and, more recently, the latest Millennium trainsets. Both G and T Sets are formed of two unpowered driving trailers with a pantograph (D cars), and two intermediate motor cars (N cars).

SPECIFICATION

Number series: T1-T112, G1-G20
Total built: T Sets - 225 driving trailers, 225 motor cars. G Sets - 41 driving trailers, 40 motor cars (up to 112 and 20 sets respectively)
Builder: Goninan
Date introduced: 1988, 1994
Track gauge, ft/ins (mm): 4 ft 8.5 in (1,435)
Unit configuration: T-M-M-T
Power supply system: 1.5 kV DC
Electrical equipment: Mitsubishi - GTO chopper control, eight nose-suspended DC traction motors per 4-car set
Power rating, hp (kW): 1,820 (1,360)
Design speed, mph (km/h): 70 (115)
Additional features: multiple working, air-conditioning

X'TRAPOLIS EMU

Connex Trains Melbourne X'TRAPOLIS emu

Among the latest passenger trains to be introduced in Australia are these state-of-the-art emus supplied by Alstom for the former Hillside Trains suburban network in Melbourne, now operated as Connex Trains Melbourne.

SPECIAL FEATURES

This fleet of new emus was ordered from Alstom in 1999 to replace life-expired vehicles built by Hitachi in the 1970s. The contract followed the award of a franchise to a Connex-led consortium to take over the formerly state-run Hillside Trains suburban network in Melbourne. Assembly of the first 10 trains was carried out at Alstom's Aytré (La Rochelle) plant in France. The remaining units were assembled at Ballarat, the former workshops of the Public Transport Corporation of Victoria which were acquired by Alstom in 1999. Features of the trains also include carbon steel bodyshells and three pairs of sliding doors per car side.

SPECIFICATION

Total built: 58
Builder: Alstom
Date introduced: 2002
Track gauge, ft/ins (mm): 5 ft 3 in (1,600)
Unit configuration: M-T-M
Power supply system: 1.5 kV DC
Electrical equipment: Alstom - three-phase asynchronous traction motors
Design speed, mph (km/h): 80 (130)
Additional features: air-conditioning, external and internal passenger information displays, interior CCTV

CLASS XP DIESEL POWER CAR

Countrylink Class XP

Based on the design of the power car of the former British Rail's HST high-speed diesel trainset, the Class XPs are used by Countrylink, the long-distance passenger business of the State Rail Authority of New South Wales, over a network linking Sydney with ten destinations.

PRINCIPAL MODIFICATIONS

Originally fitted with Paxman Valenta 12RP200L power units.

SPECIAL FEATURES

This Australian adaptation of the UK's HST high-speed diesel trainset has since the early 1980s been the principal equipment on long-distance passenger services in New South Wales, including both daylight and overnight services between Sydney and Melbourne (590 miles/950 km). The first 15 power cars were built by Comeng, followed by four more from ABB. Like some of their British counterparts, they have been the

SPECIFICATION

Number series: 2000-2018
Total built: 19
Builder: Comeng, ABB
Date introduced: 1981
Track gauge, ft/ins (mm): 4 ft 8.5 in (1,435)
Axle arrangement: Bo-Bo
Power unit type: MAN B&W 12VP185 12 cylinder vee 4-stroke
Transmission: Brush - alternator, four fully suspended DC traction motors
Weight, tonnes: 74
Power rating, hp (kW): 2,000 (1,490)
Design speed, mph (km/h): 100 (160)
Additional features: operate at both ends of rakes of seven to nine trailers to form XPT trainsets, head-end power

subject of a re-engining programme with the MAN B&W (formerly Paxman) VP185 power unit. Trailers are of stainless steel construction, drawn from a pool of 52 for seated passengers, and eight sleepers.

CLASS G DIESEL LOCOMOTIVE

Pacific National Class G

Introduced by the Victoria state rail operator V/Line in 1984, the Class G is a typical Clyde Engineering GM-powered product of the period. The class is the most numerous in the Freight Australia fleet and comprises a mix of standard and broad gauge examples.

PRINCIPAL MODIFICATIONS

At least seven examples have been rebuilt with uprated engines. Class designation and number series are unchanged.

SPECIAL FEATURES

Designated Model JT26C-2SS and built by GM's Australian licensee Clyde Engineering, these locomotives were built at plants at Somerton (Melbourne) and Rosewater, near Adelaide. The legacy of the history of railway construction in Australia is evident with standard and broad gauge variants within the class, with numbers changing according to traffic needs. In their early years, Class G locomotives handled passenger as well as freight traffic. Since May 1999, surviving examples (some have been lost to crashes) have been operated by Freight Australia, the consortium led by US-based RailAmerica that took over V/Line's freight business on privatisation. However, in 2004 Freight Australia was taken over by Pacific National.

SPECIFICATION

Number series: G511-G543
Total built: 33
Builder: Clyde Engineering
Date introduced: 1984
Track gauge, ft/ins (mm): 4 ft 8.5 in (1,435) or 5 ft 3 in (1,600)
Axle arrangement: Co-Co
Power unit type: GM 16-645E3B or 16-645F3B 16-cylinder vee 2-stroke
Transmission: GM - alternator, six nose-suspended DC traction motors
Weight, tonnes: 127
Power rating, hp (kW): 3,300 (2,460) or 3,800 (2,835)
Design speed, mph (km/h): 70 (115)
Additional features: multiple working

CLASS Y DIESEL LOCOMOTIVE

Pacific National Class Y

Introduced on the former Victoria state network for branch and shunting duties in 1963, a few examples of this veteran design remained in service in 2004 both on the standard gauge system and on broad gauge lines.

SUB-TYPES

The more powerful 6-645E power unit was fitted to the last 25 locomotives (Y151-Y175). Some locomotives have GE traction motors, others GM.

SPECIAL FEATURES

In 2003 just 14 of this once large fleet of Model G6B locomotives remained on Freight Australia's stock list, mostly handling yard and pilot duties. Others have been sold, scrapped, stored or preserved. Derived from GM's G6 model of the period, the Class Y locomotives are basic single-cab DC/DC hood units with only the last 25 receiving the Series 645 engine in place of the

SPECIFICATION

Number series: Y101-Y175
Total built: 75
Builder: Clyde Engineering
Date introduced: 1963
Track gauge, ft/ins (mm): 4 ft 8.5 in (1,435) or 5 ft 0 in (1,600)
Axle arrangement: Bo-Bo
Power unit type: GM 6-567C or 6-645E
Transmission: GM/GE - generator, four nose-suspended DC traction motors
Weight, tonnes: 68
Power rating, hp (kW): 640 (480) or 750 (560)
Design speed, mph (km/h): 40 (65)
Additional features: multiple working

once-standard Series 567. Construction took place at Clyde's Granville facility in Sydney. However, in 2004 Freight Australia was taken over by Pacific National.

INTERAIL CLASS 422 DIESEL LOCOMOTIVE

Interail Class 422

Australia

Survivors of a class of 20 supplied to the New South Wales state system from the late 1960s, the two Class 422 locomotives operated by Interail, a subsidiary of QR, signal growing commercial interest in open access operations in Australia.

SPECIAL FEATURES

The 422s were acquired by the New South Wales State Rail Authority (SRA) in the late 1960s as a mixed traffic machine. Early deployment included services south from Sydney to the Victoria state border and beyond to Melbourne. Eventually made redundant by the SRA's freight successor, FreightCorp, following the arrival of more modern traction, they were sold to other operators or traction leasing companies. The largest batch, 16 machines, went to Australia Southern Railroad, but two were sold to Northern Rivers Railroad and were subsequently acquired and refurbished by Interail. This subsidiary of QR was set up to take

advantage of open access freight opportunities over the standard gauge network. The two locomotives, 42202 (above left) and 42206, are based at Casino, New South Wales.

SPECIFICATION

Number series: 42201–42220
Total built: 20
Builder: Clyde Engineering
Date introduced: 1969
Track gauge, ft/ins (mm): 4 ft 8.5 in (1,435)
Axle arrangement: Co-Co
Power unit type: GM 16-645E 16-cylinder vee 2-stroke
Transmission: DC generator, six nose-suspended DC traction motors
Weight, tonnes: 110
Power rating, hp (kW): 1,640 (2,240)
Design speed, mph (km/h): 77 (124)
Additional features: multiple working

CLASS NR DIESEL LOCOMOTIVE

Pacific National Class NR

One of Australia's most important and numerous types, Class NR was acquired by the former National Rail Corporation, which in 2002 merged with FreightCorp to form Pacific National. The locomotives' operations cover standard gauge routes in New South Wales, Victoria and into Queensland.

SPECIAL FEATURES

The 120 Class NR machines were acquired by the former public sector National Rail Corporation to modernise its ageing standard gauge traction fleet. Designated Model CV40-9i, the single-cab NRs were built by GE's Australian licensee, Goninan, and are an adaptation of the US company's Dash 9 family. An unusual feature of the class is its capability to work at variable power outputs (2,850, 3,560 or 4,020 hp/2,125, 2,655 or 3,000 kW) according to trailing loads, with commensurate operating cost benefits. Construction was shared equally by Goninan's

SPECIFICATION

Number series: NR1-NR120
Total built: 120
Builder: Goninan
Date introduced: 1996
Track gauge, ft/ins (mm): 4 ft 8.5 in (1,435)
Axle arrangement: Co-Co
Power unit type: GE FDL-16 16-cylinder vee 4-stroke
Transmission: GE - alternator, six nose-suspended DC traction motors
Weight, tonnes: 132
Power rating, hp (kW): 4,020 (3,000) (see Special Features)
Design speed, mph (km/h): 70 (115)
Additional features: multiple working

Broadmeadow (NR1-NR60) and Bassenden (remainder) plants. The 2002 sale of National Rail and the New South Wales freight operator, FreightCorp, to Patrick Corporation and Toll Holdings led to the creation of Pacific National, with the Class NR machines becoming part of the fleet. As well as operating a wide range of freight

duties, the NRs also provide traction for passenger services operated by Great Southern Railway, including some stages of the 'Indian Pacific' tourist train. A small number of locomotives notionally assigned to such operations have received highly elaborate paint schemes based on aboriginal culture. Some others have received liveries intended to relate then to specific types of traffic, while there has been progressive repainting of National Rail-branded units into Pacific National colours. Many members of the class carry names of locations served by the former National Rail network.

CLASS 48 DIESEL LOCOMOTIVE

Pacific National Class 48

Introduced by the New South Wales Government Railways in 1959, these Alco-engined veterans have long been a common feature of freight operations in the state. Although in declining numbers in their final years, examples remain in service with Pacific National, while others have been sold to other operators or are preserved.

SUB-TYPES

4801-4845 (Mark 1) GE generator and traction motors, 4846-4885 (Mark 2) AEI generator, GE traction motors, 4886-48165 (Mark 3 and 4) AEI generator and traction motors.

PRINCIPAL MODIFICATIONS

Seven of the class were rebuilt by FreightCorp from the late 1990s to handle transfer traffic between port terminals in the Sydney area. Designated Class PL (or Portlink locomotives), they feature new cabs and a very low short hood.

SPECIFICATION

Number series: 4801-48165
Total built: 165
Builder: A E Goodwin
Date introduced: 1959
Track gauge, ft/ins (mm): 4 ft 8.5 in (1,435)
Axle arrangement: Co-Co
Power unit type: Alco 6-251B
Transmission: GE, AEI - generator, six nose-suspended DC traction motors
Weight, tonnes: 75
Power rating, hp (kW): 1,045 (780)
Design speed, mph (km/h): 75 (120)
Additional features: multiple working

SPECIAL FEATURES

One of several Alco-engined types that can still be seen in Australia, the Class 48 locomotives are a licence-built example of Alco Model DL531. Between 1959 and 1970 165 of these locomotives were supplied by A E Goodwin for service on the railways of New South Wales. Most of the earliest-built machines have been withdrawn or sold.

CLASS 81 DIESEL LOCOMOTIVE

Pacific National Class 81

Australia

Acquired by the former State Railway Authority of New South Wales (SRA) in the 1980s for its heaviest freight services, including Hunter Valley coal traffic, the Class 81s now form a key element of the fleet of private sector operator Pacific National.

SPECIAL FEATURES

A major expansion of its capability to handle Hunter Valley coal traffic was a principal factor leading the SRA to acquire the first examples of this versatile class. Designated Model JT26C-2SS and built around the proven GM 645E3B power unit, the Class 81 features a full-with body with twin cabs on a rigid underframe. Production at Clyde Engineering's Bathurst, New South Wales, plant extended from 1982 to 1991. Ownership of most of the class transferred to FreightCorp when it was set up in 1996 but 13 became part of the National Rail Corporation fleet. The entire build was reunited when that company and FreightCorp were merged to become Pacific National.

SPECIFICATION

Number series: 8101–8184
Total built: 84
Builder: Clyde Engineering
Date introduced: 1982
Track gauge, ft/ins (mm): 4 ft 8.5 in (1,435)
Axle arrangement: Co-Co
Power unit type: GM 16-645E3B 16-cylinder vee 2-stroke
Transmission: GM - alternator, six nose-suspended DC traction motors
Weight, tonnes: 126
Power rating, hp (kW): 3,000 (2,240)
Design speed, mph (km/h): 70 (115)
Additional features: multiple working

CLASS 82 DIESEL LOCOMOTIVE

Pacific National Class 82

Successor to the New South Wales State Railway Authority's Class 81 was the Class 82, featuring a 12-cylinder version of GM's 710 series engine in place of the 16-645E3B unit installed in the earlier design. Heavy haul coal traffic features prominently in the class's work

SUB-TYPES

Introduced at the same time as Class 82 and employing a 16-cylinder version of the 710G3A engine is the more powerful Class 90 (31 examples, Nos 9001-9031). Of generally similar appearance, these locomotives are distinguishable from Class 82 by having a single cab.

SPECIAL FEATURES

Introduced in 1994 to replace older machines, Class 82 is among the earliest Australian applications of GM's then new 710 series power unit. Unlike the Class 81, these locomotives

SPECIFICATION

Number series: 8201-8258
Total built: 58
Builder: Clyde Engineering
Date introduced: 1994
Track gauge, ft/ins (mm): 4 ft 8.5 in (1,435)
Axle arrangement: Co-Co
Power unit type: GM 12-710G3A 12-cylinder vee 2-stroke
Transmission: GM - alternator, six nose-suspended DC traction motors
Weight, tonnes: 132
Power rating, hp (kW): 3,250 (2,425)
Design speed, mph (km/h): 75 (120)
Additional features: multiple working

feature twin cabs and narrow hood. They are also heavier than Class 81, with resulting tractive effort benefits. While extensively employed on Pacific National's coal operations, including some in South Australia, the class is also widely used on general freight traffic.

CLASS 70 AND 94 DIESEL LOCOMOTIVES

Pilbara Rail Classes 70 and 94

Australia

While most recently delivered diesel locomotives for Australian operators have been built under licence by domestic suppliers, these Dash 9 heavy haulers came straight from GE's Erie, Pennsylvania plant. Examples have been procured for both Hamersley and Robe River lines, now operated as a single entity, Pilbara Rail.

SPECIAL FEATURES

These Model CM44-9CW/DASH 9-44CW locomotives serve separate iron ore lines running from the Pilbara region to Dampier and Cape Lambert on the northwest coast of Western Australia. Together the two lines carry more than 110 million tonnes annually. The fleets have progressively grown to their present levels as successive batches of locomotives have been delivered since 1995. Parent company changes which combined ownership of the formerly separate Robe River Iron Associates and the Hamersley line, plus the prospect of some inter-

SPECIFICATION

Number series: Hamersley locomotives - 7061-7098, Robe River locomotives - 9401-9409, 9428-9434
Total built: 38 + 16
Builder: General Electric
Date introduced: 1995
Track gauge, ft/ins (mm): 4 ft 8.5 in (1,435)
Axle arrangement: Co-Co
Power unit type: GE 7FDL-16 16-cylinder vee 4-stroke
Transmission: GE - alternator, six nose-suspended DC traction motors
Weight, tonnes: 197
Power rating, hp (kW): 4,600 (3,430)
Design speed, mph (km/h): 65 (105)
Additional features: multiple working, microprocessor control, dynamic braking

working to exploit new ore reserves, has led to the creation of Pilbara Rail to handle the common management of rail operations and locomotive fleets.

CLASS 300 TILTING TRAINSET

QR Class 300

Introduced by QR to give a boost to commercial speeds and journey quality on its electrified Brisbane-Rockhampton route, the Class 300s were Australia's first tilting trainsets. The operator has since added a diesel version to its fleet but remains the country's sole user of tilt technology.

SUB-TYPES

In 2003 QR introduced two diesel-powered seven-car tilting trainsets employing technology derived from that of the Class 300 units.

SPECIAL FEATURES

While 1980s electrification of QR's 386 mile (622 km) Brisbane-Rockhampton route included work to ease alignments, the line still features many curves. This was a key factor in the railway's decision to introduce tilting trainsets for principal services over this section, enabling journey times to be cut by up to a third. Supplied by a consortium of Australian and Japanese companies,

SPECIFICATION

Number series: 301, 302
Total built: 2
Builder: Evans Deakin Industries, Hitachi, Itochu
Date introduced: 1998
Track gauge, ft/ins (mm): 3 ft 6 in (1,067)
Unit configuration: M-T-M-M-T-M
Power supply system: 25 kV AC 50 Hz
Electrical equipment: Hitachi - IGBT inverters, 16 fully suspended AC traction motors with flexible drives
Power rating, hp (kW): 4,075 (3,040)
Design speed, mph (km/h): 105 (170)
Additional features: active tilting, regenerative braking, air-conditioning, onboard information/entertainment systems

the stainless steel-bodied Class 300 trainsets employ active tilting technology already proven in Japan, coupled with the latest Hitachi IGBT inverter control and AC traction motors. One of the trains established a new Australian rail speed record in May 1999 - 130.4 mph (210 km/h).

CLASS 2300 DIESEL LOCOMOTIVE

QR Class 2300

Rebuilds carried out from the late 1990s of earlier GM types have created this class of medium-powered general-purpose locomotives which is concentrated mainly around Brisbane and in southeast Queensland.

SPECIAL FEATURES

Designated Model GTL22CU, these 60 machines are rebuilds of earlier Class 1550, 2400, 2450 and 2470 locomotives originally built in the 1970s by Comeng and Clyde Engineering. Rebuilding with an uprated power unit and modernised transmission resulted in a 65 per cent increase in output to create a versatile unit that is used on freight and, to a lesser extent, passenger services.

SPECIFICATION

Number series: 2301-2392 (with gaps)
Total built: 60
Builder: rebuilt by QR workshops from Comeng/Clyde-built locomotives
Date introduced: 1997
Track gauge, ft/ins (mm): 3 ft 6 in (1,067)
Axle arrangement: Co-Co
Power unit type: GM 12-645E3C 12 cylinder vee 2-stroke
Transmission: GM - alternator, six nose-suspended DC traction motors
Weight, tonnes: 95
Power rating, hp (kW): 2,475 (1,850)
Design speed, mph (km/h): 62 (100)
Additional features: multiple working

CLASS 2800 DIESEL LOCOMOTIVE

QR Class 2800

The 50 GE-powered Class 2800 diesel-electrics form an important component of the QR fleet, handling a variety of freight traffic ranging from coal hauls to fast container services.

SPECIAL FEATURES

While QR's diesel fleet is mostly GM-powered, the railway also operates two classes with General Electric power units. The latest and more powerful of these is the Class 2800, introduced in 1995. Built by GE's Australian licence-holder A Goninan (now United Goninan), they are designated Model CM30-8, a narrow gauge example of GE's Dash 8 family and feature twin cabs and a narrow hood. Geared for 68 mph (110 km/h) operation, they are QR's fastest diesel locomotive.

SPECIFICATION

Number series: 2801-2850
Total built: 50
Builder: Goninan
Date introduced: 1995
Track gauge, ft/ins (mm): 3 ft 6 in (1,067)
Axle arrangement: Co-Co
Power unit type: GE 7FDL-12 12-cylinder vee 4–stroke
Transmission: GE - alternator and six nose-suspended DC traction motors
Weight, tonnes: 116
Power rating, hp (kW): 3,000 (2,240)
Design speed, mph (km/h): 68 (110)
Additional features: multiple working

CLASS 3100/3200 ELECTRIC LOCOMOTIVES

QR Class 3100/3200

The Queensland state network's electric locomotive fleet consists entirely of Bo-Bo-Bo types, of which Classes 3100 and 3200 are the most numerous. They are principally employed on haulage of coal, QR's most significant freight commodity.

SPECIAL FEATURES

Some fitted with Locotrol remote control working equipment. The 50 locomotives forming Class 3500/3600 are distinguishable from their contemporary Class 3100/3200 cousins by their corrugated bodysides. Essentially similar mechanically and in terms of performance, they employ ASEA traction equipment. Construction was undertaken in Queensland at Walkers' Maryborough plant. As with Class 3100/3200 machines, some are fitted with Locotrol equipment for remote operation in the heaviest train formations. QR acquired 30 Class 3900 machines, higher-geared versions of Class

SPECIFICATION

Number series: 3101-3168, 3205-3286
Total built: 86 (20 + 66)
Builder: Comeng
Date introduced: 1986
Track gauge, ft/ins (mm): 3 ft 6 in (1,067)
Axle arrangement: Bo-Bo-Bo
Power supply system: 25 kV AC 50 Hz
Electrical equipment: GE, Hitachi - thyristor control, six nose-suspended DC traction motors
Weight, tonnes: 110
Power rating, hp (kW): 3,870 (2,900)
Design speed, mph (km/h): 50 (80)
Additional features: multiple working

3500/3600. Some of these have been re-designated Class 3550 for coal traffic.

CLASS 4000 DIESEL LOCOMOTIVE

QR Class 4000

The most recent diesel locomotive additions to the QR fleet - and the railway's most powerful - are these GM-powered machines acquired mainly for coal and mineral traffic. More of the type were on order for delivery in 2004-05.

SPECIAL FEATURES

Designated Model GT42CUAC, this class was designed by GM's Australian licensee Clyde Engineering and built at the Maryborough, Queensland, plant of Walkers Pty. Both companies are now part of Evans Deakin Industries. The single-cab Class 4000 employs the 12-cylinder version of GM's 710 series engine and Siemens AC traction motors with a microprocessor control system, creating one of the world's most powerful narrow gauge diesel locomotive designs. Duties include hauling coal and mineral traffic over QR's non-electrified routes.

SPECIFICATION

Number series: 4001-4049
Total built: 49 (including units on order in 2004)
Builder: Clyde Engineering, Walkers
Date introduced: 2000
Track gauge, ft/ins (mm): 3 ft 6 in (1,435)
Axle arrangement: Co-Co
Power unit type: General Motors 12N-710G3B-ES 12-cylinder vee 2-stroke
Transmission: General Motors, Siemens - alternator and six nose-suspended AC traction motors
Weight, tonnes: 120
Power rating, hp (kW): 3,300 (2,460)
Additional features: multiple working, radial steering bogies

CLASS IMU EMU

QR Class IMU

Introduced for operation on QR's Gold Coast line north of Brisbane, the IMU express emus are the latest expression of this operator's pattern of procuring trains of this type from local builder Walkers, now part of Evans Deakin, and Bombardier predecessors ASEA and Adtranz. The generally similar SMU units operate many QR suburban services.

SUB-TYPES

QR also operates 42 Class SMU three-car emus which are technically similar to the IMU sets. They are numbered in the 2xx series.

SPECIAL FEATURES

The Class IMU units were introduced to provide express services on its Gold Coast route and are essentially a higher geared version of the now more numerous Class SMU trains introduced in 1994. They feature stainless steel bodyshells with GRP front-ends and like all QR emus were

SPECIFICATION

Number series: 101-114
Total built: 14
Builder: Walkers (now Evans Deakin Industries)
Date introduced: 1995
Track gauge, ft/ins (mm): 3 ft 6 in (1,067)
Unit configuration: M-M-T
Power supply system: 25 kV AC 50 Hz
Electrical equipment: Adtranz - GTO converter, eight fully suspended, longitudinally mounted three-phase asynchronous traction motors
Power rating, hp (kW): 1,930 (1,440)
Design speed, mph (km/h): 87 (140)
Additional features: regenerative braking, air-conditioning

assembled at the Walkers (now Evans Deakin Industries) plant at Maryborough. The traction package includes the less common configuration of longitudinal motors with spiral bevel gear drives. As well as air-conditioning, the trains incorporate GPS global positioning equipment for stop/station announcements, onboard CCTV cameras and wheelchair-accessible toilets.

CLASS 442 DIESEL LOCOMOTIVE

Silverton Rail Class 442

Silverton Rail, a minor operator based in Melbourne, continues to operate members of this Alco-engined Co-Co design originally supplied to the New South Wales state system. Other survivors are in the Australian traction leasing market.

SPECIAL FEATURES

Originally built for the former New South Wales Government Railways, later the State Railway Authority of New South Wales, this once 40-strong mixed traffic class was a version of Alco's DL500 model, locally built and adapted for Australian requirements. Construction was interrupted after the first 34 machines were built due to the insolvency of A E Goodwin, leading to Comeng completing the contract. Disposal of the class at the end of its career with the state operator saw some examples go to Morrison Knudsen for spares recovery, 15 others to CFCLA,

SPECIFICATION

Number series: 442s1-442s6
Total built: 40
Builder: A E Goodwin, Comeng
Date introduced: 1971
Track gauge, ft/ins (mm): 4 ft 8.5 in (1,435)
Axle arrangement: Co-Co
Power unit type: Alco 12-251C 12 cylinder vee 4-stroke
Transmission: AEI/GE/Mitsubishi - generator, six nose-suspended DC traction motors
Weight, tonnes: 115
Power rating, hp (kW): 2,000 (1,490)
Design speed, mph (km/h): 75 (120)
Additional features: multiple working

a leasing company, and eight to Silverton Rail. Six of these entered service, handling contract freight operations, infrastructure work and acting as traction for lease.

CLASS N DIESEL LOCOMOTIVE

V/Line Class N

Principal traction in Victoria for V/Line country passenger services is this fleet of GM-powered twin-cab machines, one of few types in Australia equipped to provide head-end power for coaching stock.

SPECIAL FEATURES

Introduced in the 1980s by V/Line primarily for long-distance passenger services in Victoria, the N Class were built by General Motors' Australian licensee Clyde Engineering at its Somerton plant, near Melbourne, receiving the JT22HC-2 model designation. They feature twin full-width cabs and a narrow hood and are equipped with head-end power for onboard services. All remained with the V/Line passenger business when this and the railway's freight operation were separately privatised but they returned temporarily to state ownership in 2002 when National Express Group withdrew from the franchise it had won earlier. All are named after cities and towns in Victoria.

SPECIFICATION

Number series: N451-N475
Total built: 25
Builder: Clyde Engineering
Date introduced: 1985
Track gauge, ft/ins (mm): 5 ft 3 in (1,600)
Axle arrangement: Co-Co
Power unit type: GM 12-645E3C or 12-645E3B 12-cylinder vee 2-stroke
Transmission: GM - alternator, six nose-suspended DC traction motors
Weight, tonnes: 124
Power rating, hp (kW): 2,465 (1,840)
Design speed, mph (km/h): 75 (120)
Additional features: multiple working, head-end power

CLASS B DIESEL LOCOMOTIVE

West Coast Railway Class B

While other examples of Class B have been retired or rebuilt, these GM-powered survivors in operation until 2004 with West Coast Railway have given more than 50 years service in Victoria.

PRINCIPAL MODIFICATIONS

Eleven of the class have been refurbished and upgraded with GM 12-645E3B engines, becoming Class A. These are in service with Freight Australia (7) and V/Line (4).

SPECIAL FEATURES

Essentially an Australian adaptation of General Motors classic E series, the twin-cab Class B machines were Victorian Railways' first main line diesel locomotives. As the class reached the twilight of its career with the state operator, 11 were given a new lease of life by modernisation that included replacement of their original Series 567 engines by 645E power units. Others were scrapped or passed into preservation, and six were

SPECIFICATION

Number series: B60-B85
Total built: 26
Builder: Clyde Engineering
Date introduced: 1952
Track gauge, ft/ins (mm): 5 ft 3 in (1,600)
Axle arrangement: Co-Co
Power unit type: GM 16-567BC 16-cylinder vee 2-stroke
Transmission: GM - DC generator, six nose-suspended DC traction motors
Weight, tonnes: 114
Power rating, hp (kW): 1,600 (1,190)
Design speed, mph (km/h): 82 (133)
Additional features: multiple working

sold to West Coast Railway. This private sector operator ran country passenger services until 2004 under a Victoria state government contract between Melbourne and Warnambool (166 miles/267 km). In 2004 three of the type (B61, B65 and B76) were in operational service, sharing duties with examples of the later but generally similar single-cab Class S.

CLASS DC DIESEL LOCOMOTIVE

Toll Rail Class DC

Rebuilds of the earlier Class DA machines dating from the 1960s, the Class DCs are Toll Rail's most numerous type, handling freight duties on both North and South Islands of New Zealand.

SUB-TYPES

Up to 17 examples (some unserviceable) within the main series assigned to the Tranz Scenic passenger business and designated Class DCP.

SPECIAL FEATURES

Class DC was created by rebuilding 85 former Class DA machines, replacing their GM Series 567 power units with 12-cylinder 645C engines, modernising the transmission and providing a low short hood in place of the full height version originally fitted. Originally concentrated on North Island, the class is now also seen on South Island. In 2003 some 50 remained in service, with many others stored out of use.

SPECIFICATION

Number series: 4006-4951
Total built: 85
Builder: Rebuilt Clyde Engineering, NZR
Date introduced: 1978
Track gauge, ft/ins (mm): 3 ft 6 in (1,067)
Axle arrangement: A1A-A1A
Power unit type: GM 12-645C 12-cylinder vee 2-stroke
Transmission: GM - alternator, four nose-suspended DC traction motors
Weight, tonnes: 83
Power rating, hp (kW): 1,650 (1,230)
Design speed, mph (km/h): 62 (100)
Additional features: multiple working

OTHER COUNTRIES OPERATED

One example of the class was shipped to Tasmania in 1988, operating there as Tasrail Class DC.

CLASS DFT DIESEL LOCOMOTIVE

Toll Rail Class DFT

Another GM-powered rebuild on the New Zealand system is Class DFT, upgraded from older units by engine output improvements. Examples of the class operate freight services throughout the Toll Rail network.

SPECIAL FEATURES

Class DFT was created by providing turbocharging for the engines of 30 former Class DF machines originally built by General Motors at its London, Ontario, plant. The modifications were made by the former Tranz Rail in its own workshops between 1992-97. By 2003, 25 of the class were active on freight traffic on both North and South Islands.

SPECIFICATION

Number series: 7008-7335
Total built: 30
Builder: GM, Canada, rebuilt by Tranz Rail
Date introduced: 1992
Track gauge, ft/ins (mm): 3 ft 6 in (1,067)
Axle arrangement: Co-Co
Power unit type: GM 12-645 12-cylinder vee 2-stroke
Transmission: GM - alternator, six nose-suspended DC traction motors
Weight, tonnes: 88
Power rating, hp (kW): 2,450 (1,830)
Design speed, mph (km/h): 80 (112)
Additional features: multiple working

CLASS DX DIESEL LOCOMOTIVE

Toll Rail Class DX

Toll Rail's most powerful diesel locomotives are these GE-built Model U26C machines dating from the 1970s. Initially confined to North Island, they now work the heaviest freight services throughout New Zealand.

SUB-TYPES

No 5362 was rebuilt with its engine uprated to 3,200 hp (2,390 kW) and a new-design cab, becoming Class DXR No 8007. Other examples within the main class that have undergone upgrading and modernisation are designated Classes DXC or DXH. Some are modified with low level air intakes for tunnel operations.

SPECIAL FEATURES

While much of the Toll Rail diesel fleet is of GM origin, other builders are represented, including GE. Between 1972-76 the company supplied 49 of these machines, which remain Toll Rail's most powerful diesel locomotives. Initially used on

SPECIFICATION

Number series: 5016-5517
Total built: 49
Builder: GE
Date introduced: 1972
Track gauge, ft/ins (mm): 3 ft 6 in (1,067)
Axle arrangement: Co-Co
Power unit type: GE 7FDL-12 12-cylinder vee 4-stroke
Transmission: GE - alternator, six nose-suspended DC traction motors
Weight, tonnes: 99
Power rating, hp (kW): 2,750 (2,050) or 3,000 (2,240)
Design speed, mph (km/h): 75 (120)
Additional features: multiple working

North Island, where they handled some passenger traffic as well as heavy freight services. Examples were later moved to South Island where duties include coal traffic over the steeply graded Greymouth-Christchurch route that includes the formerly electrified section between Otira and Arthur's Pass.

CLASS EF ELECTRIC LOCOMOTIVE

Toll Rail Class EF

These 'Tri-Bo' locomotives were supplied to the former New Zealand Railways by British manufacturer Brush in the late 1980s to operate over a steeply graded section of the North Island Main Trunk line.

SPECIAL FEATURES

Now New Zealand's only operational main line electric locomotives, Class EF was procured to serve the 1980s electrification of the Palmerston North-Hamilton section of the North Island Main Trunk line. Unlike the earlier 1.5 kV DC electrification of the Wellington suburban network, this main line project employed 25 kV AC. UK builder Brush Traction constructed the locomotives at its Loughborough plant, adopting a Bo-Bo-Bo axle arrangement to cope with the sharp curves of the steeply graded Main Trunk line. In 2004 17 of the class remained in traffic, two of them assigned to Tranz Scenic, New

SPECIFICATION

Number series: 30007-30249 (with gaps)
Total built: 22
Builder: Brush Traction
Date introduced: 1988
Track gauge, ft/ins (mm): 3 ft 6 in (1,067)
Axle arrangement: Bo-Bo-Bo
Power supply system: 25 kV AC 50 Hz
Electrical equipment: Brush Traction - thyristor control, six nose-suspended DC traction motors
Weight, tonnes: 106.5
Power rating, hp (kW): 4,020 (3,000)
Design speed, mph (km/h): 68 (110)
Additional features: multiple working, rheostatic braking

Zealand's long-distance passenger operator. The remainder were used by privatised freight company Toll Rail.

European
Trains

CLASSES 1014/1114 ELECTRIC LOCOMOTIVE

Austrian Federal Railways (ÖBB) Class 1014/1114

This lightweight dual-voltage design was introduced by ÖBB in the mid-1990s for cross-border services linking Austria with the Czech Republic, Hungary and Slovakia. The type is primarily, though not exclusively, used on passenger services.

SPECIAL FEATURES

Classes 1014 and 1114 are similar in all their basic characteristics, with the higher weight of the former achieved by ballasting. This makes them more suitable for freight traffic. The locomotives' dual-voltage capability avoids the need for traction changes at the borders with neighbouring networks in the Czech Republic, Hungary and Slovakia, all of which partly or wholly employ the 25 kV electrification system. Production of the type was limited in favour of large orders for the more powerful Siemens-built Class 1116 'Taurus' machines.

SPECIFICATION

Number series: 1014.003-1014.018, 1114.001-1114.002
Total built: 18
Builder: SGP
Date introduced: 1993
Track gauge, ft/ins (mm): 4 ft 8.5 in (1,435)
Axle arrangement: Bo-Bo
Power supply system: 15 kV AC 16.7 Hz/25 kV AC 50 Hz
Electrical equipment: BES (ABB, Elin and Siemens) - three-phase asynchronous traction motors
Weight, tonnes: Class 1014 – 74, Class 1114 - 64
Power rating, hp (kW): 4,020 (3,000)
Design speed, mph (km/h): 100 (160)
Additional features: thyristor control, push-pull operation

CLASSES 1042.500/1142.500 ELECTRIC LOCOMOTIVE

Austrian Federal Railways (ÖBB) Class 1042.500/1142.500

Austria

For many years the backbone of the ÖBB main line fleet, this numerous electric locomotive family which first appeared in the late 1960s is now in the twilight of its career. As an all-purpose design, examples are to be found throughout the Austrian network.

PRINCIPAL MODIFICATIONS

Class 1142.500 locomotives are former 1042.500 machines converted between 1995 and 2001 for push-pull operation. They also feature other detail differences. ÖBB decided not to treat similarly the first 20 of the class due to differences in their electrical equipment.

SPECIAL FEATURES

Class 1042.500 was a more powerful and faster development of the 60-strong 1042 series introduced in 1963 and represented the final ÖBB application of the single-phase AC traction drive system. Until the arrival in large numbers of Class 1044, these machines were the principal main line traction on the Austrian network and are still widely used on a range of duties, including the suburban push-pull traffic for which most of the class was adapted.

SPECIFICATION

Number series: 1042.501-1042.520, 1142.531-1142.707
Total built: 197
Builder: SGP
Date introduced: 1967
Track gauge, ft/ins (mm): 4 ft 8.5 in (1,435)
Axle arrangement: Bo-Bo
Power supply system: 15 kV AC 16.7 Hz
Electrical equipment: Brown Bover, Elin-Union, Siemens – tap changer control and fully suspended traction motors
Weight, tonnes: 83.8
Power rating, hp (kW): 5,100 (3,810)
Design speed, mph (km/h): 93 (150)
Additional features: rheostatic braking

CLASSES 1044/1144 ELECTRIC LOCOMOTIVE

Austrian Federal Railways (ÖBB) Class 1044/1144

Dating from the 1970s, this thyristor-controlled type was developed following the success in Austria of the similarly equipped Class 1043 machines (since retired) built in Sweden. The class is used throughout the Austrian national network and can be seen on both passenger and freight traffic.

SUB-TYPES

Class 1144.2 locomotives originally built as Class 1044.2. Reclassification followed replacement of non-standard multiple-unit equipment with ÖBB standard system.

PRINCIPAL MODIFICATIONS

The first of the class, No 1044.01, was rebuilt in 1987 for operation at speeds of up to 137 mph (220 km/h) and renumbered 1044.501. It was withdrawn in 2001.

Some Class 1144 locomotives have been equipped with remote radio control for banking duties on mountain lines.

SPECIFICATION

Total built: 216
Builder: SGP
Date introduced: 1974
Track gauge, ft/ins (mm): 4 ft 8.5 in (1,435)
Axle arrangement: Bo-Bo
Power supply system: 15 kV AC 16.7 Hz
Electrical equipment: Brown Boveri, Elin, Siemens - fully suspended traction motors
Weight, tonnes: 83
Power rating, hp (kW): 6,700 (5,000)
Design speed, mph (km/h): 100 (160)
Additional features: thyristor control, multiple-unit operation, rheostatic braking

SPECIAL FEATURES

Austria's first thyristor-controlled main line electric locomotive design was built by SGP, now part of Siemens Transportation Systems. Two prototype machines were supplied to ÖBB in 1974 and 1975, with series deliveries commencing in 1978. Class 1044.2 first appeared in 1989. Design features include a low-level traction system and axially sprung bogie wheelsets.

CLASS 1163 ELECTRIC LOCOMOTIVE

Austrian Federal Railways (ÖBB) Class 1163

Austria

ÖBB is one of only a small number of operators to employ electric traction for heavy yard shunting. Class 1163 is the most recent of several series of machines of this type to be acquired by the Austrian operator and examples can be seen at the country's major yards, especially those around Vienna and Salzburg, as well as performing light main line freight duties.

SPECIFICATION

Number series: 1163.01-1163.020
Total built: 20
Builder: SGP
Date introduced: 1994
Track gauge, ft/ins (mm): 4 ft 8.5 in (1,435)
Axle arrangement: Bo-Bo
Power supply system: 15 kV AC 16.7 Hz
Electrical equipment: Adtranz - three-phase drive system
Weight, tonnes: 80
Power rating, hp (kW): 2,145 (1,600)
Design speed, mph (km/h): 75 (120)

SPECIAL FEATURES

Class 1163 is a 15 kV-only development of the more numerous Class 1063 dual-voltage design, 50 of which were produced between 1983 and 1991. The use of a three-phase drive system avoids the thermal problems associated with conventional traction motors and ensures high tractive effort in the lower speed range without excessive component wear. The centre-cab design with low bonnets and a distinctive reverse-raked cab ensures optimum visibility and improved safety for yard personnel.

CLASS 2016

Austrian Federal Railways (ÖBB) Class 2016 'Hercules'

This medium-powered multi-purpose diesel-electric locomotive design, dubbed the Eurorunner by its builders, was developed by Siemens Transportation Systems primarily for the European market. Austrian Federal Railways (ÖBB) was the lead customer for the type.

SPECIAL FEATURES

An anticipated market for the replacement of locomotive fleets dating from the 1960s and 1970s together with opportunities created by open access to many European rail networks were drivers in Siemens' decision to create an off-the-shelf main line diesel type. In Austria Class 2016 was introduced to replace older types such as Classes 2043 and 2143 and was given the formal nickname Hercules. Low exhaust emission levels and reduced noise are features of the Eurorunner. The ÖBB machines are equipped with driver vigilance and radio communications equipment that enable them also to be used for cross-border operations in Germany and Slovenia.

SPECIFICATION

Number series: 2016.001–2016.070
Total built: 70
Builder: Siemens Transportation Systems
Date introduced: 2002
Track gauge, ft/ins (mm): 4 ft 8.5 in (1,435)
Axle arrangement: Bo-Bo
Power system: Diesel
Transmission: Siemens, electric – three-phase generator, three-phase traction motors
Power unit type: MTU 16V 4000R41
Weight, tonnes: 80
Power rating, hp (kW): 2,680 (2,000)
Design speed, mph (km/h): 87 (140)

Assembly of Class 2016 was done at the Munich plant of Siemens subsidiary Krauss-Maffei.

OTHER COUNTRIES OPERATED

In 2003 five Eurorunner locomotives were supplied to Kowloon-Canton Railway Corporation, Hong Kong, China. Other examples are owned by Siemens leasing subsidiary, Dispolok, for hire to European operators.

CLASS 2143 DIESEL LOCOMOTIVE

Austrian Federal Railways (ÖBB) Class 2143

Austria

Class 2143 is one of two types of medium-powered diesel-hydraulic locomotives built for ÖBB by Austrian domestic builders in the 1960s and 1970s to handle both passenger and freight traffic on non-electrified and secondary lines.

SPECIAL FEATURES

Together with the generally similar Jenbacher Werke-built Class 2043, of which a similar number was constructed, the 2143 series has been a major component of ÖBB's main line diesel locomotive fleet since the 1960s. Consequently the Austrian system has been one of few in Europe on which diesel-hydraulic traction is widely employed for line haulage. With most main lines electrified, the use of diesel traction is mostly confined to branch lines and secondary routes. Deliveries of Siemens-built Class 2016 machines and the less powerful Vossloh Class 2070 locomotives are expected to lead to the retirement of the class.

SPECIFICATION

Number series: 2143.001–2143.077
Total built: 77
Builder: SGP
Date introduced: 1965
Track gauge, ft/ins (mm): 4 ft 8.5 in (1,435)
Axle arrangement: B-B
Power unit type: SGP T 12c
Transmission: Voith hydraulic
Weight, tonnes: 65
Power rating, hp (kW): 1,475 (1,100)
Design speed, mph (km/h): 62 (100)
Additional features: equipped to provide electric train heating, some fitted for multiple-unit operation

CLASS 5047 DMU

Austrian Federal Railways (ÖBB) Class 5047

This modern single-unit railcar is widely used on branch and minor lines throughout the ÖBB network, often coupled to trailer cars.

SPECIAL FEATURES

Class 5047 was introduced in 1987 to improve the economics of lightly used services while offering standards of accommodation that matched contemporary main line stock. As well as being able to operate with other Class 5047 units, these vehicles are also paired with Class 6547 driving trailers.

SPECIFICATION

Number series: 5047.001–5047.100
Total built: 100
Builder: Jenbacher Werke
Date introduced: 1987
Track gauge, ft/ins (mm): 4 ft 8.5 in (1,435)
Unit configuration: M
Power unit type: Daimler Benz OM444 LA
Transmission: Voith hydraulic
Power rating, hp (kW): 560 (419)
Design speed, mph (km/h): 75 (120)
Additional features: hydrodynamic braking, equipped for driver-only operation

CLASS 4020 EMU

Austrian Federal Railways (ÖBB) Class 4020

Built from 1978 to 1987, these suburban emus are extensively employed in commuter traffic around Vienna and other Austrian cities. It is the most numerous ÖBB emu type.

PRINCIPAL MODIFICATIONS

To adapt Class 4020 units for safe operation in tunnels in Vienna, modifications to the emergency braking system have been made. Modified vehicles are renumbered in the 4020.2xx/3xx series.

SPECIAL FEATURES

Designed for suburban services entailing frequent stops and demanding good acceleration, these one-class three-car units were built over a 10-year period by SGP. They are finished in ÖBB's distinctive blue and white S-Bahn livery.

SPECIFICATION

Number series: originally 4020.001–4020.120, undergoing renumbering to 4020.201–4020.320, intermediate trailers and driving trailers numbered in 7020 and 6020 series respectively.
Total built: 120
Builder: SGP
Date introduced: 1978
Track gauge, ft/ins (mm): 4 ft 8.5 in (1,435)
Unit configuration: M–T–T
Power supply system: 15 kV AC 16.7 Hz
Electrical equipment: Brown Boveri, Elin, Siemens
Power rating, hp (kW): 4 x 400 (4 x 300)
Design speed, mph (km/h): 75 (120)

CLASS TEP60 DIESEL LOCOMOTIVE

Belarus Railways (BCh) Class TEP60

Belarus Railways is one of several ex-Soviet railway systems still operating this mass-produced diesel-electric passenger locomotive dating from the 1960s.

SPECIAL FEATURES

Along with the contemporary M62 and the later and more powerful Class TEP70 types, the TEP60 has served as a mainstay of long-distance passenger operations over non-electrified lines of countries that once formed part of the Soviet Union. Built at the Kolomna plant in the Moscow region, the type was still in production in the mid-1980s, by which time many hundreds of examples had been supplied to the former Soviet Railways. Most ended up on the present Russian Railways system but small numbers are operated by other operators, including BCh. The duties of its small fleet includes cross-border passenger services into neighbouring countries that share

SPECIFICATION

Builder: Kolomna
Date introduced: 1960
Track gauge, ft/ins (mm): 5 ft 0 in (1,520)
Axle arrangement: Co-Co
Power unit type: Kolomna 11D45
Transmission: Kharkov, electric - DC generator with axle-hung DC traction motors
Weight, tonnes: 127
Power rating, hp (kW): 2,960 (2,210)
Design speed, mph (km/h): 100 (160)

1,520 mm gauge tracks. Unlike the M62, the TEP60 was not exported.

OTHER COUNTRIES OPERATED

Lithuanian Railways (LG), Russian Railways (RZhD), Ukrainian Railways (UZ).

CLASS 62 DIESEL LOCOMOTIVE

Belgian Railways (SNCB/NMBS) Class 62

The Belgian diesel locomotive fleet has been hit recently by mass withdrawals, caused by the decline in freight traffic, and displacement from passenger services by new multiple-units. The Class 62 is now the only survivor in any numbers, but is also slated for reduction by half.

SUB-TYPES

6301-6333 are the standard design. 6391-6393 are fitted with Flexicoil suspension.

PRINCIPAL MODIFICATIONS

Many have push-pull apparatus and electric-heat equipment. Some are being fitted with automatic train equipment for use on the Leige-Leuven high-speed line.

SPECIAL FEATURES

Visually similar to the practically defunct 1950s Co-Co design that was prevalent in countries such as Belgium, Denmark, Hungary and Luxembourg, the smaller home-produced Bo-Bo version is now

SPECIFICATION

Number series: 6201-6333, 6391-6393
Total built: 136
Builder: BN/ACEC
Date introduced: 1961
Track gauge, ft/ins (mm): 4ft 8.5 in (1,435)
Axle arrangement: Bo-Bo
Power unit type: General Motors GM 12-567C
Transmission: Electric, four axle-hung traction motors
Weight, tonnes: 78-80
Power rating, hp (kW): 1,400 (1,050)
Design speed, mph (km/h): 75 (120)
Additional features: Steam-heat boiler, BN design bogies

on borrowed time, and only half the fleet will be in service by the mid-2000s. Modern dmus have stolen much of their traditional local passenger work, but freight occupies their time, often in multiple. The design was originally trialled with six prototypes, and many have been modified for specific roles, always with the ultra-reliable General Motors engine. Some SNCB disposals have been acquired by other operators.

CLASS 13 ELECTRIC LOCOMOTIVE

Belgian Railways (SNCB/NMBS) Class 13

This new dual-voltage electric locomotive was acquired to eliminate the need for locomotive changes on the important trans-Europe corridor from the Belgian North Sea ports. To replace older types, more have been purchased by Luxembourg (CFL) and are operated in a common pool with their Belgian sisters.

SPECIAL FEATURES

Poor reliablity on services caused by enforced locomotive changes through the Antwerp-Luxembourg-Metz freight corridor has been eased by the new Class 13, which is also available for high-speed passenger services between Antwerp-Charleroi, Ostend-Eupen, and Lièege-Luxembourg. It will allow the withdrawal of many older electric and diesel types by 2005. The performance of the first examples was disappointing, but has been rectified after protracted negotiations with the manufacturer that resulted in later than expected deliveries. The Belgian Class 13 should not be confused with the externally similar, but

SPECIFICATION

Number series: 1301-1360
Total built: 60
Builder: Alstom GEC Alsthom/BN
Date introduced: 1998
Track gauge, ft/ins (mm): 4 ft 8.5 in (1,435)
Axle arrangement: Bo-Bo
Power supply system: 3 kV DC/25 kV AC 50 Hz
Electrical equipment: Alstom, three-phase asynchronous AC traction motors
Weight, tonnes: 90
Power rating, hp (kW): 6,650 (5,000)
Design speed, mph (km/h): 125 (200)
Additional features: push-pull equipment

technically quite different French (SNCF) BB36000 dual-voltage design, of which 85 units have been ordered and are seen operating the same geographical region.

OTHER COUNTRIES OPERATED

Luxembourg (CFL Class 3000)

CLASS 16 ELECTRIC LOCOMOTIVE

Belgian Railways (SNCB/NMBS) Class 16

Belgium

This remarkable (and complex) design can operate over four different power systems, allowing it to work through France, the Netherlands and Germany. Their current sphere of operation is Ostend-Brussels-Liege-Cologne, but TGVs have stolen their most prestigious duties.

SUB-TYPES

Four were built with Siemens voltage converters, four with ACEC equipment.

PRINCIPAL MODIFICATIONS

1601/2/8 are painted in grey and blue livery sponsored by the Maärklin model train company.

OTHER COUNTRIES OPERATED

The complete electrification of the lines across the Benelux countries into Paris in the mid-1960s compelled Belgian Railways to consider a more modern version of its already successful tri-voltage Class 15, but this time also able to work into France. The first four, originally

SPECIFICATION

Number series: 1601-1608
Total built: 8
Builder: BN
Date introduced: 1966
Track gauge, ft/ins (mm): 4 ft 8.5 in (1435)
Axle arrangement: Bo-Bo
Power supply system: 1.5 kV DC/3 kV DC/15 kV AC 16.7 Hz/25 kV AC 50 Hz
Electrical equipment: ACEC – silicon rectifiers/resistance control with four frame-mounted DC traction motors
Weight, tonnes: 83
Power rating, hp (kW): 2,780 (2,073)
Design speed, mph (km/h): 100 (160)
Additional features: three pantographs, two for AC and one for DC operation

numbered 160.001-160.004 have Siemens AC/DC rectifiers, and the second batch have ACEC rectifiers. In 1974, the first two locomotives were fitted with a fourth pantograph, to allow holiday trains to be worked through to Switzerland, without the need to change haulage. Locomotive 1607 was destroyed in a collision at Ostend station in February 1994.

CLASS 20 ELECTRIC LOCOMOTIVE

Belgian Railways (SNCB/NMBS) Class 20

The world's first series-built electric locomotive to employ thyristor chopper control of traction motor voltage has been a mixed success. The first examples drastically reduced double-heading on the busy Ostend-Brussels-Luxembourg main line, but are now on freight.

SPECIAL FEATURES

The principal contractor for the design of this sophisticated class was Belgian electrical company ACEC, which developed the advanced traction equipment. The six separately-excited traction motors are fully suspended in bogies designed in Switzerland by SLM and built under licence in Belgium by BN. Electrically controlled rheostatic braking is independently excited, and the high adhesion factor has allowed an axle load of only 18.5 tonnes. Early on, Class 20 had more than its fair share of teething troubles, but has now had several good years, and following the introduction of Class 13 has been cascaded to freight duty on

the Antwerp-Montzen route towards the German border, replacing diesels under the wires.

SPECIFICATION

Number series: 2001-2025
Total built: 25
Builder: BN
Date introduced: 1975
Track gauge, ft/ins (mm): 4 ft 8.5 in (1,435)
Axle arrangement: Co-Co
Power supply system: 3 kV DC
Electrical equipment: ACEC - six frame-suspended traction motors
Weight, tonnes: 110
Power rating, hp (kW): 6,850 (5,150)
Design speed, mph (km/h): 100 (160)
Additional features: Chopper control, rheostatic brakes

CLASS 22 ELECTRIC LOCOMOTIVE

Belgian Railways (SNCB/NMBS) Class 22

Belgium

A general-purpose locomotive that is still seen on the Belgian network, the Class 22 is the oldest electric types still operating, and widely regarded as almost indestructible.

SPECIAL FEATURES

The class 22 general-purpose locomotives are now the elder statesmen of Belgian electric types, dating back to 1954, and the last 12 members of the class were originally dual voltage (1.5 kV and 3 kV DC). Originally designated Class 122, they were renumbered in 1970. They have been noted for their outstanding reliability and all but one of the class was still in service in early 2004. Despite their low power compared to other types, Class 22 is normally to be found on peak-hour passenger services throughout the country, but they are also noted in some numbers on freight in the north, including Antwerp. Their withdrawal was in prospect in 2004.

SPECIFICATION

Number series: 2201-2250
Total built: 50
Builder: BN
Date introduced: 1954
Track gauge, ft/ins (mm): 4 ft 8.5 (1,435)
Axle arrangement: Bo-Bo
Power supply system: 3 kV DC
Electrical equipment: SEMG/ACEC – four axle-hung traction motors
Weight, tonnes: 87
Power rating, hp (kW): 2,500 (1,880)
Design speed, mph (km/h): 80 (130)

CLASS 11/12/21/27 ELECTRIC LOCOMOTIVE

Belgian Railways (SNCB/NMBS) Classes 11/12/21/27

The most common type seen in Belgium has been built in four different versions, and although usurped in some areas by more modern types is still the backbone of the freight business conveyed under the wires. A long working life is anticipated.

SUB-TYPES

Class 11 series was built specificially for the Brussels Midi-Amsterdam push-pull service. Class 12 are dual-voltage to work into France, Class 21 for multi-purpose domestic duties. Class 27 is the most powerful version.

SPECIAL FEATURES

Specific traffic needs identified in the 1980s prompted Belgian Railways to create four specific sub-types of a basic design. The lowest-numbered Class 11s replaced worn-out inter-city emus between Brussels and Amsterdam with Dutch coaches, while the dual-voltage '12s' used to work to Paris but have now been cascaded to freight only, primarily between Gent and Lille, Chatelet and Aulnoye in France. The Class 21s and their powerful Class 27 sisters bear the brunt of freight and locomotive-hauled trains all over the country. Class 27 is fitted for multiple operation, has automatic couplers and was the first Belgian locomotive type to be equipped with rheostatic brakes. The opening in 2007 of the new high-speed line between Belgium and the Netherlands will see Class 11 transferred to cross-border freight work.

SPECIFICATION

Number series: 1181-1192, 1201-1212, 2101-2160, 2701-2760
Total built: 144
Builder: BN
Date introduced: 1985, 1986, 1984, 1981 respectively
Track gauge, ft/ins (mm): 4 ft 8.5 in (1,435)
Axle arrangement: Bo-Bo
Power supply system: Class 11 - 1.5 kV DC/3.5 kV DC, Class 12 - 3 kV DC/25 kV AC 50 Hz, Class 21 - 3 kV DC, Class 27 - 3 kV DC
Electrical equipment: ACEC/SEMG - four axle-hung traction motors
Weight, tonnes: 85
Power rating, hp (kW): Class 11/12/21 - 4,400 (3,310), Class 27 - 5,650 (4,250)
Design speed, mph (km/h): 100 (160)
Additional features (Various): chopper control, Flexicoil suspension, push-pull equipment, automatic couplers

CLASS 41 DMU

Type: Belgian Railways (SNCB/NMBS) Class AR41 DMU

Locomotive-hauled trains and the remaining early 1950s railcars operating on Belgian branch lines have been replaced by a new fleet of Alstom 'Coradia' dmus whose high levels of comfort are designed to attract new business.

SPECIAL FEATURES

Diesel locomotives and hauled stock, and the remaining Class 44/45 dmus, were ousted on routes such as Ronse-Gent-Geraardsbergen, Eeklo-Gent, Antwep-Neerpelt, Mol-Hasselt and Charleroi-Couvin. The new steel-bodied Coradia dmus were constructed at GEC Alsthom's Barcelona (Spain) factory, and are formed of two cars, permanently coupled, seating 150 passengers. Areas are reserved for the disabled, bicycles and large parcels. Delivery fell a year behind schedule because of a variety of teething troubles, but was completed by the end of 2002.

SPECIFICATION

Number series: 4101-80
Total built: 80
Builder: Alstom
Date introduced: 2000
Track gauge, ft/ins (mm): 4 ft 8.5 in (1,435)
Unit configuration: M+M
Transmission: Hydraulic
Power rating, hp (kW): 645 (485)
Design speed, mph (km/h): 75 (120)
Additional features: four-unit coupling capability

CLASS AM66 EMU

Belgian Railways (SNCB/NMBS) Class AM66 and AM70 emu

The AM66 and AM70 emus are now the second oldest electric suburban passenger unit design operating in Belgium, and a familiar sight across most of the country. Most of their former top-grade duties have been handed to more modern types.

SUB-TYPES

The original AM66 series, 601–40, was built in 1966, while those built four years later are classified AM70A (formerly on Brussels Airport services – 595-600), AM70 (641-644) and AM70Th (thyristor control).

SPECIAL FEATURES

During the 1960s, systemwide electrification created a need for a large new fleet of units, and the construction contract was awarded to a consortium of BN, ABR, Familleureux, Ateliers Braine-le-Comte and Ragheno, with electrical equipment from ACEC. A special batch of six units

SPECIFICATION

Number series: 595-676
Total built: 82
Builder: AM 66/70/70A - BN, Rag, BLC, ABR, AM70Th - CWFM
Date introduced: 1966/70
Track gauge, ft/ins (mm): 4ft 8.5 (1,435)
Unit configuration: M+M
Power supply system: 3 kV DC
Electrical equipment: ACEC
Power rating, hp (kW): 900 (680)
Design speed, mph (km/h): 90 (140)
Additional features: electro-pneumatic brakes, some with Timken roller bearings

with fewer seats and more luggage capacity was built in 1970 for an airport shuttle service between Brussels North and Central stations, but since 1984 have been displaced by more modern types such as AM80. The AM70Th was the first in Belgium to be equipped with thyristor control.

175

CLASS AM80/82/83 EMU

Belgian Railways (SNCB/NMBS) Class AM80/82/83

Standardisation of the Belgian coach fleet from the 1970s onwards resulted in the 'M4' concept being adopted for electric multiple-units as well as hauled stock.

SUB-TYPES

Classes AM80 (301-335 built 1980), AM82 (336-370 built 1982), AM83 (371-440 built 1983).

PRINCIPAL MODIFICATIONS

Some units are now fitted variously with Faiveley and Brecknell-Willis pantographs.

SPECIAL FEATURES

Nicknamed Break units (the French word for estate car), the 140 units are familiar throughout the country on both inner and outer suburban duties. At the time of their introduction, their modern interiors were in sharp contrast to the early-post war trains they replaced. Delivered in

SPECIFICATION

Number series: 301-440
Total built: 140
Builder: BN
Date introduced: 1980
Track gauge, ft/ins (mm): 4 ft 8.5 in (1,435)
Unit configuration: M+T+M
Power supply system: ACEC
Electrical equipment: ACEC - four DC traction motors
Power rating, hp (kW): 1,650 (1,240)
Design speed, mph (km/h): 100 (160)
Additional features: Thyristor control, electro-pneumatic and regenerative braking, pressure ventilation

three batches in two-car formations, all have since been augmented with new centre cars built by BN (now Bombardier). They may only work in multiple with members of the same type.

CLASS AM96 EMU

Belgian Railways (SNCB/NMBS) Class AM96 EMU

The latest Belgian Railways three-car inter-city emu has dramatically improved the quality of service on principal corridors that include journeys into France, and displaced outdated 30-year-old Class AM80/82/83 units on domestic services through the capital city of Brussels and into Luxembourg.

SUB-TYPES

441-490 are dual-voltage for use in France, and 501-570 single-voltage for domestic use.

SPECIAL FEATURES

Deliveries of Class AM96 emus were completed at the end of 2000, and they are easily identified by the rubber rings fitted to their nose ends to protect the central driver's cabin and form a secure cushion between two units. The first batch of dual-voltage units is based at Ostend and works routes around the French border, including Antwerp/Ostend-Lille, and Herstal-Lieège-

SPECIFICATION

Number series: 441-490, 501-570
Total built: 120
Builder: BN
Date introduced: 1996
Track gauge, ft/ins (mm):
Unit configuration: M+T+M
Power supply system: 441-490 - 3 kV DC, 501-570 - 3 kV AC/25 kV AC 50 Hz
Electrical equipment: ACEC - four fully suspended traction motors
Power rating, hp (kW): 1,850 (1,400)
Design speed, mph (km/h): 100 (160)
Additional features: Electronic information panels, on-train phone

Charleroi-Lille. The second tranche of 70 units is for domestic use only and they spend their time on services radiating from Brussels to Charleroi, Antwerp, Knokke/Blankenberge, Gent, Hasselt, and also into Luxembourg. They are maintained at Hasselt and Stockem depots.

CLASSES 43/44/45 ELECTRIC LOCOMOTIVE

Bulgarian State Railways (BDZ) Classes 43/44/45

Versions of this versatile Czech-built design form the major part of the BDZ electric locomotive fleet and are seen throughout the country, handling both passenger and freight traffic.

SUB-TYPES

Refurbishment by Koncar in Zagreb, Croatia, has seen some Class 43 and 44 locomotives renumbered in the 43.300 series. Modifications include provision of thyristor control equipment. At least two Class 43 have been re-geared for 68 mph (110 km/h) operation and renumbered in the 43.500 series.

SPECIAL FEATURES

These three classes of AC electric locomotive are improved and more powerful versions of BDZ's Class 41 and 42 machines, also built by Skoda and introduced in the 1960s to handle traffic on the country's expanding electrified main line network. They were designed as mixed traffic locomotives

SPECIFICATION

Total built: Class 43 – 56, Class 44 – 87, Class 45 - 59
Builder: Skoda
Date introduced: 1971, 1975, 1982 respectively
Track gauge, ft/ins (mm): 4 ft 8.5 in (1,435)
Axle arrangement: Bo-Bo
Power supply system: 25 kV AC 50 Hz
Electrical equipment: Skoda, CKD – solid state rectifiers and DC traction motors
Weight, tonnes: 84
Power rating, hp (kW): 4,050 (3,020)
Design speed, mph (km/h): 80 (130) (Class 45 – 68 (110))
Additional features: multiple-unit operation

and together with the more powerful Romanian-built Class 46 Co-Cos form the core of the BDZ electric traction fleet. Itself derived from a large family of Skoda-built DC-only predecessors, the company designated these Bulgarian machines Type 68E.

CLASS 32 EMU

Bulgarian State Railways (BDZ) Class 32

This is a standard gauge version of a Latvian-built standard suburban emu design that can also be found in various configurations on railways once part of the Soviet Union and its satellites.

SPECIAL FEATURES

BDZ's Class 32 emus are a reminder of Soviet-era central planning, when production of vehicles of a particular type was concentrated on one plant. In the case of emus the RVR facility at Riga, Latvia, specialised in the manufacture of large numbers of these vehicles which in their Russian versions are members of the ER2 (DC) and ER9 (AC) families. They are rugged units and by today's standards unsophisticated. The BDZ examples mainly work Sofia area suburban services. These and the Class 412 units active in Serbia are thought to be the only standard gauge versions of this numerous group of vehicles.

SPECIFICATION

Number Series: From 32.001
Builder: Riva Carriage Building Works (RVR)
Date introduced: 1970
Track gauge, ft/ins (mm): 4 ft 8.5 in (1,435)
Unit configuration: T-M-M-T
Power supply system: 25 kV AC 50 Hz
Electrical equipment: RVR
Power rating, hp (kW): 1,770 (1,320)
Design speed, mph (km/h): 80 (130)
Additional features: unusually fitted with Russian-type SA3 automatic couplers

OTHER COUNTRIES OPERATED

These include: Belarus (Class ER9), Estonia (Class ER2 in four- and six-car versions), Latvia (Class ER2 in four- and eight-car versions), Lithuania (Class ER9), Russia (Class ER2 family units in eight-, 10- and 12-car versions and Class ER9 family units in 10- and 12-car versions), Serbia (Class 412), Ukraine (Classes ER2 and ER9), and Uzbekistan (Classes ER2 and ER9).

CLASS 1141 ELECTRIC LOCOMOTIVE

Croatian Railways (HZ) Class 1141

Class 1141 is the Croatian representative of a large family of electric locomotives mostly built in the former Yugoslavia under licence from the Swedish company ASEA. As well as surviving in several of the new nations to emerge in the Balkans, examples of the type are also active in Romania and Turkey. All derivatives of the highly successful Swedish Rc series, these Yugoslav-built machines are examples of one of the world's most successful electric locomotive designs.

SUB-TYPES

Class 442 is a development of the Class 441 design but with thyristor control equipment and an improved cab design. Sixteen examples were built by Koncar from 1981, the survivors operating in Croatia as Class 1142.

SPECIFICATION

Total built: 87 (Croatian share of a total build of 284)
Builder: SGP Graz, Rade Koncar
Date introduced: 1967
Track gauge, ft/ins (mm): 4 ft 8.5 in (1,435)
Axle arrangement: Bo-Bo
Power supply system: 25 kV AC 50 Hz
Electrical equipment: ASEA, Elin, Rade Koncar, Sécheron – tap-changer control, silicon rectifiers, fully suspended DC traction motors
Weight, tonnes: 78-82
Power rating, hp (kW): 5,170 (3,860)
Design speed, mph (km/h): 75 (120) or 87 (140)
Additional features: Class 1141.1 – rheostatic brakes, multiple-unit control, flange lubrication, Class 1141.2 – 87 mph (140 km/h) gearing.

PRINCIPAL MODIFICATIONS

By 2002 HZ had commissioned the refurbishment

of 16 Class 1141.2 locomotives to equip them with thyristor control. They form the Class 1141.3 sub-series.

SPECIAL FEATURES

Trials conducted by the former Yugoslav Railways (JZ) with a Swedish Class Rb1 locomotive in Romania led to the adoption of this type in the late 1960s for the Belgrade-Zagreb main line electrification. Under a licensing agreement with ASEA of Sweden, construction of the type extended to 284 examples of several variants between 1967 and 1989, all becoming JZ Class 441. The first 80 were built in Austria by SGP, with remaining examples constructed at the Zagreb plant of Rade Koncar. Well adapted to conditions in the former Yugoslavia, which feature sharp curves and steep grades, these locomotives are of a design already well proven in Sweden although by then ASEA was delivering thyristor-controlled versions of the type for domestic services.

OTHER COUNTRIES OPERATED

Bosnia-Herzegovina Railways (ZBH) (nine Class 441) and (ZRS) (number unknown), Macedonian Railways (MZ) (eight Class 441, three Class 442*), Montenegrin Railways (ZCG), Serbian Railways (ZS) (96 Class 441, including ZCG examples). (*MZ Class 442 are Class 441 machines acquired from HZ, Croatia, and modernised by Koncar.) Between 1976 and 1980 Koncar supplied 130 examples of this type to Romanian State Railways (CFR).

181

CLASS 1061 ELECTRIC LOCOMOTIVE

Croatian Railways (HZ) Class 1061

The break-up of the former Yugoslavia resulted in the establishment of separate railway undertakings for the new nations and a consequent distribution of the Yugoslav Railways traction and rolling stock fleet. Survivors of the 50 Italian-built former Class 362 articulated 3 kV DC electric locomotives were divided between the railways of Croatia and Slovenia.

SUB-TYPES

Two former Class 362 machines were rebuilt in 1988 and 1993 after crashes to operate from a 25 kV AC 50 Hz power supply system forming part of the HZ fleet and are designated Class 1161.

PRINCIPAL MODIFICATIONS

Refurbishment work on Class 1061 started in 2000 by Koncar Electric Locomotives of Zagreb includes modernisation of electrical equipment and the provision of improved cabs, altering the locomotives' front-end appearance.

SPECIFICATION

Number series: 1061.001-1061.023, from 1061.101
Total built: 50 (including Slovenian Railways examples)
Builder: Ansaldo, OMFP
Date introduced: 1960
Track gauge, ft/ins (mm): 4 ft 8.5 in (1,435)
Axle arrangement: Bo-Bo-Bo
Power supply system: 3 kV DC
Electrical equipment: Ansaldo, Asgen – resistance control, axle-hung DC traction motors
Weight, tonnes: 108-112
Power rating, hp (kW): Class 1061.0 - 3,540 (2,640), Class 1061.1 - 4,220 (3,150)
Design speed, mph (km/h): 75 (120)
Additional features: rheostatic braking

SPECIAL FEATURES

Initially acquired by Yugoslav Railways for the steeply graded Rijeka-Karlovac line, the former Class 362 machines were based on the design of contemporary Italian State Railways locomotives, featuring a two-section body carried on three two-axle bogies.

CLASS 121–3/140/141 ELECTRIC LOCOMOTIVE

Czech Railways (CD) and Slovakian Railways (ZSSK) Classes 121/122/123/140/141

Now in their final years, survivors of this once large family of locomotives are representatives of Czechoslovakia's first foray into domestic mass production of electric locomotives. Examples survive on lighter duties in both the Czech Republic and Slovakia. The type's builders, Skoda, achieved some export success with the design.

SUB-TYPES

A sole modified example of this type, numbered 124.601, is retained by CD as a GSM-R radio communications test locomotive.

SPECIAL FEATURES

The first examples of this group of classes were 100 Czechoslovak State Railways Class E499.0, the few survivors of which are now designated Class 140. Using technology imported from Switzerland in bogie design and flexible drive systems, these multi-purpose machines initiated the production of modern locomotives in the former

SPECIFICATION

Number series: 121.001-121.085, 122.001-122.055, 123.001-123.030, 140.001-140.100, 141.001-141-060
Total built: Class 121 – 85, Class 122 – 55, Class 123 – 30, Class 140 – 100, Class 141 - 60
Builder: Skoda
Date introduced: 1960, 1967, 1971, 1953, 1957 respectively
Track gauge, ft/ins (mm): 4 ft 8.5 in (1,435)
Axle arrangement: Bo-Bo
Power supply system: 3 kV DC
Electrical equipment: Skoda - resistance control, fully suspended DC traction motors
Weight, tonnes: 85-88
Power rating, hp (kW): Class 122 and 123 – 2,670 (1,990), remainder – 2,725 (2,032)
Design speed, mph (km/h): Class 121, 122 and 123 – 56 (90), Class 140 and 141 – 75 (120)

Czechoslovakia. They are distinguishable from later series by their six porthole-style windows on each side of the body. The E499.0 series was followed in 1959 by the first of 60 Class E499.1.

CLASSES 150/151 ELECTRIC LOCOMOTIVE

Czech Railways (CD) Classes 150/151

The most powerful electric locomotives in the CD fleet are 26 of these handsome 3 kV DC machines, 13 of which have been refurbished and modified for fast passenger service. Like all Czech main line electric locomotives, they were built by Skoda. Similar machines, but in a dual-voltage version, are in service in Slovakia.

PRINCIPAL MODIFICATIONS

Since 1992 at least 13 examples of Class 150 have undergone extensive refurbishment by Skoda, including modifications to adapt the locomotives for 100 mph (160 km/h) passenger operations. Work included re-gearing and upgrading the bogies, suspension improvements and the provision of train protection equipment.

SPECIAL FEATURES

Nicknamed 'Gorillas', the Class 150 and 151 machines are a DC-only version of the former Czechoslovak State Railways Class ES499.0 dual-

SPECIFICATION

Total built: 27 (13 converted to Class 151)
Builder: Skoda
Date introduced: 1978
Track gauge, ft/ins (mm): 4 ft 8.5 in (1,435)
Axle arrangement: Bo-Bo
Power supply system: 3 kV DC
Electrical equipment: Skoda - rheostatic control, fully suspended DC traction motors
Weight, tonnes: 82
Power rating, hp (kW): 5,360 (4,000)
Design speed, mph (km/h): Class 150 – 87 (140), Class 151 – 100 (160)
Additional features: rheostatic brakes

voltage locomotives that became ZSSK (Slovakia) Class 350. They were originally supplied by Skoda as Class E499.2 (manufacturer's designation 65E). Designed for fast passenger work, with fully suspended traction motors, the Class 150s as built had a top speed of 87 mph (140 km/h) but track improvements in the Czech Republic have increased demand for faster traction, leading to the modification programme detailed above.

CLASSES 181/182/183 ELECTRIC LOCOMOTIVE

Czech Railways (CD) and Slovakian Railways Classes 181/182/183

Built in the 1960s and 1970s for heavy freight work, survivors of CD's and ZSSK's Classes 181, 182 and 183 six-axle DC electric locomotives still play an important role in handling both domestic and transit traffic in both countries. A large number of similar machines was exported to the former Soviet Union.

SPECIAL FEATURES

Skoda's response to a demand from the former Czechoslovak State Railways for a rugged, heavy-haul freight locomotive for its growing electrified network took the form of two prototype machines built in 1958 that became the forerunners of the type featured here. Formerly Class E669, 361 more examples of this design were subsequently built, with progressive improvements introduced over a production period that extended into the early 1970s. At the beginning of 2003 around 135 examples remained in traffic in the Czech Republic and nearly 100

SPECIFICATION

Number series: 181.001-181.150, 182.001-182.168, 183.001-183.043
Total built: 361
Builder: Skoda
Date introduced: Class 181 – 1961, Class 182 - 1971
Track gauge, ft/ins (mm): 4 ft 8.5 in (1,435)
Axle arrangement: Co-Co
Power supply system: 3 kV DC
Electrical equipment: Skoda - rheostatic control, axle-hung DC traction motors
Weight, tonnes: 120
Power rating, hp (kW): 3,500 (2,610) or 3,740 (2,790)
Design speed, mph (km/h): 56 (90)

more, including all of Class 183, in Slovakia.

OTHER COUNTRIES OPERATED

The design of this class was adopted in a passenger version by the former Soviet Railways (SZhD), surviving as Class ChS2/ChS2T .

185

CLASSES 162/163/263/362/363

Czech Railways (CD) and Slovakian Railways (ZSSK) Classes 162/163/263/362/363

Generically known by the popular name 'Perschings', this large family of second generation mixed traffic locomotives is in service with both CD and ZSSK in AC (Class 263), DC (Class 163) and dual-voltage (Classes 362 and 363) versions, forming a major part of both operators' electric traction stock. A small number were also sold to an Italian operator, the North Milan Railway.

SUB-TYPES

CD operates small numbers of Classes 162 and 362, both 87 mph (140 km/h) variants of Classes 163 and 363 respectively. The design of the later Class 371 and 372 (below right) dual-voltage machines and their German Rail (DB) Class 180 dual-voltage counterparts is based on that of the Class 162/163/263/362/363 family.

SPECIAL FEATURES

Representing the second generation of (then)

SPECIFICATION

Total built: Classes 162 and 163 – 180 (including locomotives sold to FNM, Italy), Class 263 – 12, Classes 362 and 363 - 182
Builder: Skoda
Date introduced: 1984, 1984, 1981 respectively
Track gauge, ft/ins (mm): 4 ft 8.5 in (1,435)
Axle arrangement: Bo-Bo
Power supply system: 3 kV DC/25 kV AC 50 Hz/3 kV DC/25 kV AC 50 Hz
Electrical equipment: Skoda, CKD (Skoda only Class 263), thyristor control, axle-hung DC traction motors
Weight, tonnes: 85, 85, 87
Power rating, hp (kW): 4,100 (3,060) (some Class 163 4,660 (3,480))
Design speed, mph (km/h): 120 (193) (Classes 162 and 362 - 140 (87))
Additional features: rheostatic braking, automatic speed control

Czechoslovak electric locomotive development, these machines are products of the Skoda plant at Pilsen that supplied various Eastern Bloc countries with traction of this type. Designated Types 71E,

70E and 69E respectively by Skoda, these locomotives feature electronic stepless control. Bogies are interchangeable between all three classes. The three classes were delivered with the former Czechoslovak State Railways designations of E499.3, S499.2 and ES499.1 respectively.

OTHER COUNTRIES OPERATED

The share-out of the traction resources of the former Czechoslovak State Railways on the separation of the Czech Republic and Slovakia as separate nations saw examples of all three classes passing to what has become the ZSSK fleet in Slovakia. Locomotives there carry the same class designations and there are also Class 162 and Class 362 variants comparable with those in the Czech Republic.

CLASSES 230/240/340 ELECTRIC LOCOMOTIVE

Czech Railways (CD) and Slovakian Railways (ZSSK) Classes 230/240/340

The first AC main line locomotive type to appear in former Czechoslovakia is characterised by a unique appearance, thanks to innovative body construction techniques. Not only do many examples of Classes 230 and 240 survive as the major component of the CD AC-only fleet – a few have recently been modernised and converted into dual-voltage machines.

PRINCIPAL MODIFICATIONS

In 2003 three CD Class 240 locomotives were refurbished and modified as two-voltage machines (25 kV AC 50 Hz/15 kV AC 16.7 Hz) to operate cross-border traffic linking the Czech Republic and Austria. These became Class 340.

SPECIAL FEATURES

The trend in the 1960s among several Eastern European railways to adopt the 25 kV AC system instead of DC for future electrification schemes led Skoda to develop its first main line AC

SPECIFICATION

Number series: 230.001-230.110, 240.001-240.145
Total built: Class 230 – 110, Class 240 – 145
Builder: Skoda
Date introduced: 1966, 1968
Track gauge, ft/ins (mm): 4 ft 8.5 in (1,435)
Axle arrangement: Bo-Bo
Power supply system: 25 kV AC 50 Hz
Electrical equipment: Skoda, tap-changer control, silicon rectifiers and fully suspended DC traction motors
Weight, tonnes: 88, 85
Power rating, hp (kW): 4,130 (3,080)
Design speed, mph (km/h): Class 230 – 68 (110), Class 240 – 75 (120)
Additional features: some equipped with rheostatic brakes

locomotive designs. A six-axle prototype built in 1963 was followed by a series order for Bulgaria, where examples survive as Class 42. After the construction of two prototypes, series production commenced for the Czechoslovak system, eventually totalling 255 examples.

CLASSES 750/752/753/754/755 DIESEL

Czech Railways (CD) and Slovakian Railways (ZSSK) Classes 750/752/753/754/755

This large family of distinctive mixed traffic and passenger diesel locomotives was built in the 1960s and 1970s for the former Czechoslovak State Railways. Never the most reliable machines, numbers of the original Class 753 and 754 types have been greatly depleted by withdrawals, while some examples have undergone life-extending modernisation and refurbishment.

SUB-TYPES

Class 750 has been created since 1991 by replacing the steam-heat boiler of Class 753 machines with electric equipment. In 2003 CD operated well over 100 examples and ZSSK retained nearly 50. Class 752 is a solitary example of a Class 753 re-engined with a CKD K6S 310 DR power unit in an (apparently unsuccessful) attempt to improve reliability. ZSSK's predecessor ZSR commissioned the re-engining of a Class 753 with a Pielstick power unit to create a Class 755 machine but this is no longer in traffic.

SPECIFICATION

Total built: Class 753 – 407, Class 754 – 84
Builder: CKD
Date introduced: 1968, 1975
Track gauge, ft/ins (mm): 4 ft 8.5 in (1,435)
Axle arrangement: Bo-Bo
Power unit type: CKD K12V 230 DR
Transmission: CKD, electric - generator and axle-hung DC traction motors
Weight, tonnes: 73, 74
Power rating, hp (kW): 1,775 (1,325), 1,960 (1,460)
Design speed, mph (km/h): 62 (100)
Additional features: Class 753 built with steam heating boilers, subsequently removed, Class 754 built with electric train-heating.

SPECIAL FEATURES

First examples of this conventional diesel-electric locomotive appeared in the 1960s as 10 Class T478.3 prototypes, leading to an eventual build of 397 examples of the type that became CD/ZSSK Class 753. The Class 754 (originally T478.4) followed in 1975 with an uprated version of the CKD K12V 230 DR 12-cylinder power unit.

189

CLASSES 770/771 DIESEL LOCOMOTIVE

Czech Railways (CD) Class 770/771

With more than 8,000 examples produced since 1963, most of them to Soviet Railways, this is one of the world's most numerous locomotive types. This basic, rugged design is used primarily for heavy shunting and trip freight work in many parts of Eastern Europe and beyond.

SUB-TYPES

Classes 770.8 and 771.8, now part of the ZSSK fleet in Slovakia, are 5 ft 0 in (1,520 mm) gauge machines originally supplied for the broad gauge iron ore line between Kosice and the Ukraine.

PRINCIPAL MODIFICATIONS

Class 773 has been created in Slovakia by rebuilding Class 771 machines with 1,740 hp (1,300 kW) Caterpillar engines, electronic control equipment and new-style body with low hoods.

SPECIAL FEATURES

The Class T669.0 prototype of this design was

SPECIFICATION

Total built: Class 770 – 109, Class 771 – 207 (includes locomotives assigned to Slovakia)
Builder: CKD, SMZ Dubnica
Date introduced: 1963
Track gauge, ft/ins (mm): 4 ft 8.5 in (1,435)
Axle arrangement: Co-Co
Power unit type: CKD K6S 310 DR
Transmission: CKD electric - generator and axle-hung DC traction motors
Weight, tonnes: 115, 116
Power rating, hp (kW): 1,330 (993)
Design speed, mph (km/h): 56 (90)
Additional features: multiple-unit operation

built for the former Czechoslovak State Railways in 1963. This machine became the pattern for a further 108 locomotives that became Class 770, followed by 195 Class 771 (ex-Class T669.1) from 1969. The mechanical design is of the 'hood' type, with an off-centre cab and high bonnets, riding on two three-axle bogies. In 2004 around 100 examples each remained in service with CD and ZSSK.

190

CLASS 471 EMU

Czech Railways (CD) Class 471

Czech Railways' first example of a double-deck emu is this innovative domestically built design introduced on Prague suburban services in 2000. An intercity variant has also been ordered.

SPECIAL FEATURES

These double-deck aluminium-bodied vehicles were developed for CD to replace Class 451 and 452 units on Prague suburban services. Originally ordered as four two-car and six three-car sets, all ten were eventually supplied in three-car formations of one powered car and two trailers. The type was first deployed on the Prague-Kolín line in 2000. A dual-voltage (3 kV DC/25 kV AC 50 Hz) development of the design was in production in 2004. Designated Class 675, five six-car units were ordered in 2002 with the first example scheduled for delivery in 2004.

SPECIFICATION

Number series: 471.001-471.010 (intermediate and driving trailers numbered in 071 and 971 series respectively)
Total built: 10
Builder: CKD Vagónka, Studénka
Date introduced: 1997
Track gauge, ft/ins (mm): 4 ft 8.5 in (1,435)
Unit configuration: M-T-T
Power supply system: 3 kV DC
Electrical equipment: Skoda, IGBT control equipment
Power rating, hp (kW): 2,680 (2,000)
Design speed, mph (km/h): 87 (140)
Additional features: rheostatic braking

CLASSES 809/810/811 DMU

Czech Railways (CD) and Slovakian Railways (ZSSK) Class 809/810/811

For its branch line and local services CD employs large numbers of this 1970s-built family of two-axle railcars and trailers, with similar equipment also in use in neighbouring Slovakia. Recently, while also examining closely the economics of such operations, both railways have been exploring refurbishment or replacement options for older examples.

SUB-TYPES

ZSSK operates two 5 ft 0 in (1,520 mm) gauge Class 810.8 railcars.

PRINCIPAL MODIFICATIONS

In 2001 a CD Class 810 railcar was rebuilt by Pars nova to serve as a possible prototype for large-scale refurbishment of these vehicles. Equipped with a Liaz 320 hp (240 kW) engine and Voith transmission, the unit became Class 812. The following year a Class 912 driving trailer for use the Class 812 unit was produced from a Class 010 trailer. This features a part-low-floor layout.

SPECIFICATION

Builder: Vagónka Studénka
Date introduced: 1975
Track gauge, ft/ins (mm): 4 ft 8.5 in (1,435)
Unit configuration: single car
Power unit type: Liaz ML634
Transmission: Praga, hydro-mechanical
Power rating, hp (kW): 210 (156)
Design speed, mph (km/h): 50 (80)

SPECIAL FEATURES

With over 500 examples in the CD fleet and more than 120 listed by ZSSK (which only operates the Class 810 version of this design), these numerous but rather basic lightweight railcars play an important role in meeting the regional transport demands of both railways. Introduced in 1975 as Czechoslovak State Railways Class M152, the Studénka-built vehicles provide seating for 55 passengers and standing room for 40 more. They are often used with trailer cars, as well as in multiple with members of the same class.

CLASS EA ELECTRIC LOCOMOTIVE

Danish State Railways (DSB)/Railion Denmark Class EA

Electrification of parts of the Danish main line network in the 1980s led to the introduction of the country's first electric locomotive type, Class EA. Separation of DSB's passenger and freight businesses in 2001 led to examples the 22-strong fleet being deployed by both companies.

SPECIAL FEATURES

Jointly developed by Siemens, Thyssen Henschel and BBC and based on the design of German Rail's Class 120 machines, the Danish Class EA three-phase electric locomotives were acquired by DSB for both passenger and freight traffic on lines newly electrified in the 1980s. Ten locomotives were built initially, two by Thyssen Henschel and the remainder under licence in Denmark by Scandia. These were followed in 1992-93 by 12 more featuring design improvements. The separation in 2001 of DSB's passenger and freight business saw 10 of the class

SPECIFICATION

Number series: 3001-3022
Total built: 22
Builder: Thyssen Henschel/Siemens/Scandia
Date introduced: 1984
Track gauge, ft/ins (mm): 4 ft 8.5 in (1,435)
Axle arrangement: Bo-Bo
Power supply system: 25 kV AC 50 Hz
Electrical equipment: BBC - three-phase traction technology and asynchronous traction motors
Weight, tonnes: 80
Power rating, hp (kW): 5,360 (4,000)
Design speed, mph (km/h): 108 (175)
Additional features: multiple-unit operation, push-pull operation

assigned to freight operator Railion Denmark, with the other 12 remaining with DSB for passenger traffic.

CLASS EG ELECTRIC LOCOMOTIVE

Railion Denmark Class EG

This powerful dual-voltage adaptation of Siemens Class 152 'EuroSprinter' electric locomotive family was ordered by Danish State Railways to haul heavy cross-border freight traffic between Sweden and Germany via Denmark.

SPECIAL FEATURES

Thirteen examples of this six-axle adaptation of Siemens' first generation four-axle EuroSprinter locomotive family were ordered by Danish State Railways (DSB) to handle freight traffic generated by the commissioning of the Öresund Link between Denmark and Sweden. With a combination of bridges and tunnels, the link features sharp transition gradients over which the Class EG locomotives are designed to haul 2,000 tonne trains in all weather conditions. In addition, the locomotives have a dual-voltage capability, enabling them to work on the Swedish and German 15 kV systems as well as the domestic Danish 25 kV, thus avoiding the need for traction changes at borders. Since the Class EG locomotives were ordered,

SPECIFICATION

Number series: 3101-3113
Total built: 13
Builder: Siemens Transportation Systems
Date introduced: 1999
Track gauge, ft/ins (mm): 4 ft 8.5 in (1,435)
Axle arrangement: Co-Co
Power supply system: 25 kV AC 50 Hz/15 kV AC 16.7 Hz
Electrical equipment: Siemens SIBAS 32 traction control system, water-cooled traction converters, three-phase nose-suspended traction motors
Weight, tonnes: 129
Power rating, hp (kW): 8,710 (6,500)
Design speed, mph (km/h): 87 (140)
Additional features: wheel-mounted brake discs

OTHER COUNTRIES OPERATED

Although operators in several countries employ four-axle versions of the first generation EuroSprinter design, these Danish machines remain the only six-axle examples of the type.

CLASS ME DIESEL LOCOMOTIVE

Danish State Railways (DSB) Class ME

Denmark

The most modern example of DSB's long-standing preference for General Motors-powered main line diesel locomotives is Class ME, which is used exclusively on passenger services in Denmark.

PRINCIPAL MODIFICATIONS

Locomotives 1528-1537 are equipped with passenger alarm overrides to enable them to work services through the Storebaelt tunnel, with the sub-class designation MEO. Twenty examples of the class feature modified push-pull equipment to enable them to work with Bombardier-built double-deck stock.

SPECIAL FEATURES

DSB's GM-powered three-phase Class ME locomotives now represent this operator's main traction for its principal passenger services over non-electrified lines. In 2003 the type commenced operations with newly delivered Bombardier-built double-deck push-pull coaches on services mainly east of the Great Belt.

SPECIFICATION

Number series: 1501-1537
Total built: 37
Builder: Thyssen-Henschel/Scandia
Date introduced: 1981
Track gauge, ft/ins (mm): 4 ft 8.5 in (1,435)
Axle arrangement: Co-Co
Power unit type: General Motors 16-645-E3B
Transmission: General Motors electric - alternator with BBC three-phase drives
Weight, tonnes: 115
Power rating, hp (kW): 3,040 (2,270)
Design speed, mph (km/h): 108 (175)
Additional features: multiple-unit operation, push-pull operation

Examples of the class are painted in all-over red and all-over dark blue liveries, as well as DSB's traditional black, red and white colour scheme.

IC3 (CLASS MFA/FF/MFB) DMU

Danish State Railways (DSB) IC3

A revolutionary design at the time of its introduction, the IC3 dmu brought high-speed intercity running to the existing Danish network with a vehicle concept that took account of the country's relatively short transits and the need to split or join trains en route. The IC3's basic design subsequently spawned emu and regional diesel derivatives and has achieved some export success for its manufacturers.

SUB-TYPES

Emu derivatives of the IC3 design operate in Denmark: 44 DSB IR4 four-car regional units and 24 'Øresund' four-car dual-voltage (15 kV/25 kV) units, DSB's share of a fleet jointly operated with SJ, Sweden, over the fixed link between the two countries. SJ owns 18 similar units as Class Y31. An adaptation of the IC3 design for light, regional lines dubbed 'Flexliner' has been acquired in small numbers by the operators of some Danish local

railways. These feature a partial low floor in one of the two cars.

SPECIAL FEATURES

Introduced in 1989, the IC3 dmus provided an inspired solution to DSB's aim of accelerating and improving the quality of its principal intercity

services. The three-car aluminium-bodied articulated trainsets are not only capable of running at up to 112 mph (180 km/h), they also offer the good acceleration needed between the frequent stops that characterise DSB services of this type. Together with the close coupling of cars provided by articulation, the inflated rubber seals around the front ends provide additional streamlining when units are coupled. In this configuration the driver's consoles can be swung to one side to allow passage between trains.

OTHER COUNTRIES OPERATED

The largest user of this type outside Denmark is Israel Railways (left lower), with nearly 40 examples in service by 2003, most of them locally assembled, 20 units designated Class Y2 (above) are operating regionally sponsored services in Sweden, 23 of a CAF-built non-articulated derivative with active tilt are in service with

SPECIFICATION

Number series: 5001–5092
Total built: 92
Builder: ABB Scandia
Date introduced: 1989
Track gauge, ft/ins (mm): 4 ft 8.5 in (1,435)
Unit configuration: M-T-M
Power unit type: KHD-Deutz BFBL-513-cp
Transmission: ZF - hydromechanical gearbox, Kaeble-Gmeinder - final drive
Power rating, hp (kW): 1,340 (1,000)
Design speed, mph (km/h): 112 (180)
Additional features: articulated configuration, multiple-unit operation of up to five units, multiple-unit operation with IR4 emus, some fitted with either German or Swedish ATC equipment for international operations

RENFE's Regionales business unit in Spain, forming Classes 594 and 594.1.

An adaptation of the IC3 front-end concept is applied to Belgian National Railways Class AM96 emus.

S-TRAIN EMU

Danish State Railways S-Tog S-Train

One of the more distinctive types of vehicle in this book is the large fleet of suburban emus that Danish State Railways' Copenhagen area commuter subsidiary has put into service since 1995. Members of an eventual fleet of 960 cars have seen the progressive replacement of older equipment dating from the 1960s and 1970s.

SPECIAL FEATURES

The S-Train concept was developed uniquely for S-Tog by the German train-builder Linke-Hofmann-Busch (now ALSTOM LHB), responding to the operator's demands for a high-capacity design particularly adapted to the Danish capital's needs. Each eight-car set is formed of two articulated half-sets running on single-axle air-suspended bogies. The axles are steered by a linkage system of rods connected to their adjacent carbody articulations. All but one of the five axles of each half-set are motored. The

SPECIFICATION

Total built: 105 eight-car and 30 four-car trainsets
Builder: ALSTOM (LHB)/Siemens
Date introduced: 1995
Track gauge, ft/ins (mm): 4 ft 8.5 in (1,435)
Unit configuration: M-M-M-M+M-M-M-M (eight-car), M-M+M-M (four-car)
Power supply system: 1.5 kV DC
Electrical equipment: Siemens - with asynchronous AC traction motors suspended transversely
Power rating, hp (kW): eight-car – 1,930 (1,440), four car – 965 (720)
Design speed, mph (km/h): 75 (120)
Additional features: 3 + 3 seating in a 3.6 m wide body, full width interconnection gangways.

carbody is formed of extruded aluminium sections. Axle load is a mere 10.5 tonnes. Delivery of eight pre-series units was made on 1995-97. Subsequent orders will see an eventual fleet of 105 eight-car and 30 four-car sets.

CLASS 1500 DIESEL LOCOMOTIVE

Estonian Railways (EVR) Class 1500

Denmark/Estonia

The presence of US business interests in the consortium that took over Estonian rail freight operations when that country's government privatised its network was undoubtedly a factor in the acquisition of secondhand American main line diesel locomotives. These and a batch of less powerful sister locomotives in Estonia in 2001 were the first large-scale application of a US domestic diesel design in Europe.

SPECIAL FEATURES

Increasing the efficiency of the traction fleet was seen as essential by the Baltic Rail Services consortium that took over Estonian Railways in 2001. This was achieved by obtaining two batches of General Electric-built locomotives that were surplus to requirements in the US. These C36-7 and C30-7A machines were re-gauged and refurbished at GE plants in Mexico with the latest electronic control equipment, becoming types C36-7i and C30-7Ai respectively. The more powerful C36-7i is featured here. The C30-7Ai machines, of which EVR has 19 examples, are a 12-cylinder variant of the same basic design. By

mid-2003 all of both types had been commissioned, enabling EVR to retire the surviving M62 and 2TE116 locomotives. The American machines are reported to have acquitted themselves well on the heavy freight flows operated between Russia and Estonia's Baltic ports.

OTHER COUNTRIES OPERATED

The General Electric C36-7 model is widely used in North America. The type is also in use in Brazil.

SPECIFICATION

Number series: 1500-1557
Total built: 58
Builder: General Electric
Date introduced: 2001 (built 1984-85)
Track gauge, ft/ins (mm): 5 ft 0 in (1,520)
Axle arrangement: Co-Co
Power unit type: GE 7FDL16
Transmission: GE electric – alternator and axle-hung DC traction motors
Weight, tonnes: 160
Power rating, hp (kW): 3,600 (2,640)
Design speed, mph (km/h): 70 (112)

CLASS Dr16 DIESEL LOCOMOTIVE

Finnish Railways (VR) Class Dr16

The most powerful and newest main line diesel locomotives on the Finnish network are these single-cab machines introduced in 1987 for both passenger and freight services over non-electrified lines. The locomotives' builders, Valmet, designated the type the M-series.

SPECIAL FEATURES

Class Dr16 is a workmanlike design intended to meet VR's limited requirement for a traction unit more powerful than the numerous Class Dv12 for its non-electrified lines. Two Wärtsilä-engined prototypes delivered in 1987 were quickly followed by 21 more, but with the French-designed Pielstick engine, to form the present class.

SPECIFICATION

Number series: 2801-2823
Total built: 23
Builder: Valmet
Date introduced: 1987
Track gauge, ft/ins (mm): 5 ft 0 in (1,524)
Axle arrangement: Bo-Bo
Power unit type: Wärtsilä Vasa 8 V22 or Pielstick PA4-V200 VG
Transmission: Strömberg - microprocessor control with AC axle-hung traction motors
Weight, tonnes: 84
Power rating, hp (kW): 2,010 (1,500) or 2,250 (1,677)
Design speed, mph (km/h): 87 (140)
Additional features: multiple-unit operation, electric train-heating

CLASS SR1 EELECTRIC LOCOMOTIVE

Finnish Railways (VR) Class Sr1

Finland was comparatively late to adopt electrification of its main line network, not extending the wires outside the Helsinki suburban area until the 1970s. Reflecting the fact that it shares a track gauge with its eastern neighbour, VR turned to the former Soviet Union to build its first electric locomotives, the Class Sr1, but used a domestic supplier for their traction control equipment.

SPECIAL FEATURES

The Class Sr1 was developed in collaboration with Strömberg by the Soviet All-Union Electric Locomotive Research and Design Institute (VELNII) specifically to meet VR requirements. The result was a design with an axle-load of 21 tonnes, much lower than that of contemporary Soviet electric locomotives. Until the arrival in 1996 of the first Class Sr2 locomotives, the Sr1 was VR's only electric locomotive type. Today Class Sr1

SPECIFICATION

Number series: 3001-3112
Total built: 112
Builder: Novocherkassk Electric Locomotive Works
Date introduced: 1973
Track gauge, ft/ins (mm): 5 ft 0 in (1,520)
Axle arrangement: Bo-Bo
Power supply system: 25 kV AC 50 Hz
Electrical equipment: Strömberg - thyristor control with Novocherkassk fully suspended traction motors
Weight, tonnes: 84
Power rating, hp (kW): 4,155 (3,100)
Design speed, mph (km/h): 87 or 100 (140 or 160)
Additional features: rheostatic braking, multiple-unit operation

machines can be seen throughout the Finnish electrified network on both passenger and freight main line services, occasionally operating in pairs.

CLASS SM4 EMU

Finnish Railways (VR) Class Sm4

Expansion of the Helsinki suburban network in the 1990s and the need to upgrade its rolling stock fleet led VR to order the first batch of these stylish emus from Italian builder Fiat Ferroviaria.

SPECIAL FEATURES

Having established itself in the Finnish market with the supply of Class Sm3 Pendolino high-speed tilting trainsets, Fiat Ferroviaria was selected again by VR to modernise its Helsinki suburban and outer suburban fleet with an initial order for 10 of these aluminium-bodied part-low-floor two-car emus. Assembly of the vehicles was subcontracted by Fiat to CAF in Spain. Fiat Ferroviaria subsequently became part of ALSTOM Transport, which assumed responsibility for the follow-up orders that were set to expand the fleet.

SPECIFICATION

Number series: 6301-6310/6401-6410 (cars individually numbered)
Total built: 10 (20 more ordered in 2002 for delivery 2004-05, 20 more on option)
Builder: Fiat Ferroviaria
Date introduced: 1999
Track gauge, ft/ins (mm): 5 ft 0 in (1,524)
Unit configuration: M-M
Power supply system: 25 kV AC 50 Hz
Electrical equipment: Parizzi
Power rating, hp (kW): 1,600 (1,200)
Design speed, mph (km/h): 100 (160)
Additional features: regenerative braking, air-conditioning, GPS-driven passenger information system, onboard CCTV, entrance height 580 mm above rail

TGV DUPLEX

French Railways (SNCF) TGV-Duplex

By the early-1990s SNCF's Paris-Lyon high speed railway was becoming a victim of its own success with trains full and the line approaching maximum capacity. TGV Duplex was the innovative solution, adding 40% more capacity than a standard 2+8 TGV set within the same strict weight limits.

SPECIAL FEATURES

The double deck trains have allowed extra capacity on the Paris-Lyon route and work many trains to Marseille and the French Riviera. The new generation power cars are based on those used for TGV-A and TGV-R but feature disc brakes, a revised streamlined cab and central driving position. An initial batch of 30 trains was followed by further orders to provide extra capacity on the new TGV Méditerranée line from summer 2000. The latest units are allocated to the Paris-Marseille route.

SPECIFICATION

Number series: 201-264
Total built: 64 (including units on order in 2004)
Builder: Alstom
Date introduced: 1995
Track gauge, ft/ins (mm): 4 ft 8.5 in (1,435)
Unit configuration: Bo-Bo+2-2-2-2-2-2-2-2+Bo-Bo
Power supply system: 25 kV AC 50Hz, 1.5 kV DC
Electrical equipment: 8 x FM47 1,100 kW synchronous motors
Power rating, hp (kW): 11,700 (8,800) on 25 kV AC 50 Hz, 4,900 (3,680) on 1.5 kV DAC 16.7 Hz
Design speed, mph (km/h): 186 (300)
Additional features: TVM430 cab signalling, new generation power cars

203

TGV FAMILY

French Railways (SNCF) TGV Sud-Est and TGV-Poste (TGV-PSE), TGV Atlantique (TGV-A), TGV Réseau

The TGV family is probably the world's best known and most successful group of high-speed trains. Since the introduction of the first Paris-Sud-Est (PSE) sets in 1978, TGVs have revolutionised rail travel in many parts of France, neighbouring countries, and also in the Far East.

SUB-TYPES

Three and half TGV-PSE sets are used for postal traffic between Paris, Macon and Cavaillon on the Sud-Est high-speed line. They have no passenger accommodation and are painted in Poste yellow. Nine PSE sets are dedicated to Paris-Switzerland

'Lyria' service and have 15 kV AC 16.7 Hz equipment. 34 TGV- Réseau sets have 3 kV DC equipment for international services to Belgium and a further six trains have similar equipment for operation into Italy.

PRINCIPAL MODIFICATIONS

The PSE sets have progressively lost their original distinctive orange and white livery in favour of the standard blue and grey as recent refurbishment has taken place. For the new TGV Est line from Paris to Strasbourg, 40 TGV-R sets are to be extensively refurbished and six TGV-A

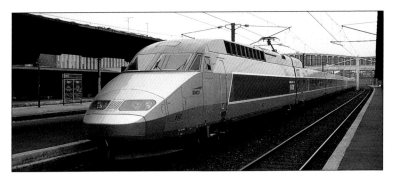

sets are to be fitted with tilt equiment for the Paris-Limoges line.

SPECIAL FEATURES

Alstom and its partners have gradually developed TGV technology to offer higher speeds, better comfort and more capacity and has successfully exported the concept to Spain and South Korea. PSE sets work to the south and east of France and Switzerland, TGV Atlantique over a wide area to the south and west of the country and TGV-R right across France and to Belgium and Italy.

OTHER COUNTRIES OPERATED

Thalys TGVs (above left) work from France to Belgium, Holland and Germany, AVE (above) and Euromed trains in Spain are based on TGV-A technology, also TGV South Korea, where 44 trainsets have been built for the country's new high-speed line.

SPECIFICATION

Number series: TGV-PSE - 01-102, 110-118, TGV-A 301-405, TGV-R - 501-550, 4501-4540
Total built: 304
Builder: Alsthom, Francorail-MTE, De Dietrich
Date introduced: TGV-PSE - 1978, TGV-A - 1988, TGV-R - 1992
Track gauge, ft/ins (mm): 4 ft 8.5 in (1,435)
Unit configuration: TGV-PSE and TGV-R – M-T-T-T-T-T-T-M, Bo-Bo+Bo-2-2-2-2-2-2-2-Bo + Bo-Bo, TGV-A – M-T-T-T-T-T-T-T-T-T-M Bo-Bo + 2-2-2-2-2-2-2-2-2-2+Bo-Bo, TGV-R - Bo-Bo+2-2-2-2-2-2-2-2-2+Bo-Bo
Power supply system: All sets 25 kV AC 50 Hz, 1.5 kV DC, plus some TGV-PSE with 15 kV AC 16.7 Hz equipment and some TGV-R with 3 kV DC
Electrical equipment: TGV-PSE - 12 525 kW traction motors, TGV-A, TGV-R - 8 FM47 1,100 kW synchronous motors
Power rating, hp (kW): TGV-PSE - 8,400 (6,300), TGV-A/R – 11,700 (8,800)
Design speed, mph (km/h): 186 (300)
Additional features: TVM300 or 430 cab signalling

CLASS CC6500 ELECTRIC LOCOMOTIVE

French Railways (SNCF) Class CC6500

The most powerful locomotives in the SNCF fleet (and Europe) when they were constructed, this type was for many years associated with 125 mph (200 km/h) expresses such as 'Le Capitole' and the 'Etendard'. Subjected to many modifications over the years, including adaptation for third rail operation they are now freight engines, and destined for early retirement.

SUB-TYPES

For many years CC6539-6559 were fitted with third rail power collection equipment for use on the Chambéry-Modane line in the Savoy Alps. Until 1995/96 CC6575-78 were numbered CC21001-004 to denote their 1.5 kV/25 kV AC dual-voltage capabilit. However this equipment was removed and the locomotives standardised.

PRINCIPAL MODIFICATIONS

For many years the CC6500s were fitted with 'préannonce' cab signalling for operation at 200 km/h but this has been removed as all locomotives are now freight only and restricted to 160 km/h.

SPECIFICATION

Number series: CC6501-6578
Total built: 78
Builder: Alsthom/MTE
Date introduced: 1969
Track gauge, ft/ins (mm): 4 ft 8.5 in (1,435)
Axle arrangement: C-C
Power supply system: 1.5 kV DC
Electrical equipment: Alsthom – frame-mounted monomotors
Weight, tonnes: 115-118
Power rating, hp (kW): 7,850 (5,900)
Design speed, mph (km/h): 125 (200)
Additional features: rheostatic braking, electro-pneumatic braking, driver- guard communication, snowploughs, gear selection: low (160 km/h) with high tractive effort for freight and high (200 km/h) for express passenger.

SPECIAL FEATURES

The ability of the CC6500s to haul heavy 'rapide' trains at high speed is legendary and SNCF is now putting this power to use on its freight trains. All locomotives are now restricted to 100 mph (160 km/h) and widely used in the south and south east of France and on the former PLM main line to Paris.

CLASS BB9200/16000/25200 ELECTRIC LOCOMOTIVE

French Railways (SNCF) Classes BB9200/BB16000/BB25200

This family of locomotives represents the classic Paul Arzens designs of the 1950s, with some locomotives appearing as late as 1977 to meet specific needs. Although displaced by modern types and TGVs on front line services, they are still widely seen at speeds of up to 200 km/h.

SUB-TYPES

BB9701-9704 were modified from BB9200s with TDM push-pull equipment for Paris-Laroche-Migennes outer suburban services, and BB16101-115 between Paris Nord and St Lazare. Dual-voltage locomotives are split into three sub-classes, mainly for freight work, with a small batch on Rhône-Alpes regional push-pull trains.

PRINCIPAL MODIFICATIONS

Within the classes there are various modifications, including two types of push-pull equipment.

SPECIAL FEATURES

The 1.5kV DC BB9200s were front line passenger traction from Paris to the south of France and the first locomotives in Europe to run at 200km/h

SPECIFICATION

Number series: BB9201-9292, BB9701-9704, BB16001-16061, BB16100-16115, BB25101-25125, BB25150-25190, BB25203-25253
Total built: 287
Builder: Schneider-Jeumont, CEM, MTE
Date introduced: 1957
Track gauge ft/ins (mm), 4 ft 8.5 in (1,435)
Axle arrangement: Bo-Bo
Power supply system: BB9200 - 1.5 kV DC, BB16000 - 25 kV AC 50 Hz, BB25100/150/200 - 1.5 kV DC/25 kV AC 50 Hz
Electrical equipment: BB9200 - Alsthom traction motors (BB9200), all other types - Jeumont
Weight, tonnes: BB9200 - 82, BB16000 - 88, BB25100/150/200 - 85
Power rating, hp (kW): BB9200 - 5,130 (3,850), BB16000 - 5,500 (4,130), other types - 4,550 (3,400) on 1.5kV DC 16.7 Hz/5,500 (4,130) on 25kV AC 50 Hz
Design speed, mph (km/h): 100 (160)
Additional features: rheostatic braking, TDM push-pull equipment, snowploughs

until replaced by CC6500s from 1969. North and east of Paris the BB16000s took over on newly electrified 25 kV AC routes in the early-1960s. Both BB9200 and BB16000 are still predominantly passenger types.

CLASSES BB7200/15000/22200

French Railways (SNCF) Classes BB7200/BB15000/BB22200

This 1970s family of locomotives was developed by Alsthom/MTE to increase train speeds and loadings over the important Toulouse and Bordeaux main lines, and the dual-voltage BB22200 is now the most widely distributed of all French locomotive types.

SUB-TYPES

BB7200 is DC-only with fixed gearing, with cowcatchers, electro-pneumatic brakes and driver- guard communication for passenger (160 or 200 km/h) or freight (100 km/h); BB15000 is 25kV AC only and BB22200 is dual-voltage.

PRINCIPAL MODIFICATIONS

BB7201-7235, BB7343-7380, BB7411-7440 are restricted to 100 km/h for freight work, BB7261-7263 have 'preannonce' cab signalling for 200 km/h operation, BB7281-7296 modified for hauling Spanish Talgo stock, and BB15001-15014,

BB15030-15049 have forced air-ventilation for traction motors, BB22379/80 and BB22399-405 were modified for operation through the Channel Tunnel to Britain in 1994/95 and eight locomotives have TVM430 cab signalling for 200 km/h parcels trains over high-speed lines.

SPECIAL FEATURES

Developed from earlier generations of French electrics such as CC6500, they retain the monomotor bogie configuration with one large traction motor per bogie. BB15000, the first to appear, remains front line traction for passenger services on the Est Region, particularly between Paris and Strasbourg. BB7200 is common in the south and south-west of France, while the dual-voltage BB22200 is seen anywhere from the Channel coast to the Mediterranean and the Spanish border.

OTHER COUNTRIES OPERATED

Similar locomotives were built by Alsthom for Morocco (Class E-1300) and the Netherlands (Classes 1600 and 1700) (above).

SPECIFICATION

SPECIFICATION

Number series: BB7201-7440, BB15001-15065, BB22201-22405
Total built: BB7200 - 240, BB15000 - 65, BB22200 - 205
Builder: Alsthom/MTE
Date introduced: BB15000 - 1971, BB7200/22200 - 1976
Track gauge: ft/ins (mm) 4 ft 8.5 in (1,435)
Axle arrangement: B-B
Power supply system: BB7200 - 1.5 kV DC, BB15000 - 25 kV AC 50 Hz, BB22200 - 1.5 kV DC/25 kV AC 50 Hz
Electrical equipment: Alsthom - TAB674 frame mounted monomotors
Weight, tonnes: BB7200 - 90 BB15000/22200 - 84, 90
Power rating, hp (kW): BB7200 - 5,370 (4,040), BB15000 - 5,850 (4,400), BB22200 - 5,800 (4,360)
Design speed, mph (km/h): 125 (200)
Additional features: rheostatic braking, self-ventilating motors, multiple working

CLASS BB8500/16500/17000/20200/25500

French Railways (SNCF) Classes BB8500/BB16500/BB17000/BB20200/BB25500

This vast family of medium-power locomotives was the first to feature Alsthom's monomotor bogies with alternative gear ratios for express passenger and slower-moving freight work. The ageing type is in steady decline following deliveries of new dual-voltage freight locomotives and TER dmus and emus.

SUB-TYPES

BB8500 is a straight 1.5 kV DC mixed traffic design, and BB16500 its 25 kV AC equivalent. The dual-voltage BB25500 version can work all over France. BB17000 is similar to BB16500 but only used on Paris area suburban work. The smallest sub-class is BB20200, fitted with 15 kV AC 16.7 Hz equipment for cross-border freights into Germany and Switzerland.

PRINCIPAL MODIFICATIONS

BB16540 modified in 1960s with 1.5 kV DC

equipment as a prototype for BB25500 class, and GPS satellite tracking for use on heavy block freight trains. In the 1990s a few BB16500s were equipped with TDM multiple-working equipment for operating as distributed power in ultra-heavy freight trains. Many BB16500, BB17000 and BB25500 are fitted for push-pull operation at 90 mph (140 km/h).

SPECIAL FEATURES

BB16500, the earliest series, remains in large numbers in north and east France, with batches dedicated to freight and regional passenger work on 25 kV AC lines. BB17000 is similar but dedicated to suburban passenger work from Paris Est, Nord and St Lazare.

BB8500 is the 1.5 kV mixed traffic equivalent and used singly or in pairs on freight and around Paris, Toulouse and Bordeaux on local passenger trains.

ELECTRIC LOCOMOTIVES

Early locomotives are increasingly used for empty stock movements in Paris.

BB25500 is widely distributed and used on both freight and regional passenger work around Paris, Lyon, Dijon and Rennes and on the Marseille-Nice-Ventimiglia route. Its dual-voltage capability is still highly valued despite the arrival of more modern types.

OTHER COUNTRIES OPERATED

Turkish State Railways (TCDD) operates 15 Class E 40 locomotives based on the 25 kV AC variant of this design. Twelve Class 2600 25 kV AC 'export design' derivatives were also supplied to CP in Portugal, followed by a further nine built locally by Sorefame. These differ in appearance, having cabs similar to those of the SNCF BB7200/BB15000/BB22200 family.

SPECIFICATION

Number series: BB8501-8646, BB16501-16794, BB17001-17105, BB20201-20213, BB25501-25694
Total built: 752
Builder: Alsthom
Date introduced: BB8500/BB25500 - 1964, BB16500 - 1958, BB17000 - 1965, BB20200 - 1969
Track gauge, ft/ins (mm): 4 ft 8.5 in (1,435)
Axle arrangement: B-B
Power supply system: 1.5 kV DC or 25 kV AC 50 Hz or both (BB25500), BB20200 - 15 kV AC 16.7 Hz
Electrical equipment: Alsthom - frame-mounted monomotors
Weight, tonnes: 71-81
Power rating, hp (kW): 3,900 (2,940), BB16500 only - 3,450 (2,580),
Design speed, mph (km/h): 90 (140)
Additional features: alternative gear ratios for freight and passenger work, Multiple working, rheostatic brakes, push-pull equipment, TDM, GPS satellite tracking, one-person operation (BB17000), snowploughs

CLASS BB27000 ELECTRIC LOCOMOTIVE

French Railways (SNCF) Class BB27000

BB27000 is part of Alstom's budget-priced modular Prima locomotive family to replace life-expired BB16500s, and tri-voltage versions are expected to start operation into Germany and Switzerland, eliminating time-consuming locomotive changes at borders.

SUB-TYPES

A total of 54 BB37000 locomotives have been ordered with tri-voltage 15 kV AC equipment for operation outside France into Germany and Switzerland. A single BB37500 prototype has also been ordered with 3 kV DC equipment to work in Belgium.

SPECIAL FEATURES

By the late-1990s SNCF's freight division was in desperate need of modern traction as it relied on several classes of low-powered locomotives dating back to the 1950s and 60s. Modern 'universal' locomotives (BB26000 and BB36000) were over-specified and expensive, forcing SNCF Fret to seek a cheaper option. By early-2004 BB27000s were increasingly common in northern France,

SPECIFICATION

Number series: BB27001-27180, BB37001-37029, BB37501
Total built: 210 (under construction)
Builder: Alstom
Date introduced: 2000
Track gauge, ft/ins (mm): 4 ft 8.5 in (1,435)
Axle arrangement: Bo-Bo
Power supply system: 1.5 kV DC/25 kV AC 50 Hz/3 kV DC/15 kV AC 16.7 Hz
Electrical equipment: Alstom - asynchronous semi-suspended traction motors
Weight, tonnes: 90
Power rating, hp (kW): 5,600 (4,200)
Design speed, mph (km/h): 90 (140)
Additional features: Multiple-working, rheostatic and regenerative braking

proving their worth on routes requiring dual-voltage capability. Tri-voltage BB37000 has been built to achieve the long-held ambition of running across national brorders without the need for long and expensive delays to services while locomotives from other networks are obtained and attached.

CLASS BB36000 ELECTRIC LOCOMOTIVE

French Railways (SNCF) Class BB36000

France

Known as the 'Astride', the BB36000 was designed as a 'universal' locomotive capable of heavy freight work and 125 mph (200 km/h) passenger operation, but has failed to live up to expectations and is now mainly seen on freight.

SUB-TYPES

Locomotives modified for Modalohr trains are reclassified as BB36300.

PRINCIPAL MODIFICATIONS

Seven locomotives fitted with TDM multiple-working and fire extinguishing equipment for use on Modalohr piggyback trains carrying complete lorries between France and Italy.

SPECIAL FEATURES

The first 30 were ordered from Alstom in place of the final 30 BB26000 'Sybics' and are a development of that type, although with asynchronous traction motors and 3kV DC equipment for operation in Belgium and Italy. A further 30 locomotives were added to the order and deliveries continued until 2001. The type has

SPECIFICATION

Number series: BB36001-36060
Total built: 60
Builder: Alstom
Date introduced: 1996
Track gauge, ft/ins (mm): 4 ft 8.5 in (1,435)
Axle arrangement: Bo-Bo
Power supply system: 1.5 kV DC/25 kV AC 50 Hz/3 kV DC
Electrical equipment: Synchronous traction motors
Weight, tonnes: 89
Power rating, hp (kW): 7,450 (5,600)
Design speed, mph (km/h): 90 (140)
Additional features: rheostatic and regenerative braking, multiple working

been a disappointment, although it does now work regularly outside France as planned. A small sub-fleet is dedicated to Modalohr lorry trains between France and Italy, and more could be converted if this traffic increases as planned. SNCF locomotives work into Belgium and Italy using their 3 kV DC capability.

CLASS BB63500 DIESEL LOCOMOTIVE

French Railways (SNCF) Class BB63500

This is one of the most widespread locomotive classes in France, seen in most corners of the country on shunting and local trip freight work. The type has been retained in preference to the older and less powerful BB63000. Variants of the type have also been exported to several countries.

SUB-TYPES

BB63400 are identical locomotives financed by Eurofima. BB63000 is a similar but lower-powered type now being phased out by SNCF, and BB64700/TBB64800 (now considered a completely separate type) is a small class of 'master and slave' units for heavy shunting at large marshalling yards.

PRINCIPAL MODIFICATIONS

The BB63500s have electric train supply, and BB63721–750, BB63811–63885 and BB63981–64020 have multiple working equipment. BB64700 has been substantially modified for heavy shunting work.

SPECIFICATION

Number series: BB63501-64080
Total built: 580
Builder: Brissonneau et Lotz
Date introduced: 1956
Track gauge, ft/ins (mm): 4 ft 8.5 in (1,435)
Axle arrangement: Bo-Bo
Power unit type: SACM MGO V12SH
Transmission: Electric
Weight, tonnes: 64–68
Power rating, hp (kW): 800 (605)
Design speed, mph (km/h): 55 (90)
Additional features: multiple working, electric train supply, cab signalling for high speed lines

SPECIAL FEATURES

The BB63500 is a more modern version of the BB63000, introduced in 1953. Heavier freight trains have seen the type used in pairs or even in threes. The most radical modification saw 23 BB63500 and 19 BB63000 converted to 'master and slave' heavy shunters with the former receiving larger cabs similar to BB66000 and the latter shortened and with cabs, fuel tanks and engines removed.

CLASS BB66000 DIESEL LOCOMOTIVE

French Railways (SNCF) Class BB66000

This long-serving class first appeared in 1959, and is still giving good service on a handful of passenger services as well as local freight and infrastructure work. Many have passed into private hands for construction contracts.

SUB-TYPES

BB66400 is a development of BB66000 with three-phase transmission, electric train supply and push-pull equipment for passenger work.

PRINCIPAL MODIFICATIONS

BB66700 is a recently converted small sub-class, modified for heavy shunting work with lower gearing and extra ballast weight.

SPECIAL FEATURES

Originally a mixed traffic type used singly and in pairs, BB66000 no longer has any passenger duties. Regional services are still handled by the more versatile ETS and push-pull fitted BB66400s, but even they are giving way to new multiple-

SPECIFICATION

Number series: BB66001-66318, BB66401-66506, BB66701-66734
Total built: 424
Builder: CAFL, CEM, Alsthom, Fives-Lille
Date introduced: BB66000 - 1959, BB66400 - 1968
Track gauge, ft/ins (mm): 4 ft 8.5 in (1,435)
Axle arrangement: Bo-Bo
Power unit type: SACM MGO V16BSHR
Transmission: Electric
Weight, tonnes: BB66000 - 66, BB66400 - 64, BB66700 - 71
Power rating, hp (kW): 1,375 (1,030)
Design speed, mph (km/h): 75 (120)
Additional features: multiple working, snowploughs, push-pull equipment

units. Some have been sold to private operators, while some of the earlier locomotives still with SNCF are employed on engineering projects such the Valence-Marseille Méditerranée high speed line and soon on LGV Est.

CLASS BB67000 DIESEL LOCOMOTIVE

French Railways (SNCF) Class BB67000

One of SNCF's first big mixed traffic diesel types allowed steam to be eliminated in many areas in the 1960s and early 1970s, and is still in use all over France. Electrification and line closures are rendering the earliest-built examples redundant, and others may follow.

SUB-TYPES

BB67200 are modified BB67000 with TVM300 or TVM430 cab signalling for working infrastructure/rescue trains on high-speed lines. BB67300/400 have electric train supply and more powerful engines with three-phase transmission.

PRINCIPAL MODIFICATIONS

BB67000/200 are now regarded as freight only and have their monomotor bogies locked in low gear for extra tractive effort. Many BB67000 have been rebuilt as BB67200, and 20 were converted to BB67371-390 with ETS and three-phase transmission.

SPECIAL FEATURES

Surviving BB67000 versions are now freight-only,

SPECIFICATION

Number series: BB67000-67097, BB67201-67270, BB67301-67390, BB67401-67632
Total built: 426
Builder: Brissonneau et Lotz, MTE
Date introduced: 1963
Track gauge, ft/ins (mm): 4 ft 8.5 in (1,435)
Axle arrangement: B-B
Power unit type: SEMT 16PA4
Transmission: Electric. BB67000/200/300 - monomotors, BB67400 - three-phase monomotors
Weight, tonnes: BB 67400 - 83, others - 80
Power rating, hp (kW): BB 67000/200 - 1,950 (1,470), BB67300/400 - 2,350 (1,765)
Design speed, mph (km/h): 90 (140)
Additional features: multiple working, push-pull equipment, electric train supply, snowploughs

BB67300 see limited passenger use, but BB67400s are still common all over France on regional, cross-country and a few express trains – Bordeaux-Nantes being a particular stronghold.

CLASS CC72000 DIESEL LOCOMOTIVE

French Railways (SNCF) CC72000

CC72000 is SNCF's most powerful diesel locomotive type and despite only being 92 strong can be seen over a very wide area on express and regional passenger and on heavy freight.

SUB-TYPES

CC72101-72103 were modified with Scharfenberg automatic couplers in 1999 to haul TGV Atlantique sets between Nantes and Les Sâbles d'Olonne. However with this through-service discontinued in 2003 the locomotives should revert to normal, including their former numbers

PRINCIPAL MODIFICATIONS

From 2002, Grandes Lignes sector CC72000s started to be re-engined and subsequently renumbered in the CC72100 series by adding 100 to the original number.

SPECIAL FEATURES

Operational strongholds include the Paris-Belfort route and non-electrified cross-country lines such as Lyon-Clermont Ferrand-Bordeaux and

SPECIFICATION

Number series: CC72001-72092, from CC72101
Total built: 92
Builder: Alsthom
Date introduced: 1967
Track gauge, ft/ins (mm): 4 ft 8.5 in (1,435)
Axle arrangement: C-C
Power unit type: SACM AGO V16ESHR or Pielstick V16PA4-VGA
Transmission: electric, monomotor bogies
Weight, tonnes: 114-118
Power rating, hp (kW): 3,120 (2,350)
Design speed, mph (km/h): 52/100 (85/160)
Additional features: gear selection, electro-pneumatic braking, driver-guard communication

Lyon-Tours. The uniquely French monomotor bogie design allows high tractive effort in the lower gear and up to 160km/h for express passenger in high gear. Complaints from staff and residents around depots about noise and smoke has led SNCF to examine re-engining the class and this process is now underway.

CLASS X72500 DMU

French Railways (SNCF) Class X72500 DMU

Seen in 1997 as SNCF's 'dmu of the future', the Alstom X72500 has not fulfilled its potential and lost out to subsequent Bombardier products. The two- and three-car units can be seen around Lyon, Nantes, Tours and in the Massif Central based at Brive.

SUB-TYPES

Basse Normandie region purchased 15 three-car X72500s for Paris-Granville services, although as this route has now been electrified they should be cascaded to other lines. Alstom has introduced a three-car 125 mph (200 km/h) electric version of the train – Z21500 – on Centre Region routes around Orléans, Limoges and Tours.

PRINCIPAL MODIFICATIONS

Set X72547/X72548 was taken from Alstom's production line and fitted with an experimental Fiat tilt system.

SPECIFICATION

Number series: X72501-72710
Total built: 105
Builder: GEC-Alsthom
Date introduced: 1997
Track gauge, ft/ins (mm): 4 ft 8.5 in (1,435)
Unit configuration: XB+XB or XB+XRB+XBM-M or M-T-M
Power unit type: Two MAN per car
Transmission: Voith - hydraulic
Power rating, hp (kW): 1,630 (1,200)
Design speed, mph (km/h): 100 (160)
Additional features: Scharfenberg automatic couplers, air-conditioning, passenger information systems, cameras and cab screens for one-person operation

SPECIAL FEATURES

Internally the 76 seats on the trains are very stylish and comfortable, although many technical problems have forced SNCF to retain older trains as cover. Work continues to improve the reliability of the class and allow older railcars to be retired.

CLASS T2000 RTG TURBOTRAIN

French Railways (SNCF) T2000 RTG Turbotrain

France

After experiments in the late 1960s, SNCF decided upon gas turbine propulsion for new inter-city trains to shorten journey times on key non-electrified routes.

SPECIAL FEATURES

SNCF introduced two types of gas-turbine powered inter-city multiple- unit. The second of these is the Rame à turbine à gaz (RTG), literally gas turbine unit, which for many years operated successfully at up to 100 mph (160 km/h) on the Paris St Lazare-Cherbourg and Lyon-Strasbourg routes. Electrification of these two main lines in the late-1980s and 1990s displaced the RTGs and many were retired. The remaining trains were used on Lyon-Bordeaux cross-country services until their retirement at the end of 2004. Usual operating procedure was for the lower powered turbine to be shut down once the train was underway.

SPECIFICATION

Number series: T2001-2082
Total built: 41
Builder: ANF, MTE
Date introduced: 1972
Track gauge, ft/ins (mm): 4 ft 8.5 in (1,435)
Unit configuration: M-T-T-T-M
Power unit type: Turmo XII and Turmo IIIF1 gas turbines
Transmission: Voith – hydraulic L411r
Power rating, hp (kW): 2,700 (2,020)
Design speed, mph (km/h): 100 (160)
Additional features: cab to shore radio, cowcatchers, buffet car

CLASS Z22500 EMU

French Railways (SNCF) Class Z22500 EMU

Z22500 is the latest in a long line of high-capacity emus developed for Paris commuter routes and cross-city RER lines. With two large double doors on each side, the trains allow large crowds to get on and off trains very quickly, reducing dwell times at stations.

SUB-TYPES

SNCF's contract for 53 trains was part of an order place jointly with Paris regional transport authority RATP, which has ordered a higher powered version -17 MI2N units – which operates its own Paris Reseau Express Regional (RER) Line A services alongside SNCF trains.

SPECIAL FEATURES

The trains were developed specifically for the Paris RER from a prototype car tested on RER Line A. SNCF's MI2Ns are allocated to services on RER Line E, the most recent addition to the network, which links Paris Est suburban routes with the city

SPECIFICATION

Number series: From Z22501
Total built: 410 cars in four- or five-car sets
Builder: GEC Alsthom
Date introduced: 1996
Track gauge, ft/ins (mm): 4 ft 8.5 in (1,435)
Unit configuration: 2-2+Bo-Bo+2-2+Bo-Bo+2-2T-M-T-M-T
Power supply system: 1.5 kV DC / 25 kV AC 50 Hz
Electrical equipment: Alsthom - asynchronous per set
Power rating, hp (kW): 4,000 (3,000)
Design speed, mph (km/h): 90 (140)
Additional features: three wide access doors on each side per car, CCTV cameras

centre. The design of the trains is quite different to previous double deck RER trains and the upper deck is not accessible from both doors. The original joint SNCF/RATP contract included options on 50 and 23 more units respectively.

CLASS Z23500 EMU

French Railways (SNCF) Class Z23500 EMU

Z23500, also known TER2N, is one of three major new classes of train designed to provide a new generation of high-quality regional trains across France, replacing 1960s stock with a new level of reliability and comfort.

SPECIAL FEATURES

Along with the X72500 and X73500 dmus, TER2N has provided much better accommodation for passengers, including air-conditioning and more comfortable seats. The first 80 two-car double deck trains are split between three regions, Provence-Alpes-Côte d'Azur (PACA), Rhônes-Alpes and Nord-Pas-de-Calais, based around Marseille and Nice, Lyon and Lille respectively. The concept has been developed further by Alstom and during 2004 the first TER2N Nouvelle Génération (TER2N NG) units should appear. These will be three- or four- car trains capable of 125mph (200km/h).

SPECIFICATION

Number series: Z23501-23580
Total built: 80
Builder: Alstom
Date introduced: 1998
Track gauge, ft/ins (mm): 4 ft 8.5 in (1,435)
Unit configuration: Bo-Bo+2-2M-T
Power supply system: 1.5 kV DC / 25 kV AC 50 Hz
Electrical equipment: Alsthom - asynchronous
Power rating, hp (kW): 2,000 (1,500)
Design speed, mph (km/h): 90 (140)
Additional features: air-conditioning, full disabled access

Twelve examples of the three-car version have been supplied to Luxembourg Railways.

Z27500 DMU/EMU

French Railways (SNCF) Class Z27500

The Autorail à Grand Capacité (AGC) is SNCF's new generation train for regional services, designed to replace a mixed bag of ageing dmus and locomotive-powered push-pull sets. Orders are eventually expected to total 500 trains with AGCs operating in almost every French region.

SUB-TYPES

Bombardier offers a range of options to regional customers in France – the main three being the BGC bi-mode X75500, XGC straight diesel (X76500) and ZGC dual-voltage emu (Z27500). Orders have been placed for three- and four-car versions of each type by 18 of the 20 French regions, with two levels of finish – Intercité and Grand Confort.

SPECIAL FEATURES

The train was designed as a response to Alstom's X72500 160km/h DMU.

SPECIFICATION

Number series: Z27500 (emu, 104 on order), X75500- (bi-mode, 76 on order), X76500- (dmu, 99 on order)
Total built: 324 units on order (late-2003), to rise to 500
Builder: Bombardier Transportation
Date introduced: 2004
Track gauge, ft/ins (mm): 4 ft 8.5 in (1,435)
Unit configuration: 2, 3 or 4-car dmu or emu, 3 or 4-car bi-mode
Power supply system: emus - 1.5 kV DC/25 kV AC 50 Hz, 2-car dmu - one MAN V12 D2842 LE 606 diesel, 3- and 4-car dmu two MAN V12 diesel, bi-mode - 1.5 kV DC and two MAN V12 diesel
Power rating, hp (kW): 500 (650) per car
Design speed, mph (km/h): 3-car dmu - 100 (160), 2/4-car dmu - 90 (140), 4-car emu - 135 (220)
Additional features: modular interior, seating and trim options, passenger information system, large central low-floor section, revolutionary electric/diesel bi-mode option

CLASS 101 ELECTRIC LOCOMOTIVE

German Rail (DB) Class 101

France/Germany

Class 101 was introduced in 1996 to replace Deutsche Bahn's Class 103 Co-Cos on universal front-line InterCity and EuroCity services across Germany. Like their illustrious predecessors, the 145 '101s' quickly entered service at speeds of up to 125 mph (200 km/h).

SPECIAL FEATURES

This modern design from Adtranz (now Bombardier) has not been without problems and it took until 2003 for the DB to finally eliminate the '103s', which dated back to 1969. The bogies in particular have been troublesome and the locomotives have suffered a high failure rate. DB's long-term plan was to replace the '101s' with ICE trainsets over the next decade and cascade the locomotives to freight work. However, this plan has now been shelved and they should remain on IC and EC work for the foreseeable future.

SPECIFICATION

Number series: 101.001-101.145
Total built: 145
Builder: Adtranz
Date introduced: 1996
Track gauge, ft/ins (mm): 4ft 8.5 in (1,435)
Axle arrangement: Bo-Bo
Power supply system: 15 kV AC 16.7 Hz
Electrical equipment: Adtranz - three-phase traction motors
Weight, tonnes: 87
Power rating, hp (kW): 8,500 (6,400)
Design speed, mph (km/h): 135 (220)
Additional features: multiple working, TDM push-pull equipment, steerable axle bogies, regenerative braking

OTHER COUNTRIES OPERATED

New Jersey Transit (USA)

CLASS 110 ELECTRIC LOCOMOTIVE

German Rail (DB) Class 110

Class 110 (originally E10) was the high-volume passenger version of Deutsche Bundesbahn's Einheitslok (Unity locomotive) family of the 1950s. After the arrival of the 125 mph (200 km/h) Class 103s, they were relegated to regional and secondary work.

SUB-TYPES

Classes 113/114 were originally built as uprated Class 110s for 100mph (160 km/h) Trans Europe Express (TEE) trains in the 1960s, but have now been downgraded and perform similar work to Class 110.

PRINCIPAL MODIFICATIONS

Push-pull equipment for Regional Express (RE) work.

SPECIAL FEATURES

Class 110 was originally the DB's principal express locomotive design, and although now in steady decline can be seen all over the former West

SPECIFICATION

Number series: 110.101-110.510
Total built: 410
Builder: Henschel/Krupp/Krauss-Maffei
Date introduced: 1956
Track gauge, ft/ins: 4ft 8.5 in (1,435)
Axle arrangement: Bo-Bo
Power supply system: 15 kV AC 16.7 Hz
Electrical equipment: AEG/Brown Boveri/Siemens
Weight, tonnes: 86
Power rating, hp (kW): 4,820 (3,620)
Design speed, mph (km/h): 90 (150)
Additional features: push-pull equipment, electric train supply, rheostatic braking

Germany on regional passenger work, and can always be relied upon to step into the breach during periods of system overload such as public holidays. Strongholds include the densely-populated Ruhr district, and the regional networks around Stuttgart, Munich and Frankfurt. The demoted Class 110s have replaced less powerful Class 141s, although they themselves are now being usurped by modern emus.

CLASS 111 ELECTRIC LOCOMOTIVE

German Rail (DB) Class 111

Class 111 is an improved version of Class 110, uprated for 100 mph (160 km/h) operation with better bogies. Originally used on long-distance InterCity services, it was quickly given more menial regional passenger work.

PRINCIPAL MODIFICATIONS

Push-pull equipment for Regional Express (RE) work.

SPECIAL FEATURES

Built for high speed operation over a period of some ten years, Class 111s built a strong reputation on the Rhein-Ruhr S-Bahn network, although these duties are now largely in the hands of Class 143s transferred from East Germany. The '111s' are all now allocated to DB Regio for Regional Express (RE) push-pull trains, often using modern double-deck stock. Locomotives are most often found around Munich, Hamburg, Frankfurt and the Ruhr areas. From the 1970s until the late-1990s, Class 111 could be seen on international trains from Germany through Austria to the Yugoslav and Italian borders.

SPECIFICATION

Number series: 111.001–111.227
Total built: 227
Builder: Krupp/Krauss-Maffei/Henschel
Date introduced: 1974
Track gauge, ft/ins (mm): 4 ft 8.5 in (1,435)
Axle arrangement: Bo-Bo
Power supply system: 15 kV AC 16.7 Hz
Electrical equipment: AEG/Brown Boveri/Siemens
Weight, tonnes: 83
Power rating, hp (kW): 4,800 (3,620)
Design speed, mph (km/h): 100 (160)
Additional features: push-pull equipment, electric train supply, rheostatic braking, multiple working

CLASS 120.1 ELECTRIC LOCOMOTIVE

German Rail (DB) Class 120.1

The adoption in the 1980s by DB of the three-phase Class 120.1 represented a significant shift away from separate electric locomotive designs for passenger and freight traffic to a universal machine that could handle services of both types. The 60-strong class is now based at Munich.

SPECIAL FEATURES

The Class 120.1 machines represented the first application of three-phase traction technology on a high-powered main line electric locomotive, providing DB with a unit equally capable of operating passenger services at up to 125 mph (200 km/h) or 2,700 tonne freight trains. Series construction in 1987-88 followed an extensive period evaluating five Class 120.0 prototypes built in 1979. Lightweight construction is employed, keeping the axle load to 21 tonnes, while the bogie design is an improved version of those fitted to the earlier Class 111 locomotives. Continuing developments in electric traction

SPECIFICATION

Number series: 120.101–120.160
Total built: 60
Builder: Henschel, Krauss-Maffei, Krupp
Date introduced: 1987
Track gauge, ft/ins (mm): 4 ft 8.5 in (1,435)
Axle arrangement: Bo-Bo
Power supply system: 15 kV AC 16.7 Hz
Electrical equipment: BBC - three-phase traction control, fully suspended asynchronous traction motors
Weight, tonnes: 84
Power rating, hp (kW): 7,500 (5,600)
Design speed, mph (km/h): 125 (200)
Additional features: rheostatic and regenerative brakes, multiple-unit operation, push-pull operation

technology in Germany led to the Class 120.1 design not being perpetuated beyond 60 examples. Indeed, the creation of separate passenger and freight business in Germany has to some degree led to moves away from universal traction in favour of dedicated equipment.

CLASSES 139/140 ELECTRIC LOCOMOTIVE

German Rail (DB) Classes 139/140

Developed as a freight and general-purpose version of the Class 110, this large series of electric locomotives once formed the largest type in the DB fleet, with nearly 900 examples. Today Class 139 and 140 machines are gradually being replaced by newer designs but they still remain in service in most parts of the German network.

SUB-TYPES

Class 150 was effectively a more powerful six-axle version of the Class 140.

SPECIAL FEATURES

Well justifying the term 'workhorse', this standard design has been serving the DB network in some cases for over 40 years, most but not exclusively handling freight traffic. Similar in most respects to the Class 110, these locomotives differ mainly in having lower gearing. The Class 139 machines are equipped with rheostatic braking for working more steeply graded routes. In 2003 more than 500 examples remained in service with DB,

SPECIFICATION

Total built: 879
Builder: Henschel, Krauss-Maffei, Krupp
Date introduced: 1957
Track gauge, ft/ins (mm): 4 ft 8.5 in (1,435)
Axle arrangement: Bo-Bo
Power supply system: 15 kV AC 16.7 Hz
Electrical equipment: AEG/BBC/SSW - tapchanger control with fully suspended AC traction motors
Weight, tonnes: Class 139 – 86, Class 140 – 83
Power rating, hp (kW): 4,850 (3,620)
Design speed, mph (km/h): 68 (110)
Additional features: Class 139 equipped with rheostatic braking, some equipped for multiple-unit operation.

although deliveries of more modern equipment were by then leading to regular retirements. Although generally similar in appearance and contemporary with Classes 139 and 140, Class 141 locomotives at 3,080 hp (2,300 kW) are much less powerful. They are mainly used on push-pull passenger regional and suburban services.

CLASS 143 ELECTRIC LOCOMOTIVE

German Rail (DB) Class 143

One of the last new electric types to be designed and mass-produced by the former East Germany, Class 143 has proved to be a reliable and useful all-purpose machine. Its success and versatility led to a total build of over 600. Although originally conceived as a freight unit, Class 143 is frequently seen on push-pull passenger duties.

SUB-TYPES

Although the DR Class 212 passenger design mentioned below was not initially series-produced, from 1990 both DR and DB acquired 130 examples of a slightly more powerful version of the type described here which became DB Classes 112 and 114.

SPECIAL FEATURES

Class 143 (former German State Railways (DR) Class 243) has its origins in the prototype 212.001 thyristor-controlled passenger locomotive produced by LEW in 1982. However, it was a lower-geared mixed traffic version of the design that entered production, initially becoming DR

SPECIFICATION

Number series: 143.002–143.973
Builder: LEW
Date introduced: 1984
Track gauge, ft/ins (mm): 4 ft 8.5 in (1,435)
Axle arrangement: Bo-Bo
Power supply system: 15 kV AC 16.7 Hz
Electrical equipment: LEW - DC traction motors
Weight, tonnes: 83
Power rating, hp (kW): 4,985 (3,720)
Design speed, mph (km/h): 75 (120)
Additional features: thyristor control, rheostatic braking, equipped for push-pull operation, some equipped for multiple-unit operation.

Class 243 and then DB Class 143 on re-unification of Germany. Production at LEW's Hennigsdorf plant near Berlin extended from 1982 to 1990. Although some withdrawals have taken place, the majority of the class survives and examples can be seen throughout the DB network.

CLASS 189 ELECTRIC LOCOMOTIVE

German Rail (DB) Class 189

Demand for European rail freight operators to boost the performance of their international operations, including political pressure from Brussels, has increased demand for multi-voltage locomotives capable of working across borders and from different systems of electrification. First unveiled in 2002, Siemens Class 189 was developed as a response to that need.

SPECIAL FEATURES

Developed directly from the Class 152 freight locomotive, this latest DB machine represents the third generation of Siemens' EuroSprinter family and is intended purely for freight traffic. Despite this, these machines have a high top speed of 87 mph (140 km/h), helping to share track capacity effectively with passenger services. Besides incorporating the complexities introduced by being required to operate under two AC and two DC power supply systems, the design of the Class 189 anticipates the certification

SPECIFICATION

Number series: 189.001-189.100
Total built: 100
Builder: Siemens Transportation Systems
Date introduced: 2002
Track gauge, ft/ins (mm): 4 ft 8.5 in (1,435)
Axle arrangement: Bo-Bo
Power supply system: 15 kV AC 16.7 Hz/25 kV AC 50 Hz/3 kV DC/1.5 kV DC
Electrical equipment: Siemens - water-cooled IGBT traction inverters, axle-hung AC traction motors with individual axle control
Weight, tonnes: 86
Power rating, hp (kW): 8,575 (6,400) on AC, 8,040 (6,000) on 3 kV DC, 5,630 (4,200) on 1.5 kV DC
Design speed, mph (km/h): 87 (140)
Additional features: prepared for certification in 14 European countries as well as Germany

requirements that will have to be met to enable the type to work through much of the European rail network By the third quarter of 2003, 15 Class 189s had been delivered to DB.

CLASSES 145/146/185 ELECTRIC LOCOMOTIVE

German Rail (DB) Classes 145/146/185

The latest Bombardier electric locomotive type aimed initially at the German domestic market is this modular design which is produced in freight and passenger and for single- or dual-voltage operations. A DB Cargo order for 400 units ensures that this type will become the future mainstay for the operator's international services. Examples have also been exported to Switzerland and locomotives of this type have also proved a popular 'off-the-shelf' choice with new open access operators in Germany.

SUB-TYPES

Orders placed with Bombardier for the Class 185-derived passenger Class 146.1 variant include 24 for the state transport authorities of Nordrhein-Westfalen and eight for Lower Saxony. These are for the operation of tendered services using push-pull coaching stock.

SPECIAL FEATURES

A development of the modular design concept employed for the Class 101 passenger machines, the Class 145 locomotive family was introduced to replace older types such as Class 110, 139, 140, 141 and 143, some of which have given over 30 years of service. The first order for this design was from DB Cargo for 80 Class 145s. These remain DB's only examples of this class. Subsequent orders from DB Cargo were for the dual-voltage Class 185 version, with deliveries of a huge order for 400 commencing in 2000. Class 185 is mechanically similar to the earlier Class 145 but some changes were made to body dimensions to comply with clearances outside Germany. Assembly of all variants has been undertaken at the Kassel facility formerly owned by Adtranz and now part of Bombardier Transportation. In an exercise intended to give all its products generic names rather than operators' class designations,

Bombardier gave this type the TRAXX brand name in 2003. Orders for 31 of the faster Class 146 version came from DB Regio for use on regional services in the Ludwigshafen and Rheinland-Pfalz areas. Examples of Class 145 or Class 185 have also been acquired by independent German operators, including Connex Cargo, rail4chem and Ruhrkohle AG. In addition, six Class 145s were acquired Locomotion Capital, a traction leasing company.

SPECIFICATION

Number series: 145.001-145.080, 146.001-146.031 and 146.101-146.132, 185.001-185.400
Total built (DB orders only): Class 145 - 80, Class 146 - 31 plus 32 Class 146.1 ordered, Class 185 still in production in 2004
Builder: Adtranz
Date introduced: 1998, 2001
Track gauge, ft/ins (mm): 4 ft 8.5 in (1,435)
Axle arrangement: Bo-Bo
Power supply system: Classes 145 and 146 – 15 kV AC 16.7 Hz, Class 185 – 15 kV AC 16.7 Hz/25 kV AC 50 Hz
Electrical equipment: Bombardier, GTO - thyristor control, axle-hung asynchronous traction motors
Weight, tonnes: 80-82
Power rating, hp (kW): 5,630 (4,200)
Design speed, mph (km/h): 87 (140), 100 (160), 87 (140)
Additional features: Class 146/146.1 machines have a destination indicator above the cab window, Class 185 designed to be retrofitted with interfaces for ERTMS/ETCS radio signalling equipment to allow operations in countries other than Germany, up to four Class 185 can operate in multiple.

CLASS 182 ELECTRIC LOCOMOTIVE

German Rail (DB) Class 182

The high-performance dual-voltage Class 182 represents the second generation of Siemens EuroSprinter electric locomotive family. Equally suitable for fast passenger or heavy freight traffic, the type was initially ordered by ÖBB in Austria. Others have been supplied to Hungary and hire fleet examples are also in service in Austria and Germany. Subsequent DB orders from Siemens were for the Class 189, suggesting that its fleet of this type may be limited to the 25 featured here.

SUB-TYPES

The modular design of this locomotive enables Siemens to produce versions in 15 kV only (ES 64 F), dual-voltage (ES 64 U2) and four-voltage (ES 64 F4).

SPECIAL FEATURES

The design of the Class 182 represents the latest example of Siemens' EuroSprinter group of electric locomotives, a development process that can be traced back to the DB Class 120. Among the locomotives' features is a high-performance traction drive with a separate disc brake shaft to help reduce unsprung masses. Construction of the DB order took place at the Krauss-Maffei plant, now part of Siemens.

OTHER COUNTRIES OPERATED

The operator of the largest fleet of this type is set to be Austrian Federal Railways which has ordered 400 examples as its 'Taurus' Class 1016/1116 (above). Some components are sourced in Austria and assembly is undertaken in ÖBB workshops. Hungarian State Railways operates 10 dual-voltage examples of the type (left lower) and the Austro-Hungarian GySEV company has another five. They are designated Class 1047 and 1047.5

SPECIFICATION

Number series: 182.001-182.025
Total built: 25 (for DB)
Builder: Siemens Transportation Systems
Date introduced: 2001
Track gauge, ft/ins (mm): 4 ft 8.5 in (1,435)
Axle arrangement: Bo-Bo
Power supply system: 15 kV AC 16.7 Hz/25 kV AC 50 Hz
Electrical equipment: Siemens - electronic control, water-cooled GTO traction converters, ac traction motors
Weight, tonnes: 86
Power rating, hp (kW): 8,575 (6,400)
Design speed, mph (km/h): 142 (230)
Additional features: starting tractive effort of 300 kN

respectively. Siemens' traction hire subsidiary Dispolok has acquired at least 38 examples of this design, with locomotives in service with passenger and freight operators in Austria and Germany. In 2004 Slovenian Railways (SZ) ordered 20 similar locomotives to be designated Class 541.

CLASS 215-218 FAMILY DIESEL LOCOMOTIVE

German Rail (DB) Class 215-218

This large family of locomotives helped DB to eliminate steam locomotives from the mid-1960s. Class 218s remain a common sight, but the older versions are in sharp decline, having been displaced by more efficient dmus.

SUB-TYPES

Two Class 217 are fitted with hydrodynamic brakes and used as braking locomotives by DB's research department. 218.901-910 were originally numbered 210.001-010 and fitted with a 1,150hp Lycoming gas turbine booster (removed 1983).

PRINCIPAL MODIFICATIONS

DB has experimented for many years with alternative power units including MTU and Pielstick units up to 3,000 hp. In the mid-1990s, ten Class 218s had their maximum speed increased to 100 mph (160 km/h) for Hamburg-Berlin IC services and renumbered Class 210.

SPECIAL FEATURES

Class 215 was built as a mixed traffic type with steam heat, but has been displaced by new DMU types in the last decade and the survivors are

SPECIFICATION

Number series: 215.001-150 (now Class 225), 216.001-216.010, 216.011-216.221, 217.001-217.022, 218.001-218.499, 218.901-218.910
Total built: 902
Builder: Krupp/MaK/Deutz/Henschel/Krauss-Maffei
Date introduced: Class 216 - 1964, Class 217 - 1965, Class 215/218 - 1968
Track gauge, ft/ins (mm): 4 ft 8.5 in (1,435)
Axle arrangement: B-B
Power unit type: Class 215/217 - MTU MB16V 652TB10, Class 216 - MTU MD16V 538TB10, Class 218 - MTU MA12V 956TB10
Transmission: Voith or MTU - hydraulic
Weight, tonnes: 74-80
Power rating, hp (kW): Class 215/216/217 - 1,900 (1,400), Class 218 - 2,500 (1,840)
Design speed Mph (Kph): Class 216/217 - 75 (120), Class 215/218 - 90 (140)
Additional features: all multiple working, Class 215/218 - push-pull equipment, Class 217/218 - electric train supply, Class 215/218 - steam-heating

operated by DB Cargo. Class 216/217 have been freight-only for many years and almost all were withdrawn by 2003. The largest group, Class 218 remains a common sight all over Germany on regional and express passenger trains.

CLASS 232 DIESEL LOCOMOTIVE

German Rail (DB) Class 232

Rugged and reliable, the former East German product now operates all over the reunified country and into Holland. Many are now with private freight operators and infrastructure companies, some imported from Russia.

SUB-TYPES

Class 232 is the basic freight version, 233 is fitted with push-pull for regional passenger work around Dresden, 234 is regeared for higher speed, and 241 have been rebuilt with Kolomna engines.

PRINCIPAL MODIFICATIONS

Push-pull equipment, DB experimented with various replacement power units in the late-1990s, including Caterpillar, MaK and Kolomna units. Some locomotives have extra signalling equipment for working into Belgium and Holland.

SPECIAL FEATURES

Class 232 (formerly 132) is a development of Class 230/231 (130/131), also built in the Soviet Union for Deutsche Reichsbahn. The locomotives have electric train supply and as result were retained

SPECIFICATION

Number series: 232.001-232.909
Total built: 709
Builder: Voroshilovgrad, Soviet Union
Date introduced: 1973
Track gauge, ft/ins (mm): 4 ft 8.5 in (1,435)
Axle arrangement: Co-Co
Power unit type: Kolomna 5D49
Transmission: Charkov – six electric traction motors
Weight, tonnes: 122
Power rating, hp (kW): 3,300 (2,200)
Design speed, mph (km/h): 75 (120) or 90 (140)
Additional features: electric train supply, TDM push-pull equipment, Class 241.9 has ATB signalling equipment for working in Holland.

by DB in preference to the earlier locomotives. Passenger work has rapidly declined with the introduction of new multiple units, but some regional trains around Dresden and EuroCity trains between Nürnberg and the Czech border are still handled. Many are now in service with private freight operators across Europe. To preserve their original indentity, it is German practise for rebuilds to only have the third digit of their number amended.

CLASS 290 DIESEL LOCOMOTIVE

German Rail (DB) Class 290

Deutsche Bahn's principal heavy shunting and local trip work locomotives, the Class 290-295 family was built between 1964-75 after it was found that the V60 0-6-0s were not powerful enough for some tasks.

SUB-TYPES

There are several sub-classes: Class 290.0 are original condition, 290.5 have been re-engined, Class 294 are radio-control fitted Class 290s, Class 295 are radio control fitted Class 291s, 294.901-294.910 have 1,000 kW MTU engines for heavy freight work around Saarbrücken.

PRINCIPAL MODIFICATIONS

Radio control shunting equipment, with new MTU 8V4000 R41 engines of 1,350 hp (1,000 kW) now being fitted to most Classes 290 and 294.

SPECIAL FEATURES

Class 290 is seen everywhere in Germany, but Class 291 is more restricted, generally allocated to depots in the North. 20 MaK prototypes were

SPECIFICATION

Number series: 290.001-290.408, 291.001-291.100, 291.901-291.903 (original numbers)
Total built: 408 (Class 290), 103 (Class 291)
Builder: MaK/Henschel/Deutz/Jung
Date introduced: 1964
Track gauge, ft/ins (mm): 4 ft 8.5 in (1,435)
Axle arrangement: B-B
Power unit type: MTU MB16V 652TA10
Transmission: Voith - hydraulic
Weight, tonnes: 78
Power rating, hp (kW): 1,100 (820)
Design speed, mph (km/h): 50 (80)
Additional features: automatic couplers, radio control for shunting, programmable automatic operation

quickly followed by 387 Class 290s and 103 Class 291s, including one built for the German Army (290.999). Many have been re-engined and in 2002 DB announced it had ordered 400 1,350 hp (1,000 kW) MTU engines to uprate the locomotives. The current breakdown of class numbers is 126 Class 290, 280 Class 294, 10 '294.9', 33 Class 291 and 70 Class 295.

CLASS 360, 362, 363, 364 & 365 DIESEL LOCOMOTIVE

Type: German Rail (DB AG) Classes 360, 362, 363, 364 and 365

Germany

Built from the mid-1950s for the former Deutsch Bundesbahn, these locomotives remain a standard shunting unit in Germany, although many have been withdrawn. Others have been the subject of a recent re-engining programme to prolong their service lives.

SUB-TYPES

Classes 362 and 363 have Caterpillar engines; Classes 363 and 365 ballasted for greater adhesion. Some equipped for radio remote control.

SPECIAL FEATURES

These rod-driven diesel-hydraulic shunters remain a familiar sight in German yards and stations. Construction of the class took place between 1955 and 1964, with most of the country's locomotive builders participating in the construction programme. By 2004, age, reduced shunting requirements and changes in DB's freight business had contributed to a reduction in the fleet to fewer than 500 examples. However,

some of these had undergone life-extension refurbishment that included fitting a Caterpillar Series 3412 engine.

Other countries operated: Disposals of members of this class by DB have led to examples appearing in several European countries, both with national and industrial operators.

SPECIFICATION

Number series: 360 001 -
Total built: 1,051
Builder: Deutz, Esslingen, Gmeinder, Henschel, Jung, Krauss-Maffei, Krupp, MaK
Date introduced: 1955
Track gauge, ft/ins (mm): 4 ft 8.5 in (1,435)
Axle arrangement: C
Power unit type: Mercedes Benz 12V 493 AZ; MTU GTO6 or GTO6A; Caterpillar 3412E D1-TTA
Transmission: Hydraulic - Voith
Weight, tonnes: Classes 360, 362, 364 – 49.5; Classes 363, 365 - 53
Power rating, hp (kW): 650 (480)
Design speed, mph (km/h): 37 (60)

CLASS 420 EMU

German Rail (DB) Class 420

Class 420 has been the standard emu for S-Bahn (suburban) services around the major population centres of Frankfurt, Stuttgart and Munich for over 30 years, but is now rapidly being displaced by more modern types.

SPECIAL FEATURES

The construction of the standard S-Bahn emu in large numbers over a 13-year period was a result of close collaboration between a wide variety of German builders, most now taken over - Linke-Hoffman-Busch/Messerschmitt-Bolkow-Blohm/Orenstein & Koppel/Uerdindgen/Waggon-Union, and the first sets entered service in Munich in time for the 1972 Olympic Games staged there. Electrical equipment was procured from AEG and Brown-Boveri (now Bombardier), and Siemens. Increasing numbers of units are stored out of service following replacement by Class 423 emus.

SPECIFICATION

Number series: 420.001-420.489
Total built: 489
Builder: LHB/MBB/Orenstein & Koppel/Uerdingen/Waggon-Union
Date introduced: 1969
Track gauge, ft/ins (mm): 4 ft 8.5 in (1,435)
Unit configuration: M-M-M
Power supply system: 15 kV AC 16.7 Hz
Electrical equipment: 4 x 200 kW traction motors per car
Power rating, hp (kW): 3,240 (2,400)
Design speed, mph (km/h): 75 (120)
Additional features: multiple working

OTHER COUNTRIES OPERATED

In 2003 15 ex-Munich units were hired to Storstockholms Lokaltrafik (SL Class X420) for use on suburban services out of Stockholm.

CLASS 423 EMU

German Rail (DB) Class 423

Developed as a replacement for Class 420 emus and locomotive-operated push-pull sets used for S-Bahn services around several of Germany's major conurbations, Class 423 was already set to number over 450 when orders in hand in 2004 had been completed. In common with other recent DB emu designs, an articulated configuration is adopted, reducing weight and maintenance requirements.

SPECIAL FEATURES

Increasingly evident on suburban services in the Rühr, Munich and Stuttgart areas and destined also to operate around Frankfurt, Class 423 is DB's latest standard S-Bahn emu. The use of aluminium for construction of the bodyshell and articulation is intended to reduce weight and therefore traction power requirements. Three pairs of doors per side of each car ensure fast passenger handling at stations.

SPECIFICATION

Number series: 423.001/423.501–423.456/423.956
Total built: 456 (including units on order in 2004)
Builder: Alstom LHB
Date introduced: 1998
Track gauge, ft/ins (mm): 4 ft 8.5 in (1,435)
Unit configuration: M-T-T-M
Power supply system: 15 kV AC 16.7 Hz
Electrical equipment: Adtranz - three-phase asynchronous traction motors
Power rating, hp (kW): 3,162 (2,360)
Design speed, mph (km/h): 87 (140)
Additional features: aluminium bodyshell

CLASSES 424/425/426 EMU

German Rail (DB) Class 424/425/426

S-Bahn services in some of Germany's largest cities are being improved with new rolling stock, with mixed success because many features have proved unreliable, particularly in cold weather.

SUB-TYPES

Class 424 - four-car units, Class 425 - four-car with revised lower-density seating, Class 426 - two-car versions of Class 425.

SPECIAL FEATURES

A new family of articulated emus has been developed to replace older types including Class 420/421. The first, Class 424, entered service on the Hannover S-Bahn in time for EXPO 2000, but is also suitable for other suburban services. Adtranz was responsible for the mechanical parts, Siemens principal electrical equipment, and GTO traction converter and motors. Class 425, (216 units, entering service from 2000) feature lower passenger capacity and higher maximum speed

SPECIFICATION

Number series: 424.001-424.040, 425.001-425.156, 425.201-40/50-69, 425.401-425.420, 426.001-43
Total built: 40; 216 (including units on order in 2004); 43
Builder: Bombardier (Adtranz/DWA), Siemens
Date introduced: 1998; 1999; 1999
Track gauge, ft/ins (mm): 4 ft 8.5 in (1,435)
Unit configuration: M-T-T-M; M-T-T-M; M-M
Power supply system: 15 kV AC, 16.7 Hz
Electrical equipment: Bombardier (Adtranz) three-phase asynchronous traction motors
Power rating, hp (kW): Class 424/425 - 3,200 (2,350), Class 426 - 1,600 (1,175).
Design speed, mph (km/h): Class 424/425.2/425.4 - 87 (140), Class 425.0/426 - 100 (160).
Additional features: full-width gangways for unrestricted view. Underfloor traction equipment, regenerative braking.

for regional services. Units are in service in Essen, Magdeburg, Trier, Saarbrücken, and Köln areas. A further order for 20 units, Class 425.4, was placed by DB for summer 2004, to be operated by the Verkehrsunternehmen Rhein-Neckar.

CLASS 612 DMU

German Rail (DB) Class 612

The policy decision to replace locomotive haulage on many regional express services has gained momentum since 2000, but the plan to build units capable of tilting (thus avoiding expensive track modifications) has been hampered by their unreliability.

SUB-TYPES

16 units have been modified to Class 612.4/612.9 with better seating and a catering area. These carry DB's white and red InterCity livery.

SPECIAL FEATURES

Painful experience with the fleet of 50 Class 611 Adtranz tilting dmus delivered from 1996 led to the search for a simpler-lower cost design for regional express services. The first 50 Class 612s were ordered in 1994, featuring a more rounded front end design, modified passenger accommodation and door locations, and two Cummins engines instead of MTU 183TD

equipment, offering a slightly higher power output. In 1998, a further 104 Class 612 sets were ordered, 75 for local passenger duties, and the rest for long distance operation. Subsequent orders were to bring the fleet size to 201 units. New centre trailers are being considered with low floors to help wheelchair users. Sixteen units have been upgraded internally as Class 612.9 to replace the unsuccessful Siemens Class 605 ICE TD tilting dmus on the Nürnberg-Dresden route.

SPECIFICATION

Number series: 612.001-612.200/612.501-612.700; 612.4xx/612.9xx; 612.901/612.902
Total built: 201
Builder: (Adtranz) Bombardier
Date introduced: 1998
Track gauge, ft/ins (mm): 4 ft 8.5 in (1,435)
Unit configuration: M-M
Power unit type: two Cummins QSK19 12 cyl
Transmission: hydraulic
Power rating, hp (kW): 1,500 hp (1,118)
Design speed, mph (km/h): 100 (160)
Additional features: multiple working

CLASS 628 DMU

German Rail (DB) Class 628

Locomotive-hauled trains on non-electrified lines have rapidly been replaced over the last thirty years by squadron introduction of Class 628 dmus, now the commonest type.

SUB-TYPES

The two design prototype sub-classes are 628.0 and 628.1, the former with two motor cars, the latter motor car and unpowered trailer. Class 628.0 units have corrugated lower bodysides; remaining vehicles are flush-sided. The production series (starting 628.2) has more powerful engines and lower density seating. Class 628.4 has an even higherrated engine and wider middle doors.

SPECIAL FEATURES

Life-expired dmu types and locomotive-hauled local trains are now hard to find following investment in a massive fleet of two-car units for both ex-Deutsche Bundesbahn and former East German routes. The production series, Class 628.2,

SPECIFICATION

Number series: 628.001-628.009, 628.101-628.103, 628.201-628.350, 628.401-704, 628.901-628.906
Total built: 471
Builder: Class 628.0/628.1 - LHB, Uerdingen; Class 628.2/628.4 - AEG, Duewag, LHB, MBB, Uerdingen
Date introduced: Class 628.0 - 1974; Class 628.1 - 1981; Class 628.2 - 1987; Class 628.4 - 1993; Class 628.9 - 1995
Track gauge, ft/ins (mm): 4 ft 8.5 in (1,435)
Unit configuration: Class 628.0/628.9 M+M, others M+T
Power unit type: Class 628.0 - xxx, Class 628.1 - xxx, Class 628.2 - Daimler Benz OM 444A, Class 628.4/628.9 - MTU.
Transmission: Voith - Hydraulic
Power rating, hp (kW): Class 628.0 - 700 (520), Class 628.1 - 350 (260), Class 628.2 - 550 (410), Class 628.4 - 650 (485), Class 628.9 - 1,300 (970)
Design speed, mph (km/h): 75 (120)

was introduced from 1986, and a start was made in 2001 to upgrade the units with smarter interiors. Class 628.4, dating from 1995, is the most modern single-engine type.

CLASS 643/644 'TALENT' DMU

German Rail (DB) Class 643/644

Originally developed by Waggonfabrik Talbot of Aachen, the Talent modular regional vehicle concept, has found a good market in both diesel and electric versions. The DB example is in service in both diesel-electric (Class 644) and diesel-hydraulic (Class 643) variants.

SPECIAL FEATURES

Classes 643 and 644 are articulated between intermediate cars, using non-powered Jacobs bogies. To minimise weight, composites are used for the side panels and the roof is formed of aluminium sandwich material. Door entry height is 31.5 in (800 mm) and in the intermediate car of a Class 644 this extends for the whole vehicle. Both DB classes are mostly based in the west of the country, with particular concentrations around Cologne and Düsseldorf. The Class 643.2 units are used on Eurobahn-branded services around Aachen, including a cross-border service into the Netherlands. The Talent design is also a

SPECIFICATION

Number series: Class 643.0 - 643.001-643.075/643.501-643.575; Class 643.2 - 643.200-643.226/643.700-643.726; Class 644 - 644.001-644.063/644.501-644.563
Total built: Class 643.0 - 75 (plus 12 three-car Class 643.3 on order in 2004); Class 643.2 - 27; Class 644 - 63
Builder: Bombardier Transportation
Date introduced: 1999; 2002; 1998
Track gauge, ft/ins (mm): 4 ft 8.5 in (1,435)
Unit configuration: M-M or M-T-M (articulated)
Power unit type: Class 643.0/643.2 - 2 x MAN 6-cylinder; Class 644 - 2 x MTU 12-cylinder
Transmission: Class 643 - Voith hydrodynamic; Class 644 - ELIN electric, with three-phase asynchronous traction motors
Power rating, hp (kW): Class 643.0 - 2 x 345 (257); Class 643.2 - 2 x 420 (315); Class 644 - 2 x 677 (505)
Design speed, mph (km/h): Class 643 - 75 (120); Class 644 - 87 (140)
Additional features: multiple-unit operation; Class 644 have rheostatic braking

popular choice for Germany's independent operators, users including Ostmecklenburgische Eisenbahn and Regio-Bahn GmbH.

CLASS 642 'DESIRO' DMU

German Rail (DB) Class 642

DB's Class 642 regional dmu is just one representative example of a generic vehicle design developed by Duewag (now Siemens) that has been produced in both diesel and electric powered versions for several operators in Germany as well other European railway undertakings. Along with dmus similar in concept from other builders, the highly successful Class 642 is playing a significant role in the revival of local and regional passenger services in Germany, replacing locomotive-hauled formations.

SPECIAL FEATURES

The Class 642 is an articulated unit using a centre non-powered Jacobs bogie. The two outer bogies are powered. Each car is provided with one door per side with a low entry level (22.6 in/575 mm) which extends to some 60 per cent of the interior. The DB Regio fleet is particularly concentrated in the east and southeast of Germany. Under its Siemens Desiro brand name, the type has also

been sold to several independent operators in Germany, including the Connex subsidiary LausitzBahn, the Nord-Ostsee-Bahn and the Vogtlandbahn (above right). The DB Classes 424 and 426 are emu derivatives of the Desiro design but are visually dissimilar.

SPECIFICATION

Number series: 642.001-642.234/642.501-642.642.734 (cars numbered individually)
Total built: 228 for DB
Builder: Siemens Transportation Systems
Date introduced: 1999
Track gauge, ft/ins (mm): 4 ft 8.5 in (1,435)
Unit configuration: M-M (articulated)
Power unit type: 2 x 370 hp (275 kW) MTU
Transmission: hydrodynamic, five-speed automatic, cardan shaft drive
Power rating, hp (kW): 740 (550)
Design speed, mph (km/h): 75 (120)
Additional features: aluminium bodyshell construction; hydrodynamic and electropneumatic brakes and track brakes; multiple-unit operation; retention toilets

OTHER COUNTRIES OPERATED:
Siemens export orders for its Desiro model include: Austria (ÖBB), 20 Class 5022 dmus; Greece (OSE), 20 five-car 25 kV emus; Hungary (MÁV), 13 Class 6342 dmus; Romania (CFR Calatori), 120 Class 99 dmus; Slovenia (SZ), 10 two-car (above) and 20 three-car Class 312 3 kV DC emus. Twelve examples of an emu version have also been supplied for Kuala Lumpur's Express Rail Link airport service in Malaysia.

CLASS 648 DMU

German Rail (DB) Class 648

Class 648 is Alstom LHB's response to the German market's requirements lightweight low life-cycle cost diesel railcars for local and regional services. Vehicles of this type have been procured by independent operators in Germany and beyond and DB also operates a single-car version.

SUB-TYPES

Class 648.1 units have a floor height of 780 mm compared with 598 mm for Class 648.2. DB also operates 30 single-car vehicles of generally similar design (Class 640).

SPECIAL FEATURES

Alstom Transport's German subsidiary Alstom LHB developed this vehicle, which it brands Coradia LINT 41 to meet demand in Germany and elsewhere for a low-cost dmu for regional services. This two-car version is articulated and features a stainless steel bodyshell with a partial low floor. At the time this book was compiled DB

SPECIFICATION

Number series: 648.001-648-006/648.501-506; 648-101-648-121/648.601-648.621; 648.201-207, 251-275/648.701-707, 751-775
Total built: 6 (plus 55 on order in 2004)
Builder: Alstom LHB
Date introduced: 2000
Track gauge, ft/ins (mm): 4 ft 8.5 in (1,435)
Unit configuration: M-M
Power unit type: MTU 6R 183 TD 6-cylinder of 422 hp (315 kW)
Transmission: hydrodynamic
Power rating, hp (kW): 844 (630)
Design speed, mph (km/h): 75 (120)
Additional features: two-class accommodation; retention toilet

operated just six Class 648 units, based at Kiel depot. However, further orders were placed in three batches during 2003 for 55 more, to be delivered between June 2004 and September 2005. The LINT 41 design has also proved a popular choice with private operators in Germany. Users include AKN/Hochbahn, MecklenburgBahn, Nord-Ostsee Bahn (Connex) and LNVG/NordWestBahn.

ICE-1/ICE-2 HIGH-SPEED TRAINSETS

German Rail (DB) ICE-1 and ICE-2

Germany's first series-built high-speed trainsets, the ICE-1s, were introduced in 1990, initially on the Hamburg-Munich route. Each set comprises two power cars and a variable number of trailers. The ICE-2 units are shorter trailer formations with just one power car and driving trailer.

SUB-TYPES

A Class 410 ICE-S trainset comprising two power cars based on the Class 402 design and three trailers is used by DB for test purposes.

SPECIAL FEATURES

The Class 401 design team achieved an all-up weight of just 77 tonnes while incorporating the high power output needed for trains formed of up to 14 trailers. The ICE-2 units are effectively 'half-sets', enabling two trains to be operated in multiple over trunk sections of route and then split to serve separate destinations. Class 402 power cars are essentially similar to the Class 401

SPECIFICATION

Number series: ICE-1 - 401.001–401.020, 401.052–401.090, 401.501–401.520, 401.552–401.590; ICE-2 - 402.001–402.046
Total built: Class 401 - 120; Class 402 - 46
Builder: (power cars) Krauss-Maffei, Krupp, Thyssen-Henschel; (trailers) ABB/Henschel, Duewag, DWA, LHB, MAN, MBB, Waggon-Union
Date introduced: ICE-1 - 1990; ICE-2 - 1995
Track gauge, ft/ins (mm): 4 ft 8.5 in (1,435)
Unit configuration: ICE-1 - two Class 401 power cars plus 11 to 14 trailers; ICE-2 - one Class 402 power car + up to six trailers plus driving trailer
Power supply system: 15 kV AC 16.7 Hz
Electrical equipment: ABB, AEG, Siemens - thyristor/GTO thyristor control
Power rating, hp (kW): 6,430 (4,800) per power car
Design speed, mph (km/h): 174 (280)
Additional features: multiple-unit operation (ICE-2); rheostatic braking; fully suspended disc brakes

vehicles but incorporated fully automatic end couplers and electro-pneumatically operated nose doors from new to facilitate the joining and dividing of pairs of ICE-2s.

CLASS 403/406 ICE-3 HIGH-SPEED TRAINSET

German Rail (DB) Class 403/406 ICE-3

The second generation of German high-speed trainsets moved away from the 'power car plus trailers' configuration in favour of distributed power to produce a true emu. Introduced from 2000, the stylish ICE-3 units have since established themselves as the epitome of rail travel in Germany, as well as attracting export business from other countries in Europe.

SPECIAL FEATURES

One significant gain, largely due to a combination of distributing traction equipment throughout the train and the use of aluminium extrusions for bodyshell construction, is a reduction in axle loading to under 17 tonnes. All electrical equipment is located beneath car floors and 50 per cent of axles are powered. Not only does this deliver very rapid acceleration, it also enables the ICE-3 sets to cope with the very sharp gradients on new high-speed lines such as Cologne-Frankfurt, where they are mostly employed. Their

SPECIFICATION

Number series: cars individually numbered in the 403.0xx, 403.1xx, 403.2xx, 403.3xx, 403.4xx, 403.5xx, 403.6xx, 403.7xx and 403.8xx series; similar numbering applies to Class 406
Total built: Class 403 - 37; Class 406 - 13; 13 additional Class 403 on order for delivery 2004
Builder: Siemens Transportation Systems, Bombardier Transportation (Adtranz), Alstom LHB
Date introduced: 2000
Track gauge, ft/ins (mm): 4 ft 8.5 in (1,435)
Unit configuration: M-T-M-T-T-M-T-M
Power supply system: Class 403 - 15 kV AC 16.7 Hz; Class 406 - 25 kV AC 50 Hz, 15 kV AC 16.7 Hz, 1.5 kV DC
Electrical equipment: Siemens, Bombardier - three-phase asynchronous traction motors
Power rating, hp (kW): 10,720 (8,000)
Design speed, mph (km/h): 205 (330); Class 406 137 (220) on DC
Additional features: multiple-unit operation

parent depot in Munich. The three-voltage Class 406 sub-series is intended for cross-border operations.

CLASS 411/415 ICE-T EMU

German Rail (DB) Class 411/415 ICE-T

To bring the ICE concept to a wider section of its passenger market, DB in the late 1990s acquired the first examples of this tilting electric version of its flagship train. Intended to improve speeds and comfort on existing electrified lines, ICE-T has proved a success, leading to orders in 2002 for a second series of these units. The type's ICE TD diesel equivalent, Class 605, proved unsuccessful and has been withdrawn from service.

SPECIAL FEATURES

Journey time savings of between 15 and 20 per cent are claimed for the Class 411 and 415 ICE-T tilting emus thanks to their active tilt capability, which on conventional routes displaces the train by up to 8° to enable curves to be taken at higher speeds. This facility, coupled with a top speed potential of 143 mph (230 km/h) where infrastructure permits, has allowed the ICE-T units to demonstrate significant improvements on the DB Reise & Touristik long-distance routes on which they are used. As with the ICE-3 trainsets, ICE-T has a bodyshell formed of aluminium

SPECIFICATION

Number series: Class 411 cars individually numbered in the 411.0xx, 411.1xx, 411.2xx, 411.5xx, 411.6xx, 411.7xx and 411.8xx series; Class 415 cars individually numbered in the 415.0xx, 415.1xx, 415.5xx, 415.6xx and 415.7xx
Total built: Class 411 - 32; Class 415 - 11; 28 additional Class 411 (ICE-T2) on order for delivery from 2004
Builder: Siemens Transportation Systems, Bombardier Transportation (DWA)
Date introduced: 1999
Track gauge, ft/ins (mm): 4 ft 8.5 in (1,435)
Unit configuration: Class 411 - T-M-M-T-M-M-T; Class 415 - T-M-M-M-T
Power supply system: 15 kV AC 16.7 Hz
Electrical equipment: Siemens - GTO converters, microprocessor control, three-phase traction motors longitudinally mounted
Power rating, hp (kW): Class 411 - 5,360 (4,000); Class 415 - 4,020 (3,000)
Design speed, mph (km/h): 143 (230)
Additional features: Fiat active tilting system; Class 411 includes restaurant car, Class 415 has bistro; high level of onboard facilities

extrusions, although it is of a narrower profile than that of its non-tilting sisters to provide structural clearances in tilt mode. Some Class 415 ICE-T diagrams see the type working into Switzerland.

VOSSLOH G2000 DIESEL LOCOMOTIVE

Vossloh Type G2000

To meet the demand for traction from new operators taking advantage of EU 'open access' rules, diesel locomotive manufacturer Vossloh has developed a product range to meet various power needs. The distinctive G2000 was the most powerful type in production in early 2004 and had already attracted customers in Germany, Italy and Switzerland.

SPECIAL FEATURES

While not in service in great numbers, the Vossloh G2000 diesel-hydraulic is included here to reflect one of the trends in European traction - standard off-the-shelf locomotive designs that can be procured or leased in small numbers to enable emerging operators to take advantage of EU rules allowing open access to the Continent's rail networks. Two prototypes/demonstrators were rolled out in 2000. Production of an initial batch of 30 series machines followed from 2001, with examples supplied to various private German

SPECIFICATION

Number series: various
Total built: in current production
Builder: Vossloh
Date introduced: 2000
Track gauge, ft/ins (mm): 4 ft 8.5 in (1,435)
Axle arrangement: B-B
Power unit type: Caterpillar CAT 3516
Transmission: Voith - hydraulic
Weight, tonnes: 87
Power rating, hp (kW): 3,000 (2,240)
Design speed, mph (km/h): 75 (120)
Additional features: options up to 3,620 hp (2,700 kW); options up to 87 mph (140 km/h); asymmetric cab (full width option)

freight operators and to four companies in Italy. One of these, Swiss Rail Cargo Italy, is a subsidiary of Swiss Federal Railways. These feature full-width cabs and are designated Class Am 840.

CLASS A9400 DIESEL LOCOMOTIVE

Hellenic Railways Organisation (OSE) Class A-9400

The metre-gauge system in the south of the country from Athens to the Peloponnese is not electrified, and relies upon relatively antique motive power of various nationalities. Class A-9400 is used for shunting, freight and infrastructure duties, but can occasionally be seen on passenger trains.

SPECIAL FEATURES

The Greek metre-gauge diesel locomotive fleet is small and showing its age. However, there is still plenty of employment, and it is often only a lack of spares that forces withdrawal. Class A-9401, delivered from Mitsubishi of Japan in 1967, is the only diesel-hydraulic design. Three of the class are now out of service. Following conversion of the depot at Piraeus to standard gauge, the survivors are maintained at Kalamata. A passenger duty for the class has been the early morning train to Kisparissia with one former dmu trailer and a luggage van.

SPECIFICATION

Number series: A9401–A9420
Total built: 20
Builder: Mitsubishi
Date introduced: 1967
Track gauge, ft/ins (mm): 3ft 3.375in (1,000)
Axle arrangement: B-B
Power unit type: two G-M V8-71N
Transmission: Niigata - hydraulic
Weight, tonnes: 48
Power rating, hp (kW): 643 (480)
Design speed, mph (km/h): 56 (90)

CLASS A-470 DIESEL LOCOMOTIVE

Hellenic Railways Organisation (OSE) Class A-470 (to become Class 220)

The Class A-470s are OSE's most modern diesel locomotives, and are designed to be rebuilt as electric locomotives when the need arises. It remains to be seen if this will ever happen as OSE has taken delivery of Siemens EuroSprinter locomotives - similar to the Spanish (RENFE) Class 252 and Portuguese (CP) Class 5600 - for front line work.

SPECIAL FEATURES

The Class A-470s (220s) were built for the most important services on the main Athens-Thessaloniki corridor, which is gradually being modernised and electrified. The first batch was built by Adtranz in Germany and Switzerland, although the last ten, for delivery in 2004, were built under the Bombardier banner. The design is based on the Adtranz '12X' demonstrator, from which the large family of Class 145/185 electric locomotives was also developed, and the two MTU engines, similar to those fitted to OSE's Class 601

SPECIFICATION

Number series: A-471 - A-496 (220 001-220 036)
Total built: 36 (including examples on order in 204)
Builder: Adtranz (Bombardier)
Date introduced: 1998
Track gauge, ft/ins (mm): 4 ft 8.5 in (1,435)
Axle arrangement: Bo-Bo
Power unit type: two MTU 12V396 TC 13 1,000 kW
Transmission: electric, three-phase
Weight, tonnes: 90
Power rating, hp (kW): 2,700 (2,000)
Design speed, mph (km/h): 125 (200)
Additional features: electric train supply

and 651 intercity dmus, can be quickly lifted out and replaced by modular electrical equipment for 25kV AC operation.

CLASS 620 DMU

Hellenic Railways Organisation (OSE) Class 620

Local and middle distance trains are now in the hands of relatively modern train sets, and the German-built Class 620 type are employed on stopping trains around Thessaloniki and the Athens suburbs.

SUB-TYPES

A further 15 units of similar design were ordered for delivery in 2004. They are designated Class 621.

SPECIAL FEATURES

Twelve two-car diesel-hydraulic dmus (formerly Class 700), each seating 144 second class passengers, were supplied from Germany in 1990 to improve stopping services, including around Thessaloniki and between the capital city of Athens and Chalkis. They carry blue and red livery, and are numbered to conform to UIC guidelines.

SPECIFICATION

Number series: 620.001-620.012
Total built: 12
Builder: MAN, Hellenic Shipyards
Date introduced: 1990
Track gauge, ft/ins (mm): 4 ft 8.5 in (1,435)
Unit configuration: M+M
Power unit type: two MAN D2842
Transmission: Voith - hydraulic
Power rating, hp (kW): 825 (610)
Design speed, mph (km/h): 75 (120)
Additional features: there is one spare power car.

CLASS A-500 DIESEL LOCOMOTIVE

Hellenic Railways Organisation (OSE) Class A-500

The modest volume of freight carried by OSE is primarily hauled by two classes of similar MLW Co-Co locomotives, both with American-styled bodies. Marginally the younger design but less numerous, Class 501 is being refurbished.

SPECIAL FEATURES

OSE operates two similar MLW locomotive types, both imported from Canada. The original type and less powerful, Class A-451, dates back to 1973 and numbers 20 examples. They are being refurbished to resemble the stronger A-501 type, of which eight of the original ten survive. The electronic equipment of these is being modernised to standard General Electric 'Dash' standards, and the power unit rebuilt with a twin aftercooler and new turbocharger. The electric train-heat equipment has been removed and the maximum speed reduced from 92 mph (150 k/mh) for freight work.

SPECIFICATION

Number series: 501-510
Total built: 10
Builder: MLW
Date introduced: 1974
Track gauge, ft/ins (mm): 4 ft 8.5 in (1,435)
Axle arrangement: Co-Co
Power unit type: Alco V16-251F
Transmission: General Electric - electric
Weight, tonnes: 124
Power rating, hp (kW): 3,520 (2,610)
Design speed, mph (km/h): 70 (112)
Additional features: Electric train supply equipment removed

CLASSES 601/651 DMUS

Hellenic Railways Organisation Classes 601/651

Greece

While their role has been somewhat diminished by electrification of the Athens-Thessaloniki main line, these diesel-electric units still provide many key OSE intercity services.

SPECIAL FEATURES

East German industry supplied the first 12 (Class 601) of these stylish intercity units shortly before re-unification of the country. By the time the second series was ordered in 1994, LEW's Hennigsdorf plant near Berlin had been acquired by AEG. For this follow-up order a third trailer car was ordered to produce a formation of two power cars and three trailers. The body-mounted engine in each power car is similar to that fitted to the Class A-470 (Class 220) diesel-electric locomotives, simplifying maintenance routines. These trains' multiple-unit capability enables OSE to combine sets for trunk runs before separating them to serve different final destinations.

SPECIFICATION

Number series: (power cars) 601-624, 651-666
Total built: 12; 8
Builder: LEW; AEG (Adtranz), DWA
Date introduced: 1989; 1995
Track gauge, ft/ins (mm): 4 ft 8.5 in (1,435)
Unit configuration: M-T-T-M; M-T-T-T-M
Power unit type: two MTU 12V396 TC 13
1,000 kW
Transmission: electric
Power rating, hp (kW): 2,665 (1,990)
Design speed, mph (km/h): 100 (160)
Additional features: multiple working

CLASS M41 DIESEL LOCOMOTIVE

Hungarian State Railways (MÁV) Classes M41.2 and M41.23 (to become Classes 2241 and 2341)

The versatile mixed traffic diesel-hydraulic design was introduced in the 1970s and handles lighter duties over non-electrified lines of the MÁV network.

PRINCIPAL MODIFICATIONS

The Class M41.23 sub-class has resulted from a re-engining programme which commenced in 2000-01, when alternative 16-cylinder replacement power units by Caterpillar and MTU were fitted to two members of the class. MÁV was reported to be planning five such conversions.

SPECIAL FEATURES

Nicknamed 'Rattlers' by enthusiasts, the M41 diesel-hydraulics are versatile medium-powered lightweight machines used throughout the MÁV system on both passenger and freight services. Constructed by Ganz-Mávag at its Budapest facility, production extended from 1972 to 1984. By early 2004 a few withdrawals had occurred

SPECIFICATION

Number series: M41.2101-M41.2214; re-engined examples renumbered in the M41.23xx series. Renumbering as Classes 2241 and 2341 respectively was due to be completed by the end of 2004.
Total built: 114
Builder: Ganz-Mávag
Date introduced: 1973
Track gauge, ft/ins (mm): 4 ft 8.5 in (1,435)
Axle arrangement: B-B
Power unit type: Pielstick 12PA4-185
Transmission: Voith/Ganz - hydraulic
Weight, tonnes: 66
Power rating, hp (kW): 1,775 (1,325)
Design speed, mph (km/h): 62 (100)
Additional features: electric train-heating

but the class remained largely intact, although more retirements were planned.

OTHER COUNTRIES OPERATED

Designated model DHM-7 by its builders, examples of this design were supplied to Greece and to Tunisia, where they survive as SNCFT Class 040-DL.

CLASS M44 DIESEL LOCOMOTIVE

Hungarian State Railways (MÁV) Class M44.0, M44.4 and M44.5 (to become Classes 2044, 2444 and 2544)

Hungary

In recent years MÁV has undertaken a refurbishment and re-engining programme to prolong the working lives of some of these useful machines.

PRINCIPAL MODIFICATIONS

Class M44.4 results from a programme started in 2001 to refurbish and re-engine 36 of the class with Caterpillar engines, improved control systems and other improvements. The project was adopted as an alternative to ordering new locomotives. Class M44.5 locomotives are also refurbished examples of the type with electronic control equipment but retaining their original Ganz engines.

SPECIAL FEATURES

Used primarily for shunting and light duties in many parts of the Hungarian network, 200 of these locomotives were built by Ganz-Mávag between 1956 and 1971. By late 2003 some 50 of

SPECIFICATION

Number series: M44.001-M44.200; M44.401-M44.436; M44.501-M44-530
Total built: 200
Builder: Ganz-Mávag
Date introduced: 1956
Track gauge, ft/ins (mm): 4 ft 8.5 in (1,435)
Axle arrangement: Bo-Bo
Power unit type: Ganz-Jendrassik XVI Jv 170/240 (Class M44.4 Caterpillar 3508 Di-TA)
Transmission: electric - Ganz Electric, DC generator and four nose-suspended DC traction motors
Weight, tonnes: 66
Power rating, hp (kW): 590 (440)
Design speed, mph (km/h): 50 (80)

the original series remained in service with MÁV, alongside examples refurbished as described above. The Austro-Hungarian Györ-Sopron-Ebenfurt Railway (GySEV) in western Hungary operates 14 M44s, re-engined with Deutz power units, and four more are retained for works trains by the HEV suburban railway in Budapest. Locomotives of this design are also used by industrial operators.

257

CLASS M62 DIESEL LOCOMOTIVE

Hungarian State Railways (MÁV) Classes M62/M62.3/M62.5 (to become Classes 2062, 2362 and 2862)

Included here as an example of this classic Soviet-built diesel locomotive design, the Hungarian M62s were among the first of their type to enter service. Despite heavy withdrawals in recent years, some look set to outlive their counterparts in other countries thanks to MÁV's plans to re-engine members of the class.

SUB-TYPES

Eighteen Class M62.5 5 ft 0 in (1,524 mm) gauge machines were supplied to MÁV for cross-border operations into Ukraine. A few survived at Záhony depot in 2004 and two were slated for re-engining.

PRINCIPAL MODIFICATIONS

The Class M62.3 sub-class has resulted from a re-engining programme which commenced in 2000-01, when alternative 16-cylinder replacement power units by Caterpillar and MTU were fitted to two members of the class. MÁV was reported to be planning 11 such conversions using the MTU engine.

SPECIFICATION

Number series: M62.001-M62.273; M62.501-M62.518. Re-engined examples numbered in the M62.3xx series. Renumbering as Classes 2241 and 2341 respectively was due to be completed by the end of 2004.
Total built: 288 for MAV, including 18 for 1,524 mm gauge
Builder: Lugansk
Date introduced: 1965
Track gauge, ft/ins (mm): 4 ft 8.5 in (1,435) (Class M62.5 - 5 ft 0 in (1,524 mm) gauge)
Axle arrangement: Co-Co
Power unit type: Kolomna 14D40
Transmission: Charkov - electric, DC generator and nose-suspended DC traction motors
Weight, tonnes: 116.5
Power rating, hp (kW): 1,972 (1,472)
Design speed, mph (km/h): 62 (100)

SPECIAL FEATURES

The shrinking MÁV 'Sergei' fleet represents just a small part of the production of this once-important diesel type by the Lugansk plant, Ukraine. Nearly 2,500 examples were supplied to former Soviet satellite countries in Europe, while some 2,000 more went to Soviet Railways (SZD). SZD examples include twin- and triple-section variants. The M62 originated with two prototypes

produced at Lugansk in 1962 and is powered by a Kolomna 12-cylinder two-stroke 'vee' engine with conventional DC/DC transmission. No train-heating equipment is fitted, requiring MÁV to use generator cars when using the type in passenger traffic. Once the most numerous diesel type on the Hungarian system, some 50 examples remained in service at the beginning of 2004.

OTHER COUNTRIES OPERATED

Other European systems supplied by Lugansk with locomotives of this type included the former Czechoslovakia, East Germany and Poland. Several former Soviet states still use broad gauge examples of the type (see also Russian Railways Class 2M62). M62s were also supplied to Cuba and North Korea, where they have been joined by secondhand examples from Eastern Europe.

CLASS Bzmot DMU

Hungarian State Railways (MÁV) Classes Bzmot 200, 300 and 400 (to become Classes 6012 and 6112)

Europe

Seen all over the MÁV network are these Czech-built railbuses which handle short-distance services and operate secondary lines. Some have been modernised to act as feeders for intercity services.

PRINCIPAL MODIFICATIONS

Sub-class Bzmot 400 comprises 23 examples modernised and upgraded with Volvo engines in 1997 to provide 'InterPici' branded services running over short distances to feed traffic into MÁV intercity trains.

SPECIAL FEATURES

Supplied by the Czech builder Vagónka Studénka, this numerous family of two-axle railbuses provides local and feeder services throughout the Hungarian network, often operating with Class Btzx unpowered driving trailers. The class suffered a setback in 2003 when many examples were 'grounded' due the discovery of axle defects but there has been a gradual return to traffic.

SPECIFICATION

Number series: Bzmot 001-Bzmot 251, Bzmot 301-Bzmot 400, Bzmot 401-Bzmot 423. Renumbering as Classes 6012 and 6112 (Class Bzmot 400) was due to be completed by the end of 2004.
Total built: 232
Builder: Vagónka Studénka
Date introduced: 1977
Track gauge, ft/ins (mm): 4 ft 8.5 in (1,435)
Unit configuration: M (single-car)
Power unit type: Rába D10, MAN D2866 or Volvo
Transmission: Voith - hydromechanical
Power rating, hp (kW): 276 or 305 (206 or 228) (Class Bzmot 400 - 280 (375))
Design speed, mph (km/h): 50 (80) (Class Bzmot 400 - 56 (90))
Additional features: multiple-unit operation

OTHER COUNTRIES OPERATED

Similar vehicles operate in the Czech Republic and Slovakia (CC and ZSSK Classes 809, 810 and 811).

260

CLASS BVhmot/BVmot EMU

Hungarian State Railways (MÁV) Classes BVhmot and BVmot (to become Classes 5041 and 5141)

Intercity and suburban variants of essentially the same design, these AC-powered vehicles were built domestically in small numbers for MÁV in the mid-1990s.

SPECIAL FEATURES

The 100 mph intercity version of this design was introduced in 1995 on the Budapest-Györ-Csorna-Szombathely route, replacing locomotive-hauled equipment. They followed 20 Class BDVmot three-phase emus supplied by the same builders from 1988, and like those feature a single powered car, two intermediate trailers and an unpowered driving car (designated Class Bmxtz). They have not been entirely successful, on some occasions operating as unpowered vehicles hauled by a Class V43 electric locomotive. While broadly similar technically, the suburban BVmot suburban units feature a less streamlined front-end and two pairs of twin doors located at bodyside spacings one-third and two-thirds per car in place of the single doors at both ends of each intercity unit car. Developed as prototypes for a new fleet of Budapest commuter trains, their construction was limited to two examples built in 1996.

SPECIFICATION

Number series: BVhmot 001-BVhmot 003; BVmot 200-BVmot 201. Renumbering as Classes 5041 and 5141 respectively was due to be completed by the end of 2004.
Total built: Classes BVhmot - 3; Class BVmot - 2
Builder: Ganz-Mávag (subsequently Ganz-Hunslet)
Date introduced: 1995; 1996
Track gauge, ft/ins (mm): 4 ft 8.5 in (1,435)
Unit configuration: M-T-T-T
Power supply system: 25 kV AC 50 Hz
Electrical equipment: ABB, Ganz Ansaldo - microprocessor control, three-phase AC traction motors
Power rating, hp (kW): 2,350 (1,755)
Design speed, mph (km/h): 100 (160); 75 (120)
Additional features: rheostatic braking

CLASS V43 ELECTRIC LOCOMOTIVE

Hungarian State Railways (MÁV) Class V43 (to become Classes 1143 and 1243)

Introduced from the 1960s to a design developed by the 50 Hz Group, the V43 mixed traffic machines have since formed the principal electric locomotive type to serve the Hungarian network.

SUB-TYPES

Class V43.2 (1243) is the result of a refurbishment scheme that saw 30 of the class modernised with thyristor control equipment, suspension improvements and push-pull equipment.

SPECIAL FEATURES

The V43s are an interesting fusion of German body construction techniques and French practice in the adoption of single-motor bogies. The first seven locomotives were constructed at Krupp in West Germany before production shifted to Hungary, with Ganz-Mávag undertaking assembly and Ganz Electric Works manufacturing the traction equipment. While some withdrawals have taken place, the type still remains the staple

SPECIFICATION

Number series: V43.1001–V43.1379, with gaps for locomotives converted to Class V43.2 and numbered in the V43.2xxx series and examples transferred to GySEV. Renumbered as Classes 1143 and 1243 respectively.
Total built: 379
Builder: Krupp, Schneider, Ganz-Mávag
Date introduced: 1963
Track gauge, ft/ins (mm): 4 ft 8.5 in (1,435)
Axle arrangement: B–B
Power supply system: 25 kV AC 50 Hz
Electrical equipment: Alsthom, BBC, Brown Boveri, Ganz Electric Works, MTE, Oerlikon, SSW - silicon rectifiers, fully suspended DC traction motors
Weight, tonnes: 80
Power rating, hp (kW): 2,975 (2,220)
Design speed, mph (km/h): 80 (130)
Additional features: multiple-unit operation; single-motor bogies

electric locomotive type on the MÁV network. In 2003 15 similar locomotives numbered in the V43.3xx series were active on the Austro-Hungarian Györ-Sopron-Ebenfurt Railway in Hungary, having been transferred from MÁV.

CLASS V63 ELECTRIC LOCOMOTIVE

Hungarian State Railways (MÁV) Class V63 (to become Classes 1063 and 1163)

Until the arrival in 2002 of the Siemens-built Class 1047 'Taurus' machines, the V63s were MÁV's most powerful electric locomotive type. Examples of the type undertake some of the heaviest duties on the Hungarian electrified network and some have been re-geared for fast passenger services.

SUB-TYPES

Sub-class V63.1 is formed of 10 examples of the class regeared for 100 mph (160 km/h) express passenger operations.

SPECIAL FEATURES

Known popularly as the 'Gigant' class, this indigenous Hungarian design appeared as two prototypes in 1975, one geared for 75 mph (120 km/h) and one for 100 mph (160 km/h), and was intended for the heaviest passenger and freight duties on the MÁV network. Five 83 mph (133 km/h) pre-production machines (V63.003-

SPECIFICATION

Number series: V63.001-V63.049; V63.1xx series. Renumbering as Classes 1063 and 1163 respectively was due to be completed by the end of 2004.
Total built: 56
Builder: Ganz-Mávag
Date introduced: 1975
Track gauge, ft/ins (mm): 4 ft 8.5 in (1,435)
Axle arrangement: Co-Co
Power supply system: 25 kV AC 50 Hz
Electrical equipment: Ganz Electric Works - thyristor control, nose-suspended DC traction motors
Weight, tonnes: 116
Power rating, hp (kW): 4,930 (3,680) continuous
Design speed, mph (km/h): Class V63 (1063) - 75 (120); Class V63.1 (1163) - 100 (160)
Additional features: rheostatic braking

V63.007) were ordered from Ganz-Mávag/Ganz Electric Works before production of the standard 75 mph version commenced in Budapest in the mid-1980s. The two prototypes and most of the pre-production locomotives have been out of service for some time.

263

CLASS 071 DIESEL LOCOMOTIVE

Irish Rail (IE) Class 071

Ireland's first high-power Co-Co for express passenger and heavy freight work, has accelerated passenger services and increased freight train weights. It is a rugged, reliable mixed traffic design.

SPECIAL FEATURES

The Class 071s were ordered by Irish Rail in the mid-1970s to accelerate InterCity services on radial routes from Dublin to Belfast and to the south and west of the Republic. Designed to operate both daytime passenger and overnight 'liner' freight trains, they have proved to be very good value for money. From 1994 they were largely relegated to secondary passenger and freight duties with the introduction of the 201 Class. Northern Ireland Railways followed Irish Rail's example in 1980 when it took delivery of similar locomotives as part of an upgrade of cross-border services. Although fitted with electric train supply this has not been used for

SPECIFICATION

Number series: 071-088
Total built: 18
Builder: General Motors USA
Date introduced: 1976
Track gauge: 5 ft 3 in (1,602)
Wheel arrangement: Co-Co
Power unit type: GM 12-645E3C of 2,475 hp
Transmission: electric
Weight, tonnes: 99
Power rating, hp (kW): 2,475 (1,830)
Design, speed, mph (km/h): 90 (150)
Additional features: multiple working

many years and the third locomotive - delivered in 1984 - was not equipped.

OTHER COUNTRIES OPERATED

UK (Northern Ireland Railways) Class 111.

CLASS 141/181 DIESEL LOCOMOTIVE

Irish Rail (IE) Class 141/181

Ireland

Small mixed traffic design adapted for Irish railways from General Motors 'switcher' types. A feature of Irish railways since the early-1960s when they were instrumental in eliminating the country's last steam locomotives.

SPECIAL FEATURES

The 141 Class was based on good experience gained with the single-cab Class 121 ordered from General Motors in the early 1960s, although the design was adapted with a cab at each end for operational convenience. The type has always been used singly on lighter trains or in pairs on heavier freight and passenger work. Their reliability shamed earlier British-built types from Metropolitan-Vickers, which were eventually rebuilt with GM engines. Following the first batch in 1962, CIE took delivery of 12 similar, but higher-powered locomotives in 1966. These simple, reliable workhorses are now reaching the

SPECIFICATION

Number series: 141-177, 181-192
Total built: Class 141 - 37, Class 181 - 12
Builder: General Motors, USA
Date introduced: Class 141 - 1962, Class 181 - 1966
Track gauge, mm: 5 ft 3 in (1,602)
Wheel arrangement: Bo-Bo
Power unit type: Class 141 - GM 8-567CR, Class 181 - 8-B645E
Transmission: electric
Weight, tonnes: 67
Power rating, hp/kW: Class 141 - 950 (700), Class 181 - 1,100 (820)
Design, speed, mph (km/)h: 80 (130)
Additional features: multiple working

end of their lives, but remain common on secondary passenger work and on freight and infrastructure trains.

CLASS 201 DIESEL LOCOMOTIVE

Irish Rail (IE) Class 201

The most modern locomotive class in Ireland, introduced in 1994, is used on front-line passenger and heavy freight work in the Republic. It also provides traction for high profile cross-border 'Enterprise' trains.

SPECIAL FEATURES

By the early 1990s Irish Rail was ready to replace its life-expired 001 Class Co-Cos dating from 1955, and not surprisingly turned to General Motors for new locomotives. The 34 Class 201s are the most powerful locomotives ever to run on Irish railways and dominate InterCity passenger services to the south and west of Ireland. As part of its share of a comprehensive upgrade of Dublin-Belfast services, Northern Ireland Railways bought two of the locomotives, which are used as part of a common 'Enterprise' pool and painted green and grey to match the dedicated coaching stock. The type also sees use on freight work. Unusually for GM products, Irish Rail has had

SPECIFICATION

Number series: 201-234
Total built: 34
Builder: General Motors EMD, Canada
Date introduced: 1994
Track gauge, mm: 5 ft 3 in (1602)
Wheel arrangement: Co-Co
Power unit type: GM 12-710G3B
Transmission: electric
Weight, tonnes: 112
Power rating, hp/kW: 3,200 (2,385)
Design, speed, mph (km/h): 100 (160)
Additional features: multiple working, TDM push-pull control, electric train supply

many problems with its Class 201s, particularly with engine fires and bogie cracks.

CLASS 2900 DMU

Irish Rail (IE) Class 2900

The 2900 Class is Irish Rail's latest - and largest - multiple-unit fleet with 20 four-car sets delivered in 2003/04 for Dublin area suburban services.

SPECIAL FEATURES

Dmus - known as railcars in Ireland - have seen something of a resurgence over the past few years as IE has ordered several batches of trains from Japan and Spain to cope with an explosion in commuting by rail. The 2900s are IE's first modern four-car trains and the first in recent times to feature a full-width cab at each end. After initial teething troubles the trains went into service in mid-2003, replacing locomotive-hauled trains on Dublin's northern suburban line. The success of the trains, and continuing overcrowding, led IE to order further Class 2900 cars in late-2003.

SPECIFICATION

Number series: 2901-2920
Total built: 20
Builder: CAF
Date introduced: 2003
Track gauge, ft/ins (mm): 5 ft 3 in (1,602)
Unit configuration: M-M-M-M
Power unit type: 1 x MAN D2876 per car
Transmission: hydraulic, Voith T211
Power rating, hp (kW): 400 (294)
Design speed, mph (km/h): 75 (120)
Additional features: Cummins diesel engine to power on-board systems, CCTV, air conditioning, passenger-driver two-way communication, passenger information system

DART CLASS 8201 EMU

Irish Rail (IE) Class 8201

The need for 35 per cent extra capacity on the electrified Dublin Area Rapid Transit (DART) suburban network between Howth/Malahide and Greystones has seen further orders for electric train sets.

SPECIAL FEATURES

These five two-cars units were ordered from Alstom Transporte and completed at its plant in Barcelona, Spain in 2000, and officially launched on July 6 - just eight days before a depot fire destroyed two of the original LHB (German) series. The first new stock since DART opened in 1983/84, the 8201 units comprise a power car and driving trailer, each with seating for 40 passengers and space for a further 185 standing and one in a wheelchair. A further 24 four-car units, numbered in the 8501/8601 series, have been supplied from Mitsui, Japan. The new trains, which are maintained at Fairview depot, have been financed with European Union and Irish government funding.

SPECIFICATION

Number series: 8201-5, 8401-5
Total built: 5
Builder: Alstom
Date introduced: 2000
Track gauge, ft/ins (mm): 5 ft 3 in (1,602)
Unit configuration: M-T
Power supply system: 1.5 kV DC
Electrical equipment: xxxx traction motors
Power rating, hp (kW): 760 (560)
Design speed, mph (km/h): 87 (140)
Additional features: compatible with other DART stock, multiple working, automated information system.

CLASS D445 DIESEL LOCOMOTIVE

Italian Railways (FS Trenitalia) Class D445

Italy has only limited need for diesel locomotives, and the most recent high-volume design is seen on passenger duty all over the country on non-electrified routes.

SUB-TYPES

D445.1036-D445.1105 push-pull fitted.

SPECIAL FEATURES

The initial series of Class D445 was constructed between 1974-1976, and are a commonplace sight on passenger services. The second batch of locomotives, which dates from 1981-1988 was fitted with push-pull equipment from new, hence the slightly greater weight. In common with other FS main line diesel locomotive designs introduced in the 1960s and 1970s, the D445s feature single-motor bogies, a solution then also favoured by French traction engineers but not widely adopted elsewhere. The locomotives have not been affected by the national policy of sectorisation, which has segregated batches of other classes for inter-city, regional passenger and freight use.

SPECIFICATION

Number series: D445.1001-D445.1150
Total built: 150
Builder: D445.1001-D445.1035 - Savagliano, D445.1036-D445.1150 - Reggiane/Omeca/Casertane
Date introduced: 1974
Track gauge, ft/ins (mm): 4 ft 8.5 in (1,435)
Axle arrangement: B-B
Power unit type: D445.1001-D445.1035 - Fiat 2112 SSF, D445.1036-D445.1150 - Fiat 210.12 SSF
Transmission: electric, Ansaldo
Weight, tonnes: D445.1001-D445.1035 - 72, D445.1036-1150 D445.1150 - 76
Power rating, hp (kW): 1,700 (1,250)
Design speed, mph (km/h): 80 (130)
Additional features: electric train-heating

CLASS D145 DIESEL LOCOMOTIVE

Italian Railways (FS Trenitalia) Class D145

These two similar centre-cab locomotive designs are employed almost exclusively by the freight sector on heavy yard shunting and trip working, with the occasional station pilot passenger duty.

SPECIAL FEATURES

Heavy shunting work is carried out by these two types. The D145.1000 series, powered by two Fiat engines, is allocated to Turin, Bologna, Rome and Udine. Class D145.2000, which is of similar design but a single power with an awkwardly-shaped stepped bonnet and a single BRIF power unit, shares similar duties. None have any diagrammed passenger work.

SPECIFICATION

Number series: D145.1000-D145.1038; D145.2001-D145.2062
Total built: 100
Builder: D145.1000-D145.1038 - Savagliano, D145.2001-D145.2062 - TIBB/ABB
Date introduced: D145.1000-D145.1038 - 1982, D145.2001-D145.2062 - 1989
Track gauge, ft/ins (mm): 4 ft 8.5 in (1435)
Axle arrangement: Bo-Bo
Power unit type: D145.1000-D145.1038 - 2 x Fiat 8297.22, D145.2001-D145.2062 - BRIF 1D 36
Transmission: electric, TIBB/Parizzi
Weight, tonnes: D145.1000-D145.1038 - 72, D145.2001-D145.2062 - 73
Power rating, hp (kW): D145.1000-D145.1038 - 620 (460), D145.2001-D145.2062 - 680 (50)
Design speed, mph (km/h): 62 (100)

CLASS E464 ELECTRIC LOCOMOTIVE

Italian Railways (FS Trenitalia) Class E464

While passenger operators have increasingly opted for emus for regional and suburban services over electrified lines, possession of a large fleet of comparatively modern coaching stock led Trenitalia to select a locomotive-hauled push-pull solution.

SPECIAL FEATURES

Manufactured at the Vado Ligure plant of Adtranz (now Bombardier Transportation), the Class E464 was specifically developed for Trenitalia to power push-pull passenger trains. It features a single aerodynamically styled main driving cab, the locomotive end normally coupled to the train possessing just a small shunting cab and a gangway to the adjoining passenger coach. The locomotive is also provided with a luggage area, accessible from the train. Deliveries of an initial order for 50 machines commenced in April 1999. Subsequent contracts have seen the number of Class E464s ordered rise to 288, with deliveries planned to continue until 2006. Among

SPECIFICATION

Number series: E464.001–E464.180
Total built: 180 (plus 108 on order 2003)
Builder: Adtranz
Date introduced: 1999
Track gauge, ft/ins (mm): 4 ft 8.5 in (1,435)
Axle arrangement: Bo-Bo
Power supply system: 3 kV DC
Electrical equipment: Adtranz (now Bombardier Transportation), GTO converter, frame-suspended three-phase asynchronous traction motors
Weight, tonnes: 72
Power rating, hp (kW): 4,020 (3,000) continuous
Design speed, mph (km/h): 100 (160)
Additional features: rheostatic and regenerative braking; multiple-unit operation; can also operate from a 1.5 kV DC power supply, at reduced performance

locomotives being replaced by the type on Trenitalia's regional services are Class E646 Bo-Bo-Bos dating from the 1960s. In 2003 the Italian regional operator Ferrovia Emilia Romagna (FER) ordered three Class E464 locomotives.

CLASSES E402A/E402B ELECTRIC LOCOMOTIVES

Italian Railways (FS Trenitalia) Classes E402A/E402B

Among the most recent purely Italian electric locomotive designs, the 5,600 kW E402 machines were developed for both high-speed passenger and heavy freight traffic. The numerically larger E420B series is a dual-voltage version equipped to work into neighbouring Austria and Switzerland.

SPECIAL FEATURES

Class E402 originated with five prototypes, the first of which appeared in 1988. Two of those survive and have been equipped to match the specification of the series-built machines. Their appearance is quite different from the main fleet, with prominent side grilles and sharply angled nose-ends. Construction followed initially of 45 3 kV Dc-only series-built Class E402A machines. They were followed by 80 dual-voltage examples. The type's design provides for the fast running required to operate over the 'Direttissima' high-speed lines as well as incorporating a

SPECIFICATION

Number series: E402.001-E402-050 (E402A); E402.101-E402.180 (E402B)
Total built: 50 (including five prototypes); 80
Builder: Ansaldo, Breda, Fiat
Date introduced: prototypes - 1988; production series - 1994
Track gauge, ft/ins (mm): 4 ft 8.5 in (1,435)
Axle arrangement: Bo-Bo
Power supply system: 3 kV DC; 3 kV DC/15 kV AC 16.7 Hz
Electrical equipment: Ansaldo - three-phase asynchronous traction motors
Weight, tonnes: 84; 87.5
Power rating, hp (kW): 7,500 (5,600)
Design speed, mph (km/h): 137 (220)

capability to handle heavy freight traffic. In fact, most are used by FS Trenitalia's passenger division on domestic intercity services.

CLASS E636 ELECTRIC LOCOMOTIVE

Italian Railways (FS Trenitalia) Class E636

Class E636 has its roots in some of the very earliest Italian electric locomotive designs, and was constructed in large numbers from 1940 as the national system was systematically electrified.

SUB-TYPES

420 built with frame-suspended traction motors, 49 with nose-suspended motors. A four-axle derivative of this design, Class E424, was introduced by FS from 1943.

SPECIAL FEATURES

Class E636 is modelled on the now defunct Class E626 which also once numbered 448 examples built from 1927 for the first main line electrified to the new standard 3 kV dc system (Benevento-Foggia). The E636, which has the same electrical equipment but differs mechanically, comprises two symmetrical halves, articulated at the centre and carried on three two-axle welded steel

SPECIFICATION

Number series: E636.001-E636.469
Total built: 469
Builder: Breda/Savigliano/OM/Reggiane/TIBB/Ansaldo/Pistoiesi
Date introduced: 1940
Track gauge, ft/ins (mm): 4 ft 8.5 in (1,435)
Axle arrangement: Bo-Bo-Bo
Power supply system: 3 kV DC
Electrical equipment: Breda/Savigliano/CGE/Marelli/TIBB/Ansaldo
Weight, tonnes: 101
Power rating, hp (kW): 2,550 (1,890)
Design speed, mph (km/h): 70 (110)
Additional features: push-pull fitted

bogies, useful on sharply curved routes before bogie technology improved. The first 108 locomotives were constructed between 1940-42, but war halted further production until 1952. Numbers of the class have been depleted in recent years by deliveries of new electric locomotives.

CLASS E444 ELECTRIC LOCOMOTIVE

Italian Railways (FS Trenitalia) Class E444

Italy's first design of high-speed passenger locomotive is still doing what it was built for, although the appearance of Class E444 has been dramatically altered by the fitting of new driving cabs.

PRINCIPAL MODIFICATIONS

New cabs. The E444s' original top speed was 170 km/h, and a number were briefly designated E447 for 200 km/h operation, but conversions were cancelled when it discovered that they could all run at this speed without damage.

SPECIAL FEATURES

Known as 'Super Tortoises' because of their slothful appearance, the E444s were first employed on the Firenza-Roma Direttissima route. Four less powerful prototypes (now all withdrawn) pre-dated the production series by three years, and first-built E444.001 is intended for museum display. For added crew protection, the E444s

have been fitted with new cabs. At the time of sectorisation of the national railway business, Class E444s were briefly allocated to freight, but it was quickly realised they were not best suited to this work. They are allocated to two principal depots at Milano and Roma.

SPECIFICATION

Number series: E444.005-E444.117
Total built: 117
Builder: Savigliano/TIBB/Casaralta/Sofer/Fiat/Reggiane/Breda
Date introduced: 1967
Track gauge, ft/ins (mm): 4 ft 8.5 in (1,435)
Axle arrangement: Bo-Bo
Power supply system: 3 kV DC
Electrical equipment: Savigliano/TIBB/Alce/Ocren/Asgen/Marelli/Cesa/Breda/Italtrafo - resistance control, four fully suspended DC traction motors
Weight, tonnes: 83
Power rating, hp (kW): 5,390 (4,020)
Design speed, mph (km/h): 125 (200)
Additional features: high-speed capability, rheostatic brakes

CLASS E632/E633 ELECTRIC LOCOMOTIVE

Italian Railways (FS Trenitalia) Class E632/E633

Italy

After years of little change in Italian design policy, the emergence in 1979 of Class E633 heralded a new generation of electric locomotives, for use on both and passenger and freight services, and from northern Italy into France. Two years later, the E632 higher-speed passenger version appeared.

SUB-TYPES

E632 - suburban passenger, E633.0 - passenger and freight, E633.2 - multiple working

SPECIAL FEATURES

E632 and E633 are technically similar, and following the introduction of more modern locomotives are now sharing many duties. The E632 is the higher-speed passenger version, mainly for push-pull suburban services, but more recently faster, long-distance services. The class is being increased in size by the conversion of

SPECIFICATION

Number series: E632.002-E632.066, E633.001-E633.111, E633.201-E633.251
Total built: 215
Builder: E632- Savigliano/TIBB, E633 - Savigliano/TIBB
Date introduced: E632 - 1982, E 633 - 1979
Track gauge, ft/ins (mm): 4 ft 8.5 in (1,435)
Axle arrangement: B-B-B
Power supply system: 3 kV DC
Electrical equipment: E632 - Ansaldo/Marelli/TIBB
E 633- Savligliano/TIBB/Sofer
Weight, tonnes: E632 - 103, E 633 - 104
Power rating, hp (kW): 5,830 (4,320)
Design speed, mph (km/h): E632 - 100 (160), E633 - 80 (130)
Additional features: push-pull operation, monomotor bogies, rheostatic brakes.

Trenitalia Regionali's 50 E633s to E632, with a change in gear ratio and modification of electronic and pneumatic equipment. The prototype E632.001 has been scrapped.

CLASS E656 ELECTRIC LOCOMOTIVE

Italian Railways (FSS) Class E656

SUB TYPES

There are a number of minor variations, mainly electrical, between production batches. E656.551–E656.608 are push-pull fitted.

PRINCIPAL MODIFICATIONS

FS Cargo has begun regearing its E656s to increase tractive effort, and others are being modified, improving their ability to start. These are now classified E655.

SPECIAL FEATURES

The E656, which is another asymmetrical articulated design, is nicknamed 'The Alligator', and the commonest locomotive type in Italy. It is technically a development of the established E636 design. Although they have been superseded on Italy's fastest expresses because of their limited speed capability compared with more modern designs, the Class E656 fleet is still the backbone

SPECIFICATION

Number series: E656.001–E656.608
Total built: 453
Builder: Sofer/Casalralta/Catertane/TIBB/Reggiane
Date introduced: 1975
Track gauge, ft/ins (mm): 4 ft 8.5 in (1,435)
Axle arrangement: Bo-Bo-Bo
Power supply system: 3 kV DC
Electrical equipment: Italfrafo/Asgen/TIBB/Marelli/Ansaldo/Retam/Lucana
Weight, tonnes: 120
Power rating, hp (kW): 5,670 (4,200)
Design speed, mph (km/h): 93 (150)

of the national motive power fleet with an important role on both regional services and freight.

CLASS ALn 668 DMU

Italian Railways (FSS) Class ALn 668

The Fiat railcar, which was in production for over 30 years and underwent several facelifts, is employed on almost all non-electrified lines in Italy, in a variety of formations, in multiple, and with or without trailers.

SUB-TYPES

1201 series (1979): As 1001 series, 244 kW, revised bodyshell. 1401 series (1956): Earliest design, with five-speed gearbox, 220kW engines, later versions with corridor connections. 1501 series (1965): Four-speed gearboxes, 228 kW engines, corridors. 1601/1701 series (1970): Four speed gearbox, 228 kW engines, work in Sicily and Verona. 1801 series (1971): 228 kW, longer wheelbase. 1901/1001 series (1975): 340 kW, revised bodyshell. 2401 series (1959): As 1400, B-2 wheel arrangement. 3001 series (1980): As 1901 series, central door. 3101 series (1980): As 3101 series, multiple working. 3301 series (1982): As 3101 series, final version

SPECIFICATION

Number series: ALn 668.1001–ALn 668.1120, ALn 668.1201–ALn 668.1260, ALn 668.1401–ALn 668.1480, ALn 668.1501–ALn 668.1575, ALn 668.1601–ALn 668.1633, ALn 668.1701–ALn 668.1720, ALn 668.1803–ALn 668.1885, ALn 668.1901–ALn 668.1942, ALn 668.2401–ALn 668.2440, ALn 668.3001–ALn 668.3040, ALn 668.3101–ALn 668.3250, ALn 668.3301–ALn 668.3340
Total built: 738
Builder: Fiat/Pistoliesi/Savagliano
Date introduced: 1956
Track gauge, ft/ins (mm): 4ft 8.5 in (1,435)
Unit configuration: 1-A-1 (Howard: M-M or M-T?)
Power unit type: Fiat
Transmission: Mechanical
Power rating, hp (kW): 150-230 (110-170)
Design speed, mph (km/h): 70-80 (110-130)

SPECIAL FEATURES

ALn 668 is an umbrella classification for units carrying 68 passengers, and the types of power unit, transmissions, corridor connections and door arrangements have all changed during the production run, which ended in 1983.

CLASS ETR 460 HIGH-SPEED TILTING TRAINSET

Italian State Railways (FS Trenitalia) Class ETR 460

The classic Pendolino family of tilting trainsets has revolutionised intercity operations in many parts of Italy, enabling speeds to be accelerated on conventional routes to bring dramatic cuts in journey times. The technology developed by Fiat and now owned by Alstom has also been adopted by rail operators in several other countries. The FS ETR 460 trainsets represent the third generation of Italian tilting technology and form the basis for derivatives used elsewhere.

SUB-TYPES

Some Class ETR 460 equipped to operate from French 1.5 kV DC power supply but with a reduced continuous output of 5,250 hp (3,920 kW). See also references to ETR 470 and ETR 480 below. An ATR 410 diesel-powered prototype was built in 1997 but has not entered series production.

SPECIFICATION

Number series: ETR 460.001–ETR 460.029. Two-digit set numbers also carried on driving cars.
Total built: 29
Builder: Fiat Ferroviaria
Date introduced: 1992
Track gauge, ft/ins (mm): 4 ft 8.5 in (1,435)
Unit configuration: M-M-T-M-M-T-M-M
Power supply system: 3 kV DC
Electrical equipment: Parizzi - GTO inverter control, three-phase asynchronous traction motors
Power rating, hp (kW): 7,880 (5,880) continuous
Design speed, mph (km/h): 137 (220)
Additional features: Fiat active tilting system; rheostatic brakes; self-steering bogies

SPECIAL FEATURES

Fiat Ferroviaria initiated tilting train development in the 1960s in a bid to raise the speeds at which fast passenger trains could negotiate curves. This culminated in the supply to FS from 1985 of 15 ETR 450 none-car Pendolino electric tilting trainsets. Their success led to orders for the first batch of 10 ETR 460s. Like their predecessors, these are nine-car trains but improvements in traction technology enabled Fiat's designers to power just six of the cars rather than eight as in the ETR 450. The trains' active tilting system displaces each car's body by up to 8°. Seating is provided for 458 passengers and both external and interior styling is by Giugiaro, a leading Italian design consultancy. Subsequent FS orders for ETR 460s brought the fleet up to 29 examples, together with 15 Class ETR 480 trainsets. These are essentially similar but were built to be readily adapted to become dual-voltage units, enabling them to work from the 25 kV AC 50 Hz power supply system being adopted for new Italian high-speed lines under construction.

OTHER COUNTRIES OPERATED

The performance of the Pendolino concept has attracted operators outside Italy and trains of this type using the Fiat (now Alstom) tilting system are in service in: Czech Republic (seven CD Class 680) (left lower); Finland (VR Class Sm3, 18 in service or on order, seven on option); Portugal (10 CP 'Pendoluso' trainsets) (above); Slovenia (three SZ Class 310); Spain (10 RENFE Class 490); Switzerland (nine Cisalpino Class ETR 470). Derived designs using the Fiat tilting system include: Germany (20 Class 610 dmus); Switzerland (34 SBB ICN trainsets, 10 on option); UK (53 Virgin Trains Class 390).

RENFE, Spain, has also ordered 20 examples of a Class 104 non-tiling design based on the Pendolino bodyshell.

CLASS ETR 500 HIGH-SPEED TRAINSET

Italian State Railways (FS Trenitalia) Class ETR 500

The ETR 500 trainsets employ the same power cars-plus-trailers configuration as their French TGV and German ICE 1 contemporaries. Orders placed in 2003 will see the DC-only power cars relegated to haulage of conventional stock.

PRINCIPAL MODIFICATIONS

Class E404.5 power cars are undergoing modifications to their traction equipment to raise their output when operating from an AC power supply to 5,900 hp (4,400 kW).

SPECIAL FEATURES

The first 30 ETR 500 trainsets were ordered before FS determined that future electrification of high-speed lines should be at 25 kV AC. As a result, they are formed of two Class E404.1 power cars equipped only for the 3 kV system and 11 light alloy trailers. The second batch of trains features Class E404.5 dual-voltage power cars capable of operating under both systems, albeit at reduced

SPECIFICATION

Number series: (power cars) E404.100-E404.150; E404.500-E404.559. Power cars also carry two-digit set numbers with '-A' or '-B' suffixes.
Total built: 60 trainsets
Builder: Consorzio Trevi (Alstom, Ansaldo, Breda (the two last-mentioned now Ansaldobreda), Bombardier (formerly Adtranz), Firema)
Date introduced: 1992
Track gauge, ft/ins (mm): 4 ft 8.5 in (1,435)
Unit configuration: two power cars plus 11 trailers
Power supply system: 30 trainsets - 3 kV DC; 30 trainsets - 3 kV DC/25 Kv AC 50 Hz
Electrical equipment: Consorzio Trevi - inverter and three-phase asynchronous traction motors
Power rating, hp (kW): on 3 kV DC - 2 x 5,900 (2 x 4,400) continuous; on 25 kV AC - 2 x 4,420 (2 x 3,300) continuous
Design speed, mph (km/h): 186 (300)

output on AC. FS was also reported to be considering lengthening the ETR 500 trainsets to 12 trailers by procuring additional cars.

CLASS 760/761 'TAF' EMU

North Milan Railway (FNME) Class 760/761

Italy

The North Milan Railway is an independent commuter system serving the northern suburbs of Milan. These high-specification double-deck emus were supplied from the late 1990s under a joint procurement programme with FS Trenitalia.

SPECIAL FEATURES

Between 1997 and 2001 72 of these high-density suburban emus were procured under a joint programme by Italian State Railways (FS Trenitalia) and FNME. Deliveries of the initial 19 supplied to the latter commenced in 1998. Subsequent orders placed in 2001 saw FS receive 27 more and FNME five, bringing the fleets to 80 and 24 respectively. The units are used in Italy's largest cities, including Milan, where duties undertaken by the FNME fleet include serving the cross-city 'Passante' line. Trains of this type also serve Milan's Malpensa Airport and carry 'Malpensa Express' branding. Seating capacity of

SPECIFICATION

Number series: EA 760 001–EA 760 024/EA 761 001–EA 761 024
Total built: 24 (for FNME)
Builder: Ansaldo, Breda/Ansaldobreda, Firema
Date introduced: 1998
Track gauge, ft/ins (mm): 4 ft 8.5 in (1,435)
Unit configuration: M-T-T-M
Power supply system: 3 kV DC
Electrical equipment: Adtranz (now Bombardier Transportation), Ansaldo (now Ansaldobreda) – GTO inverters, microprocessor control, three-phase traction motors
Power rating, hp (kW): 3,360 (2,510)
Design speed, mph (km/h): 87 (140)
Additional features: regenerative and rheostatic braking; air-conditioning; audio and visual passenger information systems

each four-car unit is for 841, with standing room for 372 more. A wheelchair space is also provided and there is a retention toilet.

CLASS 2TE10M/2TE10U DIESEL LOCOMOTIVE

Latvian Railway Class 2TE10M and 2TE10U

Developed during the Soviet era and built at Lugansk, now in Ukraine, locomotives of the characteristic twin-section 2TE10 family were built in great numbers and are seen on most railway systems in countries that once formed part of the USSR.

SUB-TYPES

Principal variants of the 2TE10M and 2TE10U include the 2TE10MK, with Kolomna 5D49 engines, and two 2TE10G gas-fuelled prototypes. Three-section 3TE10M and two- and four-section 2TE10S and 4TE10S versions were also developed from the 2TE10M, the last two types modified for operation in the extremely cold climates of northern Russia. The 2TE10U design was produced in three-section 3TE10U and 3TE10US versions and as a 2TE10UT 75 mph passenger variant.

SPECIAL FEATURES

Using two 10-cylinder two-stroke 10D100 series engines, the Class 2TE10 diesel-electric design first

SPECIFICATION

Total built: (for Soviet Railways and its successors) approx 3000; approx 500
Builder: Lugansk Diesel Locomotive Works
Date introduced: (in Latvia) 2TE10M - 1981; 2TE10U - 1990
Track gauge, ft/ins (mm): 5 ft 0 in (1,520)
Axle arrangement: Co-Co+Co-Co
Power unit type: Kharkov 10D100 10-cylinder two-stroke
Transmission: electric - Kharkov DC generators and nose-suspended DC traction motors
Weight, tonnes: 2 x 138
Power rating, hp (kW): 2 x 2,950 (2 x 2,200)
Design speed, mph (km/h): 62 (100)

emerged in the USSR in 1962 as the 2TE10L, meeting a need for a rugged heavy freight machine capable of operating in the harshest environments. An improved development of the type, the 2TE10V emerged in 1974 and was the first to feature the characteristic forward-raked windscreen.

CLASS DR1 DMU

Pasazieru Vilciens Class DR1A, DR1P and DR1Am

Under the Soviet regime the RVR plant at Riga, Latvia, was the principal manufacturer of dmus for those republics that had a requirement for vehicles of this type. Introduced in 1963, the DR1 family was built for several railways, albeit not in great numbers. With much of the Latvian system diesel-operated, units of this type provide most domestic passenger services. These are run by Pasazieru Vilciens, a joint stock company created by splitting Latvian Railway.

PRINCIPAL MODIFICATIONS

Class DR1Am is a refurbished version of Class Dr1A, with an MTU engine and Voith transmission. Ten three-car units were introduced by LDZ from 1997.

SPECIAL FEATURES

The DR1 family was the first Soviet dmu design. Series production of the original DR1 series extended from 1966 to 1970, when manufacture commenced of Class DR1P. In all, 72 sets were produced of a formation comprising two powered

SPECIFICATION

Total built: 149 cars in service in Latvia in 2003
Builder: RVR
Date introduced: 1973 (in Latvia)
Track gauge, ft/ins (mm): 5 ft 0 in (1,520)
Unit configuration: M-T-T or M-T-T-T-T-T
Power unit type: DR1A - Zvezda M756; DR1P - Zvezda M746; DR1Am - MTU
Transmission: Kaluga - hydraulic (DR1A) or hydro-mechanical (DR1P) (DR1Am - Voith hydraulic)
Power rating, hp (kW): 985 (735); 985 (735); 1,000 (745)
Design speed, mph (km/h): 75 (120)

cars with floor-mounted engines and four trailers. The improved Class DR1A entered series production in 1976. Train configuration of the Latvian examples comprises one powered car with two or five trailers, one of which is a driving trailer. These operate the majority of internal services.

OTHER COUNTRIES OPERATED

Belarus, Russian Federation and Ukraine.

CLASS 1800 DIESEL LOCOMOTIVE

Luxembourg Railways (CFL) Class 1800

CFL's 1800s are Luxembourg's most powerful diesel type and identical to the Belgian Class 55. In the twilight of their lives, they are used singly or in pairs on freight.

SUB-TYPES

1801-1804 and 1815-1820 have steam heating boilers for passenger work.

SPECIAL FEATURES

Originally a mixed traffic type, Class 1800 is now freight-only, and examples can be seen working heavy trains around the south of the country, usually in connection with the extensive steel industry in that area. They can be seen working alongside survivors of neighbouring Belgian Railways' Class 55s and on trains to and from the border. The class has been in decline as new CFL 3000 Class and identical Belgian 1300 dual-voltage electric locomotives have taken over many international freight workings.

SPECIFICATION

Number series: 1801-1820
Total built: 20
Builder: Brugeoise et Nivelles (BN), Belgium
Date introduced: 1963
Track gauge, ft/ins (mm): 4ft 8.5in (1,435)
Axle arrangement: Co-Co
Power unit type: General Motors 16-567C
Transmission: electric - DC generator and four DC nose-suspended traction motors
Weight, tonnes: 110-114
Power rating, hp (kW): 1,940 (1,435)
Design speed, mph (km/h): 75 (120)
Additional features: steam heating, rheostatic braking

OTHER COUNTRIES OPERATED

Class 55 in Belgium is of the same design.

CLASS 3600 ELECTRIC LOCOMOTIVE

Luxembourg Railways (CFL) Class 3600

While this distinctive centre-cab type has been eliminated in France, where it originated, a few examples survive in Luxembourg, operating both freight and passenger traffic.

SPECIAL FEATURES

The CFL Class 3600 machines are similar to French National Railways (SNCF) Class BB12000, 148 of which were built from 1954 for the pioneering Valenciennes-Thionville 25 kV electrification. Their unusual construction sees the transformer positioned beneath the cab floor, with control equipment and auxiliary machinery located in the two hoods either side of the driver's cab. In late 2004 four of the CFL fleet survived handling a variety of duties. However, the arrival of new dual-voltage electrics suggests that the long-term survivors of class are living on borrowed time.

SPECIFICATION

Number series: 3601-3620
Total built: 20
Builder: Alsthom, MTE
Date introduced: 1958
Track gauge, ft/ins (mm): 4 ft 8.5 in (1,435)
Axle arrangement: Bo-Bo
Power supply system: 25 kV AC 50 Hz
Electrical equipment: MTE, SW - tap-changer control, silicon rectifiers, fully suspended traction motors
Weight, tonnes: 84
Power rating, hp (kW): 3,550 (2,650)
Design speed, mph (km/h): 75 (120)
Additional features: flexible cardan shaft drive

OTHER COUNTRIES OPERATED

Similar BB12000 locomotives were in service with SNCF in France until 2000.

CLASS 2000 EMU

Luxembourg Railways (CFL) Class 2000

The 22 two-car Class 2000 EMUs form the backbone of the CFL passenger fleet, working throughout the country's electrified network and over the border into north-east France.

ADDITIONAL FEATURES

Multiple working, automatic plug doors, one-person operation.

SPECIAL FEATURES

Class 2000 was developed from the French Class Z11500s and to maximise efficiency of their emu fleets, SNCF and CFL share duties between Luxembourg and Nancy, and some SNCF Z11500 work trains on CFL routes. The emus often work in pairs on busier trains, but look likely to be replaced on these by locomotive-hauled double deck sets in the next few years. Luxembourg is also developing a tram-train network around its capital that will see many local CFL trains replaced by light rail vehicles.

SPECIFICATION

Number series: 2001-2022
Total built: 22
Builder: De Dietrich
Date introduced: 1990
Track gauge, ft/ins (mm): 4 ft 8.5 in (1,435mm)
Unit configuration: M-T
Power supply system: 25 kV AC 50 Hz
Electrical equipment: 4 x 305kW Alsthom traction motors
Power rating, hp (kW): 1,650 (1,220)
Design speed, mph (km/h): 100 (160)

OTHER COUNTRIES OPERATED

Similar Z11500s operate in north eastern France and share duties in this area with CFL units.

CLASS 6400 DIESEL LOCOMOTIVE

Railion Benelux Class 6400

PRINCIPAL MODIFICATIONS

6461-6475 have electric train heating capability. 6412, 6476-6479 are equipped for hump shunting, and radio remote control. 6491-6499 can run in Germany, 6501-6504 have been used for banking between Venlo and Kaldenkirchen. 6505-6520 can run into Belgium.

SPECIAL FEATURES

The need to replace a number of elderly Bo-Bo types (Classes 2200 and 2400) employed on trip freight workings since the 1950s prompted Netherlands Railways to procure a centre-cab design that would also be at home on heavy shunting duties, offering almost twice the power output of the locomotives they superseded. They are frequently seen triple heading 5,200 tonne iron ore trains from the port of Rotterdam to Venlo. The last ten locomotives of the class appeared new in the red livery of NS Cargo (now

SPECIFICATION

Number series: 6401-6520
Total built: 120
Builder: Maschinenfabrik Kiel (MaK), now Vossloh
Date introduced: 1988
Track gauge: 4 ft 8.5 in (1,435)
Wheel arrangement: Bo-Bo
Power unit type: MTU 12V396TC14
Transmission: electric, 4 three-phase asynchronous BBC traction motors
Weight, tonnes: 80
Power rating, hp (kW): 1,600 (1,180)
Design, speed, mph (km/h): 62 (100)
Additional features: multiple working, up to four locomotives

Railion Benelux), and the rest will follow after overhaul.

OTHER COUNTRIES OPERATED

The Dutch locomotives are a version of the standard type DE 1002 from MaK. Examples have been in service with Eurotunnel, the Bentheimer Eisenbahn in Germany and various other private and industrial operators.

CLASS 1200 ELECTRIC LOCOMOTIVE

Netherlands (ACTS) Class 1200

The American-design NS 1200 Class is the longest-serving locomotive in the Netherlands. Following withdrawal of the fleet from service in 1998 after almost 50 years service, a small number have been overhauled for further use with a private freight owner.

SPECIAL FEATURES

The NS 1200 Class is based an American design by Baldwin, assembled under licence in the Netherlands by Werkspoor in 1951-1953, with bogies imported from Philadelphia and electrical components made by Heemaf under licence from Westinghouse. For many years, '1200s' were the prime choice for long-distance inter-city trains between Zandvoort aan Zee and Maastricht/Heerlen. After replacement by more modern French-design Class 1600s, five 'Baldwins' were sold to private freight operator ACTS for waste and container trains between Rotterdam and Onnen (Groningen) or Leeuwarden. They carry

SPECIFICATION

Number series: 1251-1255
Total built: 5
Builder: Werkspoor (under licence from Baldwin)
Date introduced: 1951
Track gauge, ft/ins (mm): 4 ft 8.5 in (1,435)
Axle arrangement: Co-Co
Power supply system: 1.5 kV DC
Electrical equipment: Heemaf (under licence from Westinghouse)
Weight, tonnes: 108
Power rating, hp (kW): 3,000 (2,208)
Design speed, mph (km/h): 95 (150)

a new blue livery with a wide yellow stripe. Two are in museums, and one ACTS locomotive, 1253, has been sold to a passenger charter company.

PLAN T and PLAN V EMU

Netherlands Railways (NS) Plan T and Plan V

The 'Hondekop' or 'Doghead' EMU - so nicknamed because of the mournful look of its front end, has been a feature of Netherlands Railways for almost 50 years. The oldest types introduced in 1954 have now gone and the survivors have been displaced from most of their prestigious inter-city services.

SPECIAL FEATURES

This is the most familiar shape of passenger unit is seen throughout the Netherlands. After the success of four-car units (Plan T), a two-car version for local/regional trains was introduced (Plan V), built by Werkspoor in the Netherlands and the last batches Talbot in Aachen (Germany). The types feature different luggage compartments and seating arrangements. The two-car sets are normally used for local and regional trains, and are destined to be a common sight all over the country for some time following mechanical and

SPECIFICATION

Number series: 401-438, 441-483, 502-531, 801-965
Total built: 277
Builder: Allan/Werkspoor and Talbot
Date introduced: 401-438 - 1966, 441-483 - 1969, 502-531 - 1964, 801-965 - 1972
Track gauge, ft/ins (mm): 4 ft 8.5 in (1435)
Unit Configuration: 401-438 - M-M, 441-483 - M-M, 502-531 - M-M-M-T (B+BD+AB+B), 801-965 - M-M
Power supply system: 1.5 kV DC
Electrical equipment: Heemaf traction motors. 401-438, 441-483 - 4, 502-531 - 8, 801-965 - 4
Power rating, hp (kW): 401-438, 441-483 - 775 (580), 502-531 - 1,610 (1,200), 801-965 - 775 (580)
Design speed, mph (km/h): 140 (225)
Additional features: gangwayed within units, multiple working. 401-438 luggage compartment, 441-483 no luggage compartment, 502-531 built with buffet car, 801-965 built with post compartment

internal refurbishment. The units are in either two- or four-car formations.

CLASS DM90 DMU

Netherlands Railways (NS) Class DM90

DM90 is Netherlands Railway's most modern DMU type, introduced in 1996 to modernise several widely scattered non-electrified lines across the country. The most distinctive feature is the wide body.

SPECIAL FEATURES

Extensive teething troubles with 'DM90s' meant that older types remained in service for much longer than planned, but the trains have settled down and now work services around Roermond, Zwolle, Venlo and Arnhem. They are known by NS as 'Buffel' (Buffaloes) due to their bulky appearance. From 2000 onwards, local services in the Netherlands have been handed over to private operators, which has led to a number of 'DM90s' being hired or leased by NS to operators such as Syntus.

SPECIFICATION

Number series: 3401-3453
Total built: 53
Builder: Talbot
Date introduced: 1996
Track gauge, ft/ins (mm): 4ft 8.5 in (1,435)
Unit configuration: M-M
Power unit type: Cummins NTA 855 R4
Transmission: Voith - hydraulic,
Power rating, hp (kW): 860 (640)
Design speed, mph (km/h): 85 (140)
Additional features: Automatic plug doors, one-person operation, cycle racks

CLASS SGM SPRINTER FAMILY

Netherlands Railways (NS) Class SGM

SUB-TYPES

2001-2008 are prototype two-car trains without toilets and gangways. Others have a trailer added for extra capacity.

MAJOR MODIFICATIONS

2836-2880 were converted earlier types with the addition of a trailer and removal of first class seating in one driving car.

SPECIAL FEATURES

In the mid-1970s, the 'Sprinter' emus were introduced on the Zoetermeer Stadslijn, a circular route with very frequent stops near Den Haag. The type was subsequently developed and more units were introduced to work high-frequency stopping services around Den Haag and Rotterdam to Roosendaal, Amsterdam and Hoek van Holland. From 2003, units were heavily

refurbished by NedTrain, losing their familiar yellow for a more modern blue, white and yellow style.

SPECIFICATION

Number series: 2001-08, 2021-35, 2836-95
Total built: 83
Builder: Talbot
Date introduced: 1975
Track gauge, ft/ins (mm): 4 ft 8.5 in (1,435)
Unit configuration: M-M or M-T-M
Power supply system: 1.5 kV DC
Electrical equipment: Oerlikon
Power rating, hp (kW): 950 (1,280)
Design speed, mph (km/h): 80 (125)
Additional equipment: Automatic plug doors, disc brakes, toilet and gangways (except 2001-2008), public address system

CLASS IC3 EMU

Netherlands Railways (NS) Class IC3

For longer distance trains, Netherlands Railways has high-quality trains capable of reversing quickly without having to run round or provide spare locomotives. They feature a distinctive design with the driver's cab mounted in a pod above a through gangway.

SUB-TYPES

4001-4007, prototype trains built in 1977, originally had different interiors to production sets. Others are three-car and four-car.

MAJOR MODIFICATIONS

4001-4007 have been rebuilt internally to conform with production sets.

SPECIAL FEATURES

In 1977, seven prototype Intercity trains were introduced. Running in multiple on busy core sections of main line, these emus can provide services to or from several destinations, dividing

SPECIFICATION

Number series: 4001-4097, 4201-4230
Total built: 127
Builder: Talbot
Date introduced: 1977
Track gauge, ft/ins (mm): 4 ft 8.5 in (1,435)
Unit configuration: M-T-T or M-M-T-T
Power supply system: 1.5 kV DC
Electrical equipment: Oerlikon
Power rating, hp (kW): 4001-4097 - 1,700 (1,260), 4201-4230 - 2,550 (1,890)
Design speed: 100 (160)
Additional equipment: Automatic plug doors, disc brakes, toilet and through gangways, public address system, cycle racks, pantry for trolley catering service

at each end of their journey. The trains are used on the Rotterdam-Amsterdam-Groningen-Leeuwarden and Amsterdam-Enschede routes, among others, removing the need for locomotive-hauled trains. The trailer cars were used as the basis for NS' ICR locomotive-hauled stock, used on both internal Dutch IC routes and on Brussels-Amsterdam 'Benelux' trains.

CLASS DD IR-M EMU

Netherlands Railways (NS) Class DD IR-M

The latest fleet of double-deck IR-M emus was ordered in the mid-1990s to cater for a rapid increase in passenger numbers on routes from Amsterdam. They have better seating and air-conditioning to provide extra comfort

SUB-TYPES

Units are formed into three-, four- and six-car sets.

SPECIAL FEATURES

IR-M emus are designed for high-speed travel medium-distance interurban services where better seating is a pre-requisite. The continuing steep rise in passenger numbers in 2000-02 led NS to order extra coaches for many units, extending them to six car-lengths. This process continued into 2003, allowing the withdrawal of older single-deck emus dating from the 1950s and 1960s, modernising the fleet and increasing capacity.

SPECIFICATION

Number series: 8201-8281, 8401-8481, 8489-8681, 8701-8733, 9401-9481, 9501-9513
Total built: 290
Builder: Talbot
Date introduced: 1994
Track gauge, ft/ins (mm): 4 ft 8.5 in (1,435)
Unit configuration: three-, four- or six-car
Power supply system: 1.5 kV DC
Electrical equipment: Holec DMKT 60/45 three-phase traction motors
Power rating, hp (kW): 2,160 (1,600)
Design speed, mph (km/h): 125 (200)
Additional features: Air-conditioning, automatic plug doors, multiple working equipment, automatic couplers

DDAR/mDDM EMU

Netherlands Railways Class mDDM

The mDDM power cars are among the most remarkable vehicles currently operating in Europe, featuring passenger accommodation above what is effectively a Bo-Bo-Bo locomotive. They were ordered in the mid-1990s to work with double-deck DDM trailer cars.

PRINCIPAL MODIFICATIONS

DDM trailer cars were originally powered by NS Class 1700 electric locomotives, now replaced by new mDDM power cars. 14 sets have removable seats in the lower deck to create extra summer bicycle space

SPECIAL FEATURES

The mDDM power cars were ordered in the mid-1990s to work with double-deck DDM trailer cars that operated for over ten years with Alsthom Class 1700 locomotives. Auto-couplers are fitted for multiple working, including with the

SPECIFICATION

Number series: 7801-7879
Total built: 50
Builder: Talbot
Date introduced: 1997
Track gauge, ft/ins (mm): 4 ft 8.5 in (1,435)
Unit configuration: M-T-T-T
Power supply system: 1.5 kV DC
Electrical equipment: Holec
Power rating, hp (kW): 3,250 (2,400)
Design speed, mph (km/h): 85 (140)
Additional features: Automatic couplers, wide plug doors. DDM driving trailers - pantographs that can be raised to power on-board systems when not attached to a power car or locomotive

remaining Class 1700-powered DDM sets. The trains mainly work on interurban services in northern Holland and were acquired after tests with French double-deck stock offered NS a solution to capacity problems on routes where longer trains were not an option.

CLASS El 14 ELECTRIC LOCOMOTIVE

CargoNet Class El 14

Netherlands/Norway

These powerful electric locomotives were introduced in the late 1960s as mixed traffic machines for recently electrified lines. Today they provide front-line power for Norway's national freight operator, CargoNet.

SPECIAL FEATURES

Electrification of NSB's Dovre line and a requirement for more powerful traction on the difficult Bergen line led to orders for 31 of this successful six-axle locomotive type. Its design is to some degree based on that of the Swiss Federal Railways (SBB) Class Ae 6/6, including the bogies. Intended originally as a mixed traffic type, the El 14 has a comparatively light axle-load of 17.5 tonnes. Together with lateral sideplay in the bogie wheelsets, this adapted the type well for NSB's mountain routes. All of the class survived at the end of 2003, by which time they had been assigned to CargoNet, the rail freight company set up jointly by NSB Goods and the Swedish freight

SPECIFICATION

Number series: 14.2164-14.2190, 14.2197-14.2200
Total built: 31
Builder: Thune
Date introduced: 1968
Track gauge, ft/ins (mm): 4 ft 8.5 in (1,435)
Axle arrangement: Co-Co
Power supply system: 15 kV AC 16.7 Hz
Electrical equipment: NEBB - tap-changer control, fully suspended AC traction motors
Weight, tonnes: 105
Power rating, hp (kW): 6,805 (5,075)
Design speed, mph (km/h): 75 (120)
Additional features: rheostatic braking

operator, Green Cargo. Consequently most now carry CargoNet's black livery. The concentration of the El 14s on freight duties saw their maximum service speed reduced in 1997 from 75 to 62 mph (120 to 100 km/h).

CLASS El 17 ELECTRIC LOCOMOTIVE

Norwegian State Railways (NSB) Class El 17

Introduced in 1981 for fast passenger services, this German-built light three-phase electric locomotive type has to some degree been replaced on front-line NSB services by more modern emus.

SPECIAL FEATURES

Derived to some degree from the pioneering German Class 120s, the El 17s are claimed by Norwegians to be the first three-phase main line electric locomotives to enter regular service (the DB machines serving as test units at the time). When introduced, the El 17s were often paired with the new Type B7 coaches, which had been prepared for retrofitting with a tilting system but never modified. These combinations were used on key routes such as Oslo-Trondheim. However, in their early days the class did not prove especially successful and its comparatively low power and light axle-load rendered it unsuitable for freight - or indeed heavier passenger services on the most

SPECIFICATION

Number series: 17.2221-17.2232
Total built: 12
Builder: Henschel (Thyssen-Henschel)
Date introduced: 1981
Track gauge, ft/ins (mm): 4 ft 8.5 in (1,435)
Axle arrangement: Bo-Bo
Power supply system: 15 kV AC 16.7 Hz
Electrical equipment: NEBB, ABB - three-phase asynchronous traction motors
Weight, tonnes: 64
Power rating, hp (kW): 4,560 (3,400)
Design speed, mph (km/h): 93 (150)
Additional features: regenerative/rheostatic brakes, multiple-unit operation

steeply graded routes. With the arrival of newer emus and the powerful Class El 18 electric locomotives, the El 17s now have so little work that one (17.2223) has been preserved and six more (17.2227-17.2232) have been transferred to the famous Flåm railway, where they carry a dark green livery.

CLASS Di 8 DIESEL LOCOMOTIVE

CargoNet Class Di 8

Norway

Twenty of these Siemens-built centre-cab three-phase diesel locomotives were acquired by NSB from 1997 for heavy shunting and trip freight working, displacing examples of the Di 3 'Nohab' fleet and leased machines from Sweden. They are now operated by the national operator's CargoNet freight subsidiary.

SPECIAL FEATURES

To some extent a development of the Class 6400 locomotives supplied to Netherlands Railways, the Di 8s were built at the former MaK plant at Kiel, which for a period was part of Siemens. The manufacturing facility has since been acquired by Vossloh, which continues diesel locomotive production there. Introduction of Class Di 8 eased an NSB diesel traction shortage that had been exacerbated by problems experienced with the Siemens Class Di 6 machines. Their arrival also contributed to the demise of the Class Di 3

SPECIFICATION

Number series: 8.701-8.720
Total built: 20
Builder: Siemens
Date introduced: 1997
Track gauge, ft/ins (mm): 4 ft 8.5 in (1,435)
Axle arrangement: Bo-Bo
Power unit type: Caterpillar 3516 V16
Transmission: Siemens - three-phase
Weight, tonnes: 80
Power rating, hp (kW): 2,100 (1,570)
Design speed, mph (km/h): 75 (120)

machines and allowed NSB to return to Sweden T44 locomotives that it had leased. The fleet was assigned to CargoNet in 2002.

CLASS BM 71 EMU

Flytoget Class BM 71

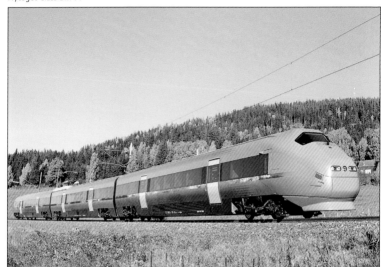

The distinctive Class BM 71 emus were introduced from 1998 to provide a dedicated high-speed service between Oslo and the new airport at Gardermoen, 46 km to the north. They are now operated by the state-owned company Flytoget. The design of these units formed the basis of NSB's Class BM 73 tilting intercity emus.

SUB-TYPES

Norwegian State Railways (NSB) operates 16 Class BM 73 and six Class BM 73B tilting four-car emus based on the design of the BM 71s.

SPECIAL FEATURES

The provision of a fast, dedicated rail service to Gardermoen was essential to the success of the project and precipitated construction of a new 48 km double-track line engineered for 125 mph (200 km/h) running. Construction of the Class BM 71 three-car emus to serve the line was undertaken by Adtranz at its now closed

SPECIFICATION

Number series: 71.001-71.016
Total built: 16
Builder: Adtranz (now Bombardier Transportation)
Date introduced: 1997
Track gauge, ft/ins (mm): 4 ft 8.5 in (1,435)
Unit configuration: M-M-M
Power supply system: 15 kV AC 16.7 Hz
Electrical equipment: Adtranz - three-phase
Power rating, hp (kW): 2,615 (1,950)
Design speed, mph (km/h): 130 (210)
Additional features: regenerative braking

Strømmen plant. The early years of these trains were dogged with running gear problems which restricted them to 100 mph (160 km/h) but these have since been resolved. The BM 71s also serve Asker, 21 km west of the capital. The company operating the trains, Flytoget AS, was originally a subsidiary of NSB but was transferred to the Ministry of Communications in 2003.

CLASS BM 72 EMU

Norwegian State Railways (NSB) Class BM 72

An innovative configuration of running gear characterises NSB's latest emu design, built by Italian manufacturer Ansaldobreda. In 2004 the type was working suburban services around Oslo and Stavanger.

SPECIAL FEATURES

A unique feature of these Italian-built emus for NSB local services is the adoption of self-steering non-powered single axles apart from beneath the cabs, where power bogies are provided. The use of this lightweight running gear, coupled with aluminium bodyshell construction, was expected to lead to a reduction in energy consumption of around 30 per cent compared with the Classes BM 68 and BM 69 units that the new trains were procured to replace. Passenger access is assisted by a low (29.5 in/750 mm) entry and floor height. Seating capacity is for 310. The first-built unit was shipped to Norway minus interior fittings for

SPECIFICATION

Number series: 72001-72036/72101-72136
Total built: 36 (plus 40 on option)
Builder: Ansaldobreda
Date introduced: 2002
Track gauge, ft/ins (mm): 4 ft 8.5 in (1,435)
Unit configuration: M-T-T-M
Power supply system: 15 kV AC 16.7 Hz
Electrical equipment: Ansaldobreda - IGBT control
Power rating, hp (kW): 3,415 (2,550)
Design speed, mph (km/h): 100 (160)
Additional features: regenerative braking, low floor access, air-conditioning

testing but it was not until 2002 that series deliveries began. Initially the type was deployed in the Stavanger area, followed by examples working in Oslo suburban services. The class is also expected to operate around Bergen and Trondheim.

CLASS ET21 ELECTRIC LOCOMOTIVE

Polish State Railways (PKP) Class ET21

Despite a substantial reduction in numbers, this veteran Polish six-axle electric freight locomotive design from the 1950s can still be seen at work on the PKP network and some examples have been given new leases of life with private operators that have taken advantage of open access to the country's rail system.

PRINCIPAL MODIFICATIONS

Some ex-PKP examples in service with industrial operators have been rebuilt and modernised.

SPECIAL FEATURES

Constructed by Pafawag at Wroclaw between 1957 and 1971, PKP's Class ET21 was the railway's standard electric freight locomotive design until production switched to the faster and more powerful ET22. By 2003 around 40 survived in PKP stock on various duties that included occasional passenger work. Most of the survivors

SPECIFICATION

Number series: From ET21-001
Total built: 500 approximately
Builder: Pafawag
Date introduced: 1957
Track gauge, ft/ins (mm): 4 ft 8.5 in (1,435)
Axle arrangement: Co-Co
Power supply system: 3 kV DC
Electrical equipment: Dolmel - resistance control with six nose-suspended DC traction motors
Weight, tonnes: 112
Power rating, hp (kW): 2,490 (1,860) continuous
Design speed, mph (km/h): 62 (100)

were based at Nowy Sacz, southeast of Krakow and at Wroclaw. Other examples have passed to private operators like CTL Polska, which operates chemicals trains both on its own system and on the PKP network.

CLASS ET22 ELECTRIC LOCOMOTIVE

Polish State Railways (PKP) Class ET22

Poland

This six-axle mixed traffic design replaced the ET21 on Pafawag's Wroclaw production line in early 1969 and with 1,183 examples built is now PKP's largest electric locomotive type, forming an important component of the freight traction fleet. In 2003 PKP commenced a programme to modernise some 600 members of the class.

SUB-TYPES

100 mph (160 km/h) Class EP23 passenger version appeared in 1974 but this variant did not enter series production. The prototype reverted to one of the standard series (ET21-121).

PRINCIPAL MODIFICATIONS

A programme to modernise 600 examples of the fleet was started by PKP in 2003. The railway expected to refurbish 50 of the class annually.

SPECIAL FEATURES

ET22 is a standard freight workhorse of PKP. At

SPECIFICATION

Number series: From ET22-001
Total built: 1,183 (may include industrial users)
Builder: Pafawag
Date introduced: 1969
Track gauge, ft/ins (mm): 4 ft 8.5 in (1,435)
Axle arrangement: Co-Co
Power supply system: 3 kV DC
Electrical equipment: Dolmel - resistance control; six spring-borne DC traction motors
Weight, tonnes: 120
Power rating, hp (kW): 4,020 (3,000) continuous
Design speed, mph (km/h): 78 (125)
Additional features: electric train-heating

the beginning of 2003 the railway's cargo subsidiary owned 954, 600 of which were regular use. Small numbers have been sold to industrial operators such as sand railways in Silesia.

OTHER COUNTRIES OPERATED

In 1973 23 similar locomotives were supplied to Morocco (ONCFM Class E-1000).

CLASSES EU07/EP07 ELECTRIC LOCOMOTIVE

Polish State Railways (PKP) Classes EU07 and EP07

The four-axle mixed traffic Class EU07 was licence-built in large numbers from the 1960s to a British design. Subsequently an express passenger variant and a twin-section freight only version were introduced, while some EU07s have been upgraded for passenger-only work to become Class EP07

SUB-TYPES

Twenty Class EU06 locomotives were supplied by AEI, English Electric and Vulcan Foundry in the UK in 1961 to form the basis of the Class EU07 family. Class EP08 (10 examples, right) is a 87 mph (140 km/h) passenger-only version, distinguishable by its orange livery. Class ET41 (200 examples) is a Cegielski-built twin-section 5,360 hp (4,000 kW) development of the EU07 introduced in 1978 for heavy freight traffic.

SPECIFICATION

Number series: EU07-001 - EU07-244; EU07-301 - EU07-542*
Total built: 486
Builder: Pafawag, HCP
Date introduced: 1963
Track gauge, ft/ins (mm): 4 ft 8.5 in (1,435)
Axle arrangement: Bo-Bo
Power supply system: 3 kV DC
Electrical equipment: Dolmel - resistance control with four spring-borne DC traction motors
Weight, tonnes: 80
Power rating, hp (kW): 2,680 (2,000) continuous
Design speed, mph (km/h): 77 (125)
Additional features: multiple-unit control; electric train heating

PRINCIPAL MODIFICATIONS

*Class EP07 are modernised examples of Class EU07. Only the class designation is changed; running numbers remain the same. Upgrading included modified gearing, but not top speed, to reduce demand on the traction motors, albeit with lower tractive effort. The traditional prominent headlights are being replaced by a more modern flush-mounted type.

SPECIAL FEATURES

Elements of contemporary British electric locomotive practice feature in the mechanical design of this important group of Polish mixed traffic machines designed to withstand tough winter conditions. These include spring-borne traction motors with quill drive. Later examples (EU07-301 onwards) from the Cegielski plant in Poznan incorporate a heavier main frame to suit them for automatic couplers and feature ribbed

bodysides but not chrome embellishments. Over 360 Class EU07 and EP07 locomotives remained in PKP stock at the beginning of 2003. They are seen over most of the Polish electrified network, principally on passenger services. Some examples are used by industrial railways in Silesia.

CLASS EP09 ELECTRIC LOCOMOTIVE

Polish State Railways (PKP) Class EP09

This domestically designed express passenger type entered PKP service in the mid-1980s, remaining in production until 1997. The class now handles many of the heavier duties on the network, including international traffic.

SPECIAL FEATURES

Class EP09 was developed by Pafawag in the 1980s in response to PKP requirements for a faster, more powerful locomotive than the EP08 for its principal express passenger services. Series construction followed testing of a prototype machine completed in 1984. The class is recognisable by its distinctive yellow and brown livery. In 2004 35 were based at Warsaw, 12 at Kroakow.

SPECIFICATION

Number series: EP09-001 - EP09-047
Total built: 47
Builder: Pafawag
Date introduced: 1986
Track gauge, ft/ins (mm): 4 ft 8.5 in (1,435)
Axle arrangement: Bo-Bo
Power supply system: 3 kV DC
Electrical equipment: Dolmel
Weight, tonnes: 84
Power rating, hp (kW): (2,920) continuous
Design speed, mph (km/h): 100 (160)
Additional features: changes introduced since production period include air-conditioned cabs and (from EP09-038) windowless doors. Some have single-arm pantographs

CLASS ET42 ELECTRIC LOCOMOTIVE

Polish State Railways (PKP) Class ET42

PKP operates three classes of twin-section electric freight locomotives. The Class ET42 machines represent a rare example of an electric locomotive export by the Soviet Union and are based on that country's domestic designs of the 1970s. They work in central Poland, mainly on coal trains.

SPECIAL FEATURES

High-powered traction requirements for its intensive coal traffic activities lead PKP in the 1970s to procure twin-section electric locomotives from three builders. These included the Soviet manufacturing plant at Novocherkassk, which supplied these machines between 1978 and 1982. Based on the Soviet Railways Class VL10 design, the ET42 features two permanently coupled single-cab sections. The entire class is based at Zdunska Wola Karsznice, near Lodz, and is mainly used on the so-called Coal Main Line from Silesia to Gdynia. At the beginning of 2003 46 examples survived.

SPECIFICATION

Number series: ET42-001 - ET42-050
Total built: 50
Builder: Novocherkassk
Date introduced: 1978
Track gauge, ft/ins (mm): 4 ft 8.5 in
Axle arrangement: Bo-Bo+Bo-Bo
Power supply system: 3 kV DC
Electrical equipment: Novocherkassk - resistance control with eight nose-suspended DC traction motors
Weight, tonnes: 164
Power rating, hp (kW): 6,000 (4,480) continuous
Design speed, mph (km/h): 62 (100)

CLASSES SM42/SP42/SU42 DIESEL LOCOMOTIVES

Polish State Railways (PKP) Classes SM42, SP42 and SU42

Built in large numbers since the 1960s, this Fablok-built single-cab Class SM42 diesel-electric design is a familiar sight on the PKP network. Class SP42 is a passenger version of the type. In recent years examples of both classes have been refurbished as the multi-purpose Class SU42.

PRINCIPAL MODIFICATIONS

Class SU42 are refurbished redundant SM42 with electric train-heating for lighter regional services. *The first 39 examples were rebuilt from SM42 with a low-voltage generator for heating, retaining their original numbers. In 1999-2000 40 SP42s were similarly converted but with a higher rated generator, numbered in the SU42-501 series.

SPECIAL FEATURES

More than 1,000 examples of this shunting and light freight design were produced at the Fablok plant in Chrzanow between 1963 and 1991. At

SPECIFICATION

Number series: From SM42/SP42/SU42-001, SU42-501*
Total built: SM42 - over 1,000 (including non-PKP examples); SP42 - 269; SU42 - 79
Builder: Fablok
Date introduced: 1963; 1970; 197x
Track gauge, ft/ins (mm): 4 ft 8.5 in (1,435)
Axle arrangement: Bo-Bo
Power unit type: HCP 8VCD22T
Transmission: electric - Dolmel, DC generator and four nose-suspended DC traction motors
Weight, tonnes: 72, 70, 72
Power rating, hp (kW): 790 (588)
Design speed, mph (km/h): 56 (90)
Additional features: SP42 - steam generator for train-heating, SU42 - electric train-heating

the beginning of 2003 977 remained in PKP stock. The slightly lighter SP42 passenger version appeared in 1970. Class SU42 locomotives are recognisable by their blue and yellow livery; SM42 and SU42 machines are painted green.

CLASS SU45 DIESEL LOCOMOTIVE

Polish State Railways (PKP) Class SU45

Poland

These medium-powered Fiat-engined diesel-electrics are modernised examples of Class SP45, introduced by PKP in the 1960s to reduce dependence on steam traction. They are used on both passenger and freight services on non-electrified lines, with a light axle-loading that suits them to secondary routes.

PRINCIPAL MODIFICATIONS

Originally Class SP45, these locomotives are examples of the class that underwent an upgrading between 1987-98 that included provision of electric train-heating. Running numbers remained unchanged.

SPECIAL FEATURES

With an axle load of just 16 tonnes, these distinctive and versatile machines handle a variety of lighter duties on the PKP network, including regional passenger services, for which their

SPECIFICATION

Number series: SU45-001 - SU45-265
Total built: 265 as SP45, 191 of which converted to SU45
Builder: HCP
Date introduced: 1967
Track gauge, ft/ins (mm): 4 ft 8.5 in (1,435)
Axle arrangement: Co-Co
Power unit type: Fiat 2112SFF, licence-built by HCP
Transmission: electric - Dolmel, DC generator with six nose-suspended DC traction motors
Weight, tonnes: 96
Power rating, hp (kW): 1,725 (1,287)
Design speed, mph (km/h): 62 (100)
Additional features: multiple-unit operation, electric train-heating

electric train-heating capability is useful. Later-built locomotives feature ribbed rather than flush bodysides. At the beginning of 2003, 157 remained in the PKP fleet.

CLASS SU46 DIESEL LOCOMOTIVE

Polish State Railways (PKP) Class SU46

PKP's most powerful diesel locomotive type is the 2,210 hp (1,659 kW) Class SU46, introduced in 1974 as a development of the SP45. They are mostly used for passenger traffic, but also occasionally appear on freight.

SUB-TYPES

In the mid-1970s two prototype Class SP47 locomotives based on the SP45 design were built. They were rated at 2,240 hp (3,000 kW), with a top speed of 87 mph (140 km/h). Both were withdrawn in the late 1990s.

SPECIAL FEATURES

The first 52 Class SU46 locomotives were built by H Cegielski between 1974 and 1977. Two more featuring detail differences were delivered in 1986. Their uses include cross-border work into Germany between Wegliniec and Horka. At the beginning of 2003 36 remained on the PKP stock list.

SPECIFICATION

Number series: SU46-001 - SU46-054
Total built: 54
Builder: HCP
Date introduced: 1974
Track gauge, ft/ins (mm): 4 ft 8.5 in (1,435)
Axle arrangement: Co-Co
Power unit type: Fiat 2112SSF, licence-built by HCP
Transmission: Dolmel - electric
Weight, tonnes: 102
Power rating, hp (kW): 2,210 (1,650)
Design speed, mph (km/h): 75 (120)
Additional features: multiple-unit control; electric train-heating

CLASS EN57 EMU

Polish State Railways (PKP) Class EN57

Poland

With over 1,100 examples built, the Class EN57 emus are widely used over the PKP electrified network, handling both commuter and longer-distance services.

SUB TYPES

Class EN71 is a four-car version of Class EN57 built in 1976. A further development of the EN71 was the ED72 for medium distance fast regional services. Pafawag built 21 of these, plus one ED73 prototype featuring performance improvements.

PRINCIPAL MODIFICATIONS

In 2002 a refurbishment programme was started, providing them with substantially improved interiors. Other examples have received new cabs, altering their front-end appearance with two windows rather than three.

SPECIAL FEATURES

Basic by today's standards, these three-car emus

SPECIFICATION

Total built: 1,134
Builder: Pafawag
Date introduced: 1962
Track gauge, ft/ins (mm): 4 ft 8.5 in (1,435)
Unit configuration: T-M-T
Power supply system: 3 kV DC
Electrical equipment: Dolmel - resistance control, four DC traction motors
Power rating, hp (kW): 815 or 940 (610 or 700)
Design speed, mph (km/h): 68 (110)

continue to play a vital role for Przewozy Regionalne (Regional Services) subsidiary. Other examples are used by PKP SKM, the division of the national operator running commuter services in the Gdańsk, Sopot and Gdynia area. Between 1962 and 1991 no fewer than 1,134 examples were placed in service by PKP. Most Class EN57s carry a blue and yellow colour scheme but some SKM units are in a cream, black and red livery.

CLASS EW58 EMU

Polish State Railways (PKP) Class EW58

This small fleet of high-density three-car commuter emus was built exclusively for the PKP SKM network serving the Gdánsk, Sopot and Gdynia area, which carries nearly 40 million passengers annually. Trains use 19 miles (31 km) of dedicated tracks alongside the PKP main line. The design has not proved successful, and in 2003 few remained in service.

SPECIAL FEATURES

A comparatively high power rating together with a 75 mph (120 km/h) top speed characterise these Pafawag-built commuter emus employed in much reduced numbers on PKP's SKM network serving the Baltic coast communities of Gdánsk, Sopot and Gdynia, where rapid acceleration and sprints between stops are required. Performance is further complemented by rheostatic braking. Also reflecting the high-density nature of the services

SPECIFICATION

Number series: EW58-001 - EW58-028
Total built: 28
Builder: Pafawag
Date introduced: 1975
Track gauge, ft/ins (mm): 4 ft 8.5 in (1,435)
Unit configuration: M-T-M
Power supply system: 3 kV DC
Electrical equipment: Dolmel
Power rating, hp (kW): 2,210 (1,650)
Design speed, mph (km/h): 75 (120)
Additional features: rheostatic braking

they operate, EW58s have three pairs of doors per side. They are finished in a red and cream colour scheme.

1400 CLASS DIESEL LOCOMOTIVE

Portuguese Railways (CP) 1400 Class

Poland/Portugal

The first British diesel export order to mainland Europe, the steeple-cab 1400 Class has been numerically the largest diesel class seen in Portugal. Although designed for all duties, it is now primarily seen on local freight workings.

SPECIAL FEATURES

In a serious attempt to rid Portuguese Railways of residual steam power, ten 1400 Class Bo-Bos were ordered from the UK, before fleet production was switched to Portugal, and the locomotives were assembled under licence at Sorefame, Lisbon. Technically, they bear a close resemblance to the once 228-strong Class 20 design used in the United Kingdom, including the distinctive whistling sound of the turbocharger. Until recently, a regular performer on the peak hour suburban passenger services out of Porto Sao Bento station, the '1400s' are reduced to much more menial duties and suffering withdrawals of accident-damaged examples. Split evenly between

SPECIFICATION

Number series: 1401-1467
Total built: 67
Builder: 1401-1410 - English Electric, UK, 1411-1467 - Sorefame, Portugal
Date introduced: 1966
Track gauge, ft/ins (mm): 5 ft 6 in (1,668)
Axle arrangement: Bo-Bo
Power unit type: English Electric 8 CSVT
Transmission: English Electric generator and four nose-suspended DC traction motors
Weight, tonnes: 64
Power rating, hp (kW): 1,000 (746)
Design speed, mph (km/h): 65 (105)
Additional features: dual air/vacuum brakes on some locomotives, inter-class multiple working

the inter-regional and regional (UVIR) and freight and logistics (UTML) sectors, they are seen throughout the country. They have regular duties along the Douro Valley. 1453 is restored to historic blue livery, but prototype 1401 has been scrapped.

1901/1931 CLASS DIESEL LOCOMOTIVE

Portuguese Railways (CP) 1901/1931 Class

These two diesel types are classic examples of the massive French export drive of the latter part of the 20th century, where a broadly standard design was modified for specialist use. At a time when investment capital was in short supply, only a small number of new locomotives of both types could be justified.

SUB-TYPES

1901-1913 are specifically geared for freight traffic, and 1931-1947 for mixed traffic duties.

SPECIAL FEATURES

Built under licence from Alsthom, France, the 1901 series is designed specifically for freight haulage, and the 1931 for mixed traffic working. This has been achieved by the use of different designs of traction motor (TAO 659 C1 for 1901, TAO 659 P for 1931). The external appearance is clearly French with the raked back cab. The early

SPECIFICATION

Number series: 1901-1913/1931-1947
Total built: 30
Builder: Sorefame under Alsthon licence
Date introduced: 1981
Track gauge, ft/ins (mm): 5 ft 6 in (1,668)
Axle arrangement: Co-Co
Power unit type: SACM AGO V12 DSHR
Transmission: Alstom - alternator and six nose-suspended DC traction motors
Weight, tonnes: 117
Power rating, hp (kW): 3,020 (2,240)
Design speed, mph (km/h): 1901-1913 - 62 (100), 1931-1947 - 75 (120)
Additional features: air brakes, multiple operation. 1901-1913 only - dynamic braking

career of 1901-1913 was dogged by power unit failures, while the 1931-1947 series suffered bogie fires, and while both types continue to play a front line role, many of the routes they have operated on have either been electrified or lost their core traffic to other transport modes.

1961 CLASS DIESEL LOCOMOTIVE

Portuguese Railways (CP) 1961 Class

The Portuguese 1961 Class is an export version of a standard MLW design with twin cabs and a full width body. The provision of train heating equipment was to allow them to handle the domestic leg of international services to Paris, displacing UK-built 1800 Class, but they are now considered second-string.

SPECIAL FEATURES

At the time of its introduction in 1979, the 1961 Class was the most powerful diesel locomotive type in Portugal, but was quickly overshadowed by the French-designed 1901/1931 Class assembled two years later. Prototype 1961 was lost in a collision on the Beria-Alta line, and the balance are normally seen in the north of the country, on passenger or freight services. Following electrification of the Beria-Alta route, they have been seen worked more in the north of the country, including cement and mixed freight

SPECIFICATION

Number series: 1961-1973
Total built: 13
Builder: MLW (now Bombardier), Montreal
Date introduced: 1979
Track gauge, ft/ins (mm): 5 ft 6 in (1,668)
Axle arrangement: Co-Co
Power unit type: MLW (now Bombardier)
Transmission: General Electric
Weight, tonnes: 115
Power rating, hp (kW): 2,270 (1,680)
Design speed, mph (km/h): 75 (120)
Additional features: electric train-heating, multiple working within class

trains in the Douro Valley and Minho lines. Privatisation may see examples sold to contractors.

2551 CLASS ELECTRIC LOCOMOTIVE

Portuguese Railways (CP) 2551 Class

The pioneering use of a stainless steel bodyshell on a powered locomotive vastly improved the power-to-weight ratio of the 2551 Class, which is regarded as having a long-term future despite the higher cost of maintenance. However, several have been lost in mishaps.

SPECIAL FEATURES

An agreement with the Budd company of Philadelphia, USA in 1955, allowed Portugal train maker Sorefame to construct vehicles with stainless steel bodies, including the 2551 Class locomotives, offering a three tonne weight saving on earlier designs. The survivors work passenger and freight services but lack electric train heating equipment to handle modern coaching stock. Two were quickly written-off in accidents, a third has been rebuilt with a conventional steel bodyshell, but mishaps in 2003 continued to take their toll.

SPECIFICATION

Number series: 2551-2570
Total built: 20
Builder: Sorefame
Date introduced: 1963
Track gauge, ft/ins (mm): 5 ft 6 in (1,668)
Axle arrangement: Bo-Bo
Power supply system: 25kV AC 50 Hz
Electrical equipment: ACEC, AEG, Alsthom, Brown Boveri, Oerlikon, MTE, Siemens - tap-hanger control with 4 x Alsthom TAO-645 A1 fully suspended DC traction motors
Weight, tonnes: 71
Power rating, hp (kW): 1,960 (2,650)
Design speed, mph (km/h): 75 (120)
Additional features: dual air/vacuum brakes, multiple working equipment

0601 CLASS DMU

Portuguese Railways (CP) 0601 Class

Stainless steel-bodied dmus were constructed on a regular basis for Portuguese rail services for 35 years until 1990. All have a broadly similar outline, and the 0601 series has been the mainstay of Algarve and Porto non-electrified services for the last quarter of a century.

SPECIAL FEATURES

The first 20 of the 0601 series were originally two-car units with two power cars. However, the second batch of six sets constructed from 1989 onwards were equipped with centre trailers, and similar vehicles were ordered at the same time to augment the earlier units. They are seen all over the country on regional services, with the original series allocated to Campolide, Setubal, Faro and Contumil, and the later batch working around the Lisbon area. 0654 has been written after collision damage, and a major refurbishment programme may take place to align them with other vehicles of the same vintage.

SPECIFICATION

Number series: 030601-030620, 030651-030656
Total built: 26
Builder: Sorefame
Date introduced: 1979
Track gauge, ft/ins (mm): 5 ft 6 in (1,668)
Unit configuration: M-T-M
Power unit type: SFAC
Transmission: Voith - hydraulic
Power rating, hp (kW): 380 (280)
Design speed, mph (km/h): 75 (120)

2101/2201 CLASS EMU

Portuguese Railways (CP) 2101/2201 Class

SPECIAL FEATURES

Once their refurbishment has been completed the 2101/2201 class are easily identified from older types by their revamped red fibreglass front ends and long bodyside windows.

The contract, awarded in 2000 to Alstom, provides for brand new Onix traction equipment (relocated under the floor) with new disc brakes. The interiors have been redesigned with air conditioning and revised seating areas, which include spaces for wheelchairs and bicycles. They are employed on suburban and stopping services over a number of routes, including Lisbon-Tomar/Faro, Coimbra-Porto/Vila Formoso, Sado-Sul, Barreiro-Setubal and Entroncamento-Castelo Branco.

SPECIFICATION

Number series: 2101-2124/2151-2186/ 2201-2215
Total built: 57
Builder: Sorefame
Date introduced: 1962
Track gauge, ft/ins (mm): 5 ft 6 in (1,668)
Unit configuration: Bo-Bo+2'2'+2'2'
Power supply system: 25kV AC 50 Hz
Electrical equipment: GEC Alstom Onix three-phase traction motors
Power rating, hp (kW): 1,730 (1,280)
Design speed, mph (km/h): 75 (120)
Additional features: air-conditioning, passenger information systems, security cameras

ESTORIL EMU

Portuguese Railways (CP) Estoril emu

The Estoril Railway from Lisbon Cais do Sodre station to Cascais is a busy, almost self-enclosed suburban system along the picturesque coast, and has enjoyed brief bursts of investment over the years. The mainstay of motive power has for many years been three-car emus.

SPECIAL FEATURES

The Estoril Railway was completely re-equipped from 1950 onwards, first with three-car units from Cravens of Sheffield (UK), and then with similar stock from domestic builder Sorefame over two decades. All have GEC traction equipment imported from the UK. Refurbishment of 34 units (3112-3124, 3201-3214) is taking place at Entroncamento Works at a third of the cost of new construction, also extending their lives by up to 30 years. They are being equipped with new front ends with an ergonomic driving position, modern interiors and dynamic braking and public

SPECIFICATION

Number series: 3101-3124, 3201-3222
Builder: 3101-3111 - Cravens (UK), 3112-3124, 3201-3222 - Sorefame
Date introduced: 3101-3111 - 1950, 3112-3124, 3201-3222 - 1959
Track gauge, ft/ins (mm): 5 ft 6in (1,668)
Unit configuration: T-M-T
Power supply system: 1.5 kV DC
Electrical equipment: GEC
Power rating, hp (kW): 1,469 (1,088)
Additional features: Multiple working

address. The rebuilding of the trains is leading to a change of unit formation, with build types now intermixed.

3400 CLASS EMU

Portuguese Railways (CP) 3400 Class

The latest emu type to operate in Portugal was delivered to CP from 2002 for Porto area suburban services. These articulated 25 kV AC units are to form the basis of DC-only and dual-voltage versions for commuter service on other parts of the Portuguese network.

SUB-TYPES

CP's contract included options covering up to 10 five-car 1.5 kV DC and up to 10 five-car dual-voltage versions of this type for Lisbon area services.

SPECIAL FEATURES

Construction of the 3400 Class emus was shared between Siemens, which provided traction and auxiliary equipment, HVAC systems and automatic couplers, and Bombardier, responsible for carbody construction and running gear. The design combines elements of Siemens' Desiro family and Bombardier's Itino vehicle concept and was

SPECIFICATION

Number series: 3401-3434
Total built: 34
Builder: Siemens Transportation Systems (as consortium leader), Bombardier Transportation
Date introduced: 2002
Track gauge, ft/ins (mm): 5 ft 6 in (1,668)
Unit configuration: M-T-T-M
Power supply system: 25 kV AC 50 Hz
Electrical equipment: Siemens
Power rating, hp (kW): 2,280 (1,700)
Design speed, mph (km/h): 87 (140)
Additional features: Jacobs-type articulated intermediate bogies, air-conditioning, GSM-controlled communications and diagnostics

developed to achieve economical operation and low energy consumption. Assembly took place at Bombardier's Amadora plant in Lisbon. Bodyshells are of stainless steel and the units are articulated, with only the leading bogies powered. In the Porto area the new trains have taken over from older emus and also serve newly electrified lines.

9500 CLASS DMU

Portuguese Railways (CP) 9500 Class

Portugal

The closure of the metre-gauge network radiating from Porto for conversion into a mixture of electrified tramway and suburban railway has now only left a few remote narrow gauge branches, and the withdrawal of the final diesel locomotives leave them all with dmus.

SPECIAL FEATURES

Of the two principal classes of metre-gauge dmu remaining in Portugal, the Class 9501s are a rebuild of units already purchased second-hand in 1980 from Yugoslavian Railways and originally designated 9700 Class. They are normally seen on branches off the Douro Valley line. Allocated to UVIR (inter-city and regional sector), they are maintained at depots at Regua and Mirendela, and four carry names, Lisboa, Bruxelas, Paris, and Strasburgo. Formerly the most common design of railcar, the now displaced 9600 series built by Alstom from 1976, have attracted interest from

SPECIFICATION

Number series: 9501-9509
Total built: 9
Builder: EMEF
Date introduced: 1996
Track gauge, ft/ins (mm): 3ft 3.375in (1,000)
Transmission: Voith - hydraulic
Power rating, hp (kW): 240 (180)
Design speed, mph (km/h): 52 (84)

countries as diverse as Argentina, Vietnam and Madagascar.

FERTAGUS 3500 CLASS EMU

Portugal 3500 Class

18 four-car double-deck electric multiple-units were ordered from Adtranz, CAF and GEC Alstom by Fertagus to operate from Lisbon over the River Tagus via the 25 April bridge.

SPECIAL FEATURES

These trains work over the Eixo Norte-Sul line between Lisbon Entrecampos and the south bank of the river Tagus, via the Ponte 25 de Abril (25 April Bridge), the rail deck of which opened in 1999. Although currently only a short line, it is to link Oriente station in Lisbon with the southern Portuguese main line, which currently runs from Barreiro ferry terminal to the Alentejo and Algarve regions. The units have a passenger capacity of 1,310 (484 seated), and their original blue and white livery has been covered over by advertising. Portuguese Railways (CP) ordered a similar series of 12 units for its Lisboa-Azabuja suburban service, and a boom in traffic for both

companies prompted consideration of a further new joint order for Lisbon suburban lines, enabling production costs to be kept down. The CP units also may get a centre trailer.

CLASS 80 and 81 DIESEL LOCOMOTIVES

Romanian State Railways (CFR) Class 80 and 81

Seen throughout the Romanian network, this medium-powered single-cab diesel-hydraulic design was built in large numbers from the mid-1960s. Examples were built with and without train-heating equipment and a variant with electric transmission was also produced.

SUB-TYPES

Class 84 and 88 are broad (5 ft 0 in/1,520 mm) gauge locomotives of this type for border area operations in eastern Romania. Classes 69 and 73 are diesel-electric versions of the design; 28 examples were supplied to CFR from 1975.

PRINCIPAL MODIFICATIONS

In 1999 four Class 80/81 locomotives were refurbished and re-engined by Alstom in collaboration with Romanian industry.

SPECIAL FEATURES

Originally designated Class 040 DHC, 632 of these

SPECIFICATION

Total built: 632 (for CFR)
Builder: August 23
Date introduced: 1966
Track gauge, ft/ins (mm): 4 ft 8.5 in (1,435)
Axle arrangement: B-B
Power unit type: Sulzer 6LDA28-B
Transmission: hydraulic - Voith
Weight, tonnes: 68
Power rating, hp (kW): 1,235 (920)
Design speed, mph (km/h):
Additional features: Class 80 has steam train-heating equipment

medium-powered diesel-hydraulic locomotives were delivered by the August 23 plant in Bucharest to CFR between 1966 and the early 1980s. They see widespread use for both freight and passenger traffic, Class 80s having been built with steam train-heating equipment. Many are believed to be out of service due to a traction surplus resulting from a general decline in CFR traffic.

CLASS 60 and 62 DIESEL LOCOMOTIVES

Romanian State Railways (CFR) Class 60 and 62

Designed in Switzerland, where main line diesel locomotives are virtually unknown, and adopted as a standard by the Romanian national network, this classic design became one of the most numerous types of this form of traction to be produced in Europe. Between 1960 and the early 1990s some 2,500 examples were built.

CFR still uses these locomotives and has begun to modernise some. Others have found their way into various parts of Europe, while exported examples of variants of the type remain active in China.

SUB-TYPES

Two machines were constructed in the 1980s with domestically licence-built Alco 251 series engines, becoming Class 61. Small numbers of locomotives designated Classes 67 (62 mph gearing) and 68 (75 mph) were built for 5 ft 0 in (1,520 mm) gauge cross-border operation into the former Soviet network. As well as the 1,413 locomotives

supplied to CFR, Electroputere delivered 162 examples to industrial users in Romania, including one twin-unit locomotive supplied to a power station at Craiova.

PRINCIPAL MODIFICATIONS

In 1999, two examples were substantially rebuilt with General Motors eight-cylinder Series 710 engines with the same rating as the original 'donor' locomotives and an alternator/rectifier traction package. Successful experience led CFR in 2003 to authorise 57 similar conversions, designated Class 63. The rebuilding, carried out jointly by Electroputere and General Motors, includes provision of a new bodyshell.

SPECIAL FEATURES

Originally designated Class 060-DA, this was Romania's first main line diesel-electric type. Developed by the Swiss rail industry for CFR, the first six were assembled by SLM and Brown Boveri

and featured a 12-cylinder version of the Sulzer LDA28 twin-bank four-stroke engine. Ten more locomotives were supplied to Electroputere, Craiova, which continued production under licence for CFR until 1981 and other users until 1993. The builder designated the type LDE 2100. Inevitably variations occur in such a large fleet, the most significant adoption from 1968 of 75 mph (120 km/h) gearing in some examples (now Class 62). The CFR fleet has been depleted by retirements, disposals and conversions to Class 63.

OTHER COUNTRIES OPERATED

Outside Romania the customer taking the largest number (422) was Polish State Railways, where examples survive as Class ST43. A further 130 went to Bulgarian State Railways (BDZ Class 06), while Chinese Railways received 373 based on this design which became Classes ND2 and ND3. A sharp decline in CFR traffic in the 1990s created enough of a traction surplus for the

SPECIFICATION

Total built: 1,413 (for CFR)
Builder: SLM/Brown Boveri, Electroputere
Date introduced: 1959 (Romania 1960)
Track gauge, ft/ins (mm): 4 ft 8.5 in (1,435)
Axle arrangement: Co-Co
Power unit type: Sulzer 12LDA28
Transmission: electric - Brown Boveri, Electroputere, DC generator, DC traction motors
Weight, tonnes: 116
Power rating, hp (kW): 2,070 (1,545)
Design speed, mph (km/h): Class 60 - 62 (100); Class 62 - 75 (120)
Additional features: some equipped for multiple-unit operation

establishment of a locomotive disposal subsidiary, SAAF. As a result, small numbers of this type have found new operators in Germany, Iran, Italy and Spain. Karsdorfer Eisenbahn in Germany has 20 ex-Romanian machines (above).

CLASS 40, 41 AND 45 ELECTRIC LOCOMOTIVES

Romanian State Railways (CFR) Class 40, 41 and 45

Developed from a contemporary Swedish design, this important family of powerful six-axle rectifier electric locomotives is the principal motive power on the Romanian electrified network. Locally-built examples were also exported to neighbouring Bulgaria and Yugoslavia.

PRINCIPAL MODIFICATIONS

One member of Class 40 or 41 was modified in the 1970s with 125 mph (200 km/h) bogies, becoming the sole example of Class 42. From 1999 a modernisation programme covering 24 Class 40 and 41s was initiated for CFR's passenger division, upgraded machines becoming Class 45. Modifications include new control and diagnostics equipment, multiple-unit control, push-pull equipment, and gearing for 100 mph (160 km/h).

SUB-TYPES

Two examples of a thyristor-controlled 80 mph

SPECIFICATION

Total built: 932
Builder: Swedloc, Electroputere
Date introduced: 1965
Track gauge, ft/ins (mm): 4 ft 8.5 in (1,435)
Axle arrangement: Co-Co
Power supply system: 25 kV AC 50 Hz
Electrical equipment: ASEA, Electroputere - tap-changer control, silicon rectifiers, fully suspended DC traction motors
Weight, tonnes: 120-126
Power rating, hp (kW): 6,835 (5,100) continuous
Design speed, mph (km/h): Class 40 - 75 (120); Class 41/45 - 100 (160)
Additional features: rheostatic braking; some Class 40 ballasted to 126 tonnes

(130 km/h) Class 46 freight version of the design were built in the 1980s but this variant did not enter series production.

CLASS ChS4T ELECTRIC LOCOMOTIVE

Russian Railways (RZhD) Class ChS4T

Class ChS4T is one of several electric passenger locomotive designs supplied to Soviet Railways by Skoda, in the former Czechoslovakia. More than 500 of these silicon rectifier machines were built, most remaining in Russia after the Soviet Union was dismantled.

SUB-TYPES

Of similar appearance is RZhD Class ChS4T, a 3 kV DC version of this design.

SPECIAL FEATURES

With Soviet electric locomotive plants mainly committed to the production of freight machines during the 1960s and 1970s, the Ministry of Railways turned to the former Czechoslovakia for its passenger traction needs. Class ChS4T was procured for express passenger services on AC lines and was a development of the fibreglass-bodied ChS4 design built from 1965. The later design featured here reverted to steel body

construction, some featuring flush sides, others ribbed. Mostly used in the west of Russia, Class ChS4T is primarily used on passenger services, albeit at speeds lower than the design maximum of 112 mph.

OTHER COUNTRIES OPERATED

Examples are also active in Belarus.

SPECIFICATION

Number series: ChS4T-001 – ChS4T-510
Total built: 510
Builder: Skoda
Date introduced: 1971 (prototype); 1973 (series production)
Track gauge, ft/ins (mm): 5 ft 0 in (1,524)
Axle arrangement: Co-Co
Power supply system: 25 kV AC 50 Hz
Electrical equipment: Skoda - silicon rectifiers, fully suspended DC traction motors
Weight, tonnes: 126
Power rating, hp (kW): 6,590 (4,920) continuous
Design speed, mph (km/h): 112 (180)
Additional features: rheostatic braking

CLASS ChS200 ELECTRIC LOCOMOTIVE

Russian Railways (RzHD) Class ChS200

Introduction in the late 1970s of the Skoda-built ChS200 signalled a switch to eight-axle twin-section designs for subsequent electric passenger locomotives for Soviet Railways.

SUB-TYPES

Class ChS6 was a development with lower gearing. It is also a 3 kV DC design, as is the ChS7, which employs features of the ChS200 and of the ChS4T. The ex-Soviet Czech-built twin-section electric passenger family is completed by the ChS8/ChS8T, a 25 kV AC version of the ChS7.

PRINCIPAL MODIFICATIONS

In the 1990s the surviving ChS200 locomotives underwent refurbishment and modernisation at Skoda's Plzen plant in the Czech Republic.

SPECIAL FEATURES

The need for greater haulage power on the Moscow-St Petersburg route led to the

SPECIFICATION

Number series: ChS200-001 - ChS200-012
Total built: 12
Builder: Skoda
Date introduced: 1975 (prototypes); 1979 (series production)
Track gauge, ft/ins (mm): 5 ft 0 in (1,524)
Axle arrangement: Bo-Bo+Bo-Bo
Power supply system: 3 kV DC
Electrical equipment: Skoda - rheostatic control with eight fully suspended DC traction motors
Weight, tonnes: 156
Power rating, hp (kW): 10,720 (4,000) continuous
Design speed, mph (km/h): 135 (220)
Additional features: rheostatic braking, electric train-heating

development of two prototypes. Completed in 1975, these were a development of the company's ES499.0 for Czechoslovak State Railways (now Slovakian Railways Class 350) design with high-performance bogies and suspension.

CLASSES VL10/VL10U ELECTRIC LOCOMOTIVES

Russian Railways (RZhD) Classes VL10 and VL10U

With nearly 3,000 examples built since 1961, the twin-section VL10/VL10U was the successor to the earlier VL8 and still plays a vital role in freight operations of the DC lines of Russian Railways.

SUB-TYPES

The Tbilisi-built VL11 family was a derivative of the VL10 design. The Class VL80 and VL82 families are the AC-only and dual-voltage equivalents of the VL10 and are of similar appearance.

PRINCIPAL MODIFICATIONS

In 2003 Class VL10 locomotives were undergoing modernisation at RZhD's Chelyabinsk workshops.

SPECIAL FEATURES

The twin-section VL10 did not enter series production until 1967, when the Tbilisi plant in Georgia ceased manufacture of the VL8. Incorporating some 25 per cent more power than its predecessor, the VL10 continued to be built at

SPECIFICATION

Number series: VL10-001 - VL10-1907; VL10U-001- VL10U-1030
Total built: 2,882 (total production)
Builder: Novocherkassk, Tbilisi
Date introduced: VL10 - 1961; VL10U - 1974
Track gauge, ft/ins (mm): 5 ft 0 in (1,524)
Axle arrangement: Bo-Bo+Bo-Bo
Power supply system: 3 kV DC
Electrical equipment: Novocherkassk, Tbilisi - resistance control with eight nose-suspended traction motors
Weight, tonnes: VL10 - 184; VL10U - 200
Power rating, hp (kW): 6,165 (4,600)
Design speed, mph (km/h): 62 (100)
Additional features: regenerative braking

Tbilisi until 1977. In addition, 1,010 examples were built at Novocherkassk between 1969 and 1976. Class VL10U, introduced in prototype form in 1974-75, differs mainly in being ballasted to increase the axle-load to 25 tonnes to raise tractive effort. This version was also built at both Novocherkassk and Tbilisi.

CLASSES VL60K/VL60PK ELECTRIC LOCOMOTIVES

Russian Railways (RZhD) Class VL60K/VL60PK

Europe

The six-axle VL60 was the Soviet Union's first series-built domestic AC electric locomotive type. Over 2,600 were built at Novocherkassk between 1962 and 1968. Subsequent modifications to rectifier equipment and to meet new operational needs spawned several sub-classes.

SUB-TYPES

Class 2VL60K was created from 1987 by the semi-permanent pairing of two VL60Ks.

SPECIAL FEATURES

The VL60s, which first appeared as two Class N60 prototypes in 1957, featured mercury arc rectifiers. These proved unsuccessful and from 1962 were progressively replaced with silicon rectifiers, receiving the designation Class VL60K. The VL60P (later VL60PK) higher-geared passenger version appeared in 1965, while other VL60Ks were also reclassified to meet a shortage of passenger traction on AC lines.

SPECIFICATION

Total built: 2,612 (total production)
Builder: Novocherkassk
Date introduced: VL60K - 1962; VL60PK - 1965
Track gauge, ft/ins (mm): 5 ft 0 in (1,425)
Axle arrangement: Co-Co
Power supply system: 25 kV AC 50 Hz
Electrical equipment: Novocherkassk - silicon rectifiers and six nose-suspended DC traction motors
Weight, tonnes: 138
Power rating, hp (kW): 5,425 (4,050) continuous
Design speed, mph (km/h): VL60K - 62 (100); VL60PK - 68 (110)
Additional features: multiple working; VL60PK - electric train-heating

OTHER COUNTRIES OPERATED

Members of the Class VL60 family are also active in Kazakhstan and Uzbekistan.

CLASS VL65 ELECTRIC LOCOMOTIVE

Russian Railways (RZhD) Class VL65

The first passenger locomotive design to be built at Novocherkassk for some 60 years, the VL65 was delivered from 1992. Production was limited, however, as Russian Railways sought to take advantage of the latest three-phase asynchronous traction technology.

SPECIAL FEATURES

Production of the VL65 ceased after delivery of 48 examples, enabling Novocherkassk to concentrate on the Class EP10 three-phase development of the design. The VL65s are used on RZhD's East Siberian, North Caucasian and Transbaikal lines.

SPECIFICATION

Number series: VL65-001 - VL65-048
Total built: 48
Builder: Novocherkassk
Date introduced: 1992
Track gauge, ft/ins (mm): 5 ft 0 in (1,524)
Axle arrangement: Bo-Bo-Bo
Power supply system: 25 kV AC 50 Hz
Electrical equipment: Novocherkassk
Power rating, hp (kW): 6.270 (4,680)
Design speed, mph (km/h): 75 (120)

CLASS VL80 FAMILY ELECTRIC LOCOMOTIVES

Russian Railways (RZhD) Classes VL80K, VL80T, VL80R and VL80S

Along with the contemporary six-axle VL60s, the twin-section VL80 electric locomotive in its various versions has dominated freight traffic on Soviet and now Russian AC lines for over three decades.

SUB-TYPES

Classes VL82 and VL82M are dual-voltage versions of the VL80 built in small numbers (24 and 67 respectively) between 1966 and 1979. Several experimental prototypes based on the VL80 were built to test technologies such as thyristor control and asynchronous traction motors and Class VL81, VL83 and VL84 prototypes evaluated the benefits of fully suspended traction motors but did not enter series production. Class VL10 and VL10U families are the DC-only equivalents of the VL80 family, and of similar appearance.

SPECIFICATION

Total built: VL80K - 718; VL80T - 1,073; VL80R - 373; VL80S - 2,600+ (figures indicate total production)
Builder: Novocherkassk
Date introduced: VL80K- 1963; VL80T - 1967; VL80R - 1967; VL80S - 1979
Track gauge, ft/ins (mm): 5 ft 0 in (1,524)
Axle arrangement: Bo-Bo+Bo-Bo
Power supply system: 25 kV AC 50 Hz
Electrical equipment: Novocherkassk - silicon rectifiers with eight nose-suspended DC traction motors
Weight, tonnes: VL80K/VL80T - 184; VL80R/VL80S - 192
Power rating, hp (kW): 7,930 (5,920) continuous
Design speed, mph (km/h): 68 (110)
Additional features: VL80T/VL80S - rheostatic braking; VL80R - regenerative braking; VL80S multiple working

CLASS VL85 ELECTRIC LOCOMOTIVE

Russian Railways (RZhD) Class VL85

Introduced in the mid-1980s for freight haulage on some of the former Soviet Railways' most difficult routes, including the Baikal-Amur line in Siberia, the VL85 delivers a massive continuous output of 12,540 hp (9,360 kW). Each of the twin sections of the locomotive is carried on three two-axle bogies.

SUB-TYPES

Classes VL15 and VL15S, built at Tbilisi, are DC versions of the VL-85.

SPECIAL FEATURES

The VL-85 was developed by the former Soviet Railways to provide an effective alternative to double-heading with Class VL80 machines, especially on demanding lines in harsh climatic conditions. The adoption of three two-axle bogies for each of the two sections of the locomotive was driven by the improved dynamic qualities of this arrangement compared with a Co-Co layout and regenerative rather than rheostatic braking avoids the damaging effect of the latter's heat dissapation in tunnels in permafrost areas. At least 245 are reported to have been built.

SPECIFICATION

Builder: Novocherkassk
Date introduced: 1983
Track gauge, ft/ins (mm): 5 ft 0 in (1,524)
Axle arrangement: Bo-Bo-Bo+Bo-Bo-Bo
Power supply system: 25 kV AC 50 Hz
Electrical equipment: Novocherkassk - silicon rectifiers, with 12 fully suspended DC traction motors
Weight, tonnes: 288
Power rating, hp (kW): 12,540 (9,360)
Design speed, mph (km/h): 68 (110)
Additional features: regenerative braking, multiple operation

CLASS EP10 ELECTRIC LOCOMOTIVE

Russian Railways (RZhD) Class EP10

At the time of writing existing only in prototype form, the dual-system Class EP10 represents a new generation of Russian passenger electric locomotives, incorporating asynchronous traction equipment supplied by Bombardier Transportation.

PRINCIPAL MODIFICATIONS

Class EP2 (3 kV DC only) and Class EP3 (25 kV AC only) versions of this design are projected as part of a modular family of four- and six-axle derivatives.

SPECIAL FEATURES

Mechanically derived from the earlier VL65, the dual-system EP10 incorporates the latest Western European three-phase asynchronous technology. Equipment for a prototype machine was supplied by Adtranz before its acquisition by Bombardier, resulting in EP10-001 emerging in 1998. After testing at the Scherbinka test track near Moscow,

SPECIFICATION

Number series: EP10-001
Total built: 1 (nine more on order in 2004)
Builder: Novocherkassk
Date introduced: 1998
Track gauge, ft/ins (mm): 5 ft 0 in (1,524)
Axle arrangement: Bo-Bo-Bo
Power supply system: 25 kV AC 50 Hz/3 kV DC
Electrical equipment: Bombardier Transportation - GTO control equipment and three-phase asynchronous traction motors
Power rating, hp (kW):
Design speed, mph (km/h): 100 (160)

the prototype began service trials in August 2002 on the Moscow-Rostov-Adler line, which features both AC and DC power supply systems. Traction equipment for nine series-built machines was ordered from Bombardier in December 2003, with delivery of completed locomotives expected in 2004-05. They are destined for service on the Moscow-Nizhniy Novgorod line.

CLASS TEM2 FAMILY DIESEL LOCOMOTIVE

Russian Railways (RZhD) Class TEM2 family

Series-built at the Bryansk and Lugansk plants from 1967, the type remains a familiar sight in yards in Russia and other ex-Soviet republics.

SUB-TYPES

During fleet production, various experimental versions were produced, including locomotives with alternative power units, rheostatic braking and electro-magnetic adhesion equipment. From 1989 production at Bryansk switched to the TEM2UM and TEM2UMT models. These retain the Penza engine but have traction equipment improvements.

SPECIAL FEATURES

Developed from the earlier TEM1, prototypes of this basic shunting type appeared in 1960-61 but it was not until 1967 that series production began in earnest at Bryansk. This was followed one year later by first deliveries from Lugansk. Detailed changes were incorporated in the TEM2A, which

SPECIFICATION

Total built: unconfirmed
Builder: Bryansk, Lugansk
Date introduced: 1960 (prototypes); 1967 (series production)
Track gauge, ft/ins (mm): 5 ft 0 in (1,524)
Axle arrangement: Co-Co
Power unit type: Penza PD1 six-cylinder four-stroke
Transmission: electric - six ETM nose-suspended traction motors
Weight, tonnes: TEM2/TEM2A - 120; TEM2U - 124
Power rating, hp (kW): 1,185 (883)
Design speed, mph (km/h): 62 (100)

first appeared in 1969, while TEM2U, which features both mechanical and traction equipment improvements, appeared in prototype form in 1978 before entering production from 1984. 9,000 examples are believed to have been built.

CLASS TEP70 DIESEL LOCOMOTIVE

Russian Railways (RZhD) Class TEP70

Soviet Railways' successor to the TEP60 on the Kolomna production lines as its front-line express passenger diesel was the AC/DC TEP70. Deliveries of the latest version of this design were still being made in 2003. Examples can also be found on other ex-Soviet networks.

SUB-TYPES

Two 5,920 hp (4,418 kW) Class TEP75 prototypes partly based on the design of the TEP70 and powered by a 20-cylinder Kolomna engine were delivered in 1976 and 1977. This type did not enter series production.

SPECIAL FEATURES

Developed to meet a requirement for a more powerful diesel locomotive than the TEP60 and less costly to operate than its twin-section 2TEP60 variant, the TEP70 first appeared in prototype form in 1973. Trials led to detail improvements that were introduced in the production machines,

SPECIFICATION

Total built: unconfirmed
Builder: Kolomna
Date introduced: 1973
Track gauge, ft/ins (mm): 5 ft 0 in (1,524)
Axle arrangement: Co-Co
Power unit type: Kolomna 2A-5D49 V16 four-stroke
Transmission: electric - alternator with six ETM DC fully suspended traction motors
Weight, tonnes: 129
Power rating, hp (kW): 3,945 (2,944)
Design speed, mph (km/h): 100 (160)
Additional features: rheostatic braking

built by Kolomna from 1978. The class is used on express passenger services in various parts of the Russian network.

OTHER COUNTRIES OPERATED

TEP70s are also used in Kazakhstan, Latvia, Lithuania and Ukraine.

CLASS 2M62/2M62U DIESEL LOCOMOTIVES

Russian Railways (RZhD) Classes 2M62 and 2M62U

Developed from the proven M62 (featured in the Hungary section), this twin-section diesel-electric design was a response by the Lugansk plant to a demand from Soviet Railways for increased pulling power for both freight and passenger traffic. The improved 2M62U was still in production in the 1990s and a triple-section version is also in use.

SUB-TYPES

Class 3M62U is a triple section version of this design; at least 99 examples are reported to have been built.

SPECIAL FEATURES

The 2M62 was created by the simple expedient of semi-permanently coupling two M62 locomotives built with cabs at one end only. Production took place at Lugansk between 1976 and 1987, when the improved 2M62U was introduced. This version features bogies with better dynamic and traction

SPECIFICATION

Number series: 2M62-0001 - 2M62-1261, from 2M62U-0001
Total built: 1261; 355+ (figures indicate total production)
Builder: Lugansk
Date introduced: 1976; 1987
Track gauge, ft/ins (mm): 5 ft 0 in (1,524)
Axle arrangement: Co-Co+Co-Co
Power unit type: Kolomna 14D40 12-cylinder two-stroke
Transmission: electric - DC generator and 12 ETM DC traction motors
Weight, tonnes: 240; 252
Power rating, hp (kW): 3,940 (2,940)
Design speed, mph (km/h): 62 (100)

performance and increased fuel capacity, contributing to a higher axle-loading of 21 tonnes. At least 355 2M62Us are known to have been built but with the Lugansk works located in Ukraine, Russian orders for the type diminished in favour of domestic models after the break-up of the Soviet Union.

CLASS 2TE116 DIESEL LOCOMOTIVE

Russian Railways (RZhD) Class 2TE116

This Lugansk product for Soviet Railways saw a switch to AC/DC transmission to produce a successful high-powered twin-section freight unit that remains a key element of Russian Railways' diesel traction fleet.

SUB-TYPES

Experimental variants included Class 2TE116M with rheostatic braking and Class 3TE116G triple-section gas-powered prototype. A single section export version was supplied to the former East Germany (now DB Classes 232, 233 and 234) and Bulgaria (BDZ Class 07).

SPECIAL FEATURES

For the 2TE116, Lugansk employed a 16-cylinder version of the four-stroke 5D49 engine rather than the two-stroke 14D40 power unit used in the earlier M62 locomotive family. Coupled with the adoption of AC/DC transmission, this delivered

SPECIFICATION

Number series: 2TE116-001
Total built: approximately 1,700 (total production)
Builder: Lugansk
Date introduced: 1971
Track gauge, ft/ins (mm): 5 ft 0 in (1,524)
Axle arrangement: Co-Co+Co-Co
Power unit type: Kolomna 1A-5D49/1A-5D49-2 16-cylinder four-stroke
Transmission: electric - AC alternator and 12 ETM nose-suspended DC traction motors
Weight, tonnes: 276
Power rating, hp (kW): 6,030 (4,500)
Design speed, mph (km/h): 62 (100)

a powerful heavy freight machine that was in production from 1971 until beyond the separation of the Soviet Union. The type remains in widespread use in Russia, sharing duties with the more numerous 2TE10 locomotive family of similar configuration.

CLASS ER2R/ER2T EMU

Russian Railways (RZhD) Classes ER2R and ER2T

Included as an example of Russian emu practice, these 3 kV DC units (left in picture) provide commuter services on various parts of the country's network

SUB-TYPES

Class ER2T features differences in its electrical equipment and electric braking system. The appearance of these units is similar to that of later versions of the ER9 family of 25 kV AC emus, also built by RVR.

SPECIAL FEATURES

Like most Soviet-era emus, these vehicles were designed and built at the RVR plant in Riga. They are a development of the very numerous ER2 units and feature thyristor control and electric braking. Unit lengths of 10 or twelve cars are formed by the inclusion of motor and trailer pairs of intermediate cars. The class can be seen on various parts of the Russian 3 kV DC network.

SPECIFICATION

Number series: ER2R - 7001-7089; from ER2T - 7090
Total built: 89; unconfirmed
Builder: RVR, Riga
Date introduced: 1979; 1987
Track gauge, ft/ins (mm): 5 ft 0 in (1,524)
Unit configuration: five or six M-T pairs to form 10- or 12-car sets
Power supply system: 3 kV DC
Electrical equipment: REZ - thyristor control with DC traction motors
Power rating, hp (kW): 1,285 (960) per M-T pair
Design speed, mph (km/h): 80 (130)
Additional features: multiple working within and between types; rheostatic and regenerative braking

CLASS 125.8 ELECTRIC LOCOMOTIVE

Slovakian Railways (ZSSK) Class 125.8

ZSSK's small fleet of twin-section Class 125.8 electric locomotives operate freight services over a short section of broad gauge line that penetrates Slovakia from Ukraine.

SPECIAL FEATURES

Class 125.8s were supplied by Skoda to serve the 54 mile (87 km) 5 ft 0 in (1,520 mm) coal and iron ore line from Uzghorod, Ukraine, via the Slovakian border station of Cierna nad Tisou to a steelworks at Haniska, south of Kosice. One of two classes of twin-section electrics built for the former Czechoslovak State Railways (the other is the standard gauge ZSSZ Class 131), they are fairly conventional DC machines designed solely for heavy freight traffic. Trains are usually hauled by two twin-section locomotives, with banking from a third needed on some sections of the line. Most of the class remained in service in 2004.

SPECIFICATION

Number series: 125.801-125.844 (each locomotive section individually numbered)
Total built: 22
Builder: Skoda
Date introduced: 1976
Track gauge, ft/ins (mm): 5 ft 0 in (1,520)
Axle arrangement: Bo-Bo+Bo-Bo
Power supply system: 3 kV DC
Electrical equipment: Skoda - rheostatic control with eight nose-suspended DC traction motors
Weight, tonnes: 170
Power rating, hp (kW): 5,465 (4,080) continuous
Design speed, mph (km/h): 56 (90)
Additional features: rheostatic braking, Soviet-style knuckle couplers

CLASS 425.95 EMU

Slovakian Railways (ZSSK) Class 425.95

Introduced in 2001, these Swiss-designed emus equip ZSSK's electrified metre-gauge network serving the High Tatras mountains in central Slovakia.

SUB-TYPES

In 2003 the first of six standard gauge diesel-powered Class 480 railcars based on the GTW 2/6 concept was delivered to ZSSK, also for service in the High Tatras. These feature more streamlined front-end styling.

SPECIAL FEATURES

These metre-gauge emus are representatives of the innovative Type GTW 2/6 lightweight railcar developed for local and regional services by the Swiss manufacturer Stadler. The vehicle's configuration comprises a centre powered module, in which there is no passenger accommodation, flanked by articulated driving trailers. These Slovakian examples were assembled

domestically by the EMU GTW-Vysoké Tatry consortium, entering service in 2001 on the metre-gauge system running from Poprad into the High Tatras. Their introduction led to the retirement of Class 420.95 units dating from the 1960s.

SPECIFICATION

Number series: 425.951–425.9514
Total built: 14
Builder: EMU GTW-Vysoké Tatry consortium (Stadler, Adtranz, ZOS Vrútky)
Date introduced: 2001
Track gauge, ft/ins (mm): 3 ft 3.375 in (1,000)
Unit configuration: T-M-T
Power supply system: 1.5 kV DC
Electrical equipment: Adtranz - GTO control, three-phase traction motors
Power rating, hp (kW): 805 (600)
Design speed, mph (km/h): 50 (80)
Additional features: aluminium bodyshell, multiple working

CLASS 342 ELECTRIC LOCOMOTIVE

Slovenian Railways Class 342

Now in the twilight of their careers, these successful Italian-built four-axle electric locomotives have fulfilled a useful mixed traffic role initially on the Yugoslav network and subsequently in Slovenia. In 2003 some members of the class found a new owner in their country of origin.

SPECIAL FEATURES

Using contemporary Italian technology, 40 of these machines were supplied to the former Yugoslav Railways between 1968 and 1971 to handle mixed traffic duties on the country's 3 kV DC lines. All passed to SZ when it came into existence in 1992 but their role subsequently diminished with falling traffic and many were put into store. In 2003 SZ agreed to sell eight to North Milan Railway (FNME) after refurbishment at its Ljubljana-Moste workshops.

SPECIFICATION

Number series: 342-001 - 342-040
Total built: 40
Builder: Ansaldo, OMFP
Date introduced: 1968
Track gauge, ft/ins (mm): 4 ft 8.5 in (1,435)
Axle arrangement: Bo-Bo
Power supply system: 3 kV DC
Electrical equipment: Ansaldo - rheostatic control, four fully suspended DC traction motors
Weight, tonnes: 76
Power rating, hp (kW): 3,055 (2,280)
Design speed, mph (km/h): 75 (120)
Additional features: rheostatic braking; multiple working (believed isolated on some)

OTHER COUNTRIES OPERATED

The eight examples sold to FNME in 2003 became Class E640 and were destined to work international freight services between the Milan area and Domodossola for onward movement to the Swiss network.

CLASS 644 DIESEL LOCOMOTIVE

Slovenian Railways (SZ) Class 644

Slovenia

Class 644 is one of several diesel-electric designs supplied to the former Yugoslav Railways by General Motors or company licensees in Europe. All passed to SZ, where their axle arrangement makes them a useful machine for secondary lines.

PRINCIPAL MODIFICATIONS

Steam train-heating equipment removed.

SPECIAL FEATURES

Construction of the Class 644 locomotives was undertaken by Macosa in Spain under GM licence as that company's G22U model, with a non-turbocharged 645 series engine. Ownership of all 25 passed to the Slovenian system when it was established in 1992. With a central carrying axle in each bogie, they are especially useful on SZ's secondary lines, where they now undertake mostly freight duties.

SPECIFICATION

Number series: 644-001 - 644-025
Total built: 25
Builder: Macosa (GM licence)
Date introduced: 1973
Track gauge, ft/ins (mm): 4 ft 8.5 in (1,435)
Axle arrangement: A1A-A1A
Power unit type: General Motors 12-645E
Transmission: electric - General Motors DC generator and four nose-suspended DC traction motors
Weight, tonnes: 89
Power rating, hp (kW): 1,650 (1,230)
Design speed, mph (km/h): 75 (120)
Additional features: dynamic brakes

OTHER COUNTRIES OPERATED

Various versions of the General Motors G22 family are in service in many countries.

CLASS 813.100/814.100 DMU

Slovenian Railways Class 813.100/814.100

These Fiat-built dmus dating from the 1970s have been refurbished to provide a distinctive vehicle for regional and local services in Slovenia.

SUB-TYPES

Not all have been refurbished.

SPECIAL FEATURES

These vehicles are refurbished examples of an original fleet of 29 dmus acquired from Fiat by the former Yugoslav Railways between 1973 and 1976. Their original design was based on that of the ALn 668 units being supplied to Italian State Railways at the time. A modernisation programme was started at the TVT plant in Maribor in 1988, although some vehicles remained to be treated in 2003. Refurbished units feature new cabs of more modern appearance and carry a 1xx suffix to their fleet numbers.

SPECIFICATION

Total built: 29
Builder: Fiat
Date introduced: 1973
Track gauge, ft/ins (mm): 4 ft 8.5 in (1,435)
Unit configuration: M-T
Power unit type: Fiat
Transmission: Mechanical
Power rating, hp (kW): 395 (295)
Design speed, mph (km/h): 62 (100)
Additional features: multiple working

OTHER COUNTRIES OPERATED

Similar vehicles operate in Italy as members of the ALn 668 family.

CLASS 250 ELECTRIC LOCOMOTIVE

Spanish National Railways (RENFE) Class 250

These large C-C electric locomotives were built in Spain in the mid-1980s using well-established Krauss-Maffei and Brown Boveri technology. Originally for mixed traffic use, but they are now almost exclusively employed on freight services all over the country.

SUB-TYPES

250.6 is a small sub-class of five locomotives built 1986–1988 with minor external differences and chopper control.

SPECIAL FEATURES

Like many French locomotive types, Class 250's monomotor bogies and switchable gear ratios offer high tractive effort for freight work in 'PV' low gear (62 mph - 100 km/h maximum) or higher speed (100 mph - 160 km/h), but lower starting power for passenger work. Today, the 40 locomotives are split between RENFE's Cargas (general freight) and Transporte Combinado

(intermodal) sectors and can be seen on the busy Valencia-Barcelona corridor.

SPECIFICATION

Number series: 250 001-035, 250 601-605
Total built: 40
Builder: Krauss-Maffei/Brown Boveri/CAF/MTM
Date introduced: 1982
Track gauge, ft/ins (mm): 5 ft 6 in (1,668)
Axle arrangement: C-C
Power supply system: 3kV DC
Electrical equipment: BBC
Weight, tonnes: 124
Power rating, hp (kW): 6,200 (4,600)
Design speed, mph (km/h): 100 (160)
Additional features: electric train supply, monomotor bogies with two switchable gear ratios

CLASS 251 ELECTRIC LOCOMOTIVE

Spanish National Railways (RENFE) Class 251

RENFE's Class 251 are extremely unusual in Europe, being based on a Mitsubishi B-B-B design for Japanese National Railways. The appearance is distinctly Far Eastern, and they are allocated (with the exception of the first built) to the freight sector.

SPECIAL FEATURES

Outwardly the heritage of Class 251 locomotives is obvious as they closely resemble JR Freight locomotives. RENFE's Cargas sector uses these powerful machines on heavy freight, particularly steel trains, from the industrialised north-east of Spain around León and Oviedo. Their high tractive effort in low gear (349 kN) is particularly useful for hauling heavy trains over the steep gradients in the Pajares mountains in this area. The locomotives also reach Madrid on freights from the north-east.

SPECIFICATION

Number series: 251.001-251.030
Total built: 30
Builder: Melco (Mitsubishi)/CAF/Macosa
Date introduced: 1982
Track gauge, ft/ins (mm): 5 ft 6 in (1,668)
Axle arrangement: B-B-B
Power supply system: 3 kV DC
Electrical equipment: Melco
Weight, tonnes: 138
Power rating, hp (kW): 6,250 (4,650)
Design speed, mph (km/h): 100 (160)
Additional features: electric train supply, monomotor bogies with two switchable gear ratios

OTHER COUNTRIES OPERATED

The locomotive is based on the Japanese Class EF66.

CLASS 269 ELECTRIC LOCOMOTIVE

Spanish National Railways (RENFE) Class 269

Class 269 is the most versatile and numerous of Spanish locomotive types. Batches have different characteristics for specific duties. Designed in Japan, its introduction followed the success of the earlier Classes 279 (16 units) and 289 (40 units) built for dual voltage (3 kV/1.5kV dc) operation.

SUB-TYPES

269.001-269.113 - standard type, for freight;

269.201-269.522 - higher top speed;

269.601-269.604 - streamlined body;

269.901-269.923 - regeared for Grandes Líneas 'Estrella' overnight services.

SPECIAL FEATURES

Designed by Mitsubishi and assembled in Spain, Class 269 has been re-organised in recent years, and renumbering takes place when locomotives are rebuilt and transferred to another sub-class. The original Class 269.0, now increased from 108 to 113, has lost its passenger work. The top speed

SPECIFICATION

Number series: 269.001-269.108, 269.201-269.321, 269.401-269.420, 269.501-269.522, 269.601-269.604, 269.901-269.923
Total built: 265
Builder: CAF, Macosa (under licence from Mitsubishi)
Date introduced: 1973
Track gauge, ft/ins (mm): 5 ft 6 in (1,676)
Axle arrangement: B-B
Power supply system: 3 kV DC
Electrical equipment: Cenemesa/Westinghouse/General Electric
Weight, tonnes: 88
Power rating, hp (kW): 4,185 (3,100)
Design speed, mph (km/h): 269.0 - 62/85 (100/140), 269.2, 269.6 - 62/100 (100/160), 269.4 - 100 (160), 269.5 - 56/100 (90/160), 269.6 - 125 (200), 269.9 - 85 (140)
Additional features: rheostatic braking, multiple working within class

capability dictates the role of the other types, and the most refined version is the four-strong Class 269.6, built in 1980/81 with streamlined cabs and later modernised to run at 125 mph (200 km/h).

CLASS 252 ELECTRIC LOCOMOTIVE

Spanish National Railways (RENFE) Class 252

RENFE's most modern electric locomotives are these Siemens-designed three-phase machines built in both broad gauge versions for 'classic' lines and as standard gauge variants to operate over Spain's high-speed network. They are derived from the German Class 120.

SUB-TYPES

Three versions of Class 252 are in service with RENFE: standard gauge dual-voltage; broad gauge dual-voltage and broad gauge DC only.

SPECIAL FEATURES

Class 252 is a representative of Siemens first generation EuroSprinter three-phase electric locomotive design, a development of the German Class 120. The first 15 were standard gauge machines built in Germany for use with Talgo coaching stock on RENFE's high-speed line between Madrid and Seville; four were subsequently converted to broad gauge. Two

further batches for broad gauge operations were licence-built in Spain by CAF (15 dual-voltage) and GATSA (45 3 kV DC) between 1993 and 1996. Standard gauge locomotives carry AVE livery also used by RENFE's Class 100 high-speed trainsets. Some broad gauge examples bear the Altaria and Arco colour schemes of RENFE long distance passenger subsidiaries, others are in the operator's yellow and charcoal livery.

OTHER COUNTRIES OPERATED

The Class 127 15 kV prototype locomotive on which Class 252 was based remains in Germany in the Siemens Dispolok hire pool. Similar locomotives are in Greece (24 OSE Class 120, formerly H 560, including locomotives on order) and Portugal (30 CP Class 5600) (right). German Rail Class 152 and its derived version for Korea (Korean National Railroad Class 8100) are second generation members of the EuroSprinter family.

SPECIFICATION

Number series: 252.001-252.075
Total built: 75
Builder: Siemens, CAF, GATSA
Date introduced: 1992
Track gauge, ft/ins (mm): 11 locomotives - 4 ft 8.5 in (1,435); remainder - 5 ft 6 in (1,668)
Axle arrangement: Bo-Bo
Power supply system: 252.001-252.031 - 25 kV AC 50 Hz/3 kV DC; 252.032-252.075 - 3 kV DC
Electrical equipment: Siemens - GTO thyristor converters, three-phase asynchronous traction motors
Weight, tonnes: 89 (3 kV DC-only locomotives - 87)
Power rating, hp (kW): 7,500 (5,600) continuous
Design speed, mph (km/h): 136 (220)
Additional features: rheostatic braking; bogies exchangeable between standard and broad gauge locomotives; 252.001-252.031 equipped with LZB cab signalling

CLASS 319 DIESEL LOCOMOTIVE

Spanish National Railways (RENFE) Class 319

The first major order awarded to General Motors by RENFE, Class 319 has been much-modified since its introduction in 1965, with changes, variously, to the power equipment, bogies and even external body design. The class has now settled down to three distinct sub-types.

SUB-TYPES

319.2 - new body, traction motors and generator, no train-heat, some altered to standard gauge for the Malaga-Sevilla high-speed line; 319.3 - new engine, electric train heat; 319.4 - new engine, no train heat, GM control equipment.

SPECIAL FEATURES

Originally the 1900 Class, the original ten '319s' were American imports with a single cab and steam generator inside the hood. However, the nine survivors have now been rebuilt and integrated into the same sub-class as the Valencia-produced examples which have a full-width body and two cabs. Extensive

SPECIFICATION

Number series: 319.201-319.257, 319.301-319.338, 319.401-319.410
Total built: 104
Builder: General Motors, USA/Macosa, Valencia
Date introduced: 1965
Track gauge, ft/ins (mm): 5 ft 6 in (1,676)
Axle arrangement: Co-Co
Engine: 319.2 - GM 16-657C, 319.3, 319.4 - GM 16-645E
Transmission: Electric, D77 traction motors
Weight, tonnes: 319.2 - 110, 319.3 - 119, 319.4 - 116
Power rating, hp (kW): 319.2 - 1,605 (1,190), 319.3 and 319.4 - 1,850 (1,372)
Design speed, mph (km/h): 319.2 and 319.4 - 75 (120), 319.3 - 87 (140)

rebuilding commenced in 1984, and with Class 319.2 the body was restyled halfway through the programme. Class 319.3 has been re-engined, but the installation of train-heat equipment left them underpowered. Lessons were learned from this mistake to improve the small and final no-heat Class 319.4 series.

CLASS 333 DIESEL LOCOMOTIVE

Spanish National Railways (RENFE) Class 333

The value of the Class 333 on Spanish Railways is demonstrated by the decision in 2002 to rebuild the already 28-year-old design with completely new bodyshells, bogies, and electrical equipment.

SUB-TYPES

333.0 - original design; 333.1 - new bogies, higher speed, unmodernised; 333.2 - new bogies, higher speed, modernised; 333.3 - modernised, new bodywork; 333.4 – Class 333.3 upgraded for passenger service

SPECIAL FEATURES

At its introduction, Class 333 was the most powerful locomotive in the fleet, but it lost this title to Class 354 in 1982. Built to a Scandinavian design with General Motors power units, they are seen all over the country, and continue to be upgraded. Of similar layout to the Danish Railways Class Mz, the '333' was assembled in Spain with an engine imported from North America, and electrical components from MTM.

SPECIFICATION

Number series: 333.001-333.093, 333.101-333.108, 333.201-333.204, from 333.301, 333.401-333.406
Total built: 93
Builder: Macosa (under licence from GM/Nohab)
Date introduced: 1974
Track gauge, ft/ins (mm): 5 ft 6 in (1,676)
Axle arrangement: Co-Co
Engine: GM 16-645 E3
Transmission: Electric. MTM
Weight, tonnes: 120
Power rating, hp (kW): 4,515 (3,345)
Design speed, mph (km/h): 333.0 - 95 (150), 333.1, 333.2 - 100 (160), 333.3 - 75 (120), 333.4 - 90 (145)
Additional features: multiple working

From 1994 onwards, four of the class were extensively rebuilt (Class 333.2), with new bogies for higher speed, while examples of the standard design were also upgraded with new bogies (Class 333.1). A 25-year life extension programme has begun with a complete new bodyshell and rearrangement of internal equipment.

349

CLASS 354 DIESEL LOCOMOTIVE

Spanish National Railways (RENFE) Class 354

These unusual locomotives are the third and final generation of low-profile diesel-hydraulics designed exclusively for use with Talgo's patent coaching stock. Although more modern locomotives are now freely available, Class 354s are being retained because of their high level of reliability.

SPECIAL FEATURES

Considerably more powerful than their predecessors, the '354s' were built to run at 200km/h with later variants of the Talgo coaching stock family, including the passive-tilt fitted Talgo Pendular. They operate on routes radiating from Madrid, mainly to the north and east of Spain on lines that have not yet been electrified. Although the older and less energetic Class 352s and 353s are now being retired and replaced by more conventional diesels such as Class 319 and 333, the '354s' remain busy.

SPECIFICATION

Number series: 354.001-354.008
Total built: 8
Builder: Krauss-Maffei
Date introduced: 1983/84
Track gauge, ft/ins (mm): 5ft 6in (1,668)
Axle arrangement: B-B
Power unit type: 2 x MTU 396TD13-16
Transmission: Voith L-520 rz U2 hydraulic
Weight, tonnes: 80
Power rating, hp (kW): 3,050 (2,250)
Design speed, mph (km/h): 125 (200)
Additional features: low-profile to match Talgo coaching stock

CLASSES 462, 463, 464 AND 465 EMU

Spanish National Railways (RENFE) Classes 462, 463, 464 and 465

Known as the Civia, this is the latest emu to enter service with RENFE, commencing operations in 2003. Future orders for these state-of-the-art commuter vehicles are expected to create a 248-strong class.

SUB-TYPES

Two-, three-, four- and five-car units are designated/to be designated Classes 462, 463, 464 and 465 respectively.

SPECIAL FEATURES

The need to replace older emu types such as Class 440 led RENFE to develop this design, known as the Civia, in partnership with its suppliers. The initial order was for 14 trains, comprising 11 four-car and three two-car units. A modular concept also enables Civia units to be supplied as three- and five-car sets according to operational needs. The trains' articulated configuration and lightweight construction, together with the efficiencies of a modern

SPECIFICATION

Number series: 462.001-462.003; 464.001-464.511
Total built: 3 Class 462; 11 Class 464 (plus 80 units on order in 2003)
Builder: Alstom, Bombardier, CAF, Siemens
Date introduced: 2003
Track gauge, ft/ins (mm): 5 ft 6 in (1,668)
Unit configuration: M-M; M-T-T-M
Power supply system: 3 kV DC
Electrical equipment: Alstom, Siemens - IGBT control with six three-phase traction motors
Design speed, mph (km/h): 75 (120)
Additional features: articulated, aluminium alloy bodyshells, low-floor entrance, full-width gangways, real time passenger information system

traction system, yield energy consumption savings of up to 50 per cent compared with equivalent recent designs. In October 2003 RENFE ordered 80 more Class 464s, 40 from Alstom and 40 from CAF/Siemens, all for delivery by 2007.

CLASS 1900 ELECTRO-DIESEL LOCOMOTIVE

Spanish Narrow-Gauge Railways (FEVE) Class 1900

Converted from an Alsthom diesel-electric design, FEVE's Class 1900 machines can operate autonomously on diesel power or as under electric traction from an overhead supply. Their duties include haulage of the prestigious Transcantábrico luxury train.

SPECIAL FEATURES

Main line locomotives that can operate from an electric power supply or using a diesel engine are comparatively rare. FEVE's first examples of this type appeared in 2002, created from former Class 1050 Alsthom-built single-cab diesel-electric locomotives. Apart from the bogies and frames, little remained of the 10 donors after conversion, which was undertaken by Sunsundegui of Alsasua in conjunction with FEVE. The programme was completed in 2004. The versatility of the Class 1900s enables them to operate under FEVE's 1.5 kV DC system of electrification or autonomously

SPECIFICATION

Number series: 1901–1910
Total built: 10
Builder: Sunsundegui
Date introduced: 2002
Track gauge, ft/ins (mm): 3 ft 3.975 in (1,000)
Axle arrangement: Bo-Bo
Power supply system: 1.5 kV DC
Electrical equipment: Siemens - IGBT converters, three-phase asynchronous traction motors
Power unit type: Caterpillar 3512B 12-cylinder four-stroke
Weight, tonnes: 60
Power rating, hp (kW): 1,515 (1,130)
Design speed, mph (km/h): 56 (90)
Additional features: multiple working

on diesel power, primarily handling freight services. However, the class also hauls the Transcantábrico luxury train and locomotive 1901 is painted in this train's livery.

CLASS 1600/1650 DIESEL LOCOMOTIVE

Spanish Narrow-Gauge Railways (FEVE) Class 1600/1650

Spain

State-owned FEVE (Ferrocarriles de Vía Estrecha), established in 1965 to operate Spain's extensive network of narrow gauge lines relies heavily on a small fleet of modern Bo-Bo locomotives comprising Class 1600 (single cab), and Class 1650 (twin-cab).

SPECIAL FEATURES

FEVE, whose management has been devolved to regional governments, works its motive power fleet hard because of a massive upturn in business, primarily freight. Class 1600 and Class 1650 have a punishing routine, particularly the steel trains which run between Aviles, Bilbao and Donostia, for which they are expected to haul loads of up to 500 tonnes single-handed up 1 in 50 gradients. Following problems with unreliability, the entire class is receiving new Caterpillar 3512-B power units as they become due for heavy overhaul. This will lead to massive fuel savings.

SPECIFICATION

Number series: 1601-1614, 1651-1660
Total built: 24
Builder: MTM (under licence from Alsthom)
Date introduced: Class 1600 - 1982, Class 1650 - 1985
Track gauge, ft/ins (mm): 3 ft 3.975 in (1,000)
Axle arrangement: Bo-Bo
Power unit type: SACM-MGO V16
Transmission: Electric, Alsthom
Weight, tonnes: Class 1600 - 58, Class 1650 - 60
Power rating, hp (kW): 1,590 (1,177)
Design speed, mph (km/h): 55 (90)
Additional features: multiple working

CLASS 213 EMU

Ferrocarrils de la Generalitat de Catalunya (FGC) Class 213

Services in the Barcelona area have been considerably improved since their management was transferred to FGC in 1979, and new rolling stock continues to be ordered. Class 213 entered service in 1999 following electrification of the Martorell-Igualada line.

SPECIAL FEATURES

FGC had already gained valuable experience with Alstom electrical equipment in its train sets when it ordered Class 213. This came from 16 Type 112 four-car emus ordered for the Catalunya i Sarria line in 1995 to replace older types.

The '213' is of similar format with three-phase traction motors, and its centre trailer vehicle has a low-floor section to facilitate boarding from simple platforms. The original batch of seven units will be boosted by an order for a further 13.

SPECIFICATION

Total built: 20
Builder: CAF/Alstom
Date introduced: 1999
Track gauge, ft/ins (mm): 3ft 3.975 in (1,000)
Unit configuration: M-T-M
Power supply system: 1.5 V DC
Electrical equipment: ABB three-phase traction motors
Power rating, hp (kW): 1,920 (1,440)
Design speed, mph (km/h): 55 (90)

CLASS T44 DIESEL LOCOMOTIVE

Green Cargo Class T44

Spain/Sweden

The standard Swedish centre-cab GM-powered heavy haul and shunt locomotive was built in large numbers over a period of ten years, and followed experience with an earlier (Class T43) design. A number are now operated by private companies.

SPECIAL FEATURES

The familiar GM 12-645E power unit was chosen for the final design of Swedish Bo-Bo diesel locomotive, and the three batches constructed exhibited only minor design changes. The original series has been upgraded with safety rails on the running plate, and most of the later series (and a few of the early batches) are fitted with radio control, bringing with it a reclassification 'T44R'. The 'T44' deisgn has also formed the basis for 20 Class Tb and Tc single-cab locomotives, which are effectively self-operating snowploughs, which feature retractable novel underslung turntable equipment that enables them to be turned round in any location.

SPECIFICATION

Number series: T44.259-T44.416
Total built: 123
Builder: Nohab
Date introduced: 1968
Track gauge, ft/ins (mm): 4 ft 8.5 in (1,435)
Axle arrangement: Bo-Bo
Engine: General Motors GM 12-645E
Transmission: Electric, GM EMD Type D77 traction motors
Weight, tonnes: 76
Power rating, hp (kW): 1,670 (1,235)
Design speed, mph (km/h): 95 (70)
Additional features: Multiple working with Classes 42, Tb and Tc

OTHER COUNTRIES OPERATED

Two former Swedish Class T44 have been employed by an iron ore operator LKAB in Norway, in which the SJ has a financial interest. Others are hired on an occasional basis. Israel Railways also operates a solitary example of the type.

CLASS Rc ELECTRIC LOCOMOTIVE FAMILY

Swedish Railways (SJ)/Green Cargo Class Rc1/Rc2/Rc3/Rc4/Rc6/Rm

The most dominant electric locomotive type in Scandinavia won substantial export orders and, with derived versions working as far afield as North America and Iran. Although equipment upgrades have been made over the years, the basic design has remained in place for over 40 years.

SUB-TYPES

Rc2 - higher gear ratio and tractive effort; Rc3 - express passenger type; Rc4 - upgraded electronics; Rc6 - further upgrade, better driver's cab; Rm - Lower gearing, central couplings for ore trains.

PRINCIPAL MODIFICATIONS

Some Class Rc1 have radio control equipment for heavy shunting. Class Rc2 is being progressively converted to Rc3 to allow higher speed running. All Rc5 are converted to Rc6 for the same reason.

SPECIAL FEATURES

The Rc class is based on the Rb, whose six 1962 prototypes (1001-1006, now all scrapped) pioneered the use of thyristor rectifiers, which eliminated the maintenance-heavy transformer and reduced wheel slipping. They dominated principal Swedish passenger services until the late 1980s when the most important routes radiating from Stockholm and Goteborg were upgraded for high speed tilting trains, and economies on regional routes also saw them replaced by emus. The passenger sector owns Classes Rc3 and Rc6. Others are employed on services operated by SJ's freight subsidiary, Green Cargo, and are progressively receiving an attractive green livery, while several others have been hived off to private concerns. The ten Austrian Railways Class 1043s, which are identical to the Rc2s, have been acquired for use by Swedish infrastructure authority BV, and the TGOJ and Tågab companies.

OTHER COUNTRIES OPERATED

After successful trials with Swedish prototypes 1001 and 1002, Class Rc locomotives were sold to Austria (Class 1043), Iran (Class 40-700RCH), Norway (Class El.16 - four of which are now owned by TGOJ, Sweden) and the USA (Amtrak and MARC Class AEM-7 (above) and the broadly similar NJ Transit Class ALP-44). A similar version of the design, but incorporating silicon rectifiers rather than thyristors, is covered in the entry for the Croatian Railways Class 1141.

SPECIFICATION

Number series: Rc1- 1007-1026, Rc2 and Rc3 - 1027-1056/1064-1136/1198/1255, 1043.001-1043.10, Rc4 - 1137-1200/1251-1256/1263-1322, Rc6 - 1323-1422, Rm - 1257-1262
Total built: 376
Builder: Nohab/ASJ/Motala/Hägglunds
Date introduced: 1967
Track gauge, ft/ins (mm): 4 ft 8.5 in (1,435)
Axle arrangement: Bo-Bo
Power supply system: 15kV AC 16.7 Hz
Electrical equipment: ASEA traction motors
Weight, tonnes: Rc1 - 80, Rc2, Rc3 - 77, Rc4, Rc6 - 78, Rm - 92
Power rating, hp (kW): 4,860 (3,600)
Design speed, mph (km/h): Rc1, Rc2, Rc4 - 85 (135), Rc 3, Rc 6 - 100 (160), Rm - 62 (100)
Additional features: thyristor control, multiple working

CLASS X2 EMU

Swedish Railways (SJ) Class X2

As well as successfully reviving Swedish intercity business, the X2 emu solved the problem of trying to operate fast trains on routes with severe curves. Adtranz (now Bombardier) developed this tilting train, which set a Swedish speed record of 148 mph (238 km/h) on test runs in 1993.

SUB-TYPES

Secondary routes are served by a shortened version, the X2-2. Within the main series, some units are equipped to take power from the Danish 25 kV supply and are designated X2K, while those that work to Norway are sub-class X2N or X2NK.

SPECIAL FEATURES

The X2 is the country's flagship train, having slashed Stockholm-Göteborg journey times to three hours and increased business tenfold. Since completion of the Øresund fixed link, they offer a fast service south into Denmark. Seven units (with four trailers) were repainted in a blue, red and

SPECIFICATION

Number series: 2001-2043
Total built: 43 power cars, plus driving trailers and coaches
Builder: Adtranz (now Bombardier)
Date introduced: 1990
Track gauge, ft/ins (mm): 4 ft 8.5 in (1,435)
Unit configuration: M-T (plus variable number of intermediate trailers)
Power supply system: 15 kV AC 16.7 Hz (Class X2K and X2NK also equipped for 25 kV AC 50 Hz)
Electrical equipment: four bogie-mounted asynchronous traction motors
Power rating, hp (kW): 4,400 (3,260)
Design speed, mph (km/h): 125 (200)
Additional features: tilt mechanism, automatic train control, high specification interior, conference cabin

yellow livery for services between Stockholm-Karlstad-Oslo and Göteborg-Malmö-Kobenhavn. In the early days the X2 had some problems - when the train ran over small track defects it caused the train to tilt incorrectly.

CLASS X50 EMU FAMILY

Swedish Railways Class X50/X51/X52/X53/X54

In summer 2001, Bombardier introduced the Regina series of emus for regional and local services in Sweden. The stainless steel-bodied trains are assembled in Västerås, and the first operator to run the train was Västmanlands Länstrafik (VL), a nearby operator.

SUB-TYPES

X50 - VL (Västmanlands Lokaltrafik); UL (Upplands Lokaltrafik); X51 - Tåg i Bergslagen, X-Trafik; X52 - SJ, Transitio; X53 - Västtrafik, Värmlandstrafik, X54 - VL..

SPECIAL FEATURES

There are five variations of the new electric unit: X50–X54, which work for Swedish State Railways and many other businesses operating services under contract to regional transport authorities. These units are mainly owned by these authorities and carry local branding, concealing the identities of their operators who include BK Tåg and TKAB, as well as SJ, while other vehicles are owned by

SPECIFICATION

Number series: various, according to operator
Number built: 68 (including units on order in 2004)
Builder: Bombardier
Date introduced: 2000
Track gauge, ft/ins (mm): 4 ft 8.5 in (1,435)
Unit configuration: M-M or M-T-M
Power supply system: 15 kV AC 16.7 Hz
Electrical equipment: Bombardier, three-phase traction motors
Power rating, hp (kW): 2,150 (1,590)
Design speed, mph (km/h): X50, X52, X54 - 125 (200), X51, X53 - 110 (180)
Additional features: wheelchair lift for passengers with reduced mobility

Transitio, a leasing company created by several regional authorities. One of the widest body designs seen in Europe, the Regina uses this width to provide a passenger capacity increase of 25 per cent compared with older vehicles. The type suffered early teething troubles with wheelsets, frozen water tanks and jammed pantographs. These problems have been addressed by Bombardier.

ARLANDA EXPRESS CLASS X3 EMU

Arlanda Express Class X3

The inauguration in 1999 of a new dedicated high-speed rail link between Stockholm Central station and the main airport at Arlanda 26 miles (42 km) away solved the major competitive disadvantage of poor public transport to Sweden's capital city. The trains were assembled by Alstom in the UK.

SPECIAL FEATURES

Swedish construction companies NCC and Siab, power utility Vattenfall, and British-based firms Mowlem and GEC Alstom formed the A-Train AB consortium to finance, build and operate the Arlanda Express, 15-minute interval service. Trains are operated by seven dedicated four-car electric units built by Alstom at Birmingham (the bodyshells came from Spain and the bogies from France). All vehicles have platform-level entry, and there is special provision for luggage and accommodation for wheelchairs. Target availability is 98%.

SPECIFICATION

Number series: 1-7
Total built: 7
Builder: Alstom, UK
Date introduced: 1999
Track gauge, ft/ins (mm): 4 ft 8.5 in (1,435)
Unit configuration: M-T-T-M
Power supply system: 15 kV AC 16.7 Hz
Electrical equipment: Alstom ONIX traction motors
Power rating, hp (kW): 3,000 (2,240)
Design speed, mph (km/h): 125 (200)
Additional features: automatic train protection, regenerative brakes, automatic couplings compatible with X-2000 emus, air-conditioning

CLASS IORE ELECTRIC LOCOMOTIVE

Malmtrafik I Kiruna AB (MTAB) Class IORE

Among the world's most powerful electric locomotives, these recently delivered twin-section machines are used to haul iron ore on the 335 mile (540 km) Malmbanan, which links mines at Kiruna, Malmberget and Svappavaara with the ports of Luleå (Sweden) and Narvik (Norway). Much of the line lies within the Arctic Circle.

SPECIAL FEATURES

Developed by Adtranz (now Bombardier) as a member of the Octeon (now TRAXX) three-phase locomotive family that also includes the German Class 185 and the Swiss Class 482, these massive machines were supplied as part of a major modernisation programme for the Malmbanan iron ore line. Introduction of the new locomotives from March 2001 enabled MTAB to run 68-wagon formations grossing 6,800 tonnes compared with the 4,200 tonnes to which the triple-section Class Dm3 locomotives were limited. Bodyshells for the IORE locomotives were fabricated at the former

SPECIFICATION

Number series: 101-118 (each locomotive section individually numbered)
Total built: 9 twin-section locomotives
Builder: Bombardier
Date introduced: 2001
Track gauge, ft/ins (mm): 4 ft 8.5 in (1,435)
Axle arrangement: Co-Co+Co-Co
Power supply system: 15 kV AC 16.7 Hz
Electrical equipment: Bombardier - three-phase asynchronous traction motors
Weight, tonnes: 360
Power rating, hp (kW): 14,470 (10,800) continuous
Design speed, mph (km/h): 50 (80)
Additional features: rheostatic braking

Pafawag plant in Poland, while final assembly was undertaken at Bombardier's Kassel facility. Deliveries were completed in 2004.

CLASS MX DIESEL LOCOMOTIVE

Class MX

The distinctive dognose Nohab MX diesel locomotive lives on in small numbers in Scandinavia, having found new use with privatised Swedish operators long after it was considered surplus to requirements in its native Denmark. The type is seen on a variety of passenger and freight work alongside its older and more powerful MY counterpart.

SPECIAL FEATURES

Although the Danish State Railways MX class had the same familiar outward appearance of a number of American-inspired locomotive types also built for Norway, Luxembourg and Hungary, it was unique amongst the European fleet in being fitted with the less-powerful 12-cylinder power unit. A total of 18 were sold to private Danish operators after withdrawal between 1987-93, and 11 more ended up in Sweden. Examples of 'MX' in service in Sweden are 1015 with Bantåg i

SPECIFICATION

Number series: Various
Total built: 45
Builder: Nohab
Date introduced: 1960
Track gauge, ft/ins (mm): 4 ft 8.5 in (1,435)
Axle arrangement: A1A-A1A
Engine: General Motors GM 12-567C or General Motors 12-567D1
Transmission: Electric - GM main generators and four GM DC nose-suspended traction motors
Weight, tonnes: 89
Power rating, hp (kW): 1,425 (1,047) or 1,445 (1,064)
Design speed, mph (km/h): 83 (133)

Dalarna; 1027 and 1042 with BK Tåg AB; 1013, 1014, and 1016 with Inlandsbanan AB (IBAB) (above), 1024 with Skånetåg Bulk, 1021, 1028 and 1032 with Tågab. The pioneer 1001 has been restored to original maroon livery in Denmark for special duties, and 1040 is also preserved in Norway.

CLASS Ma ELECTRIC LOCOMOTIVE

TGOJ Trafik Class Ma

TGOJ Trafik AB, whose history is closely linked to the former freight sector of Swedish Railways, operates with many refurbished older types of locomotive, of which the ASEA Class Ma continues to give good service.

SPECIAL FEATURES

Despite their age, Class Ma (and the virtually identical Ma2) are an important feature of the TGOJ fleet. They were purchased new for the company at the time its principal routes were electrified, and share the same specification as locomotives purchased from ASEA by the national Statens Jarnvagar (Swedish Railways) company. Some of these machines now form part of the TGOJ fleet. Only 19 were in traffic at the end of 2003, with the rest in store. The plan is to maintain members of the class in service for at least another five years, and the Mas are being refurbished with better drivers' cabs. They are also being repainted in the company's new livery of

SPECIFICATION

Number series: 401-409, 825-829, 831-833, 873-877, 959, 961-967
Total built: 29
Builder: ASEA
Date introduced: 1953
Track gauge, ft/ins (mm): 4 ft 8.5 in (1,435)
Axle arrangement: Co-Co
Power supply system: 25kV AC 50 Hz
Electrical equipment: ASEA
Weight, tonnes: 105
Power rating, hp (kW): 5,300 (3,960)
Design speed, mph (km/h): 62 (100)

lime green with horizontal dark blue stripes in place of the earlier red and white.

CLASS RABDe ICN HIGH-SPEED TRAINSET

Swiss Federal Railways (SBB) Class RABDe

Switzerland began high-speed train operation in 1999, when the first of these ICN (InterCity Neigezug) tilting units entered service on the Pied du Jura line between Lausanne and St Gallen. Deliveries under way in 2003-04 were destined to bring the fleet strength up to 44 trainsets.

SPECIAL FEATURES

With heavily curved alignments an inevitable characteristic of the Swiss rail network, the use of tilting technology to raise train speeds was a natural choice when SBB needed to improve performance as part of its Bahn 2000 capacity enhancement strategy. After exhaustive trials with a four-car test set, 24 examples of this design were ordered by SBB in 1996. Originally specified as seven-car sets but later expanded to nine cars, they were built by a consortium led by Adtranz and including Fiat-SIG (these companies subsequently becoming Bombardier and Alstom). This latter company was responsible for the design and development of the electric tilting

SPECIFICATION

Number series: 500.000-500.023
Total built: 44
Builder: Bombardier (formerly Adtranz), Alstom (formerly Fiat-SIG)
Date introduced: 2000
Track gauge, ft/ins (mm): 4 ft 8.5 in (1,435)
Unit configuration: M-M-T-T-T-T-M-M; M-M-T-T-T-M-M
Power supply system: 15 kV AC 16.7 Hz
Electrical equipment: Bombardier - GTO converters, eight three-phase asynchronous traction motors
Power rating, hp (kW): 6,970 (5,500)
Design speed, mph (km/h): 125 (200)
Additional features: active electric tilting, steerable bogies, multiple working, rheostatic braking

system that displaces the train's cars by up to 8°, a feature which, together with steerable axles, enables ICN to pass through curves more quickly. In 2001, orders were placed for 20 more ICN sets, this time each of seven cars, to be delivered by 2004.

CLASS Ae 6/6 (610) ELECTRIC LOCOMOTIVE

Swiss Federal Railways (SBB) Class Ae 6/6 (610)

Now in its twilight years, the Class Ae 6/6 electric locomotive was a pioneering design that signalled the transition from rigid frame to all-adhesion traction units on the Gotthard and Simplon mountain routes. Despite their age and the delivery of newer locomotives, most of Class Ae 6/6 remained in service in 2004.

SUB-TYPES

11401–11425 built with chrome waist-level bands and nose flashes.

SPECIAL FEATURES

Experience gained with the BLS Ae 4/4 and SBB Re 4/4 I four-axle bogie designs was soon applied to meeting the challenging traction requirements posed by Switzerland's mountain routes. The resulting Class Ae 6/6 was a classic type which for many years handled the heaviest trains over the Gotthard line and to a lesser extent the Simplon. Two prototype machines, 11401 and 11402, were produced in 1952 and 1953, with series deliveries commencing in 1955 and extending to 1966. By the end of 2003 the two prototypes had been withdrawn and a few other class members had been retired or stored but most remained in service with SBB Cargo, mainly handling freight services on SBB's flatter routes. Some carry their original green livery, while others have received SBB's red and grey colour scheme.

SPECIFICATION

Number series: 11401–11520
Total built: 120
Builder: SLM
Date introduced: 1952
Track gauge, ft/ins (mm): 4 ft 8.5 in (1,435)
Axle arrangement: Co-Co
Power supply system: 15 kV AC 16.7 Hz
Electrical equipment: Brown Boveri, Oerlikon - high-tension tap changer control, six single-phase fully suspended AC traction motors
Weight, tonnes: 120
Power rating, hp (kW): 5,320 (3,970)
Design speed, mph (km/h): 78 (120)
Additional features: regenerative braking, all named after Swiss cantons

CLASS Re 4/4 II (420) and Re 4/4 III (430) ELECTRIC

Swiss Federal Railways (SBB) Class Re 4/4 II (420) and Re 4/4 III (430)

Until the arrival in large numbers of the modern Class 465 and 482 machines, the Class Re 4/4 II and Re 4/4 III locomotives had been SBB's standard electric traction since the late 1960s. They still play a key role in both passenger and freight operations in Switzerland and can be seen throughout the network.

SUB-TYPES

Class Re 4/4 III differs only in having a lower gear ratio and was built for Gotthard line work. Other variations include locomotives with Austrian/German-style pantographs for cross-border working.

SPECIAL FEATURES

Developed as a standard design capable of meeting a wide range of operational needs, the first six locomotives of this versatile design were delivered as prototypes in 1964. Series production followed from 1967 and continued until 1985. The only withdrawals have been the result of

SPECIFICATION

Number series: 11101-11397
Total built: 397
Builder: SLM
Date introduced: 1964
Track gauge, ft/ins (mm): 4 ft 8.5 in (1,435)
Axle arrangement: Bo-Bo
Power supply system: 15 kV AC 16.7 Hz
Electrical equipment: Brown Boveri, Oerlikon, Sécheron - tap-changer control with four fully suspended single-phase AC traction motors
Weight, tonnes: 80
Power rating, hp (kW): 6,230 (4,650) one-hour
Design speed, mph (km/h): Re 4/4 II - 87 (140); Re 4/4 III - 78
Additional features: multiple working within class and with Classes Re 4/4 II or III and Re 6/6, regenerative braking, push-pull operation

accidents, leaving the majority of the original build still active on passenger and freight services over much of the SBB network. Four Class Re 4/4 III machines are operated by the Südostbahn, including three procured from SBB. In 2004 six Class Re 4/4 II locomotives were transferred to BLS Lötschbergbahn.

CLASS Re 6/6 (620) ELECTRIC LOCOMOTIVE

Swiss Federal Railways (SBB) Class Re 6/6 (620)

Developed for SBB's mountain routes, the powerful Re 6/6 is a development of the Re 4/4 II and Re 4/4 III designs, carried on three two-axle bogies. The class now mostly handles freight traffic but a few are assigned to passenger work.

SUB-TYPES

Two of the four prototypes, 11601 and 11602, have two-section bodies; remaining locomotives have a single rigid body.

SPECIAL FEATURES

Intended to enable increased loads to be taken over the Gotthard and Simplon mountain routes, and to avoid double-heading with Classes Re 4/4 II and Re 4/4 III, these locomotives yield a remarkable 82 per cent increase in power-to-weight ratio compared with Ae 6/6 introduced 20 years earlier. The 'Tri-Bo' axle arrangement permits higher speeds through curves and reduces rail wear. While designed to provide optimum

SPECIFICATION

Number series: 11601-11689
Total built: 89
Builder: SLM
Date introduced: 1972
Track gauge, ft/ins (mm): 4 ft 8.5 in (1,435)
Axle arrangement: Bo-Bo-Bo
Power supply system: 15 kV AC 16.7 Hz
Electrical equipment: Brown Boveri - tap-changer control with six fully suspended AC traction motors
Weight, tonnes: 120
Power rating, hp (kW): 9,700 (7,240) continuous
Design speed, mph (km/h): 87 (140)
Additional features: multiple working within class and with Classes Re 4/4 II and Re 4/4 III, regenerative braking

performance on steeply graded lines, Re 6/6 also has a top speed of 87 mph. Most of the class are assigned to SBB Cargo for freight but the first 13 are used by the passenger sector. All are named after Swiss communities and most bear their original green livery or the later red and grey.

CLASS 450 ELECTRIC LOCOMOTIVE

Swiss Federal Railways (SBB) Class 450

Designed specifically for the Zurich S-Bahn network, these single-ended three-phase machines operate intensive push-pull suburban services with dedicated rakes of double-deck stock.

SPECIAL FEATURES

Usually operating in semi-permanent formations of locomotive plus three trailers, the Class 450s are in effect power cars for Zurich's S-Bahn trainsets. Up to three of these sets can be coupled in multiple, providing seating for 1,200 passengers. A feature of the Class 450 is a bogie design that allows radial adjustment of the axles, improving tracking characteristics. The eventual displacement of these push-pull sets from Zurich S-Bahn services was foreshadowed by a 2003 SBB contract with Siemens for 35 four-car double-deck emus for these duties.

SPECIFICATION

Number series: 450.001–450.115
Total built: 115
Builder: SLM
Date introduced: 1989
Track gauge, ft/ins (mm): 4 ft 8.5 in (1,435)
Axle arrangement: Bo-Bo
Power supply system: 15 kV AC 16.7 Hz
Electrical equipment: ABB - GTO thyristors with four three-phase nose-suspended traction motors
Weight, tonnes: 78
Power rating, hp (kW): 4,290 (3,200)
Design speed, mph (km/h): 80 (130)
Additional features: multiple working, push-pull operation, regenerative braking

CLASS RBDe 4/4 (560) EMU

Swiss Federal Railways (SBB) Class RBDe 4/4 (560)

Introduced in prototype form in 1984 and known as the 'Colibri' (humming bird) type due to its colourful livery, these two-car units are widely employed on SBB local services. Examples are also operated by some independent Swiss railways.

SPECIAL FEATURES

This steel-bodied regional SBB emu first appeared in 1984, when four prototypes were delivered. Designed for one-person operation, the units are formed of one power car and one driving trailer, but the vehicles' design allows for the addition of extra intermediate cars with the necessary through control wiring. The class is widely used on SBB local services. Vehicles of this type are also operated by BLS Lötschbergbahn (Class RBDe 4/4), Mittelland Regional Railways (RM) and the South Eastern Railway (SOB) (both Class 566).

SPECIFICATION

Number series: 2100-2225 (motor cars)
Total built: 126
Builder: FFA, Schindler, SIG
Date introduced: 1984 (series production 1987)
Track gauge, ft/ins (mm): 4 ft 8.5 in (1,435)
Unit configuration: M-T (plus variable number of intermediate trailers)
Power supply system: 15 kV AC 16.7 Hz
Electrical equipment: BBC (ABB) - thyristor control with four DC traction motors
Power rating, hp (kW): 2,210 (1,650) one-hour
Design speed, mph (km/h): 87 (140)
Additional features: multiple operation, regenerative braking

CLASS 460 ELECTRIC LOCOMOTIVE

Swiss Federal Railways (SBB) Class 460

Developed as the 'Lok 2000' universal locomotive to provide the additional and more potent traction required for SBB's Bahn 2000 capacity enhancement programme, the Class 460 incorporates three-phase propulsion technology in a design that is equally at home on freight services over Switzerland's mountain routes or handling high-speed passenger traffic on the country's more level lines.

SUB-TYPES

Class 465 is a more powerful (8,575 hp/6,400 kW) version of this design. Initially eight were ordered by the Bern-Lötschberg-Simplon Railway (BLS), followed by 10 built for SBB but finished in BLS blue livery to handle piggyback services over the Simplon route. In 2003 the SBB machines were transferred to the BLS fleet.

SPECIFICATION

Number series: 460.001–460.119
Total built: 119
Builder: SLM
Date introduced: 1993
Track gauge, ft/ins (mm): 4 ft 8.5 in (1,435)
Axle arrangement: Bo-Bo
Power supply system: 15 kV AC 16.7 Hz
Electrical equipment: ABB (Adtranz) - GTO thyristors and three-phase AC traction motors
Weight, tonnes: 81
Power rating, hp (kW): 8,175 (6,100) continuous
Design speed, mph (km/h): 143 (230)
Additional features: rheostatic braking; multiple working; push-pull operation

SPECIAL FEATURES

The last major series to be built at the famous SLM plant at Winterthur, the 460s are the most modern electric locomotives in SBB's main line fleet, with examples assigned to both freight and

passenger businesses. The class is particularly used on intercity passenger services formed of IC 2000 double-deck stock. Most are finished in the standard SBB red and grey colour scheme but some carry advertising liveries.

OTHER COUNTRIES OPERATED

China (two examples supplied to Kowloon-Canton Railway Corporation); Finland (46 VR Class Sr2) (above); Norway (22 Class El 18) (below).

CLASS Re 4/4 ELECTRIC LOCOMOTIVE

BLS Lötschbergbahn (BLS) Class Re 4/4

With some visual similarities to the pioneering BLS Ae 4/4 design of 1944, the brown-liveried Re 4/4 rectifier locomotives were for many years the principal motive power on the Lötschberg system. They are now progressively being displaced by more modern traction.

SPECIAL FEATURES

At a time when Swiss Federal Railways continued to procure single-phase AC-motored main line electric locomotives, BLS chose a rectifier design with DC motors as front-line traction. Deliveries extended from 1964 to 1983. The Class Re 4/4 machines were not only intended for the BLS's steeply graded mountain routes - they were also to serve as a general purpose machine throughout the system, becoming familiar on local push-pull services as well as heavy freights. While the supremacy of the class has been challenged by

SPECIFICATION

Number series: 161-195
Total built: 35
Builder: SLM
Date introduced: 1964
Track gauge, ft/ins (mm): 4 ft 8.5 in (1,435)
Axle arrangement: Bo-Bo
Power supply system: 15 kV AC 16.7 Hz
Electrical equipment: BBC - tap-changer control, silicon rectifiers, four fully suspended DC traction motors
Weight, tonnes: 80
Power rating, hp (kW): 6,630 (4,945)
Design speed, mph (km/h): 87 (140)
Additional features: multiple working, push-pull operation, rheostatic braking

the Class 465 and more recently Class 485 machines, many examples survive handling a variety of duties.

CLASS Ge 4/4 II ELECTRIC LOCOMOTIVE

Rhaetian Railways (RhB) Class Ge 4/4 II

Switzerland's first series-built thyristor-controlled electric locomotives were these 23 machines supplied by SLM from 1973. While the more powerful Ge 4/4 III series handles the heaviest RhB services, these earlier designs continue to play a leading role in this metre-gauge railway's operations.

SPECIAL FEATURES

The first ten of these locomotives were ordered in 1970, with a mechanical design that drew on that of the SBB Class Re 4/4 II and traction control technology derived from the BLS Class Re 4/4. The class was strengthened by orders for 13 more of the type, delivered in 1984-85, making it the RhB's standard locomotive until the arrival of the Ge 4/4 IIIs. Duties on RhB include freight and secondary passenger services throughout the network.

SPECIFICATION

Number series: 611–633
Total built: 23
Builder: SLM
Date introduced: 1973
Track gauge, ft/ins (mm): 3 ft 3.975 in (1,000)
Axle arrangement: Bo-Bo
Power supply system: 11 kV AC 16.7 Hz
Electrical equipment: BBC - thyristor control with four fully suspended DC traction motors
Weight, tonnes: 50
Power rating, hp (kW): 2,270 (1,690)
Design speed, mph (km/h): 56 (90)
Additional features: multiple operation, push-pull operation, rheostatic braking

CLASS Ge 4/4 III ELECTRIC LOCOMOTIVE

Rhaetian Railways (RhB) Class Ge 4/4 III

Rhaetian Railways' latest electric locomotive type is this powerful design introduced in 1993. Like all this remarkable railway's locomotive fleet, the Ge 4/4 IIIs were built by SLM. They now handle the RhB's heaviest services, especially Chur-St Moritz passenger services and shuttles through the Vereina Tunnel.

SPECIAL FEATURES

The first nine of these state-of-the-art metre-gauge locomotives was delivered by SLM from 1993. Three more were supplied in 1999 to strengthen the fleet for car services via the Vereina Tunnel linking Klosters and Süsch. In addition to working these trains, the class is active on the Chur-St Moritz line. Most now carry advertising liveries. Locomotives of generally similar design are operated by the Bière-Apples-Morges Railway (BAM) and the Montreux-Oberland Bernois Railway (four Class Ge 4/4 800 V DC machines).

SPECIFICATION

Number series: 641-652
Total built: 12
Builder: SLM
Date introduced: 1993
Track gauge, ft/ins (mm): 3 ft 3.975 in (1,000)
Axle arrangement: Bo-Bo
Power supply system: 11kV AC 16.7 Hz
Electrical equipment: ABB - three-phase traction motors
Weight, tonnes: 62
Power rating, hp (kW): 4,290 (3,200) one-hour
Design speed, mph (km/h): 62 (100)
Additional features: multiple working, rheostatic braking

CLASS Gem 4/4 ELECTRIC LOCOMOTIVE

Rhaetian Railway (RhB) Class Gem 4/4

One of a small number of types that can operate both from an electric power supply system or on diesel power, these two unusual machines operate on RhB's Bernina line. Both have recently undergone modernisation and re-engining.

PRINCIPAL MODIFICATIONS

Both locomotives were refurbished in 2003-04, receiving new, more powerful Cummins diesel power units than those originally fitted, improved cabs and upgraded electrical equipment.

SPECIAL FEATURES

SLM originally supplied these locomotives to RhB in 1968 mainly to operate on the Bernina line between St Moritz and Tirano. Unlike the rest of the RhB network, which is electrified at 11 kV AC, this section retains the 1 kV DC system employed since its opening in 1910. The locomotives' diesel capability enable them to be used on passenger services which operate over both parts of the

SPECIFICATION

Number series: 801, 802
Total built: 2
Builder: SLM
Date introduced: 1968
Track gauge, ft/ins (mm): 3 ft 3.975 in (1,000)
Axle arrangement: Bo-Bo
Power supply system: 1 kV DC
Electrical equipment: BBC - resistance control with four nose-suspended DC traction motors
Power unit type: two Cummins QST30-L 12-cylinder four-stroke
Weight, tonnes: 50
Power rating, hp (kW): electric operation - 720 (540) continuous; diesel operation - 1,900 (1,420)
Design speed, mph (km/h): 40 (65)
Additional features: multiple working, regenerative braking in electric operation, rheostatic in diesel

system as well for snow clearance duties and as relief power on the 11 kV network at times of peak traffic demand.

CLASS HGe 4/4 ELECTRIC LOCOMOTIVE

Swiss Federal Railways (SBB)/Matterhorn Gotthard Bahn (MGB) Class HGe 4/4 (SBB Class 101)

This family of modern metre-gauge electric locomotives was supplied in the late 1980s and early 1990s for services over some of Switzerland's most spectacular tourist railways. Most are equipped to operate as rack machines on the steepest sections of the lines they operate.

SPECIAL FEATURES

The first operator to receive locomotives of this type was the Furka Oberalp Railway (FO), which in 2003 merged with the contiguous BVZ Zermatt-Bahn (BVZ) to form the MGB. The FO's eight rack-equipped examples now form an integrated fleet with the five former non-rack BVZ machines. In 1989-90, SBB acquired eight rack-equipped 15 kV examples of the type for its Brünig line between Interlaken and Lucerne, which in 2005 merged with the Luzern-Stans-Engelberg Railway to form Zentralbahn.

SPECIFICATION

Number series: SBB locos - 101.961-101.968; MGB locos - 1-5 (ex-BVZ fleet), 101-108 (ex-FO fleet)
Total built: 21
Builder: SLM
Date introduced: 1988 (on FO)
Track gauge, ft/ins (mm): 3 ft 3.975 in (1,000)
Axle arrangement: Bo-Bo
Power supply system: SBB locos - 15 kV AC 16.7 Hz; remainder - 11 kV AC 16.7 Hz
Electrical equipment: BBC/ABB
Weight, tonnes: SBB locos - 62, remainder - 64
Power rating, hp (kW): 2,225 (1,660)
Design speed, mph (km/h): 56 (90) (22 (35) on rack sections)
Additional features: ex-FO locos equipped for Abt rack system, SBB locos equipped for Riggenbach rack system; rheostatic braking

CLASS RABe EMU

BLS Lötschbergbahn (BLS) Class 525 (RABe 4/8) emu

Switzerland

Known as NINA units (Niederflur-Nahverkehr - low-floor local transport), these articulated emus were procured by BLS to replace older equipment and contribute to the creation of a Bern area S-Bahn network. The design has subsequently been adopted by several other Swiss operators.

SPECIAL FEATURES

The first eight of these vehicles was delivered from 1999 by a consortium formed by Vevey Technologies and Netherlands-based traction equipment supplier Holec (Traxis). Subsequently both companies were taken over by Bombardier and Alstom respectively, these firms fulfilling a further order for 18 units place in 2001. These were primarily intended for the Bern S-Bahn network, which BLS took over completely in 2004. The NINA design features a low floor for all of the train except the areas above the leading and trailing powered bogies, articulation using Jacobs-type bogies and full-width gangways. Other Swiss

SPECIFICATION

Number series: 525.001-525.026
Total built: 26 (including units on order in 2004)
Builder: Vevey/Bombardier
Date introduced: 1999
Track gauge, ft/ins (mm): 4 ft 8.5 in (1,435)
Unit configuration: M-T-M
Power supply system: 15 kV AC 16.7 Hz
Electrical equipment: Holec (Traxis)/Alstom
Power rating, hp (kW): 1,340 (1,000)
Design speed, mph (km/h): 87 (140)
Additional features: multiple working, part low-floor, air-conditioning, rheostatic braking

operators of NINA emus include Transports de Martigny et Régions (TMR) and Transport Régionaux Neuchâtelois (TRN) (three and two Class 527 three-car sets respectively).

CLASS 520 EMU

Swiss Federal Railways (SBB) Class 520 (Type GTW 2/8)

The inclusion in this book of SBB's Class 520 Type GTW 2/8 lightweight regional emu is a reflection of the success of the Swiss company, Stadler, in developing designs of this type to respond to a strong demand for low life-cycle vehicles of this type both from the domestic market and beyond.

SPECIAL FEATURES

Class 520 is an adaptation of Stadler's standard GTW vehicle concept, developed specifically for the Seetalbahn between Lucerne and Lenzburg. Infrastructure constraints on this line necessitated reducing the bodyshell width from the 3,000 mm of earlier members of this vehicle family to 2,650 mm. The body is constructed of aluminium extrusions and like other GTW units the vehicle is articulated around a small powered module that houses all traction equipment. Construction was undertaken at Stadler's Bussnang plant, deliveries commencing in 2002.

SPECIFICATION

Number series: 520.001-520.017
Total built: 17
Builder: Stadler
Date introduced: 2002
Track gauge, ft/ins (mm): 4 ft 8.5 in (1,435)
Unit configuration: T-M-T-T
Power supply system: 15 kV AC 16.7 Hz
Electrical equipment: Bombardier
Power rating, hp (kW): 700 (520)
Design speed, mph (km/h): 70 (115)
Additional features: articulated, full-width gangways, part low-floor, air-conditioning, retention toilets

OTHER COUNTRIES OPERATED

As well as proving highly successful in various configurations in both standard- and metre-gauge applications in Switzerland, both diesel and electric versions of the GTW family have been supplied to national operators in France, Germany, Greece, Slovakia and local and regional railways in Austria, Germany, Italy, Spain and the USA.

CLASS VL8 ELECTRIC LOCOMOTIVE

Ukrainian Railways (UZ) Class VL8

Switzerland/Ukraine

UZ still retains examples of this first Soviet twin-section electric locomotive design that dates from the 1950s. The type also operates on the Georgian and Russian systems.

SUB-TYPES

An experimental electronically controlled 6 kV DC version was produced by Tbilisi in 1966.

PRINCIPAL MODIFICATIONS

Suspension improvements were applied to some of the class during construction and to others retrospectively to enable their top speed to be increased from 50 to 62 mph (80 to 100 km/h).

SPECIAL FEATURES

The twin-section configuration adopted by Soviet Railways for the Class VL8 established a long dynasty of locomotive types employing this arrangement that continues today. In the VL8, the bogies are articulated, and traction loads are not transmitted to the bodies. Construction initially

SPECIFICATION

Number series: VL8-001–VL8-1723
Total built: 1,723 (for Soviet Railways)
Builder: Novocherkassk, Tbilisi
Date introduced: prototype - 1953; series production - 1955
Track gauge, ft/ins (mm): 5 ft 0 in (1,524)
Axle arrangement: Bo+Bo+Bo+Bo
Power supply system: 3 kV DC
Electrical equipment: Novocherkassk - resistance control, eight nose-suspended DC traction motors
Weight, tonnes: 184
Power rating, hp (kW): 5,040 (3,760) continuous
Design speed, mph (km/h): 50 (80) or 62 (100)
Additional features: regenerative braking

took place at Novocherkassk, but from 1958 the newly completed plant at Tbilisi, Georgia, also started producing VL8s. This continued until 1967, Novocherkassk having concentrated on VL10 production from 1964. In Ukraine the class is primarily used on freight traffic.

CLASS 20 DIESEL LOCOMOTIVE

Direct Rail Services (DRS) Class 20

The first production main line diesel type to be introduced to British Railways was an outstandingly successful design. It was employed on freight across virtually the entire national network.

PRINCIPAL MODIFICATIONS

Air brakes and slow speed control. 20301-20906 refurbished with additional fuel tanks.

SUB-TYPES

20001-20228 – standard version,
20301-20906 – air brake only.

SPECIAL FEATURES

Class 20 is the UK's oldest national production diesel design, and was originally intended for trip freight and station pilot work, later becoming the standard type for coal from collieries in the Midlands and Scotland, and occasional passenger relief work. Working them in pairs also provided valuable additional braking power. Although

SPECIFICATION

Number series: 20001-20906
Total built: 228
Builder: English Electric, Newton-le-Willows
Date introduced: 1957
Track gauge, ft/ins (mm): 4 ft 8.5 in (1,435)
Axle arrangement: Bo-Bo
Power unit type: English Electric 8SVT Mk2
Transmission: Electric, English Electric traction motors
Weight, tonnes: 20001-20228 - 73, 20301-20315, 20901-20906 - 76
Power rating, hp (kW): 1,000 (746)
Design speed, mph (km/h): 75 (120)
Additional features: multiple working within type and UK Classes 31, 33, 37, 55

many were scrapped following replacement by new 56s and 60s from the mid-1970s, some survivors were resurrected and after refurbishment are now owned by Direct Rail Services based at Carlisle in the North West of England. Others have been hired for Channel Tunnel construction work in the UK and France, and many, including the prototype, are preserved.

CLASS 31 DIESEL LOCOMOTIVE

FM Rail Class 31

After success in export markets including Ceylon, Brush Traction developed a mixed traffic locomotive that was quickly adopted to eliminate steam in eastern England. They have been repeatedly updated, and a number are employed by FM Rail, formerly Fragonset Railways, on contract work.

SUB-TYPES

31101-31327 – no-heat freight version,
31401-31569 – electric train heat,
31601-31602 – through wiring for electric heat controls.

PRINCIPAL MODIFICATIONS

All re-engined, steam-heat boilers removed.

SPECIAL FEATURES

Following early successes, large numbers of 31s were constructed to increase their operation to Yorkshire and the North East, and following line closures surplus examples later displaced less reliable types on the Western and Midland Regions. The original problematic Mirrlees power units were replaced with English Electric versions from 1964, while the replacement of the steam heat boiler with electric heat equipment in 70 examples allowed their use with modern coaching stock on suburban and regional services. Despite extensive refurbishment, the type was eliminated from squadron use by 2001. The prototype and many others are preserved.

SPECIFICATION

Number series: 31101-31602
Total built: 263
Builder: Brush, Loughborough, UK
Date introduced: 1958
Track gauge, ft/ins (mm): 4 ft 8.5 in (1,435)
Axle arrangement: A1A-A1A
Power unit type: English Electric 12SVT
Transmission: Electric, Brush TM73-68 traction motors
Weight, tonnes: 107-111
Power rating, hp (kW): 1,470 (1,100)
Design speed, mph (km/h): 90 (145)
Additional features: dual vacuum and air brakes

CLASS 37 DIESEL LOCOMOTIVE

EWS and Direct Rail Services Class 37

Allocated to the Eastern, Western and Scottish Regions, the Class 37 is arguably the most successful first generation mixed traffic diesel design of the early 1960s. The fleet remained practically intact for 35 years, but following delivery of new types in the late 1990s has been reduced to a handful devoted to specialist roles.

SUB-TYPES

37010-37384 - standard design, 37401-37430 - alternator fitted, electric train heat, 37503-37698 - no-heat, alternator fitted, 37701-37899 - no heat, alternator fitted, ballast weights added. Some early numbered examples have nose-end connecting doors (never used).

PRINCIPAL MODIFICATIONS

All locomotives numbered 37401 upwards have been refurbished with the main generator replaced by an alternator.

SPECIFICATION

Number series: 37010-37899
Total built: 308
Builder: English Electric, Newton-le-Willows/Robert Stephenson & Hawthorn, Darlington
Date introduced: 1960
Track gauge, ft/ins (mm): 4 ft 8.5 in (1,435)
Axle arrangement: Co-Co
Power unit type: English Electric 12CSVT
Transmission: Electric, Type 538A traction motors
Weight, tonnes: 102-120
Power rating, hp (kW): 1,300 (1,750)
Design speed, mph (km/h): 90 (145)
Additional features: Multiple working, increased fuel capacity on many examples

SPECIAL FEATURES

The reliability of the Class 37s resulted in high volume production and a quickly extended sphere of operation. Although still seen right across the UK network, principal freight operator EWS has consigned much of its fleet to store or scrap.

CLASS 47/57 DIESEL LOCOMOTIVE

Class 47/57

The 500-plus examples of the Brush Class 47 were the mainstay of British diesel express passenger and freight operation for over 40 years, but are now relegated to a support and reserve role.

SUB-TYPES

47033-47377 - freight only, 47701-47854 - electric train heat, some push-pull fitted, 57001-57012 - freight only, 57301-57314, 57601-57604 - electric train heat.

PRINCIPAL MODIFICATIONS

57001-57605 re-engined.

SPECIAL FEATURES

After successful trials with 20, fleet production was divided into passenger versions fitted with steam-heat boilers, and 81 freight versions. From the early 1970s, many were converted to electric train heat operation, and others specifically modified for push-pull or parcels operation and long-distance freight work. Since 1997, some life-

SPECIFICATION

Number series: 47033-47854, 57001-57605
Total built: 512
Builder: Brush, Loughborough/BR Crewe
Date introduced: 1962
Track gauge, ft/ins (mm): 4 ft 8.5 in (1,435)
Axle arrangement: Co-Co
Power unit type: 47033-47854 - Sulzer 12LDA28C, 57001-57605 - General Motors 645-12E3
Transmission: Electric, Brush TM64-68 traction motors
Weight, tonnes: 47033-47854 - 112-125, 57001-57604 - 116-121
Power rating, hp (kW): 47033-47854 - 2,580 (1,920), 57001-57604 - 2,500 (1,860)
Design speed, mph (km/h): 47033-47854, 57601-57604 - 95 (150), 57001-57012 75 (120)
Additional features: multiple working. 47488-47854, 57301-57604 electric train heating, some with extended fuel tanks

expired redundant Class 47s have been completely rebuilt with reconditioned General Motors engines from VMV, Paducah, Kentucky, USA with a 20-year life extension, becoming Class 57.

CLASS 55 DIESEL LOCOMOTIVE

Class 55 'Deltic'

The twin-engined 'Deltic' locomotive was the most powerful and fastest first generation diesel type that transformed performance on intercity services on the East Coast Main Line out of London. Although displaced in 1982, six of the class survive in private ownership and have been certified for use on excursions although none was active in early 2005.

PRINCIPAL MODIFICATIONS

Dual air/vacuum brakes, electric train heat equipment.

SPECIAL FEATURES

The 'Deltic' is so named because the opposed pistons in the twin Napier power units are arranged in a complex triangular fashion. Following the outstanding success of a company-owned prototype (now preserved at York Museum), a small fleet was assembled to supplant steam and speed up London-Edinburgh/Aberdeen

SPECIFICATION

Number series: 55002-55022
Total built: 22
Builder: English Electric, Newton-le-Willows
Date introduced: 1960
Track gauge, ft/ins (mm): 4 ft 8.5 in (1,435)
Axle arrangement: Co-Co
Power unit type: Two Napier Deltic D18-25
Transmission: Electric, English Electric 538A traction motors
Weight, tonnes: 105
Power rating, hp (kW): 2,460 (3,300)
Design speed, mph (km/h): 100 (160)
Additional features: electric train heat, multiple working

services, the first series-built UK diesel design capable of 100 mph (160 km/h) running.

Although expensive to maintain, they were held in high regard for two decades until replaced in 1979 by even faster 125mph (200 km/h) High Speed Trains, surviving for a couple more years on Trans-Pennine services. The six surviving 'Deltics' are being progressively renovated from museum status to full main line condition.

CLASS 60 DIESEL LOCOMOTIVE

EWS Class 60

The robust British-built Class 60 is regarded as a long-life locomotive by current operator English Welsh & Scottish Railway, which acquired the entire fleet upon privatisation. The type is seen hauling coal, construction, metals and petroleum trains across the length and breadth of the UK.

PRINCIPAL MODIFICATIONS

Some fitted with extra-capacity fuel tanks.

SPECIAL FEATURES

The Class 60 was the final British response to the need for 100 modern heavy duty freight diesel locomotives. Following consideration of the import of further General Motors (Class 59) locomotives from Canada similar to the small fleet operated by Mendip Rail, the decision was taken to buy from the UK after all, and Brush won the construction contract. After early teething troubles with computer software and bogie and structural defects, the class settled down to regular work, and has been allocated to

SPECIFICATION

Number series: 60001–60100
Total built: 100
Builder: Brush, Loughborough
Date introduced: 1989
Track gauge, ft/ins (mm): 4 ft 8.5 in (1,435)
Axle arrangement: Co-Co
Power unit type: Mirrlees 8MB275T
Transmission: Electric, Brush TM216 traction motors
Weight, tonnes: 129-131
Power rating, hp (kW): 3,100 (2,310)
Design speed, mph (km/h): 62 (100)
Additional features: multiple working, slow-speed control

depots at Toton, Nottingham (Midlands), Immingham (East Coast) and Thornaby (North East). Upon repainting in EWS red and maroon livery, Class 60s are losing their original nameplates commemorating British cultural figures, mountains and beauty spots, either running with business-related nameplates or none at all. The type is completely overshadowed by the more common Canadian-built Class 66.

CLASS 66 DIESEL LOCOMOTIVE

EWS/GBRf/Freightliner/Direct Rail Services Class 66

The decision of newly-installed private freight operator English Welsh & Scottish Railway (owned by Wisconsin Central) to acquire 250 standard North American JT42CWR locomotives modified to British loading gauge was a wise one. It has led to new levels of service reliability, prompted competing UK hauliers to follow suit, and opened up a new European market to General Motors.

SUB-TYPES

66601-66622 - modified gear ratio.

SPECIAL FEATURES

Soon after it took over the majority of UK freight operations, English Welsh and Scottish Railway placed an order for 250 identical locomotives of a proven design, and all were delivered at a rapid pace between 1998-2000, in the company's maroon and yellow livery. Rival operators Freightliner (green and yellow), GB Railfreight

(blue and orange) (right lower) and Direct Rail Services (dark blue) have followed suit, and further orders are likely. The only major modification to the original series so has been to gearing (66601-66622), although future deliveries may have revised exhaust emission arrangements.

OTHER COUNTRIES OPERATED

General Motors and train leasing companies Porterbrook Leasing and HSBC have placed small numbers of further production '66s' in the Netherlands, Belgium, Germany, Sweden and Norway, and France and Poland are in prospect. They are considered a worthwhile and cheaper alternative to multi-voltage electric locomotives and starting up a European production line is being considered.

SPECIFICATION

Number series: 66001-66250, 66401-66410, 66501-66581, 66601-66622, 66701-66722, 66951/2
Total built: 381
Builder: General Motors, Ontario
Date introduced: 1998
Track gauge, ft/ins (mm): 4 ft 8.5 in (1,435)
Axle arrangement: Co-Co
Power unit type: GM 12N-710G38-EC
Transmission: Electric, GM D43TR traction motors
Weight, tonnes: 126
Power rating, hp (kW): 3,200 (2,385)
Design speed, mph (km/h): 66001-66250, 66401-66410, 66501-66581, 66701-66722 - 75 (120), 66601-66622 - 65 (105) 66951-66952
Additional features: multiple working, slow speed control

CLASS 67 DIESEL LOCOMOTIVE

EWS Class 67

The fastest and newest British diesel locomotive is a version of Alstom's Prima design using the same General Motors engine as that employed in the successful high-volume Class 66. The unexpected loss of the postal traffic it was designed to haul has forced operator English Welsh & Scottish Railway to search for alternative employment for the type after only three years.

SPECIAL FEATURES

The desire to meet the needs of the Royal Mail for the high speed movement of letters and parcels was the inspiration behind the decision of English Welsh & Scottish Railway to order a small fleet of locomotives of the JT42 family capable of passenger work. Assembly was sub-contracted by General Motors to the Alstom plant in Spain. Although sharing the same power unit as the UK Class 66, it does not have a full loading bearing structure, being built on a conventional frame.

SPECIFICATION

Number series: 67001-67030
Total built: 30
Builder: Alstom, Valencia, Spain
Date introduced: 1999
Track gauge, ft/ins (mm): 4 ft 8.5 in (1,435)
Axle arrangement: Bo-Bo
Power unit type: General Motors 12N-710G38-EC
Transmission: Electric, GM D43FM traction motors
Weight, tonnes: 90
Power rating, hp (kW): 3,200 (2,385)
Design speed, mph (km/h): 125 (200)
Additional features: electric train heating, slow speed control

Since the loss of mail traffic early in 2004, new employment found for Class 67s, includes sub-lease to intercity companies, standby power in case of breakdowns, excursions and displacement of older EWS types.

OTHER COUNTRIES OPERATED

A similar 'JT42' design has operated in Israel since 1998, eight six-axle 'Semi-Mega' units (702-709) (above) for freight work, and 20 Class 'Mega' Bo-Bos (731-750) for express passenger duty. Ten 5 ft 6 in (1,676 mm) gauge six-axle Class M9 machines were supplied by Alstom to Sri Lanka Railways (SLR) in 2000 and 30 generally similar standard gauge locomotives were delivered to Syrian Railways (CFS) from 1999. SLR and CFS locomotives have Ruston engines.

CLASS 86/87/90 ELECTRIC LOCOMOTIVE FAMILY

Class 86/87/90

86221

The second generation of UK main line electric locomotive, built in three batches, has given good service on inter-city passenger and freight work for over four decades, but is now in decline. The oldest, Class 86 (recognised by its three cab windows), is under the greatest threat, while Class 87 (two windows) is losing its principal duties on the West Coast Main Line, and the most modern Class 90 (sleek front end) is seeking a revised role.

SUB-TYPES

86205-86261 - general passenger fleet, 86401-86430 - freight and passenger charter work, 86501, 86602-86639 - freight, train-heat equipment isolated, 87001-87035 - inter-city passenger, 90001-90050 - thyristor control, inter-city passenger and freight.

SPECIFICATION

Number series: 86205-86902, 87001-87035, 90001-90050
Total built: 186
Builder: 86205-86639 - English Electric, Newton-le-Willows and BR Doncaster, 87001-87035, 90001-90050 - BREL Crewe
Date introduced: 86205-86639 - 1965, 87001-87035 - 1973, 90001-90050 - 1987
Track gauge, ft/ins (mm): 4 ft 8.5 in (1,435)
Axle arrangement: Bo-Bo
Power supply system: 25 kV 50 Hz AC
Electrical equipment: 86205-86902 - AEI 282BZ traction motors, 87001-87035 - GEC G412AZ traction motors, 90001-90050 - GEC G412CY traction motors
Weight, tonnes: 86205-86902 - 83-85, 87001-87035 - 83, 90001-90050 - 85
Power rating, hp (kW): 86205-86261 86901/2 - 4,040 (3,010), 86401-86439-86639 - 3,600 (2,680), 87001-87035, 90001-90050 - 5,000 (3,730)
Design speed, mph (km/h): 86205-86261, 86901/2 - 125 (200), 86401-86430 100 (160), 86501, 86602-86639 - 75 (120), 87001-87035, 90001-90050 - 110 (175)
Additional features: multiple working; rheostatic braking

PRINCIPAL MODIFICATIONS

86201-86261, 86901/2 - resilient wheels and
Flexicoil suspension, 86401-86430, 86602-86639
- original design, 86501 - regeared for freight
work.

SPECIAL FEATURES

The second generation of UK main line electric
locomotive was built over a 15-year period. The
early types were fitted with axle-hung traction
motors instead of frame-mounted (a decision
later regretted and resolved by fitting revised
suspension). As UK electrification has been
extended, the type's traditional haunts of the
West Coast Main Line between London and
Glasgow has been extended to East Anglia and
occasionally the East Coast. Since privatisation,
the fleet has been subdivided into freight and
passenger sub-classes, with their number series
frequently altered to reflect a new role. Classes 86

and 87 sport similar bodyshells, while the Class 90
has a sleeker, semi-streamlined front end.
Displaced from much of its work by other types,
Class 86 is now in rapid decline, while the future
of the more modern types is also increasingly
uncertain. Two were acquired by Network Rail in
2004 for load-bank duty, being painted in all-new
yellow as 86901 and 86902. Some Class 87 have
been diverted to freight work.

CLASS 91 ELECTRIC LOCOMOTIVE

GNER Class 91

The abandonment of the Advanced Passenger Train fixed formation concept created the need for a powerful new locomotive to haul conventional stock with a tilt facility at 140 mph. Although fully stretched in their role on the East Coast Main Line, the Class 91s have never reached their technological potential.

PRINCIPAL MODIFICATIONS

Extensive refurbishment in 2001-2003.

SPECIAL FEATURES

For hauling fixed rakes of conventional coaching stock with a tilt facility (never activated), one of the Class 91's driving cabs is streamlined. The locomotive is normally seen at the northern end of Mk 4 coaches on inter-city passenger services on the East Coast Main Line between London, Leeds, Newcastle, Edinburgh and Glasgow. Although it has a high design speed, only 125 mph (200 km/h) has so far been possible, and the

SPECIFICATION

Number series: 91101-91132
Total built: 31
Builder: GEC/BREL, Crewe
Date introduced: 1988
Track gauge, ft/ins (mm): 4 ft 8.5 in (1,435)
Axle arrangement: Bo-Bo
Power supply system: 25kV 50 Hz AC
Electrical equipment: GEC G426AZ body-mounted traction motors with cardan shaft drives
Weight, tonnes: 84
Power rating, hp (kW): 6,090 (4,540)
Design speed, mph (km/h): 140 (225)
Additional features: push-pull facility; rheostatic braking

earlier intention of employment on overnight parcels and freight has also not been followed through. In 1996, Class 91s were leased to Great North Eastern Railway, whose dark blue and red livery they carry. Some of them are named after famous cities and towns on the eastern side of the UK, and recent extensive refurbishment has removed deep-seated reliability defects.

CLASS 92 ELECTRIC LOCOMOTIVE

SNCF/EWS Class 92

Ownership of the complex dual-voltage Class 92 which was developed to work from England to France through the Channel Tunnel, was shared between British Rail, SNCF (French Railways) and European Passenger Services. It has not been a success because of its large power requirement and unsuitability for working beyond Calais Fréthun yard. Despite this, the 92s remain rare examples of a third rail electric locomotive type.

SPECIAL FEATURES

The Class 92 has much of its internal equipment duplicated to ensure that a normal failure will not prevent it leaving the Tunnel. On-board control systems have taken several years to de-bug, and approval to work from Glasgow and around London was also protracted. Until December 2003 a dedicated pool of locomotives handled traffic over the Eurotunnel network through the Tunnel, these machines operating with third rail shoegear removed. Since then, all serviceable EWS examples

SPECIFICATION

Number series: 92001-92046
Total built: 46
Builder: Brush, Loughborough
Date introduced: 1993
Track gauge, ft/ins (mm): 4 ft 8.5 in (1,435)
Axle arrangement: Co-Co
Power supply system: 25 kV AC 50 HZ overhead/750 V DC third rail
Electrical equipment: ABB traction control equipment, Brush traction motors
Weight, tonnes: 126
Power rating, hp (kW): 6,760 (5,040) on AC, 5,360 (4,000) on DC
Design speed, mph (km/h): 87 (140)
Additional features: Anglo-French compatibility, including TVM 430 cab signalling equipment; rheostatic braking.

have formed a common pool authorised to work throughout between Glasgow and Calais. Nine of the class are owned by SNCF and bear the company's logo. However, operation in France is restricted by the lack of French automatic train control equipment.

CLASS 43 HIGH-SPEED TRAIN

InterCity Class 43

The High Speed Train is regarded as the traction unit that singularly rescued Britain's inter-city passenger business from the doldrums in the mid-1970s. The concept of single-ended Class 43 locomotives attached to each end of a rake of Mk 3 coaching stock has lasted the test of time, and almost all the locomotives are still in service.

PRINCIPAL MODIFICATIONS

Many have had their power units replaced with more efficient Paxman 12VP185s.

SPECIAL FEATURES

In the absence of investment in electrification on most UK main lines, a high-speed intercity diesel locomotive was devised to run at speeds of up to 125 mph (200 km/h). They revolutionised intercity services in Britain. While many still work on the London-West of England/South Wales, Edinburgh/Aberdeen and Sheffield routes for which they were built, others have been used on

SPECIFICATION

Number series: 43002-43197
Total built: 196
Builder: BREL, Crewe
Date introduced: 1976
Track gauge, ft/ins (mm): 4 ft 8.5 in (1,435)
Unit configuration: Bo-Bo
Power unit type: Paxman Valenta 12RP200L or 12VP185
Transmission: Electric, Brush TMH68-46 or GEC G417AZ traction motors
Power rating, hp (kW): 2,250 (1,680)
Design speed, mph (km/h): 125 (200)
Additional features: electric heat equipment

less demanding lines over the last decade. They continue to enjoy high quality maintenance and the increased fitting of new Paxman 12VP185 power units has enhanced their reliability. UK operators in 2005 were First Great Western, Great North Eastern Railway and Midland Mainline. A small number are also now owned by Network Rail to haul test trains, and are painted in the company's yellow livery.

CLASS 220/221 VOYAGER/SUPER VOYAGER DEMU

Virgin Trains Class 220/221 Voyager/Super Voyager DEMU

Services on over 2,700 route miles (4,400 km) of UK cross-country routes radiating from Birmingham have been revolutionised by the introduction of dedicated fixed-formation diesel-electric units. The Voyager follows standard European design, but with narrow bodies for the smaller British loading gauge.

SUB-TYPES

220001-220034 - (Voyagers) non-tilt, 221101-221144 - (Super Voyagers) tilting trains.

SPECIAL FEATURES

Voyagers and Super Voyagers operated by Virgin's CrossCountry business, have replaced life-expired locomotives on inter-regional UK routes. Class 220 are in four-coach formations. Class 221 Super Voyager is of similar design, already mostly in five-car formation, but with tilt equipment to allow high speed running on regional lines

SPECIFICATION

Number series: 220001-220034, 221101-221144
Total built: 78
Builder: Bombardier, Bruges (Belgium) and Wakefield (UK)
Date introduced: 2000
Track gauge, ft/ins (mm): 4 ft 8.5 in (1,435)
Unit configuration: M-M-M-M/M-M-M-M-M
Power unit type: Cummins QSK19
Transmission: electric - Alstom Onix 800 body-mounted three-phase traction motors with cardan shaft drive
Power rating, hp (kW): Class 220 - 3,000 (2,240); Class 221 - 3,750 (2,800)
Design speed, mph (km/h): 125 (200)
Additional features: multiple working

without the need for track re-alignment. All cars are powered. Two other UK train operators, Midland Mainline, and Hull Trains, have also bought non-tilt Voyager units for the London-Sheffield and London-Doncaster/Hull routes. They are both designated Class 222.

PENDOLINO CLASS 390 EMU

Virgin Trains Class 390 Pendolino EMU

The UK version of the Pendolino is part of a multi-billion pound modernisation scheme for the tightly curved West Coast Main Line serving the principal cities of London, Birmingham, Liverpool, Manchester and Glasgow. The full fleet was in service by the end of 2004.

SPECIAL FEATURES

The high speed tilting concept is a throwback to the early 1980s when British Rail pioneered the technology in its Advanced Passenger Train, a scheme aborted because of severe technical difficulties that could not be resolved without massive spending. The Pendolinos, which are fitted with tilting equipment, are derived from the Italian design of the same name but built to the tight British loading gauge. However, a significant difference is the adoption of electrically actuated tilting in the British trains rather than the hydraulic equipment of their

SPECIFICATION

Number series: 390001-390053
Total built: 53
Builder: Alstom, Italy/UK
Date introduced: 2001
Track gauge, ft/ins (mm): 4 ft 8.5 in (1,435)
Unit configuration: M-M-T-M-T-M-T-M-M
Power supply system: 25 kV AC 50 Hz
Electrical equipment: Alstom Onix 800 traction motors
Power rating, hp (kW): 6,835 (5,100)
Design speed, mph (km/h): 140 (225)
Additional features: multiple working, tilting equipment; rheostatic and regenerative braking

Continental counterparts. The 390s have a maximum axle-load of 14.7 tonnes and a top speed of 140 mph (225 km/h) that may never be realised because planned infrastructure improvements have been cut back. A pre-production set achieved a UK record 138mph on test in October 2002.

CLASS 373 EUROSTAR

Eurostar Class 373

London-Paris/Lille/Brussels services via the Channel Tunnel are provided by a purpose-built fleet of trains that are variously owned by SNCF, SNCB and the British Eurostar UK. Each train is two half-units comprising nine trailers, coupled in the centre with a driving motor car at each end.

SUB-TYPES

3001-3022, 3101-3108, 3201-3232 - Three Capitals ten-car half-sets; 3301-3314 - Regional Eurostar eight-car half-sets. Eighteen half-sets also equipped with 1500 V DC power equipment to work to Alpine ski resorts.

SPECIAL FEATURES

The Eurostar fleet, which is based on the French TGV design but purposely built to fit the smaller UK loading gauge, has proved a technical success, with excellent ride quality at high speed helped by the use of articulated trailers on two-axle

SPECIFICATION

Number series: 3001-3022, 3101-3108, 3201-3232, 3301-3314
Total built: 78 half-sets
Builder: GEC Alsthom/Brush/ANF/De Deitrich/BN/ACEC
Date introduced: 1992
Track gauge, ft/ins (mm): 4 ft 8.5 in (1,435)
Unit configuration: Two power cars and either 18 (Class 373) or 14 (Class 373/3) trailers
Power supply system: 25 kV AC 50 Hz overhead/3kV DC overhead/750 V DC third rail (18 half-sets also equipped for 1.5 kV DC overhead)
Electrical equipment: GEC/Brush - three-phase asynchronous traction motors
Power rating, hp (kW): 16,350 (12,200)
Design speed, mph (km/h): 185 (300)
Additional features: monocoque bodies, articulated bogies on trailers, friction and rheostatic brakes, TVM430/KVB/TBL signalling

bogies. The trains, which are reversible, have two identical halves, with separate first class accommodation and restaurant facilities.

CLASS 142/143/144 DMU FAMILY

Regional Class 142/143/144

British Rail's search for a low-cost replacement for first generation dmus rounded on a design that incorporated a bus body on a high-strength railway underframe.

PRINCIPAL MODIFICATIONS

Interiors refurbished, 142084 - Perkins 2006-TWH engine.

SPECIAL FEATURES

Following experiments with the now-withdrawn Class 140 and 141 DMU types, three manufacturers undertook a rapid construction programme, using a number of body components compatible with British Leyland road coaches. The underframe is designed to withstand high speed collisions, and although the type was intended for a short working life, their success has led to full internal modernisation for a life to 2010. Class 142 is generally seen in the North of England and South Wales, Class 143 in Wales, and Class 144 in

SPECIFICATION

Number series: 142001-142096, 143601-143625, 144001-144023
Total built: 144
Builder: 142001-142096 - BREL Derby/Leyland, 143601-143625 - W Alexander/Andrew Barclay, 144001-144023 - W Alexander/BREL Derby
Date introduced: 142001-143625 - 1985, 144001-144023 - 1986
Track gauge, ft/ins (mm): 4 ft 8.5 in (1,435)
Unit configuration: 142001-144014 - M-M, 144015-144023 M-T-M
Power unit type: Cummins LTA10-R
Transmission: Mechanical
Power rating, hp (kW): 230 (172)
Design speed, mph (km/h): 75 (120)
Additional features: multiple working

Yorkshire. Operators and liveries are many and varied but in 2004 included Arriva Trains Northern, Arriva Trains Wales, First North Western and Wessex Trains, although some of these were due to alter with further amendments to the franchise map of the British network.

CLASS 158/159 DMU

Regional Class 158/159

Following the replacement of many 1950s dmus with the basic new Sprinter, a more luxurious two-car version was built with the replacement of locomotive-hauled services in mind.

SUB-TYPES

158701-158798, 158815-158872 - standard type, 158799-158814, 159001-159022 - three-car units, 158901-158910 - owned by West Yorkshire Transport Authority.

SPECIAL FEATURES

Over 200 Sprinter Express Class 158 were built in the space of just four years, allowing the withdrawal of many worn out older types. After introduction to Scotland they took over services on cross-country routes throughout England and Wales. Sponsorship from the West Yorkshire authority allowed 15 units to be extended to three-cars, and ten additional two-car units to be constructed. A mechanically identical three-car

SPECIFICATION

Number series: 158701-158872, 158901-158910, 159001-159022
Total built: 204
Builder: BREL Derby
Date introduced: 1989
Track gauge, ft/ins (mm): 4 ft 8.5 in (1,435)
Unit configuration: 158798-158814 - M-M, 159001-159022 - M-M-M
Power unit type: 158701-158814, 158863-158872, 158901-159022 - Cummins NTA855R, 158815-158862 Perkins 2006-TWH
Transmission: Mechanical
Power rating, hp (kW): 158701-158814, 158864-158872 - 700 (520), 155863-155872, 159001-159022 - 800 (600)
Design speed, mph (km/h): 90 (145)
Additional features: multiple working

Class 159 design with modified seating works services between London Waterloo and the West Country. In 2004 operators included Arriva Trains Northern, Arriva Trains Wales, Central Trains, First North Western, ScotRail, TransPennine Express, South West Trains and Wessex Trains.

CLASS 165/166 DMU

Suburban Class 165/166

The 'Network Turbo' dmu, designed for services radiating from London's Paddington and Marylebone stations was one of the final moves by the former British Rail to improve the working lives of commuters whose daily journey until took place in tired 35-year-old units.

SUB-TYPES

165001-165039 - Paddington and Marylebone services; 165101-166221 Paddington-Oxford.

SPECIAL FEATURES

The Network Turbo, which shares the same bodyshell as Class 365/465/466 EMUs, is formed of two- and three-car units, and is seen on services radiating from London, and the three classes are mechanically virtually identical. Private train operators have customised their batches with, variously new interiors and air-conditioning. They are almost exclusively employed on Thames

SPECIFICATION

Number series: 165001-165039, 165101-165137, 166201-166221
Total built: 99
Builder: BREL/ABB York
Date introduced: 1990
Track gauge, ft/ins (mm): 4 ft 8.5 in (1,435)
Unit configuration: M-M, 165029-165039, 165101-166221 M-M-M
Power unit type: Perkins 2006-TWH
Transmission: Hydraulic - Voith
Power rating, hp (kW): 700 (520) 960 (780)
Design speed, mph (km/h): 165001-165039 - 75 (120), 165101-166221 - 90 (145)
Additional features: multiple working, swing plug doors.

Trains Paddington-Reading/Newbury/Oxford and Chiltern Railways Marylebone-Aylesbury/Banbury-Birmingham services. A couple of units have been lost in accidents.

CLASS 168/170 DMU FAMILY

Suburban Class 168/170

After a celebrated 1,064-day gap in new train orders because of the privatisation of Britain's railways, Adtranz (later Bombardier) secured the lion's share of the dmu replacement and fleet enhancement programme. The Turbostar is now the most widespread new DMU type in the UK.

SUB-TYPES

168001-168217 - Chiltern Railways, 170101-170117 - Midland Mainline, 170201-170273 - One, 170301-170392 - South West Trains, 170393-170396 - Hull Trains, 170397-170399 - short-lease units, 170401-170479 - First ScotRail, 170501-170523, 170630-170639 - Central Trains, 171721-171736 - Southern.

SPECIAL FEATURES

The design is an extensively re-worked Class 165/166 Network Turbo, and follows the original desire of Chiltern Railways for a high-speed, air-conditioned unit to upgrade its service between.

SPECIFICATION

Number series: 168001-168005, 168106-168113, 168214-168217, 170101-170117, 170201-170208, 170270-170273, 170301-170308, 170392-170399, 170401-170424, 170430-170462/170470-170479, 170501-170523, 170630-170639, 171721-171736
Total built: 166
Builder: Adtranz/Bombardier, Derby
Date introduced: 1997
Track gauge, ft/ins (mm): 4 ft 8.5 in (1,435)
Unit configuration: Two, three and four-car formations
Power unit type: MTU 6R183TD13H
Transmission: Hydraulic, Voith
Power rating, hp (kW): 422 (315)
Design speed, mph (km/h): 100 (160)
Additional features: multiple working, air conditioning, passenger information systems

Following privatisation, agreements were reached between Bombardier, leasing companies and train operators for high volume production for national service. More orders are possible beyond 2004 as UK passenger demand grows.

CLASS 180 DMU

InterCity Class 180

Service strengthening was undertaken by First Great Western on its London Paddington-Bristol/South Wales corridor with a new type of dmu - known as the 'Adelante' - that finally reached its potential in 2003 after three years of unreliability.

SPECIAL FEATURES

Alstom's troubled entry into the UK train replacement programme was compounded by control system problems in the otherwise highly-regarded dmu that has allowed private operator First Great Western to replace old locomotive-hauled trains between London and the West Country, releasing some of the hard-worked 30-year-old High Speed Train fleet to allow the running of a more intensive timetable. The trains are members of Alstom's Coradia family and are of similar general design to the less powerful two- and three-car Class 175 regional dmus employed in northwest England and North Wales.

SPECIFICATION

Number series: 180101-180114
Total built: 14
Builder: Alstom, Birmingham
Date introduced: 2000
Track gauge, ft/ins (mm): 4 ft 8.5 in (1,435)
Unit configuration: M-M-M-M-M
Power unit type: Cummins QSK19
Transmission: Hydraulic, Voith
Power rating, hp (kW): 3,750 (2,800)
Design speed, mph (km/h): 125 (200)
Additional features: Multiple working, air conditioning, passenger information system

CLASS 313/314/315/507/508 EMU FAMILY

Inner-suburban Classes 313/314/315/507/508

After trials with prototypes built in 1972, British Rail decided on a double-leaf sliding door design for suburban services, the only variation being different electrical equipment for different UK regions, notably London, Glasgow and Liverpool.

SUB-TYPES

Class 313 dual AC/DC voltage; 314, 315 - overhead AC power; Class 507, 508 third rail DC.

SPECIAL FEATURES

High-density services in London (Class 313/315), Glasgow (Class 314) and Liverpool (Class 507/508) were transformed over a period of ten years with the replacement of slam-door and sliding-door stock with a new design that concentrated on passenger comfort and ease of operation. Some spare Liverpool units have been modernised and sent to London for North Kent (South Eastern Trains Class 508/2) and North London line services (Silverlink Class 508/3). Other operators in 2004 included One (Class 315), Merseyrail (Classes 507 and 508/1), First ScotRail (Class 314), Silverlink (Class 313/1) and West Anglia Great Northern (Class 313/0)

SPECIFICATION

Number series: 313018-313064, 313101-313134, 314201-314216, 315801-315861, 507001-507033, 508103-508143, 508201-508212, 508301-508303
Number built: 217
Builder: BREL York
Date introduced: 1976
Track gauge, ft/ins (mm): 4 ft 8.5 in (1,435)
Unit configuration: Class 313, 314, 507, 508 - M-T-M, Class 315 - M-T-T-M
Power supply system: 314, 315 25 kV AC 50 Hz, 507, 508 750 V DC, 313 dual voltage
Electrical equipment: Class 313, 507, 508 - GEC G310 AZ traction motors, Class 314, 315 GEC G310 AZ/Brush TM61-53 (mixed)
Power rating, hp (kW): 445 (330)
Design speed, mph (km/h): 75 (120)
Additional features: Tightlock automatic coupling, dynamic braking, air suspension

CLASS 317/318/319/320/321/322 EMU FAMILY

Suburban Classes 317/318/319/320/321/322

Economy of design was at the forefront of British Rail thinking when the outer suburban emu fleet was considered for expansion to serve newly-electrified routes, and the already established Mk 3 coach bodyshell, still under production at the time, was modified to reduce design costs and shorten the build time. In various configurations, the units are seen all over the UK.

SUB-TYPES

Class 317 - London suburban (Liverpool Street and Thameslink); Class 318, 320 - Glasgow; Class 319 - Thameslink (central London); Class 321 - London suburban (Liverpool Street and Euston); Class 322 - London suburban (Liverpool Street), greater luggage space.

SPECIFICATION

Number series: 317301-317732, 318251-318270, 319001-319460, 320301-320322, 321301-321448, 322481-322485
Number built:
Builder: BREL York/Derby
Date introduced: 1981
Track gauge, ft/ins (mm): 4 ft 8.5 in (1,435)
Unit configuration: 317, 319, 320, 321, 322 - 4, 318 - 3
Power supply system: 25 kV AC 50 Hz
Electrical equipment: Class 317, 319 - GEC G315BZ traction motors, Class 318, 320, 321, 322 - Brush TM2141
Power rating, hp (kW): Class 317, 301- 335 (248), Class 318, 319, 320, 321, 322 - 362 (268)
Design speed, mph (km/h): Class 317, 318, 319, 321, 322 - 100 (160), 318251-318270 - 90 (145), 320301-320322 - 75 (120)
Additional features: Multiple working, driver-only operation

SPECIAL FEATURES

Experience gained at BR's Derby workshops with coaches made it the ideal choice to develop ideas for a new (Class 317) four-car unit to serve the newly-electrified London St Pancras-Bedford suburban route, and successive fleets were to be built in batches over the next ten years. All have twin-leaf sliding doors, and are driver-only operation. Classes 317 and 318 are broadly similar with front end gangway connections, but the Class 319 (above) designed for travel through London tunnels, has a flush end cab, and this was carried through the end of production with other classes. The nature of UK privatisation is that units are frequently moved between routes, the best example being the final Class 322, which has led a nomad existence working in the London, Manchester and Edinburgh areas during its short life. The emus carry many liveries, often within the same class on the same duties. Operators in

2004 included Arriva Trains Northern (Class 321/9), One (Classes 317, 321/3 and 322), First ScotRail (Classes 318 and 320), Silverlink (Class 321/4), Southern (Classes 319/0 and 319/2), Thameslink (Classes 319/0, 319/3 and 319/4) and West Anglia Great Northern (Class 317). In 1995 ABB supplied 16 dual-voltage four-car Class 325 emus to the UK postal authority, Royal Mail. Their design was based on that of the Class 319.

CLASS 332/333 EMU

Suburban and regional Classes 332/333

Siemens was a slow starter in the UK rolling stock requirement bonanza that followed privatisation, but it did manage to secure a private contract for units for the new electric service from London Paddington to Heathrow Airport.

SUB-TYPES

Class 332 - Heathrow Express (extended luggage areas, on-board video), Class 333 - West Yorkshire services operated by Arriva Trains Northern.

SPECIAL FEATURES

The launch in 1998 of the dedicated Heathrow Express airport service, not regulated by the UK Government, was supported by 14 units from Siemens, capable of fast acceleration. First class accommodation was retro-fitted, and the popularity of the service has resulted in orders for more trailers to expand the units from three to five cars. The urgent need for replacement trains

SPECIFICATION

Number series: 332001-332014, 333001-333016
Builder: CAF, Spain; Siemens, Germany
Total built: 30
Date introduced: Class 332 - 1997, Class 333 - 2001
Track gauge, ft/ins (mm): 4 ft 8.5 in (1,435)
Unit configuration: Class 332 - M-T-T-M or M-T-T-T-M; Class 333 - M-T-T-M
Power supply system: 25 kV AC 50 Hz
Electrical equipment: Siemens - IGBT converters with eight three-phase asyncronous traction motors
Power rating, hp (kW): 1,875 (1,400)
Design speed, mph (km/h): 100 (160)
Additional features: twin-leaf sliding doors, automatic train protection, rheostatic braking

for services radiating from Leeds and Bradford saw the same design adopted with a much-revised specification. Both classes were built in Spain by CAF at its Zaragoza plant, with Siemens providing the traction equipment.

CLASS 334/458/460 EMU FAMILY

Suburban and Regional Classes 334/458/460

The Juniper series, Alstom's other contribution to the modernised UK train fleet has not been an unqualified success, with late deliveries and complaints from operators of poor performance.

SUB-TYPES

Class 334 - First ScotRail Glasgow area suburban services (overhead); Class 458 - South West Trains services from London Waterloo (third rail); Class 460 - Gatwick Express (London) services (third rail).

SPECIAL FEATURES

Class 460 (above) is employed by Gatwick Express, a dedicated service from London Victoria station to Gatwick airport which chose the Juniper emu sliding-door design as the replacement for 1960s locomotives and coaches. These units are amongst the most easily recognised trains in the UK because of their front end 'Darth Vader' fairings. The driving car at the London end of each eight-car set provides stowage for checked baggage. South West Trains, the recipient of Class 458s, has had worse experiences and decided to hand them back to the leasing company. ScotRail's Class 334s have fared slightly better on Glasgow suburban duties, where they have replaced the original 1960 Class 303 'Blue Trains'.

SPECIFICATION

Number series: 334001-334040, 458001-458030, 460001-460008
Number built: 78
Builder: Alstom, Birmingham
Date introduced: 1998
Track gauge, ft/ins (mm): 4 ft 8.5 in (1,435)
Unit configuration: Class 334 - M-T-M, Class 458 - M-T-M-M, Class 460 - M-T-T-M-M-T-M-M
Power supply system: Class 334 - 25 kV AC 50 Hz, Class 458/460 - 750 V DC
Electrical equipment: Alstom ONIX 800 traction motors
Power rating, hp (kW): 540 (270)
Design speed, mph (km/h): 100 (160)

CLASS 357/375/377 EMU FAMILY

Suburban Classes 357/375/377

Major international manufacturer Bombardier scored early successes with mass orders for new London suburban emus to replace slam-door stock, and by 2003 1,318 coaches had been ordered, to be marshalled into a variety of formations. They are known as 'Electrostars'.

SUB-TYPES

357001-357228 - c2c London-Southend routes, overhead power, dual-voltage provision; 375301-375310 - South Eastern Trains London-Kent/Sussex third rail (dual-voltage potential) three-car; 375601-375630 - South Eastern Trains London-Kent/Sussex dual-voltage four-car; 375701-375830 - South Eastern Trains London-Kent/Sussex third rail four car; 375901-375927 - South Eastern Trains London outer suburban, third rail; 377101-377215 - Southern London outer suburban, dual voltage potential; 377301-377328 - Southern London outer suburban, third rail;

SPECIFICATION

Number series: 357001-357046/357201-375228, 375301-375310, 375601-375630, 375701-375715, 375801-375830, 375901-375927, 377101-377164, 377201-377215, 377301-377328, 377401-377475
Number built: 378
Builder: Adtranz/Bombardier, Derby
Date introduced: 1999
Track gauge, ft/ins (mm): 4 ft 8.5 in (1,435)
Unit configuration: Class 357 - M-M-T-M, Class 375 - M-T-M and M-M-T-M, Class 377 - M-M-T-M
Power supply system: Class 357 - 25 kV AC 50 Hz; remainder 750 V DC (but some equipped for retrofitting as dual voltage units)
Electrical equipment: Adtranz/Bombardier traction motors
Power rating, hp (kW): 2,010 (1,500) (Class 375/3 and 377/3 - 1,340 (1,000)
Design speed, mph (km/h): 100 (160)
Additional features: multiple working, regenerative braking, air-conditioning

377401-377475 - Southern London outer suburban voltage unspecified.

CLASS 360/444/450 EMU FAMILY

Suburban Classes 360/444/450

Suburban services in the south of the UK will be further transformed by 2006 with the arrival of Desiro trains from Siemens, which are direct replacements for slam-door stock, some of it approaching 50 years old. An additional series also meets extra demand on routes into Essex.

SUB-TYPES

Class 360 - London-Ipswich route, overhead power, full width cab; Class 444 - South London outer-suburban routes, third rail, low-density seating; Class 450 - South London inner suburban routes, third rail, high density seating.

SPECIAL FEATURES

A relatively modest order from First Great Eastern for the Desiro, which follows standard European practice reduced in size for the smaller UK loading gauge paved the way for major orders. The modular concept is followed, and every unit is given pre-delivery trials on the Siemens test track

SPECIFICATION

Number series: 360101-360121, 444001-444045, 450001-450100, 450201-450232
Number built: 198 (more may be ordered)
Builder: Siemens, Austria/Germany
Date introduced: 2002
Track gauge, ft/ins (mm): 4 ft 8.5 in (1,435)
Unit configuration: Class 360- M-T-T-M, Class 444 - M-T-T-T-M, Class 450 - M-T-T-M
Power supply system: 360101-360121 - 25 kV AC 50 Hz, 444001-450232 750 V DC
Electrical equipment: Siemens 1TB2016-0GB02 traction motors
Power rating, hp (kW): 1,350 (1,000)
Design speed, mph (km/h): 100 (160)
Additional features: multiple working, air-conditioning

at Wildenrath. Class 450 is a four-car design with nose-end gangway for suburban and outer-suburban services, while Class 444 is a five-car higher specification, lower-density version with a slightly longer bodyshell to run between Waterloo and the south coast. A further order has been placed for the Heathrow Express service.

CLASS 365/465/466 EMU

Suburban Classes 365/465/466 emu

The final pre-privatisation Networker and Networker Express designs for outer suburban services out of north and south-east London is easily distinguished from other types by its rounded front-end design.

SUB-TYPES

Class 365 - dual voltage;
Class 465, 466 - third rail.

SPECIAL FEATURES

These electric units are popular features of the London suburban landscape because of their ample and comfortable seating. The Class 365 dual-voltage fleet was originally split between the northern King's Cross-Peterborough/Cambridge routes and South Eastern Trains routes out of London, the former powered from overhead wires, the latter on third rail. Modification to the other power mode is relatively straightforward.

SPECIFICATION

Number series: 365501-365541, 465001-465050, 465151-465197, 465201-465250, 466001-466043
Number built: 231
Builder: 365501-365541 ABB York, 465001-465250 BREL York/Metro Cammell, Birmingham, 466001-466043 GEC Alsthom, Birmingham
Date introduced: 1991
Track gauge, ft/ins (mm): 4 ft 8.5 in (1,435)
Unit configuration: Class 365, 465 - M-T-T-M, Class 466 - M-M
Power supply system: Class 365 - 25 kV AC 50 Hz/750 V DC, Class 465, 466 - 750 V DC
Electrical equipment: Class 365 - GEC Alsthom G354CX traction motors, 465001-465197 - Brush TIM970, 465201-466043 - GEC Alsthom G352AY
Power rating, hp (kW): Class 365 - 850 (628), Class 465, 466 1,510 (1,120)
Design speed, mph (km/h): Class 365 - 100 (160), Class 465, 466 - 75 (120)
Additional features: Sliding doors, air-conditioning (Class 365)

CLASS 423 EMU

Suburban Class 423 emu

Increasingly stringent crash standards have accelerated the demise of slam-door trains in London. Class 423 is based on early post-war coach designs.

SUB-TYPES

3401-3591 - Owned by Angel Trains and HSBC Bank; 3801-3812 - owned by Porterbrook Leasing; 3901-3919 - dedicated to South London Metro service.

SPECIAL FEATURES

Class 423, also known in the UK as the 4-VEP (Vestibule Electro-Pneumatic), was the final high-volume design to be based on the Mk 1 coach. The original series was allocated to newly-electrified London Waterloo fast outer-suburban services, but the type was later built in large numbers for other routes in the South East, where station dwell times could be minimised by the considerable passenger handling capacity afforded

SPECIFICATION

Number series: 3401-3591, 3801-3812, 3901-3919
Builder: BR Derby/York
Date introduced: 1967
Track gauge, ft/ins (mm): 4 ft 8.5 in (1,435)
Unit configuration: T-T-M-T
Power supply system: 750 V DC third rail
Electrical equipment: four EE507 DC traction motors
Power rating, hp (kW): 1,000 (740)
Design speed, mph (km/h): 90 (145)
Additional features: electro-pneumatic brakes, gangway connection, multiple working

by doors along the entire train. Its poor performance in accidents, particularly the significant 1988 Clapham Junction disaster, heralded the search for a replacement, although it took over 20 years before Classes 375/377/444/450 started to appear. In 2004 the type remained in service with three operators, Southern, South Eastern Trains and South West Trains but its replacement was imminent.

411

CLASS 442 EMU

Class 442

Since the late 1980s the distinctive Class 442 emus have provided principal long-distance interurban services between London's Waterloo station and Southampton, Bournemouth and Weymouth. They feature some traction equipment from an earlier generation of vehicles that served the same route.

SPECIAL FEATURES

The 1980s electrification of the former Southern Region route west from Bournemouth to Weymouth led to the abandonment of the use of diesel locomotives for passenger services over that section in favour of emu operation throughout from London. This led to the development of the units featured here, which employ traction motors recovered from the redundant Class 432 4-REP slam-door emus that previously worked the London-Bournemouth section. Bodyshell design is a development of that employed in the Mark 3

SPECIFICATION

Number series: 2401-2424
Total built: 24
Builder: BREL
Date introduced: 1988
Track gauge, ft/ins (mm): 4 ft 8.5 in (1,435)
Unit configuration: T-T-M-T-T
Power supply system: 750 V DC third rail
Electrical equipment: English Electric, resistance control
Power rating, hp (kW): 1,605 (1,200)
Design speed, mph (km/h): 100 (160)

intercity coach, but with swing-plug doors. Corridor connections at each end of a Class 442 permit passengers and traincrew to move between coupled units. Air-conditioning is provided. The fleet is currently operated by South West Trains.

North American Trains

TYPE SW1500 DIESEL LOCOMOTIVE

General Motors SW1500

A heavy-duty yard switcher (shunter), also designed for transfer freights and main line work, it remains the standard workhorse at many freight yards across America nearly 40 years after its introduction.

SPECIAL FEATURES

General Motors' line of 'SW' (switcher) locomotives culminated in 1966 with the introduction of its new 645 two-stroke engine, offered in eight-cylinder 1,000 hp and 12-cylinder 1,500 hp versions for the SW1000 and SW1500 models. The SW1500 outsold the 1,000 hp version three-to-one and remains in service with many US railroads as a heavy-duty yard switcher (shunter). Around half were built on standard switcher bogies (trucks) with plain bearings, the others on Flexicoil bogies (trucks) for main line use on transfer freights. However, its light weight hampered its performance on the

SPECIFICATION

Number series: Various, according to railroad
Total built: 807
Builder: General Motors, USA
Date introduced: 1966
Track gauge, ft/ins (mm): 4 ft 8.5 in (1,435)
Axle arrangement: Bo-Bo
Power unit type: GM 645E
Transmission: Electric, 4 x GM traction motors
Weight, tonnes: 112
Power rating, hp (kW): 1,500 (1,119)
Design speed, mph (km/h): 65 (105)

main line. Of the original purchasers, Southern Pacific (with 240) and Penn Central (112), accounted for nearly half the total production, which ran until 1974.

TYPE F7/F9 DIESEL LOCOMOTIVE

General Motors F7/F9

The final development of General Motors' classic 'bullnose' design were built in 1957 and although designated 'F' for freight, passenger versions were also built. Their rock-solid reliability means that a small number survive in service.

SPECIAL FEATURES

Built as a freight unit or in a body four feet longer incorporating a steam-heating boiler ('FP') they made major inroads replacing steam on freight with the F7s following on from the very similar pre-war F3s. Using the uprated 567B engine and later the 567C engine, the F7s and F9s were sold as 'A' units with a cab or 'B' (booster) without cabs. Normally to be found as an A+B formation or two sets back-to-back, in later years locomotives would also be included in formations with other types. Available with different gear ratios, it proved to be a truly mixed-traffic locomotive, handling every type of traffic from the heaviest freights to fastest passenger trains, proved by sales of 3,681 F7s to 49 different US

SPECIFICATION

Number series: Various, according to railroad
Total built: 3,849 (F7), 241 (F9)
Builder: General Motors, USA
Date introduced: 1949
Track gauge, ft/ins (mm): 4 ft 8.5 in (1,435)
Axle arrangement: Bo-Bo
Power unit type: GM 16-567B (F7); GM 16-567C (F9)
Transmission: Electric, 4 x GM traction motors
Weight, tonnes: 104
Power rating, hp (kW): F7 -1,500 (1,119); F9 - 1,750 (1,305)
Design speed, mph (km/h): 50-120 (80-164) depending on which gear ratios are fitted
Additional features: multiple working; many fitted with rheostatic brakes. 301 were built with steam-heating boilers (FP series) and 60 were also equipped for third-rail current collection as dual-mode units for tunnel operation in the New York area (FL9)

railroads and 301 FP7s. By the time the F9s were built, the market for carbody locomotives had almost dried up, as railroads chose 'hood' versions for easier maintenance. Many 'Fs' were traded-in for newer GM models as parts could be re-used.

TYPE GP7 DIESEL LOCOMOTIVE

General Motors GP7

A General Motors design that saw many railroads convert from steam to diesel, it was designed for shunting in addition to branch line freight work and thus designated 'road switcher'. It is a rugged design that was so good that locomotives were rebuilt in later years, resulting in some remaining in service today. It also formed the basis of the GP design for the next 50 years.

SUB-TYPES

GP7B, (total 5) 'Booster' or 'slave' locomotives without were cabs sold to Sante Fe.

SPECIAL FEATURES

Built in response to General Motors' competitors, especially Alco, which were gaining success with a general purpose model for branch line use, the GP7 used the engine and electrical equipment from the 'F7', but on a load-bearing underframe, rather the 'Fs' load-bearing bodies. It was an instant success, with 2,610 being sold to US railroads, 112 to Canada and two to Mexico. As

SPECIFICATION

Number series: Various, according to railroad
Total built: 2,729
Builder: General Motors, USA
Date introduced: 1949
Track gauge, ft/ins (mm): 4 ft 8.5 in (1,435)
Axle arrangement: Bo-Bo
Power unit type: GM 16-567B
Transmission: Electric, 4 x GM traction motors
Weight, tonnes: 109
Power rating, hp (kW): 1,500 (1,119)
Design speed, mph (km/h): 65 (105)
Additional features: multiple working. Some fitted with rheostatic (dynamic) brakes and/or steam-heating boilers

they used standard GM parts, they remained in service with various railroads for many years, and were often rebuilt to incorporate rheostatic (dynamic) brakes, and short-height front bonnets to improve visibility. Most US railroads operated them at some time or another and today it tends to be small companies that run the survivors.

TYPE GP9 DIESEL LOCOMOTIVE

General Motors GP9

The 'GP' or 'Geeps' as they are known, are credited with completing the dieselisation of American railroads throughout the 1950s. The GP7 was upgraded with a more powerful engine and other maintenance-reducing modifications and the otherwise almost identical GP9 set a new record with the GP being America's (and therefore the world's) best-selling diesel locomotive.

SUB-TYPES
GP9B, (total 165) 'booster' or 'slave' locomotives without cabs.

SPECIAL FEATURES
During the seven years during which the GP9 and GP9B variants were built, they were sold to Mexico (10), Canada (646) with the remainder taken by various US railroads. Some were built with a low nose, a hint of things to come with later models. Like the GP7s, most were used for branch and secondary lines. Buyers could specify variations, such as steam heating boilers for

SPECIFICATION

Number series: Various, according to railroad
Total built: 4,257
Builder: General Motors, USA
Date introduced: 1954
Track gauge, ft/ins (mm): 4 ft 8.5 in (1,435)
Axle arrangement: Bo-Bo
Power unit type: GM 16-567C
Transmission: Electric, 4 x GM traction motors
Weight, tonnes: 110
Power rating, hp (kW): 1,750 (1,305)
Design speed, mph (km/h): 65 (105)
Additional features: multiple working. Some fitted with rheostatic (dynamic) brakes and/or steam-heating boilers

passenger use, or in the case of Canadian National, Flexicoil bogies (trucks) and small fuel tanks to lighten them for branch line work. Fuel tanks options ranged from 800 to 1,800 gallons. Second-hand sales in later years saw them work over a wide number of US railroads. Included in the total built are 165 GP9Bs ('boosters' without cabs) bought by the Pennsylvania (40) and Union Pacific Railroads (125).

417

TYPE SD9 DIESEL LOCOMOTIVE

General Motors SD9

General Motors' 'SD' designation meaning 'special duties', indicates a Co-Co version of its general purpose 'GP' model. The extra powered axles made them ideal for heavy-haul freights as they were less likely to slip and their design continued to be improved in later modes. Popular with many railroads, hundreds remain in service today.

SPECIAL FEATURES

Many of the major railroads saw the Co-Co version of the GP9 as the answer for heavy freight running at slow speeds for many miles. The type was in production for six years until superseded by the more powerful SD18 and SD24 series (1,800 hp and 2,400 hp respectively). Built with a full-height bonnet, some were rebuilt with lower bonnets. Their rugged and durable nature meant that like the more numerous GP9s, many remain in service, although no longer with the

SPECIFICATION

Number series: Various, according to railroad
Total built: 471
Builder: General Motors, USA
Date introduced: 1954
Track gauge, ft/ins (mm): 4 ft 8.5 in (1,435)
Axle arrangement: Co-Co
Power unit type: GM 16-567C
Transmission: Electric, 6 x GM traction motors
Weight, tonnes: 163
Power rating, hp (kW): 1,750 (1,305)
Design speed, mph (km/h): 65 (105)
Additional features: multiple working, most fitted with rheostatic (dynamic) brakes. Some had steam-heating boilers

major (Class 1) railroads which originally bought most of them.

TYPE U30C DIESEL LOCOMOTIVE

General Electric U30C

General Electric trailed behind General Motors in volume for its all-purpose 3,000hp locomotive - the U30 series - which was its best-selling model until production ended in 1976.

SUB-TYPES

U30CG: Six of these full-width body versions with steam heating boilers for passenger trains were built specifically for Santa Fe; in all other respects they were a standard U30C.

SPECIAL FEATURES

Nicknamed 'U-boats' the U30C ('U' Universal, '30' 3,000 hp, 'C' six-axles) was a direct competitor to General Motors' two-stroke 3,000 hp SD40 introduced the same year. In 1966 it was evolution rather than revolution that saw GE's existing four-stroke 16-cylinder FDL engine uprated from 2,500 hp in the U25B (Bo-Bo) and U25C (Co-Co) models that were produced from 1959. A Bo-Bo variant (U30B) was also built of which 296 were sold. GE, recognising that there

SPECIFICATION

Number series: Various, according to railroad
Total built: 598
Builder: General Electric, USA
Date introduced: 1967
Track gauge, ft/ins (mm): 4 ft 8.5 in (1,435)
Axle arrangement: Co-Co
Power unit type: GE FDL-16 of 3,000 hp
Transmission: Electric, 6 x GE-752 traction motors
Weight, tonnes: 177
Power rating, hp (kW): 3,000 (2,240)
Design speed, mph (km/h): 70 (113)
Additional features: multiple working, optional steam heating

was also a demand for an intermediate horsepower locomotive, offered the 12-cylinder 2,250 hp FDL engine in Bo-Bo and Co-Co formats in the U30 body, selling 465 and 53 locomotives respectively from 1968 to 1977. The majority of 'U-boats' were sold new to USA railroads, with only 40 U23Bs going to Mexico and none to Canada. However, second-hand sales saw them widely redistributed across USA and Mexico, where some still remain in service.

TYPE GP38 DIESEL LOCOMOTIVE

General Motors GP38

A general-purpose medium horsepower locomotive that earned a reputation for solid reliability on freight in the USA; additionally 21 were sold to Canada and six to Mexico. Its successor, the GP38-2 was one of the most successful locomotives built with more than 90 per cent still in service, 30 years after they were constructed.

SUB-TYPES

GP38AC: An option offered during 1971, the last year of GP38 manufacture, it had an AC alternator, rather than a DC generator, and 240 were built.

SPECIAL FEATURES

When the 645E engine replaced the 567 engine, the 16-cylinder GP38 was introduced as a replacement for the 1,800 hp (1,343 kW) GP28 to which it was otherwise identical. General Motors perceived there was a market for a sub-3,000 hp

locomotive without a turbocharger - which adds maintenance cost, especially if the extra power is not needed. In its six years in production, it sold reasonably well. However, sales took off when the GP38-2 was introduced in 1972. Using the same microprocessor controls and electrical equipment as the GP40-2, and fitted with an AC alternator in place of the DC generator, it became a runaway favourite. It soon gained an exceptional reputation for high availability and low operating costs, with total sales of 2,222 to 59 customers; 254 locomotives were for Canada and 153 for Mexico. Some were built for passenger use such as in 1982 for Mexico's NdeM and CH-P, that had them built with steam-heating boilers, the last North American locomotives to be so fitted. Many were built reusing parts, such as bogies (trucks), from older GM locomotives and production continued until 1986 when the 710 engine was introduced.

SPECIFICATION

Number series: Various, according to railroad
Total built: 733
Builder: General Motors, USA
Date introduced: 1965
Track gauge, ft/ins (mm): 4 ft 8.5 in (1,435)
Axle arrangement: Bo-Bo
Power unit type: GM 16-645E
Transmission: Electric, 4 x GM D77 traction motors
Weight, tonnes: 113
Power rating, hp (kW): 2,000 (1,493)
Design speed, mph (km/h): 65 (105)
Additional features: Multiple working, steam heating, and/or rheostatic (dynamic) brakes

TYPE GP39 DIESEL LOCOMOTIVE

General Motors GP39

A turbocharged version of the GP38, but with 12 rather than 16 cylinders, it was expected to become a good-selling locomotive for freight and passenger work. In its modified 'Dash 2' form, sales were better, but most railroads preferred to avoid turbochargers due to higher maintenance costs and sales remained low by GM's standards.

SUB-TYPES

GP39DC: Two locomotives built in 1970 with DC generators for Kennecott Copper.

SPECIAL FEATURES

The original version found only three customers of which the largest was the Chesapeake & Ohio, which bought 20 locomotives. In 1972, when the Dash 2 series of GM locomotives were introduced, the GP39 was dropped from the catalogue. However, somewhat to GM's surprise, sales started coming in and the GP39-2 was built to special order. The first customer was Santa Fe in 1974,

SPECIFICATION

Number series: Various, according to railroad
Total built: 23
Builder: General Motors, USA
Date introduced: 1969
Track gauge, ft/ins (mm): 4 ft 8.5 in (1,435)
Axle arrangement: Bo-Bo
Power unit type: GM 12-645E3
Transmission: Electric, 4 x GM D77 traction motors
Weight, tonnes: 113-125
Power rating, hp (kW): 2,300 (1,716)
Design speed, mph (km/h): 65 (105)
Additional features: multiple working, steam heating, and/or rheostatic (dynamic) brakes

which needed the turbocharger for operation at high altitudes, in Colorado for example, where non-turbocharged locomotives lose considerable power and smoke badly due to the lack of oxygen. Production continued for Santa Fe and other railroads until a total of 239 GP39-2s had been built, by the time the last batch of 20 was completed in 1984.

TYPE GP40 DIESEL LOCOMOTIVE

General Motors GP40

Offering 800-1,000 hp more than the GP38/GP39 models, the GP40 together with its Co-Co variant and later versions were the world's most popular diesel with 7,990 locomotives being built - most for the USA market.

SUB-TYPES

GP40TC: Eight locomotives built in 1966 for Toronto Commuter operator they had a separate auxiliary engine and generator for electric train heating. GP40P: Thirteen were built in 1968 with longer frames and a rear projection containing a steam-heating boiler for the Central Railroad of New Jersey's commuter trains.

SPECIAL FEATURES

For main line use the low-maintenance 16-cylinder 2,000 hp 645E (pressure-charged with a Roots-type blower) was offered in the GP38; the turbocharged 3,000 hp 645E3 in the GP40 and 20-cylinder 3,600 hp 645E3 (2,690 kW) in the Co-

SPECIFICATION

Number series: Various, according to railroad
Total built: 1,264
Builder: General Motors, USA
Date introduced: 1965
Track gauge, ft/ins (mm): 4 ft 8.5 in (1,435)
Axle arrangement: Bo-Bo
Power unit type: GM 16-645E3
Transmission: Electric, 4 x GM D77 traction motors
Weight, tonnes: 116-126
Power rating, hp (kW): 3,000 (2,240)
Design speed, mph (km/h): 65 (105)
Additional features: multiple working, optional electric or steam heating and/or rheostatic (dynamic) brakes

Co SD45. The new engine was similar to the old model, but its bore was increased from 567 cubic inches to 645 cubic inches. GM offered trade-ins on its original 'E' series locomotives that it sold from 1945 and the GP40 family, with higher horsepower and lower maintenance costs. Trade-ins on some models also reduced the cost as some items, such as bogies (trucks), could be re-used.

TYPE SD40 DIESEL LOCOMOTIVE

General Motors SD40

The 3,000 hp Co-Co SD40 was preferred by railroads over the Bo-Bo GP40, which was otherwise identical, on account of its better adhesion.

SUB-TYPES

SDP40: Passenger version with an extended body containing a steam-heating boiler. Six were bought by the Great Northern Railway, and 16 by the National Railways of Mexico. SD40A: A special batch of 18 built for the Illinois Central on the 5 ft longer underframe of the SD45, to allow room for larger fuel tanks.

SPECIAL FEATURES

Introduced as part of the new range of locomotives fitted with the 645 engine they were built on the same underframe as the SD38, resulting in large front and rear platforms beyond the bonnets at each end, known as 'the front porch'. Offering the same 'punch' as the GP40,

SPECIFICATION

Number series: Various, according to railroad
Total built: 1,295
Builder: General Motors, USA
Date introduced: 1966
Track gauge, ft/ins (mm): 4 ft 8.5 in (1,435)
Axle arrangement: Co-Co
Power unit type: GM 16-645E3
Transmission: Electric, 6 x GM D77 traction motors
Weight, tonnes: 167-179
Power rating, hp (kW): 3,000 (2,240)
Design speed, mph (km/h): 65 (105)
Additional features: multiple working, optional steam heating and/or rheostatic (dynamic) brakes

the advantage of putting the power through six, rather than four traction motors soon found favour with railroads when adhesion problems and traction motors failures manifested themselves on the Bo-Bo design, when pushed to its limit. Like all USA diesels, they worked in multiple on freight trains, and became part of the backbone of many railroads.

TYPE SD40-2 DIESEL LOCOMOTIVE

General Motors SD40-2

The introduction of electronic control systems in 1972 saw the 'Dash 2' range of GM locomotives introduced, of which the 3,000hp Co-Co SD40-2 was the most popular, used mainly on freight. Total sales included 744 to Canada and 107 to Mexico. In all it made the SD40-2 the most successful model in GM's history.

SUB-TYPES

SD40T-2: The 'Tunnel Motor', a variant for Southern Pacific in 1974 as a solution to cooling problems suffered by locomotives working at high altitudes in the hot exhaust-filled air of tunnels, which would cause locomotives behind the leading engine to shut down. The radiators were re-located to the top of the hood and air intakes moved to just above the frame. Of the 312 built, SP took 239 and Rio Grande bought 73.

SD40-2SS: These nine locomotives, built in 1978, were test beds with GM's advanced Super Series wheelslip control, high capacity AR16 alternator

SPECIFICATION

Number series: Various, according to railroad
Total built: 4,291
Builder: General Motors, USA
Date introduced: 1972
Track gauge, ft/ins (mm): 4 ft 8.5 in (1,435)
Axle arrangement: Co-Co
Power unit type: GM 16-645E3C
Transmission: Electric, 6 x GM D77 or D78 traction motors
Weight, tonnes: 164
Power rating, hp (kW): 3,000 (2,240)
Design speed, mph (km/h): 65-82 (105-132)
Additional features: multiple working, optional steam heating and/or rheostatic (dynamic) brakes

and larger turbocharger and were taken by Union Pacific and Burlington Northern.

SD40-2F: Production of the SD40-2 ended in February 1986. However Canadian Pacific, purchaser of the third-largest fleet of SD40-2s, persuaded GM to build a final order of 25 SD40-2s in 1988 with a full-width body, Positive Traction Control and 'comfort' cabs.

TYPE GP40-2 DIESEL LOCOMOTIVE

General Motors GP40-2

The GP40 design was reinvigorated in 1972 with the introduction of solid-state electronics and a revolutionary wheelslip system that made it a market leader in freight haulage.

SUB-TYPES

GP40-2L: 233 'lightweight frame' versions sold to Canada, with Canadian National full-width 'comfort' cab with better sound insulation, collision protection and facilities such as 'fridges and hotplates. GP40P-2: Three locomotives built for Southern Pacific with steam-heating boilers.

SPECIAL FEATURES

Externally the GP40 was hardly affected by the change to the 'Dash 2', but on the inside the traction motor and alternator were refined and the engine beefed-up with a redesigned turbocharger, camshaft bearings and pistons. The most significant improvement was the installation of a solid-state control system with

SPECIFICATION

Number series: Various, according to railroad
Total built: 1,225
Builder: General Motors, USA
Date introduced: 1972
Track gauge, ft/ins (mm): 4 ft 8.5 in (1,435)
Axle arrangement: Bo-Bo
Power unit type: GM 16-645E3
Transmission: Electric, 4 x GM D77B traction motors
Weight, tonnes: 116-128
Power rating, hp (kW): 3,000 (2,240)
Design speed, mph (km/h): 65 (105)
Additional features: multiple working, optional electric or steam heating and/or rheostatic (dynamic) brakes

interchangeable printed circuit boards. Adhesion and wheelship problems were banished with a sophisticated ground-radar system that knew how fast the locomotive was actually travelling. Sales were slow until the Chessie System, which already had over 200 GP40s, started buying the first of 350 GP40-2s, while Canadian National was also a big purchaser.

TYPE SD70/SD75 DIESEL LOCOMOTIVE

General Motors SD70/SD75

United States of America

A natural progression from the 3,800 hp SD60, this pair of 16-cylinder 4,000 hp and 4,300 hp diesel-electrics is the current pinnacle of DC traction motor designs from General Motors. Bought for heavy freight and high-speed intermodal work, they are relatively low in numbers, reflecting the move by railroads towards AC traction motors.

SUB-TYPES

SD70: Standard model with conventional cab. So far 120 have been delivered to Norfolk Southern (also the first to order SD70s), Illinois Central and Conrail. SD70I: 'I' stands for 'isolated cab' - GM's top-of-the-range WhisperCab - and Canadian National ordered 26 in 1995. It has a large full-width cab floating on rubber cushions to reduce noise and vibration to a minimum. SD70M: The most popular variant, with 1,063 locomotives built so far, it has a full-width 'Modified' North American cab (hence the 'M' designation) with

SPECIFICATION

Number series: Various, according to railroad
Total built: 1,209 (SD70), 283 (SD75)
Builder: General Motors, Canada
Date introduced: 1992/1995
Track gauge, ft/ins (mm): 4 ft 8.5 in (1,435)
Axle arrangement: Co-Co
Power unit type: GM 16-710G3 (SD75: 4,300 hp)
Transmission: Electric, 6 x GM D90TR traction motors
Weight, tonnes: 178
Power rating, hp (kW) SD70: 4,000 (2,985). SD75: 4,300 (3,209)
Design speed, mph (km/h): 70 (113)
Additional features: multiple working, rheostatic (dynamic) brakes, steering radial bogies (trucks).

soundproofing and improved collision protection. SD75M: The standard 4,300 hp model comes with a full-width North American cab and has so far sold 76 locomotives. SD75I: Isolated WhisperCab version. Of the 207 sold, more than half went to Canadian National.

TYPE DASH 7 DIESEL LOCOMOTIVE

General Electric Dash 7

From 1977 General Electric's new range of locomotives, the Dash 7 series replaced its 'U-boat' models. Apart from visual differences, it offered marked improvements in fuel economy, tractive effort, performance and reliability as it paved the way for GE's dominance from the mid-1980s and put the company 'on the map'.

SUB-TYPES

B-series locomotives are Bo-Bo; C-series are Co-Co

B23-7 (pictured right): A total of 535 of the 12-cylinder locomotives were built, making it the most popular Bo-Bo Dash 7. Conrail had 141, and Mexico 123.

BQ23-7: Ten built in 1978 for Seaboard Coast Line with an enlarged crew 'Quarters' cab without a nose.

B30-7: Fitted with the 16-cylinder 3,000 hp engine, some were built on second-hand bogies (trucks), and the 199 locomotives follow directly

SPECIFICATION

Number series: Various, according to railroad
Total built: 2,471
Builder: General Electric, USA
Date introduced: 1977
Track gauge, ft/ins (mm): 4 ft 8.5 in (1,435)
Axle arrangement: Bo-Bo (B23-7); Co-Co (C30-7)
Power unit type: GE 7FDL12 (B23-7) or GE 7FDL16 (C30-7)
Transmission: Electric, 4 or 6 x GE-752 traction motors
Weight, tonnes: 114-127 or 163-190
Power rating, hp (kW): 2,250 (1,679) or 3,000 (2,240)
Design speed, mph (km/h): 70 (113)
Additional features: multiple working, optional steam heating

from the previous U30B design.

B30-7A: A bold move by GE in 1980, using its 12-cylinder engine, uprated to 3,000 hp, rather than the 16-cylinder. The 58 locomotives bought by Missouri Pacific led the way for more variations using the same engine.

B30-7A(B): Identical to the B30-7A, apart from the lack of a cab. All 120 'B' (booster) units were built for Burlington Northern in 1982/83.

B30-7A1: Standard B307A locomotives, but with the internal equipment relocated, 22 were built to Southern's unique specifications in 1982.

B36-7: Evolved from the B30-7, it is fitted with the 16-cylinder FDL engine pushed to 3,600 hp (2,687 kW). The model was built from 1980-85 and 110 were produced for Sante Fe, Southern, Exxon, Southern Pacific and Conrail. The final order for 120 in 1985 was from Seaboard System.

C30-7: Designed to succeed the 3,000 hp U30C, GE's best-selling model in the 'U-boat' range, it achieved nearly double its sales with 1,078 locomotives between 1976-86. All used the 16-cylinder 3,000 hp FDL engine and improvements over the U30C include better performance, updated electrical equipment and fuel efficiencies. Purchasers included Burlington Northern, Mexico and Sante Fe.

C30-7A: 12-cylinder 3,000 hp engine, 50 built in 1984 for Conrail.

C36-7: Pushing for even higher horsepower, in 1978 the 16-cylinder engine was uprated to 3,600 hp (2,686 kW) and 84 were sold to Mexico and Norfolk & Western. After construction of Dash 8 models started in 1984, the C36-7 was enhanced with some of the former's components and uprated again to 3,750 hp (2,798 kW). Orders for 85 from Conrail and Missouri Pacific took production up to 1985.

SPECIAL FEATURES

With all models having the suffix '-7' (indicating 1977, their year of design), the Dash 7 series paved the way for General Electric to make inroads into the domestic diesel market. Launched in the middle of the coal boom (following the oil crisis) when potential for locomotive sales was good, the Dash 7 series was in production until 1985. Dash 7s were continuously improved, resulting in a 16 per cent fuel saving between the first and last batches, while later builds incorporated some Dash 8 electronics and components. With a wide range and willingness to recycle parts from traded-in locomotives such as bogies (trucks) from competitor General Motors' products, Dash 7 production kept GE busy during lean times.

Additionally, GE brought out the Super 7 series of Bo-Bo (12-cylinder 2,250 hp) and Co-Co (16-cylinder 3,000 hp) locomotives. While not strictly Dash 7s (and not included in the headline totals), 261 locomotives were re-manufactured from 1989-94. More than a rebuild, but not quite new, they used frames, bogies (trucks), fuel tanks and alternator from traded-in U-boats, with Dash 7 and Dash 8 technology. Bought by many railroads, including in Mexico, it is effectively an honorary Dash 7.

OTHER COUNTRIES OPERATED

The design was also a success overseas, with 420 for Chinese Railways (Class ND5) from 1984-86 (not included in the overall totals).

TYPE DASH 8 DIESEL LOCOMOTIVE

General Electric Dash 8

The result of a programme to improve the Dash 7 design, the key difference was the Dash 8's sophisticated microprocessor controls, which took GE into third-generation locomotive technology. The Bo-Bo versions were popular for the growing number of high-speed intermodal trains, but as train weights grew, the Co-Co version took over as GE established itself as North America's market-leading locomotive builder.

SUB-TYPES

B-series locomotives are Bo-Bo; C-series are Co-Co B32-8: Three 1984-built prototypes with 12-cylinder 3,150 hp engine. B36-8: Single 3,600 hp Dash 8 prototype built in 1982 with 16-cylinder engine. B39-8: Production run (1984-88) of 145 3,900hp 16-cylinder Dash 8s, of which 100 were leased to Burlington Northern and the rest bought by Southern Pacific. Dash 8-40B: Immediate successor to the B39-8, production started before the last B39-8s were finished.

Almost identical, power was increased to 4,000 hp, but inside was a host of improvements from software upgrades to engine enhancements. In just over a year until May 1989, 151 were built for Conrail, Cotton Belt, Sante Fe, Susquehanna and others, mainly for high-speed intermodal trains. Dash 8-40BW: Identical to the 8-40B, except for a full-width North American 'comfort' cab, 83 were bought by ATSF in 1991. Dash 8-32B: Medium horsepower offering, using 12-cylinder 3,200 hp engine of which 46 were sold. The Co-Co version never found any takers. Dash 8-32BWH: Modified 8-32B with electric train heating, and full-width North American cab to Amtrak specifications which bought 20 in 1991 as part of an order for the first Genesis locomotives. C36-8: A one-off 3,600 hp prototype built in 1983 using the 16-cylinder engine, to refine the Dash 8 design. C32-8: Ten pre-production C39-8s sold to Conrail in 1984; they had the 12-cylinder engine rated at 3,150 hp

(effectively a Dash 8 version of the C30-7A).
C39-8: Production version of the 16-cylinder
3,900 hp Co-Co. Introduced from 1984 it was the
first Dash 8 model to enter full production and
161 were sold to Norfolk Southern and Conrail
until 1987. Dash 8-40C: A seamless transition
from the C39-8 in 1987 with an almost symbolic
increase to 4,000 hp from the 16-cylinder four-
stroke engine. The standard cab version sold to
Union Pacific (256), CSX (147), Chicago & North
Western (77), Norfolk Southern (75) and Conrail
(25) giving a total of 580 sold in five years.
Dash 8-40CM: Full-width body version with
'comfort cab' to Canadian National design, which
bought 30 examples in 1990. They were the first
GE locomotives sold to a major (Class 1) railroad
in Canada since 1950 and were followed by orders
from other Canadian railroads, including 55 to
Canadian National, to give a total of 84. Dash 8-
40CW: Establishing a new standard for GE
locomotives, 903 of these 4,000 hp 8-40s with a

SPECIFICATION

Number series: Various, according to railroad
Total built: 2,242
Builder: General Electric, USA
Date introduced: 1983
Track gauge, ft/ins (mm): 4 ft 8.5 in (1,435)
Axle arrangement: Bo-Bo (Dash 8-40B); Co-Co
(Dash 8-40C)
Power unit type: GE 7FDL16
Transmission: Electric, 4 or 6 x GE-752AG
traction motors
Weight, tonnes: 130 or 181
Power rating, hp (kW): 4,000 (2,985)
Design speed, mph (km/h): 70 (113)
Additional features: multiple working

full-width Canadian-style North American
'comfort' cab were sold from 1989 with many
purchasers (including Union Pacific, Sante Fe, CSX
and Conrail buying in large numbers) until the
end of Dash 8 production in 1984. Dash 8-44CW:
Introduced in 1993, the final version had its 16-
cylinder engine rated at 4,400 hp and 53 were
built for CSXT.

TYPE SD60 DIESEL LOCOMOTIVE

General Motors SD60

Marking a step-change for GM, this new design heralded its third-generation diesel-electric locomotives, using the new 710 engine and totally revised electronic controls. During the 11 years of production, the SD60s were bought by major 'Class 1' railroads as modern, heavy-freight movers.

SUB-TYPES

SD60F: Built specifically for Canadian National, the 64 locomotives have full-width bodies and 'comfort cabs' featuring more space, improved collision protection, better sound insulation and good crew facilities.

SD60M: Introduced from 1989, they have large full-width cabs (similar to the SD60F) described as North American modified (hence the 'M' designation) 'comfort' cabs. A total of 461 were built until 1993, although some railroads continued to buy standard SD60s, which remained

SPECIFICATION

Number series: Various, according to railroad
Total built: 1,147
Builder: General Motors, Canada
Date introduced: 1984
Track gauge, ft/ins (mm): 4 ft 8.5 in (1,435)
Axle arrangement: Co-Co
Power unit type: GM 16-710G
Transmission: Electric, 6 x GM D87B traction motors
Weight, tonnes: 166 (sub-types 166-179)
Power rating, hp (kW): 3,800 (2,836)
Design speed, mph (km/h): 70 (113)
Additional features: multiple working, rheostatic (dynamic) brakes

in production until 1991. SD60M purchasers were Union Pacific (281), Conrail (75), Burlington Northern (100) and Soo Line (5).

SD60I: An advance on the North American Modified cab, the full-width Isolated WhisperCab (hence 'I') was introduced in 1993. Unlike previous cabs, it is not welded to the frame, but floats on a cushion of rubber mounts to further reduce noise and vibration. A total of 81 were built, all for Conrail, over two years.

SD60MAC: Four prototypes, built in 1991/2 and owned by GM Electro-Motive Division (EMD) to test Siemens AC traction equipment, they were delivered to Burlington Northern and returned to GM in 1998.

SPECIAL FEATURES

The year 1984 was a landmark for General Motors as it launched its new 710 two-stroke engine, and ushered in a third generation of locomotives - the 16-cylinder 60 series. The totally redesigned control system, run by three microprocessors, used new wheelslip technology and pushed the high horsepower race ahead. Its predecessor, the SD50s, which used the 16-cylinder 645 engine, (pushed to its limit at 3,500 hp) and SD40-2 electronics, resulted in sales of only 487. But the new 60-series saw its first bulk order of 50 from Norfolk Southern, just months after its launch. In a repeat of GM's 'three-for-four' sales tactics when the 3,000 hp SD40 was launched to replace first-generation 'E' and 'F' series diesels, three SD60s had almost the same horsepower as four SD40s, with the advantage of much improved adhesion.

From 1993, when the new 'comfort' cab was introduced, some buyers took the sub-type, whilst others, including CSX, Kansas City Southern and Norfolk Southern, continued to buy the standard version with conventional cabs. Locomotive sales continued to boom for GM through the early 1990s, with more orders that it could handle at London, Ontario, Canada, and assembly under contract at other locations became commonplace. A Bo-Bo version - the GP50 - was otherwise identical to its Co-Co brother and 380 were sold, with Sante Fe taking 126, including 23 cab-less GP60Bs (the first 'B' booster units built by GM since 1963). Other buyers included Southern Pacific (195), Norfolk Southern (50) and Rio Grande (3). Changing trends saw the former all-purpose Bo-Bo fall from grace - the Co-Co SD60 outsold the Bo-Bo GP50 by three-to-one - and when the final GM 'Geep' was built in February 1994, it appeared to close the book on main line freight Bo-Bo designs after 45 years.

TYPE DASH 9 DIESEL LOCOMOTIVE

General Electric Dash 9

Representing the current pinnacle in DC diesel locomotive design, the 4,400 hp 44CW and its 4,000 hp 40CW heavy freight sister continue to win sales, selling almost double that of its General Motors competitor, and confirming its number one position in North America.

SUB-TYPES

Dash 9-40C: Initially resistant to the North American cab and 4,400 hp, Norfolk Southern specified traditional standard cabs and a 4,000 hp rating in 120 locomotives built in 1995. They were the last GE locomotives for the home market with standard cabs.

Dash 9-40CW: Subsequent orders totalling 856 of the 4,000 hp version for Norfolk Southern, which has bought nearly half the total Dash 9 production. With a North American cab, but standard cab controls, production started in 1996 and deliveries continue. Changes to the computer control and fuel racks means the engine can be easily uprated to 4,400 hp if desired.

Dash 9-44CW: The standard 4,400 hp version, still in production, of which 1,768 have been built so far. Chicago & North Western was the first to place orders in 1993, and other buyers include Sante Fe, North Western, Canadian Pacific and Southern Pacific.

Dash 9-44CWL: Canadian National's version of the 4,400 hp model with its own full-width 'comfort' cab design, of which it bought 23, followed by BC Rail taking four. For later orders, both took the standard 44CW design.

SPECIAL FEATURES

The Dash 9 took GE into the third generation of diesels, following the success of the popular Dash 8. Fitted with the North American 'comfort' cab, the current high-horsepower DC model from GE features improvements introduced on late model

Dash 8s, such as a split cooling system, on-board diagnostics and upgraded microprocessor controls. It also introduced GE's new HiAd (High Adhesion) low-weight bolsterless bogies (trucks) with microprocessor-controlled wheelslip for much improved adhesion, even in wet weather.

OTHER COUNTRIES OPERATED

The design has also proved popular in the export market with versions sold to Australia and Brazil, confirming GE's dominance abroad.

SPECIFICATION

Number series: Various, according to railroad
Total built: 2,771 (44CW: 1,768, 40CW: 856)
Builder: General Electric, USA
Date introduced: 1993
Track gauge, ft/ins (mm): 4 ft 8.5 in (1,435)
Axle arrangement: Co-Co
Power unit type: GE 7FDL16 (40CW: rated at 4,000 hp)
Transmission: Electric, 6 x GE-752AH traction motors
Weight, tonnes: 181
Power rating, hp (kW): 44CW: 4,400 (3,284). 40CW: 4,000 (2,985)
Design speed, mph (km/h): 74 (119)
Additional features: multiple working

TYPE SD70MAC DIESEL LOCOMOTIVE

General Motors SD70MAC

The world's first production AC-powered diesel locomotive proved an instant hit, with three SD70MACs able to replace five SD40-2s on heavy coal trains. The new steering bogie and AC traction motors have revolutionised the North American locomotive market.

SPECIAL FEATURES

Main operators are Burlington Northern Sante Fe, CSX, TFM (Mexico), and the Alaska Railroad. GM was the first locomotive builder to introduce AC power, with four SD60MAC locomotives for Burlington Northern in 1991, following a tie-up with Siemens of Germany, which supplied its vast AC traction knowledge normally used for multiple-units. The quartet was so successful that BN ordered 350 4,000 hp locomotives with AC drive before they had been designed. Although AC power adds considerably to the new cost of a locomotive, its capabilities outweigh this. Coupled with GM's steering bogie (the HTCR), the additional adhesion that AC traction motors can

SPECIFICATION

Number series: Various, according to railroad
Total built: 1,007
Builder: General Motors, Canada
Date introduced: 1993
Track gauge, ft/ins (mm): 4 ft 8.5 in (1,435)
Axle arrangement: Co-Co
Power unit type: GM 16-710G3C-ES
Transmission: Electric, 6 x Siemens 1TB2630 AC traction motors
Weight, tonnes: 188
Power rating, hp (kW): 4,000 (2,985)
Design speed, mph (km/h): 70 (113)
Additional features: multiple working, rheostatic (dynamic) brakes, steering radial bogies (trucks), isolated WhisperCab

provide, together with their smaller size and greater robustness, meant that the SD70MAC became a rapid best-seller and now more than 800 locomotives work for BNSF on its Powder River Basin coal traffic. GM continues to offer the design in its catalogue and although it fitted its 'Isolated' WhisperCab as standard from 1995, the model designation was not changed.

TYPE AC4400CW DIESEL LOCOMOTIVE

General Electric AC4400CW

An AC traction motor version of the 4,400hp Dash 9-44CW, its appearance is very similar. Over 2,200 examples have been constructed for domestic US railroads.

SPECIAL FEATURES

Unlike GM, whose locomotives have one bank of inverters per bogie, meaning an entire bogie has to be isolated if a traction motor fails, GE plumped for one inverter per traction motor. This results in a large box on the side of the locomotive behind the cab, containing 36 Gate Turn On (GTO) inverters to chop rectified DC power from the alternator into three-phase AC for the traction motors. Despite offering the higher adhesion and lower maintenance of AC power, many railroads preferred GM's steering radial bogie. This led GE to develop its own version in 1996, making competition neck-and-neck, although some, notably Union Pacific, decided to stick with the HiAd bogie.

SPECIFICATION

Number series: Various, according to railroad
Total built: 2,249
Builder: General Electric, USA
Date introduced: 1993
Track gauge, ft/ins (mm): 4 ft 8.5 in (1,435)
Axle arrangement: Co-Co
Power unit type: GE 7FDL16
Transmission: Electric, 6 x GEB13 AC traction motors
Weight, tonnes: 190
Power rating, hp (kW): 4,400 (3,284)
Design speed, mph (km/h): 74 (119)
Additional features: multiple working
Main operators: CSXT, Union Pacific, Chicago & North Western, Southern Pacific

TYPE SD80MAC DIESEL LOCOMOTIVE

General Motors SD80MAC

The introduction of AC traction motors removed the limits placed on DC motors, so in 1995 GM revived its 20-cylinder engine to create a 5,000 hp monster as it competed head-on with General Electric in the horsepower race.

SPECIAL FEATURES

In a head-to-head horsepower race with arch rival General Electric following the introduction of AC traction motors, General Motors revived its 20-cylinder engine and took the lead in 1995 by building two 5,000 hp demonstrators, based on the 4,000 hp SD70MAC. Four months later the first of a 28-strong order for Conrail was delivered, but with no other takers for the design, Conrail also bought the demonstrators. Since then, the high horsepower stakes have risen again and it is unlikely that any more of these models will be built.

SPECIFICATION

Number series: 4100-4129
Total built: 30
Builder: General Motors, Canada
Date introduced: 1995
Track gauge, ft/ins (mm): 4 ft 8.5 in (1,435)
Axle arrangement: Co-Co
Power unit type: GM 20-710G3B-ES
Transmission: Electric, 6 x Siemens 1TB2830 AC traction motors
Weight, tonnes: 190
Power rating, hp (kW): 5,000 (3,731)
Design speed, mph (km/h): 70 (113)
Additional features: multiple working, rheostatic (dynamic) brakes, steering radial bogies (trucks), isolated WhisperCab.

TYPE AC6000CW DIESEL LOCOMOTIVE

General Electric AC6000CW

United States of America

Although it entered the AC traction motor market two years after competitor GM, GE quickly stole a march, outselling its rival by almost two-to-one in the AC heavy freight high-horsepower race.

SUB-TYPES

AC6000CW (Upgradeable): While GE was testing its 6,000 hp prototypes, it began building 'convertible' versions fitted with the 16-cylinder engines used in the AC4400CW, intended to be upgraded when the 6,000 hp engine was perfected. Only Union Pacific placed orders, taking 106 that have yet to be upgraded.
AC6000CW: Available with GE steering bogies or the lower-spec HiAd bogie, the 16-cylinder HDL 6,000 hp version is the current model and has been bought by Union Pacific (80) and CSXT (117).

SPECIAL FEATURES

At the same time as rival General Motors announced a 6,000 hp AC locomotive (SD90MAC),

SPECIFICATION

Number series: Various, according to railroad
Total built: 305
Builder: General Electric, USA
Date introduced: 1995
Track gauge, ft/ins (mm): 4 ft 8.5 in (1,435)
Axle arrangement: Co-Co
Power unit type: GE 7HDL16 (or 7FDL16)
Transmission: Electric, 6 x GEB13 AC traction motors
Weight, tonnes: 193 (or 187)
Power rating, hp (kW): 6,000 (4,478) or 4,400 (3,284)
Design speed, mph (km/h): 75 (121)
Additional features: multiple working

so did General Electric. It developed a 16-cylinder HDL engine with German partner Deutz and the prototypes started service testing in 1995. Unlike GM, the GE 6,000 hp engine has performed well. UP, which has GM and GE 6,000 hp locomotives and has traditionally been a supporter of high-horsepower models, could hold the key to future orders.

TYPE SD90MAC DIESEL LOCOMOTIVE

General Motors SD90MAC

The next step for AC traction - and apparently one too far - was to exploit its haulage capability by building a 6,000 hp locomotive. However, most of the fleet is running with temporary 4,300 hp engines, until the higher-rated design is perfected.

SUB-TYPES

SD90/43MAC: 'Upgradeable' version fitted with GM's two-stroke 16-cylinder 4,300 hp 710 engine. Outwardly identical to the SD80MAC, they can be fitted with a 6,000 hp engine when the design is perfected and are known as 'convertibles'. Of the 410 built, Union Pacific has 309; Canadian Pacific 61, and leasing company CIT Financial 40.

SD90MAC-H: Fitted with 6,000 hp engine, 22 were built for UP from 1996-1999.

SD90MAC-H II: Phase 2, with redesigned cab and reliability refinements including an improved version of the engine. Only 46 have been built to date for UP (40) and CP (4) plus two test beds.

SPECIFICATION

Number series: Various, according to railroad
Total built: 478
Builder: General Motors, Canada
Date introduced: 1995
Track gauge, ft/ins (mm): 4 ft 8.5 in (1,435)
Axle arrangement: Co-Co
Power unit type: GM 16V265H or 16-710G3-ES
Transmission: Electric, 6 x Siemens 1TB2830 AC traction motors
Weight, tonnes: 188-192
Power rating, hp (kW): 6,000 (4,478) or 4,300 (3,209)
Design speed, mph (km/h): 70 (113)
Additional features: multiple working, rheostatic (dynamic) brakes, steering radial bogies (trucks), isolated WhisperCab.

SPECIAL FEATURES

With the horsepower race hitting fever pitch in the early 1990s as AC traction took off, both General Electric and General Motors offered 6,000 hp locomotives. Remarkably both builders

received orders, even while the locomotives were on the drawing board despite neither manufacturer having a suitable engine. However, armed with orders from Union Pacific, GM abandoned its two-stroke roots from the 1930s and in 18 months conceived and built a 6,000 hp four-stroke 16-cylinder engine. Soon, teething troubles hit and rather than delay the order GM agreed with UP to build the first batches as 'convertibles' with the 4,300 hp engine used in the SD75 - effectively creating an AC version of the SD75. Although only intended to be a temporary measure, difficulties refining the 6,000 hp engine have lead to the SD90/43 designation (for 4,300 hp) to avoid confusion with real 6,000 hp locomotives.

The 6,000 hp 265H engine finally appeared in 1996, but was still plagued with problems that kept UP's fleet of 22 sidelined, often for months. Still trying to perfect the design, a Phase 2 version appeared in 1998 with more engine design changes, but it was months before the finished locomotives were released to UP. In the meantime, CP cut its order for SD90MAC-H II locomotives back from 20 to four.

TYPE F40PH DIESEL LOCOMOTIVE

General Motors F40PH

Built to replace the 'F' series passenger locomotives, they were for many years the standard North American passenger locomotive and until their eventual retirement in 2002 formed the backbone of Amtrak's fleet. Based on the successful GP40-2 (Dash 2) micro-processor controlled freight design, production ran for 17 years until replaced by the more modern F59PH model.

SUB-TYPES

F40PH-2: built from 1985-88 (total 131), identical to the main series which continued to be built, but offered fuel rack adjustments to uprate the power unit to 3,200 hp (2385 kW).

F40-PH-2C: in total 26 were built in 1987/8 for Massachusetts Bay Transportation Authority and incorporate a separate Cummins engine-alternator set to provide electric train heating to allow all the main engine's output to be used for traction power. To accommodate this,

SPECIFICATION

Number series: Various, according to railroad
Total built: 471
Builder: General Motors, USA
Date introduced: 1976
Track gauge, ft/ins (mm): 4 ft 8.5 in (1,435)
Axle arrangement: Bo-Bo
Power unit type: GM 16-645E
Transmission: Electric, 4 x GM D77 traction motors
Weight, tonnes: 117.7-127.7
Power rating, hp (kW): 3,000 (2,238)
Design speed, mph (km/h): 103 (166)
Additional features: multiple working; electric train heating

the locomotive is 8 ft 1 in longer.

F40PH-2M: four non-turbo-charged locomotives (2,000 hp/1,492 kW) built for Speno rail-grinding trains, they have flush-fronted cabs.

F40PHM-2: built in 1992/3 they are mechanically identical to the other 3,200 hp F40s, but have a sloping cab, rather than a stub nose. They were the last locomotives built at GM's La Grange

plant, USA, before production transferred to London, Ontario, Canada. La Grange continues to manufacture power units and traction equipment.

SPECIAL FEATURES

Replacing the 'F' series locomotives, the FP40 family was for many years America's standard passenger locomotive. Essentially a freight GP40-2 Bo-Bo, it is encased in a non-load bearing body and supplies electric train heating (head-end power), requiring the 16-cylinder engine to run at nearly full throttle, even when it is stationary.

To overcome the loss of power for traction due to the diversion of some electricity to the train, later models were uprated by 200 hp simply by adjusting the fuel racks, a retrospective modification made to many of the original locomotives too.

Amtrak placed the first order, for 30 FP40s, for use on short-haul services, and the Co-Co SDP40F, which had bodies 16 ft longer to incorporate steam-heating boilers, on long distance trains. However a series of inexplicable derailments of the rear bogie on the latter saw 123 SDP40Fs rebuilt after around five years as Bo-Bo FP40s.

For the FP40 to cope with the longer distances, the original 1,500 gallon fuel tank was enlarged to 1,800 gallons and the electric train generator's output increased from 500 to 800 kW.

Best known for its success as Amtrak's workhorse, it has also proved itself as a commuter locomotive - the original intention of the design - with major purchasers including Boston's Massachusetts Bay Transportation Authority (above), New Jersey Transit and California's CalTrain.

Amtrak procured the largest number of the units (210), followed by VIA Rail, Canada (59), plus many other commuter operators.

TYPE F59PH DIESEL LOCOMOTIVE

GO Transit General Motors F59PH

This design formed the platform for a new range of passenger diesels from GM. It went on to become a standard passenger locomotive, with additional sales of 23 to Metrolink.

SPECIAL FEATURES

Designed to replace the FP40H, the F59PH was commissioned and designed in conjunction with Ontario's state-owned commuter operator GO Transit. The concept was a 3,000 hp locomotive using the 12-cylinder 710 engine (which replaced the 645 power unit from 1984 and remains in production) plus an independent engine-generator set providing the electric train heating supply. The package was presented in a full-width body with a Canadian National-style 'comfort' cab, offering improved collision protection and sound-proofing. General Motors was initially reluctant to embrace the idea, but GO Transit made a strong case and the first one was delivered in May 1988. The design has proved to be successful, both technologically and commercially, and GO Transit placed further orders, eventually replacing all its F40s, and buying more for expansion, although later selling four on to Dallas. Meanwhile, Metrolink in Los Angeles ordered 17, and later a further six for its October 1992 launch of LA commuter services.

SPECIFICATION

Number series: GO Transit 520-564, Metrolink 874-887
Total built: 72
Builder: General Motors, USA
Date introduced: 1988
Track gauge, ft/ins (mm): 4 ft 8.5 in (1,435)
Axle arrangement: Bo-Bo
Power unit type: GM 12-710G3B
Transmission: Electric, 4 x GM D87B traction motors
Weight, tonnes: 117.7
Power rating, hp (kW): 3,000 (2,238)
Design speed, mph (km/h): 63 (101)
Additional features: multiple working, electric train heating

TYPE F59PHI DIESEL LOCOMOTIVE

General Motors F59PHI

Designed for Amtrak-California, these are mechanically identical to the F59PH. The additional 'I' designation (for 'isolated cab') belies its modern streamlined appearance, compared with the previous boxy design and it remains in GM's catalogue as a standard passenger locomotive for which, in North America at least, there is no direct competitor.

SPECIFICATION

Number series: Various, according to railroad
Total built: 74
Builder: General Motors, USA
Date introduced: 1994
Track gauge, ft/ins (mm): 4 ft 8.5 in (1,435)
Axle arrangement: Bo-Bo
Power unit type: GM 12-710G3B-EC
Transmission: Electric, 4 x GM D87BTR traction motors
Weight, tonnes: 121
Power rating, hp (kW): 3,000 (2,238)
Design speed, mph (km/h): 110 (176)
Additional features: multiple working; electric train heating.

SPECIAL FEATURES

Designed specifically for Amtrak-California, the appearance was radically altered with a glass-fibre streamlined nose. Nine were ordered by the California Department of Transportation for the state-funded services. They feature 'isolated' cabs for sound and vibration reduction and a streamlined body with side-skirts over the fuel tanks and side panels designed to blend in with double-decker coaches ordered for the same service. The F59PHI, or California F59 as it is also known, proved popular with other operators as well as Amtrak, which placed follow-on orders. Main operators are Amtrak (36), Amtrak-California (16), Greater Vancouver Translink (5), Metrolink (8), Trinity Railway Express (6), Seattle Sound Transit Board (11) (above), Montreal Transport Agency (7), North County Transit (2) and North Carolina (2).

TYPE GENESIS DIESEL LOCOMOTIVE

General Electric Genesis

Winning a major contract from Amtrak in 1991 to supply 4,000 hp passenger locomotives saw a new GE design, which went on to form the basis of a successful good-selling and smart-looking range of passenger diesels, introducing AC traction motors along the way.

SUB-TYPES

Dash 8-40BP: The first series of Genesis diesels, like all the range, has high-speed German bogies (trucks) with Flexicoil suspension; 46 of the 16-cylinder-engined locomotives were built for Amtrak in 1993.

P32AC-DM: The second series of Genesis locomotives built from 1995 and still in the current catalogue, it uses the 12-cylinder FDL engine rated at 3,200 hp (2,388 kW) and introduced AC traction motors to passenger diesels. An electro-diesel, it can run on 650V third rail to New York's Grand Central and Penn

SPECIFICATION

Number series: Various, according to railroad
Total built: 327
Builder: General Electric, USA
Date introduced: 1993
Track gauge, ft/ins (mm): 4 ft 8.5 in (1,435)
Axle arrangement: Bo-Bo
Power unit type: (Dash 8-40BP) GE 7FDL16
Transmission: Electric, four GE AC traction motors
Weight, tonnes: 119
Power rating, hp (kW): 4,000 (2,985)
Design speed, mph (km/h): 115 (185)
Additional features: multiple working, electric train heating

stations. To date, 53 have been bought by Amtrak, Metro North and the Connecticut Department of Transportation for work around New York.

P42DC: By far the best-selling Genesis, with 228 built since introduction in 1996, it is the latest model and successor to the Dash 8-40BP, giving

4,200 hp (3,134 kW) from the same 16-cylinder engine. Proving that AC has not yet won the day in the passenger market, the DC powered-machine, with updated microprocessor controls, on-board diagnostics and remote engine starting, is rapidly replacing GM's F40PHs to become Amtrak's standard locomotive, of which it has bought 207. GE won a new customer in 2001 when VIA took its first GE diesels with an order of 21 of the type.

SPECIAL FEATURES

In a full-width body with streamlined nose, from the outside all Genesis diesels look the same, and that's largely due to Amtrak's 1991 requirements which called for a 4,000 hp locomotive weighing less than the 3,000 hp F40, while fitting through the tight Hudson River tunnels. The specification also called for electric train heating (supplied by an auxiliary alternator) which would operate from the engine running at lower engine speed while standing at stations (unlike GM's which requires the engine to run at almost full throttle, even when stationary) and be adaptable to an electro-diesel or straight electric. Inside is a host of the latest microprocessor technology and the successful design is now established as the market leader.

TYPE DE30AC/DM30AC DIESEL/ELECTRO-DIESEL

Long Island Railroad DE30AC/DM30AC

GM's first AC-powered passenger locomotives, these machines were custom-designed for the Long Island Rail Road, which remains the only operator. After a shaky start they are now good performers.

SPECIAL FEATURES

The 46 locomotives (half of which are electro-diesels) were part of orders including 120 double-deck coaches to run through trains, eliminating the need for passengers to change trains at Jamaica station from diesel multiple-units to electric multiple-units. The technical specification is based on GM's SD70MAC and SD80MAC locomotives. Half the fleet comprises the DM30AC (dual-mode), which has shoes for 650 V third-rail pick up, crucial in the electric-only zone through the East River Tunnel to Penn station. They are the railroad's first purpose-built passenger locomotives in decades and a requirement in the contract saw them assembled

SPECIFICATION

Number series: DE30AC: 400-422, DM30AC: 500-522
Total built: 46
Builder: General Motors, USA
Date introduced: 1997
Track gauge, ft/ins (mm): 4 ft 8.5 in (1,435)
Axle arrangement: Bo-Bo
Power unit type: GM 12N-710G3B-EC
Additional power source: DM30AC locomotives, 650 V DC third-rail
Transmission: Electric, 4 x AC-1TB2624 traction motors
Weight, tonnes: 128
Power rating, hp (kW): 3,000 (2,239)
Design speed, mph (km/h): 100 (160), (80 (130) in electric mode_
Additional features: multiple working, disc brakes, electric train heating. Dual-mode DM30AC can also operate on third rail.

at Super Steel Schenectady in Glenville, New York. To ensure they could match timings of the multiple-units they replaced to maintain headways, the design called for high power on the third rail.

TYPE AEM-7 ELECTRIC LOCOMOTIVE

General Motors AEM-7

Designed to replace the rugged and reliable classic GG1 electric locomotives, by then 40 years old, on the Northeast Corridor, these European-designed locomotives were the USA's first high-speed electrics. They are based on a contemporary Swedish design.

SPECIAL FEATURES

To replace the ageing GG1 electric locomotives on the New York-Philadelphia-Washington 'Northeast Corridor' Amtrak had bought 27 E60CP Co-Co electrics from General Electric in 1973. However, their rough-riding at speed meant they were unable to meet this requirement so Amtrak looked to Europe, with its lengthy experience of high-speed electrics. It chose the Rc4 design by ASEA, of which 150 had been supplied to Sweden and a further 15 (Class El 16) to Norway. However a 'Buy American' campaign saw ASEA licence the design to GM, which used some ASEA parts. AEM-7 stands for the 'A' in ASEA, 'EM' for

SPECIFICATION

Number series: Amtrak 900-953, Septa 2301-2307, MARC 4900-4903
Total built: 67
Builder: General Motors, USA under licence from ASEA
Date introduced: 1979
Track gauge, ft/ins (mm): 4 ft 8.5 in (1,435)
Axle arrangement: Bo-Bo
Power supply system: 12.5 kV AC 25Hz or 60Hz or 25 kV AC 60Hz
Electrical equipment: Thyristor control, 4 fully suspended DC traction motors with flexible hollow shaft drive.
Weight, tonnes: 91.6
Power rating, hp (kW): 7,000 (5,224)
Design speed, mph (km/h): 125 (200)
Additional features: Multiple working, electric train heating, regenerative braking

General Motors' Electro-Motive Diesels, and '7' for 7,000 hp. The route was upgraded for higher speeds and they are reliable locomotives, which until the recent arrival of the Acela high-speed trainsets, were used on all frontline services.

TYPE ALP-44 ELELCTRIC LOCOMOTIVE

General Motors ALP-44

Almost identical to the AEM-7 125 mph (200 km/h) passenger electrics built under licence by General Motors, this follow-on order by New Jersey Transit, was built in Sweden.

SPECIAL FEATURES

General Motors stopped building the AEM-7 in 1988 (constructed under licence from ASEA), so when the New Jersey Department of Transportation (NJ Transit) wanted to buy new electric locomotives, it ordered 15 ALP-44s built by ASEA (ABB Traction) in Sweden. Apart from some minor bodyside differences, they are identical to the AEM-7 and are used on commuter services. Although Septa ordered one ALP-44, delivered in 1996, to run alongside its seven AEM-7s, it remains a solitary example.

SPECIFICATION

Number series: New Jersey Transit 4400-4431, Septa 2308
Total built: 33
Builder: ABB Traction
Date introduced: 1979
Track gauge, ft/ins (mm): 4 ft 8.5 in (1,435)
Axle arrangement: Bo-Bo
Power supply system: 12.5 kV AC 25Hz or 60Hz or 25 kV AC 60Hz
Electrical equipment: Thyristor control, 4 fully suspended DC traction motors with flexible hollow shaft drive.
Weight, tonnes: 92.5
Power rating, hp (kW): 7,000 (5,224)
Design speed, mph (km/h): 125 (200)
Additional features: multiple working, electric train heating, regenerative braking

TYPE HHP-8 ELECTRIC LOCOMOTIVE

Amtrak HHP-8

Ordered as part of an upgrade of the Northeast Corridor, which included new tilting EMUs, these 8,000 hp electric locomotives were bought for semi-fast services, branded Acela Regional.

SPECIAL FEATURES

The Acela HHP-8 (meaning High Horse Power 8,000 hp) was ordered in March 1996 as part of Amtrak's plan to improve speeds on the crucial Washington-New York-Boston 'Northeast Corridor'. The former Northeast Direct trains now run faster as the 'Regional' service. The double-cabbed locomotives, unusual for the USA, haul conventional double-deck coaches on the semi-fast Regional Acela service, with stops including Providence, New York, Philadelphia and Baltimore. The locomotives were built by Bombardier in its American factories, with Alstom electrical components, and are based on the French Class BB36000 locomotive, which also sees service in Belgium and Luxembourg. Although

SPECIFICATION

Number series: 650-664
Total built: 15
Builder: Bombardier/Alstom
Date introduced: 1998
Track gauge, ft/ins (mm): 4 ft 8.5 in (1,435)
Axle arrangement: Bo-Bo
Power supply system: 12.5 kV AC 60Hz, 11 kV AC 25Hz or 25 kV AC 60Hz
Electrical equipment: Alstom, 4 x 4FXA4559 AC traction motors.
Weight, tonnes: 100.7
Power rating, hp (kW): 8,000 (5,970)
Design speed, mph (km/h): 135 (217)
Additional features: multiple working, electric train heating, regenerative braking, cab signalling

well regarded and now having their first heavy overhauls, their entry into service was beset by a variety of teething troubles including bogie problems.

ACELA EXPRESS HIGH-SPEED TILTING TRAINS

Amtrak Acela Express tilting trains

Ordered for a major upgrade of the 457-mile Northeast Corridor, these 150 mph (240 km/h) tilting trains are based on the French TGV.

SPECIAL FEATURES

Ordered in March 1996 as a design and build contract from a consortium of Bombardier and Alstom, these are the first modern 'complete' trains, rather than locomotives and coaches which have traditionally been used in the country. The Acela Express ('Acela' for 'acceleration' and 'excellence') will eventually replace all Metroliner services. Based on the French TGV and its variants, but without articulation, it can run up to 100 mph without tilt, or 150 mph with tilt activated. The original order for 18 sets was increased by two more in July 1998. Each set comprises a power car at each end and six intermediate coaches offering passenger comforts such as at-seat audio and sockets for laptops. Launched in October 2000, services began in December, but

SPECIFICATION

Number series (power cars): 2000-2039
Total built: 20
Builder: Bombardier/Alstom consortium
Date introduced: 2000
Track gauge, ft/ins (mm): 4 ft 8.5 in (1,435)
Axle arrangement: Bo-Bo
Power supply system: 12.5 kV AC 60Hz, 11 kV AC 25Hz or 25 kV AC 60Hz
Electrical equipment: Alstom, 4 x 4FXA4550 three-phase AC traction motors
Weight, tonnes: 90.7
Power rating, hp (kW): 6,169 (4,603)
Design speed, mph (km/h): 150 (240)
Additional features: multiple working, regenerative braking, disc and tread brakes, cab signalling

were plagued by a series of teething troubles, especially with the tilt system, culminating in legal action from 2001–2004 between the consortium and Amtrak. However, the trains are popular with passengers and rapid revenue increases are justifying the investment, as the sets settle down with improving reliability.

BUDD RAIL DIESEL CARS (RDC) DMU

VIA Rail Budd RDC-1

Budd built more than 300 Rail Diesel Cars (RDCs) in the 1950s for relatively low traffic passenger routes, and they are credited with saving many smaller rural and inter-urban passenger services in the USA and Canada.

SPECIAL FEATURES

More than 300 Budd single-car DMUs were built during the 1950s, following the demonstration of a prototype in 1949. Their distinctive stainless steel construction, with corrugated sides, was similar to the company's passenger coaches. The idea came about when Budd decided to marry General Motors' V6 diesel engine (designed for powering battle tanks) with torque-converters, also used by the army. Each engine powers the inside axle of each bogie. With rapid acceleration, air-conditioning and disc brakes with anti-slide protection, they were modern for their time. Their ever-lasting stainless steel bodywork and the ease with which engines could be replaced contributed

SPECIFICATION

Number series: 6126-6250
Total in service: 5
Builder: The Budd Co, Philadelphia, USA
Date introduced: 1956
Track gauge, ft/ins (mm): 4 ft 8.5 in (1,435)
Engine: 2 x General Motors 6-110 6-cylinder two-stroke of 275 hp
Transmission: Hydraulic
Weight, tonnes: 57.5
Power rating, hp (kW): 550 (410)
Design speed, mph (km/h): 85 (136)
Additional features: multiple working, air-conditioning, inter-car gangways

to their longevity. Budd RDCs ran many stopping trains in rural Canada, although now just five are left in service with VIA Rail, working Vancouver's Malahatt service and Sudbury-White River, Ontario, services. In 1997 Via Rail sold 13 RDCs to Trinity Railway Express, Dallas, USA. These have been extensively refurbished by AMF Transport and now include space for four wheelchairs per vehicle.

RTL TURBOLINER TRAINS

Amtrak RTL Turboliner

Used on services into New York, the small fleet with 125 mph potential is undergoing a major rebuild and refurbishment after 25 years' service.

SPECIAL FEATURES

Fixed-formation passenger trains have never caught on in the USA due to their inability to cope with varying passenger numbers. However, in 1969 two French-built Turboliner passenger trains ran on Penn Central's Providence-New York service. Amtrak, which took over the route, followed this up with six French ANF Turboliners, classed RTLI. In 1976 it ordered seven more similar trains (RTLII) from Rohr (which later exited the rail market). The five-car formation seats around 260 passengers, compared with 350 in a conventional train. To allow them to work through tunnels into Penn Central station, barred to diesels, one trailer car has a single traction motor. Due to upgrade work needed to track and signalling they never reached their 125 mph (200 km/h) top speed, with 110 mph (176 km/h) being

SPECIFICATION

Number series: 2131-62
Total built: 7 sets
Builder: Rohr Industries
Date introduced: 1976
Track gauge, ft/ins (mm): 4 ft 8.5 in (1,435)
Axle arrangement: B-B
Power unit type: Gas Turbine of 1,400 hp or 650V DC third rail
Transmission: Voith hydraulic or one electric traction motor on third rail
Weight, tonnes: 67
Power rating, hp (kW): 1,140 (850) or 295 (220) on third rail
Design speed, mph (km/h): 125 (200), 45 (72) on third rail

the normal maximum and much lower speeds over most routes. In 2000 Amtrak placed a contract with Super Steel in Schenectady, New York State, to undertake an extensive rebuild of all seven units, including a new streamlined steel cab, more powerful 1,600 hp (1,194 kW) gas turbines and mechanical systems for continued use in New York State. The first two were finished in 2000 and entered traffic in 2003.

TYPE M2 EMU

Metro-North Railroad M2

Until recently the General Electric M2 electric multiple units formed the backbone of New York's Metro-North Railroad operations. Introduced from 1973, the two-car units - operating in multiple up to 12 cars - are now being replaced by class M7 EMUs.

SPECIALFEATURES

Although two-car units, they normally work in multiple of up to 12 cars, especially in rush hours. Introduced from 1973, they were the latest in technology, offering rapid acceleration and good passenger comfort.

A subsidiary of New York State's Metropolitan Transportation Authority, Metro-North was founded in 1983 when the Metropolitan Transportation Authority assumed control of Conrail commuter operations in the states of New York and Connecticut on behalf of the Connecticut Department of Transportation, on what was a main line of the former New Haven & Hartford Railroad.

SPECIFICATION

Number series: Various
Total built: 242 x 2-car units
Builder: General Electric
Date introduced: 1973
Track gauge, ft/ins (mm): 4 ft 8.5 in (1,435)
Unit configuration: M-M
Power supply system: 11 kV AC 60 Hz
Electrical equipment: General Electric 4 x 160 hp (120 kW) DC traction motors per car
Power rating per car, hp (kW): 640 (480)
Design speed, mph (km/h): 100 (160)
Additional features: inter-unit gangways, air-conditioning, multiple working

Having just celebrated its 20th anniversary, MTA Metro-North Railroad, one of five commuter operators in New York and the second largest commuter railroad in the United States, provides approximately 250,000 passenger trips each weekday and 73 million trips per year. The M2 EMUs replaced Budd M1 EMUs, but in turn they are now starting to be replaced by 858 class M7 EMU vehicles, delivery of which started in 2003.

CLASS MR-90 EMU

Agence Métropolitaine de Transport (AMT) Bombardier/General Electric Class MR-90

Brand new Bombardier-built electric multiple-units delivered in 1994 for the totally rebuilt and modernised Deux-Montagnes to Montreal Central commuter line. Opened as an electrified railway in 1918, this route still had some of the original 1914-built locomotives in service in 1995.

SPECIAL FEATURES

Delivered in 1994 for the long-overdue total modernisation of the commuter system formerly run under contract by Canadian National, the CSD289 million work was announced in 1992 but not completed until 1995. It included station refurbishment and replacement of catenary and signalling. Unusually, the cars have a single centre sliding door for high platform boarding, plus end plug-doors. The new stock replaced a motley collection of best described as a working museum. From 1992, CN leased 35 coaches, built in 1954, from VIA Rail. The system was opened in 1918 and electrified at 2.4 kV DC overhead (increased to

SPECIFICATION

Number series: 400-456 even numbers only (driving motor), 401-449 odd numbers only (trailer), 481-487 (non-motored driving trailer).
Total built: 58 cars
Builder: Bombardier, La Pocatière, Quebec, Canada
Date introduced: 1995
Track gauge, ft/ins (mm): 4 ft 8.5 in (1,435)
Unit configuration: Various, typically M-T-M or M-T
Power supply system: 25 kV AC 60 Hz
Electrical equipment: General Electric; each motor car has 4 x 380 hp (284 kW) AC traction motors
Power rating per car, hp (kW): 1,520 (1,134)
Design speed, mph (km/h): 75 (120)
Additional features: air-conditioning, inter-unit gangways

3 kV DC in the early 1980s). The route and service was gradually cut back from the early 1960s. Now the Agence Métropolitaine de Transport (AMT) system is booming, with plans for route extensions and additional stock.

South American Trains

Ex-RENFE CLASS 321 DIESEL LOCOMOTIVE

América Latina Logística (ALL-BAP) Class 321

Twenty locomotives were acquired second hand from Spanish National Railways (RENFE) in 1979 and are used today by the Buenos Aires al Pacifico/ San Martín (BAP) railway, which was formed in 1992 when the Argentinian rail system was privatised and is now operated by América Latina Logística. They all see intensive use.

SPECIAL FEATURES

The Class 321s are primarily allocated to freight duties over the sprawling ALL-BAP system, which links Buenos Aries with Mendoza and San Juan in the foothills of the Andes and close to the border with Chile in the west of the country. The locomotives share many features with North American types of the 1940s and 1950s but have a flat, full width cab at each end, rather than the single-ended locomotives with bonnets favoured by US railroads. Their performance has been hampered by the poor condition of the track and

SPECIFICATION

Total built: 80 (for Spain)
Builder: Alco/CAF/SECN/Euskalduna
Date introduced: 1965-1971, sold to BAP in 1979
Track gauge, ft/ins (mm): 5 ft 6 in (1,676)
Axle arrangement: Co-Co
Power unit type: Alco 251-C
Transmission: Electric
Weight, tonnes: 119
Power rating, hp (kW): 1,850 (1,370)
Design speed, mph (km/h): 75 (120)

signalling over the branches away from the San Martin east-west main line, but this is being addressed.

OTHER COUNTRIES OPERATED

A fleet of 54 Class 321s was retained in Spain.

TYPE RSD 16 DIESEL LOCOMOTIVE

Nuevo Central Argentino (NCA) RSD 16

Argentina

The final development of General Motors' classic 'bullnose' design the last were built in 1957 and although designated 'F' for freight, passenger versions were also built and they are a true mixed-traffic locomotive. Their rock-solid reliability means that a small number survive in service.

PRINCIPAL MODIFICATIONS

Widened bogies have been fitted for operation on the 1,676 mm network.

SPECIAL FEATURES

The former General Mitre Railway network connects the industrial cities of Tucumán, Rosario and Córdoba in north central Argentina. In 1997, 13 of the company's 27 RSD-16s were available for traffic with the other 14 under repair or refurbishment. Freight hauled by the NCA locomotives includes grain - the major source of traffic - bulk cement and intermodal containers. Train weights can be up to 2,000 tonnes.

SPECIFICATION

Number in service: 27
Builder: Alco
Date introduced: 1957-1959
Track gauge, ft/ins (mm): 5 ft 6 in (1,676mm)
Axle arrangement: Co-Co
Power unit type: Alco 251-B four-stroke V12
Transmission: GE Electric
Weight, tonnes: 108
Power rating, hp (kW): 1,800 (1,340)
Design speed, mph (km/h): 76 (122)
Additional features: Westinghouse air brake, multiple working, VHF radio-based cab signalling

OTHER COUNTRIES OPERATED

Other Argentinian railway systems using the type include América Latina Logística (ALL-BAP), Transportes Metropolitanos (TMS), FerroExpresso Pampeano (FEPSA), Servicios Ferroviarios Patagonicos (SEFEPA), Ferrocarriles Mediterraneos (FeMed), and Trenes de Buenos Aires (TBA).

TYPE GT22CW DIESEL LOCOMOTIVE

Unidad Ejecutora del Programa Ferroviaria Provincial (UEPFP) GT22CW

The popular General Motors Co-Co is widespread across Argentina, having been constructed in many batches over almost two decades. Since privatisation at the start of the 1990s, the original build has been spread across several private operators in both metre and broad gauge versions.

SPECIAL FEATURES

Unidad Ejecutora del Programa Ferroviaria Provincial (UEPFP) has operated passenger trains over a wide area of Argentina since the country's federal government ended its support for such services in 1993. The company's ex-Ferrocarriles Argentinos GT22-CWs are the backbone of its operations, linking Buenos Aires with Mar del Plata on the Atlantic Coast and many other lines in the Atlantic and Pampas regions. The locomotives are powered by the renowned GM 645 series engine with six GM SIAM D75 traction motors.

SPECIFICATION

Number series: 9001 andA901 series
Total built: 250 (broad and metre gauge)
Builder: General Motors, ASTARSA (Astilleros Argentinos SA)
Date introduced: 1972, 1980, 1985, 1988
Track gauge, ft/ins (mm): 5 ft 6 in (1,676), 3 ft 3.375 in (1,000)
Axle arrangement: Co-Co
Power unit type: GM 645 series
Transmission: Electric. Six SIAM D75 traction motors
Weight, tonnes: 108
Power rating, hp (kW): 2,250 (1,680)
Design speed, mph (km/h): 87 (140)
Additional features: multiple working, Westinghouse air brakes

OTHER COUNTRIES OPERATED

The type is also operated by a host of other Argentinian operators, including FerroSur, TUFESA, Metropolitano, NCA, TBA, FEMED, and SEFEPA.

CLASS 1300 DIESEL LOCOMOTIVE

Gruppo Aziende Italiano Argentino (GAIA) Class 1300

These medium power locomotives were built between 1962 and 1969 by GAIA for the General Mitre Railway lines, and since privatisation have been divided amongst four companies.

PRINCIPAL MODIFICATIONS

Some locomotives were re-engined with 1,400hp Fiat GMD V8 A230-8 power units in 1978, followed by another batch with 1,300hp Alco 25-1B V12 engines after 1989.

SPECIAL FEATURES

Argentina's railway network is one of the largest and most developed in South America. After years of decline, the railway sector recovered rapidly as a result of privatisation, and the locomotive fleet is now hard-worked. Class 1300 was divided among four companies awarded operating concessions - Trenes Buenos Aires (TBA), Transportes Metropolitanos, Nuevo Central

SPECIFICATION

Number series: 6201-6350
Total built: 150
Builder: Gaia (Gruppo Aziende Italiano Argentino)
Date introduced: 1962-1969
Track gauge, ft/ins (mm): 5 ft 6 in (1,676)
Axle arrangement: Co-Co
Power unit type: Fiat/GM EMD/Alco
Transmission: Electric
Weight, tonnes: 93
Power rating, hp (kW): 1,233 (920), 1,300 (970), 1,400 (1045)
Design speed, mph (km/h): 70 (110)
Additional features: multiple working, Westinghouse air brakes

Argentinos amd Ferrocarriles Mediterraneos. They have Marelli generator and traction motors, and Westinghouse air-brake equipment and are primarily employed on freight duties.

RACK ELECTRIC LOCOMOTIVE

MRS Logística Hitachi rack locomotive

These very specialised locomotives were built by Hitachi in 1980 to work the 10.7 per cent Old Serra Incline in south-eastern Brazil, which is electrified and fitted with rack equipment to combat the severe gradient. Their top speed of just 28 mph (45 km/h) is indicative of their low gearing.

SPECIAL FEATURES

These rack locomotives, the only electric motive power in the MRS Logística fleet, became the responsibility of the company in 1996 when it was granted a 30-year concession to be the exclusive provider of freight services on the 1,674 km south-east rail network of Brazil. They are however restricted to just five miles (8 km of route) linking São Paulo with the port of Santos. MRS also operates the regional rail network of the Brazilian Federal Railway, but not the urban passenger lines in the metropolitan areas of Rio de Janeiro and São Paulo.

SPECIFICATION

Total built: 12
Builder: Hitachi
Date introduced: 1973
Track gauge, ft/ins (mm): 5 ft 3 in (1,600)
Axle arrangement: B-B
Power supply system: 3 kV DC
Electrical equipment: Hitachi, rheostatic control, two bogie-mounted DC traction motors with jackshaft drive for adhesion working, four nose-suspended DC traction motors for rack working
Weight, tonnes: 118
Power rating, hp (kW): 3,300 (2,460)
Design speed, mph (km/h): adhesion working - 28 (45); rack working - 19 (30)
Additional features: rheostatic braking, multiple working, rack equipment

TYPE C36ME DIESEL LOCOMOTIVE

MRS Logística C36ME (Super 7)

Brazil

The urgent need of MRS Logística to boost its fleet of medium power locomotives resulted in the arrival in December 2000 of second-hand USA-built General Electric machines acquired from three systems.

SPECIAL FEATURES

The Atchison, Topeka and Santa Fé (today Burlington Northern Santa Fe), Union Pacific, and Conrail were the providers of nine C63ME-type six-axle locomtives which after minor attention and re-gauging entered service with MRS between March and April 2001. They are powered by the same General Electric 7FDL16 engine as several other MRS-owned types, and with a multiple working facility and fuel tank capacity of 15,000 litres are capable of hauling the company's heaviest trains over the longest distances and at the highest speeds.

SPECIFICATION

Number series: 3801-3809
Number in service: 9
Builder: General Electric
Date introduced: 1977
Track gauge, ft/ins (mm): 5ft 3in (1,600)
Axle arrangement: Co-Co
Power unit type: GE 7FDL16
Transmission: Electric
Weight, tonnes: 180
Power rating, hp (kW): 3,000 (2,240)
Design speed, mph (km/h): 75 (120)
Additional features: multiple working, dynamic brakes

TYPE SD38M DIESEL LOCOMOTIVE

MRS Logística SD38M

These locomotives are virtually standard GM products adapted for use on the Brazilian rail network, and represent a sizeable proportion of the locomotive fleet of privatised company MRS Logística, which inherited over 250 locomotives in 1976 when it secured the contract to operate the country's southern network.

SPECIAL FEATURES

Janeiro, São Paulo, Belo Horizonte and the Santos-Jundiaí Railroad, the SD38Ms are used exclusively on freight in the south and east of the country. They frequently work in multiple on the heaviest freight trains. There are gaps in the fleet's number sequence.

SPECIFICATION

Number series: 5101-5144
Number in service: 34
Builder: General Motors
Date introduced: 1967
Track gauge, ft/ins (mm): 5 ft 3 in (1,600)
Axle arrangement: Co-Co
Power unit type: GM 645E
Transmission: Electric
Weight, tonnes: 163
Power rating, hp (kW): 2,000 (1,493)
Design speed, mph (km/h): 60 (97)
Additional features: multiple working, Westinghouse air brake

TYPE MX620 DIESEL LOCOMOTIVE

Ferrocarril Centro-Atlantico (FCA) MX620

The lines of the former RFFSA (the federal railways division Viação Férrea Centro-Oeste, which reaches from Goiânia and Brasília to Belo Horizonte, Cruzeiro and Angra dos Reis), rely on a fleet of locomotives that is currently being life-extended.

PRINCIPAL MODIFICATIONS

2701-2706 are a modernised version, while 6101 has been converted into a driverless 'slug' locomotive.

SPECIAL FEATURES

Alco (later Bombardier) collaborated with the construction between 1980-1982 of 74 Co-Co locomotives that were assembled by Emaq in Brazil. The diesel engine is the conventional Alco/Bombardier model 12-cylinder 251-CE. 6101 has had its cab removed for remote control operation, and is based at Divinópolis.

SPECIFICATION

Number series: 2701-2706, 6101-6174
Number in service: 74
Builder: Emaq (under licence from MLW/Bombardier)
Date introduced: 1980
Track gauge, ft/ins (mm): 3 ft 3.75 in (1,000)
Axle arrangement: Co-Co
Power unit type: Alco/Bombardier 12-251-CE
Transmission: Electric, six GE-761-PA14 traction motors
Weight, tonnes: 96
Power rating, hp (kW): 2,000 (1,493)
Design speed, mph (km/h): 64 (103)
Additional features: multiple working, dynamic brakes

TYPE DASH 9-44CW-M DIESEL LOCOMOTIVE

Central Atlantic Railway (FCA)/Ferronorte Type DASH 9-44CW-M

These locomotives were built by General Electric in 1997 for a new railway in central Brazil. Pending completion of the project some are operated by FCA. At 4,400hp (3,260kW), they are among the most powerful in South America and are similar to units built for US and Canadian railroads.

PRINCIPAL MODIFICATIONS

Widened bogies for operation on Brazilian broad gauge network

SPECIAL FEATURES

Fifty of these powerful locomotives were built from 1999 for the new 2,000 km Ferronorte broad gauge freight railway in central Brazil. Pending completion of that scheme some of the fleet has been transferred to the Central Atlantic Railway (FCA), formerly the Belo Horizonte, Salvador and Campos regions of the RFFSA national network and now owned by the Cia Vale do Rio Doce

SPECIFICATION

Number series: 9001-9050
Total built: 50
Builder: General Electric
Date introduced: 1999
Track gauge, ft/ins (mm): 5 ft 3 in (1,600)
Axle arrangement: Co-Co
Power unit type: GE 7FDL
Transmission: Electric
Weight, tonnes: 180
Power rating, hp (kW): 4,400 (3,350)
Design speed, mph (km/h): 50 (80)
Additional features: multiple working, cab signalling, automatic train control, 'black box' event recorders, electronic fuel injection

group. They are primarily used for iron ore and minerals traffic.

OTHER COUNTRIES OPERATED

Similar locomotives work in the USA and Canada, while another Brazilian operator, the Carajás Railroad (EFC), took delivery of nine GE C44-9W locomotives starting in 1999.

CLASS U20C DIESEL LOCOMOTIVE

Ferrovias Bandeirantes (Ferroban) Class 3800 and 7800

These medium power GE diesels are the largest and most powerful diesel locomotives operated by Ferrovias Bandeirantes SA (Ferroban), a company formed 1999 to take over the freight and passenger operations of the former Sao Paulo State Railways (FEPASA).

SUB-TYPES

The 3800 and 7800 series were built three years apart but are virtually identical apart from their track gauge.

SPECIAL FEATURES

The history of this locomotive type dates back to 1956, and is a story of continuous evolution, starting with a 6-cylinder power unit that was later uprated and then enlarged. The U20Cs are used in multiples of up to four locomotives on heavy freight trains on Ferroban's 5ft 3in (1,600mm) gauge lines. The company also has many smaller diesels and a number of 3kV DC

SPECIFICATION

Number series: 3801-3910, 7801-7826
Total built: 136
Builder: General Electric
Date introduced: 1974 - 3801-3910, 1977 - 7801-7826
Track gauge, ft/ins (mm): 3801 series - 3 ft 3.375 in (1,000); 7801 series - 5 ft 3 in (1,600)
Axle arrangement: Co-Co
Power unit type: GE 7FDL-12
Transmission: Electric
Weight, tonnes: 108
Power rating, hp (kW): 2,000 (1,491)
Design speed, mph (km/h): 65 (103)
Additional features: multiple working, semi-automatic couplers

electric classes for use on both its broad and metre gauge networks.

OTHER COUNTRIES OPERATED

Similar locomotives are in use with other Brazilian lines, the USA and Canada, Argentina, Bolivia, Colombia, Indonesia, Angola, Mozambique, South Africa, Sudan, Zambia, and Pakistan.

TYPE DDM-45 DIESEL LOCOMOTIVE

Estrada de Ferro Vitória-Minas Railway (EFVM) DDM-45

The Estrada de Ferro Vitória-Minas is one of the busiest Brazilian railroads, linking the iron ore mines of Minas Gerais state with the harbour at Tubarão, near Vitória, capital of Espírito Santo state. It belongs to the Brazilian mining corporation Companhia Vale do Rio Doce, which also runs another railroad in the north of Brazil, Estrada de Ferro Carajás, also used mainly for iron ore transportation.

SUB-TYPES

Six DDM-45 were rebuilt as DDM-MP in 1993 with new power units, generators, traction motors and computer control.

SPECIAL FEATURES

These curious eight-axle DDM-45s were delivered in seven batches between 1970 and 1976, and form the backbone of the Vitória a Minas Railway fleet, although the railway also operates smaller numbers of many other GM and GE locomotive

SPECIFICATION

Number series: 801-883
Total built: 83
Builder: General Motors
Date introduced: 1970
Track gauge, ft/ins (mm): 3 ft 3.375 in (1,000)
Axle arrangement: Do-Do
Power unit type: GM 20-645E3
Transmission: Electric
Weight, tonnes: 162
Power rating, hp (kW): 3,930 (2,910)
Design speed, mph (km/h): 37 (60)
Additional features: Multiple working, cab signalling, cab-shore radio

types. As well as featuring the 20-cylinder version of the 645E3 power unit, they are unusual in having four-axle bogies, even more so in that they operate on metre gauge track. Some examples of the class have been transferred to the Ferrovia Centro-Atlântico.

TYPE DASH 9-40BBW DIESEL LOCOMOTIVE

Estrada de Ferro Vitória-Minas Railway (EFVM) DASH 9-40BBW

Brazil

The 22 Dash-9s are the most powerful locomotives in the Vitória a Minas Railway (EFVM) fleet, delivering the power through four two-axle bogies. This package is more than most locomotives on wider gauges and exceptional for metre gauge operation.

SUB-TYPES

The first 12 Dash-9s were delivered from General Electric in 1996, with two more batches of the modified Dash-9WC variant arriving in 1997 (10) and 2000 (15).

SPECIAL FEATURES

The additional power offered by this useful fleet is necessary for hauling enormously heavy trains of iron ore between Companhia Vale de Rio Doce (EFVM's parent company) mines and an Atlantic Ocean port near Vitória. Unlike their General Motors DDM-45 counterparts, the GE machines employ four two-axle bogies to deliver 4,160 hp on metre gauge track.

SPECIFICATION

Number series: 1101-1137
Total built: 37
Builder: General Electric
Date introduced: 1996
Track gauge, ft/ins (mm): 3 ft 3.375 in (1,000mm)
Axle arrangement: Bo-Bo-Bo-Bo
Power unit type: GE 7FDL-16efi
Transmission: Electric
Weight, tonnes: 160
Power rating, hp (kW): 4,160 (3,085)
Design speed, mph (km/h): 37 (60)
Additional features: multiple working, cab signalling, cab-shore radio

TYPE U12B DIESEL

Flumitrens (Central) U12B

In Rio de Janeiro, suburban services have been run by a new state-owned company Flumitrens (Fluminenses Trains) since 1996, set up by the Federal government. This new company was privatised in 1999, and is now also known as SuperVia.

SPECIAL FEATURES

The four-axle U12Bs of Rio de Janeiro suburban operator Flumitrens are amongst the oldest General Electric main line locomotives operating in Brazil, having been built almost 50 years ago.

SPECIFICATION

Builder: General Electric
Date introduced: 1957
Track gauge, ft/ins (mm): 3 ft 3.375 in (1,000)
Axle arrangement: Bo-Bo
Power unit type: GE 7FDL
Transmission: four 5GE-761-A1 traction motors
Weight, tonnes: 71
Power rating, hp (kW): 1200 (890)
Design speed, mph (km/h): 60 (96)
Additional features: multiple working, dynamic brakes

CLASS 2100 EMU

Companhia Paulista de Trens Metropolitanos (CPTM) Class 2100 emu (ex-RENFE)

Second-hand emus have been purchased from Spanish Railways (RENFE) to improve commuter services over the suburban lines in São Paulo city.

SPECIAL FEATURES

In recent years, the Companhia Brasileira de Trens Urbanos - CBTU (Brazilian Company of Urban Trains) and Ferrovias Paulistas - FEPASA, have been merged in a state-owned company: Companhia Paulista de Trens Metropolitanos - CPTM (Paulista Company of Metropolitan Trains). This new company is trying to provide a better level of commuter service, including the purchasing of new and modern trains. These include this fleet of 48 former RENFE Class 440 units acquired from 1998 after refurbishment in Spain. For their new role, double lights on both sides of the main headlamps were changed from red and yellow to red and white.

SPECIFICATION

Total built: 48
Builder: CAF
Date introduced: 1964 (on RENFE)
Track gauge, ft/ins (mm): 5 ft 3 in (1,600mm)
Unit configuration: T-M-T
Power supply system: 3 kV DC
Electrical equipment: Toshiba, Sepsa - rheostatic control, four DC traction motors
Power rating, hp (kW): 1,554 (1,160)
Design speed, mph (km/h): 87 (140)
Additional features: multiple working

CLASS 1400 DIESEL LOCOMOTIVE

Antofagasta and Bolivia Railway (FCAB) Class 1400

Antofagasta is the fourth-largest city in Chile today, and a principal centre for the export of silver, copper and nitrate. The self-supporting Antofagasta and Bolivia Railway has been Chile's largest and most profitable independent line, and Class 1400 covers a varied fleet of General Motors locomotives built between 1957-1969.

SUB-TYPES

Although under one type designation, there are a host of differences between the five batches, reflecting their second-hand nature in many cases.

PRINCIPAL MODIFICATIONS

A refurbishment programme is under way.

SPECIAL FEATURES

FCAB suffers from a 40 per cent loss of power from some of its locomotives on its mountain routes, which is prompting a move towards turbo diesel-electric designs. Growth in traffic has

prompted a worldwide search for additional power, and the 17 NF 210s were acquired from Canadian National's Newfoundland system and refurbished in Antofagasta workshops. Type GR 12 is also a recent purchase.

SPECIFICATION

Total built: 30
Builder: General Motors
Date introduced: NF 210 - 1957, GR 12U - 1961, GR 12 and GR 12UD - 1962, G 22CU - 1969
Track gauge, ft/ins (mm): 3 ft 3.375 in (1,000)
Axle arrangement: Co-Co
Power unit type: NF 210, GR 12U, GR 12, GR 12UD - EMD 12-567C, G 22CU - EMD 12-645E
Transmission: Electric
Weight, tonnes: NF 210, GR 12U, GR 12, GR 12UD - 90, G 22CU - 103
Power rating, hp (kW): NF 210 - 1,410 (1,044), GR 12U, GR 12, GR 12UD - 1,435 (1,063), G 22CU - 1,660 (1,230)
Design speed, mph (km/h): 95-97 (152-156)

EFE TERRASUR EMU

(EFE) Terrasur/Chilean State Railways

Chile

EFE has established a high-quality service between Santiago and Chillan known as Terrasur with three-car units offering a high specification of internal equipment and on-train catering facilties.

SPECIAL FEATURES

Claimed to be amongst some of the highest quality trains in South America, the UTS 444 units have six access doors, and seating for 200 in 2+2 rows with a central gangway. There is a catering facility, a large space for luggage, and public address system.

SPECIFICATION

Builder: GEE, MACOSA, GEE, MELCO. Acquired for Chile by the Company Española from RENFE (Spain)
Date introduced: 1974
Track gauge, ft/ins (mm): 5 ft 6 in (1,676)
Power supply system: 3kV DC
Design speed, mph (km/h): 87 (140)
Additional features: air conditioning, reclining seats, electromagnetic braking

METROTREN CLASS UT-440 EMU

Chilean State Railways (EFE) Class UT-440

The completion of deliveries of former regional electric units from Spanish National Railways (RENFE) has allowed the introduction of two through services each day between Santiago Alameda and San Fernando, together with intermediate services.

SPECIAL FEATURES

Sixteen former RENFE (Spanish National Railways) three-car units have been imported from Spain - twelve of them for Metrotren services. There is seating capacity for 260. A small number are out of service with accident damage.

OTHER COUNTRIES OPERATED

Spain (RENFE Class 440) and exports to Brazil.

SPECIFICATION

Number series: 101-112, 201-204
Total built: 253 (16 to Chile)
Builder: MACOSA, MELCO, CAF, GEE (Spain)
Date introduced: 1974 (1997 to Chile)
Track gauge, ft/ins (mm): 5 ft 6 in (1,676)
Unit configuration: M-T-T
Power supply system: 3kV DC
Electrical equipment: Four traction motors
Power rating, hp (kW): 1,565 (1,160)
Design speed, mph (km/h): 93 (150)
Additional features: Rheostatic brakes

TYPE TE-114K DIESEL LOCOMOTIVE

Union de Ferrocarriles de Cuba (UFC) TE-114K

Chile/Cuba

Between 1978-84, Cuba imported a reported 108 Voroshilovgrad-built TE-114K locomotives for passenger and freight work. Less than half the original fleet survives in service because of problems obtaining spare parts, and because of the current general conditions and shortages they can be seen anywhere on the system.

PRINCIPAL MODIFICATIONS

Revised cooling system.

SPECIAL FEATURES

UFC, the Cuban national railroad, imported three major classes of Soviet-built equipment after 1967. The TE-114Ks (the 'K' suffix indicates a Cuban variation of the basic design) have proved a useful resource, and required little modification apart from the radiators to cope with the different climatic conditions. The design has operated much better than the imported M62K

SPECIFICATION

Total built: 108
Builder: Voroshilovgrad
Date introduced: 1978
Track gauge, ft/ins (mm): 4ft 8.5in (1,435)
Axle arrangement: Co-Co
Power unit type: 5D49
Transmission: Electric, Jaricov
Weight, tonnes: 121
Power rating, hp (kW): 2,581 (1,912)
Design speed, mph (km/h): 75 (120)

and proved to be one of the fastest and most powerful locomotive types in Cuba. By 2003, only 45 locomotives still operated, with many others laid aside due to a lack of spare parts.

TYPE MX624 DIESEL LOCOMOTIVE

Union de Ferrocarriles de Cuba (UFC) MX624

Coincidentally with the same power rating as the Soviet Class TE-144K, this type comes from a completely different manufacturing source - Bombardier of Canada. In common with other Cuban types, availability has suffered through harsh economic as well as climatic conditions.

SPECIAL FEATURES

The arrival from 2002 of 20 replacement ex-Mexican General Electric locomotives (53001-53020) gave the weary MLW MX624s a break; they are now used primarly for long-distance passenger trains from Havana to Guantanamo, Santiago, Sancti Spiritus, Holguin, Bayamo/Manzanillo and Pinar de Rio. The new GEs are in charge of almost all the freight services. In October 2001, a new service started to run from Havana to Santiago and two MX624s have proved generally most reliable.

SPECIFICATION

Number series: 52401–52450
Total built: 50
Builder: Bombardier
Date introduced: 1975
Track gauge, ft/ins (mm): 4 ft 8.5 in (1,435)
Axle arrangement: Co-Co
Power unit type: Alco 251E
Transmission: Electric, GE
Weight, tonnes: 112
Power rating, hp (kW): 2,581 (1,912)
Design speed, mph (km/h): 84 (135)

TYPE MX620

Ferrocarriles de Guatemala (FEGUA) Class MX620

Despite closure in March 1996, Guatemala's main line railway has been reconstructed following washouts of the track both east and west of Guatemala city and in spite of occupation of the route by squatters. A plan has been drawn up to renovate most of the MX620 fleet to haul services.

SPECIAL FEATURES

The railway was revived between Guatemala City and the Atlantic by the end of 1998. As part of a 50-year operating concession awarded to the Railroad Development Corporation from the USA, the plan has been to restore seven of the ten MX620s to service, as well as five General Electric Class U10s (a third of the total). The aim is to run up to two trains per day on the Atlantic corridor.

SPECIFICATION

Number series: 1000-1009
Total built: 10
Builder: Bombardier
Date introduced: 1982
Track gauge, ft/ins (mm): 3 ft (914mm)
Axle arrangement: Co-Co
Power unit type: Alco/Bombardier 12-251-CE
Transmission: Electric, six GE-761-PA14 traction motors
Weight, tonnes: 96
Power rating, hp (kW): 2,000 (1,493)
Design speed, mph (km/h): 2,000 (1,493)
Additional features: multiple working, dynamic brakes

TYPE AC4400CW DIESEL LOCOMOTIVE

Transportación Ferroviaria Mexican (TFM) AC4400CW

These leased modern General Electric machines have played a key role in revitalising the motive power fleet of TFM, which took over the North East network of the former Mexican National Railways when it was privatised in 1997.

SPECIAL FEATURES

Already described in the USA section of this book, the GE AC4400CW was one of two types selected by TFM to upgrade its traction fleet following the commencement of its 50-year concession in 1997. Built at GE's Erie, Pennsylvania, plant, the locomotives were supplied in two batches - 50 in 1998, followed by 25 more in 2000. The operator, which is part-owned by Kansas City Southern, additionally leased 75 General Motors SD70-MACs. The TFM network includes the route between Mexico City to Neuvo Laredo, forming the main access to the US network but also providing operating challenges as the line descends from 7,400 ft at Mexico's capital to some 400 ft at the Mexico-US border.

SPECIFICATION

Number series: 2600-2674
Total built: 75
Builder: General Electric
Date introduced: 1998
Track gauge, ft/ins (mm): 4 ft 8.5 in (1,435)
Axle arrangement: Co-Co
Power unit type: GE 7FDL16 four-stroke 16-cylinder 'vee'
Transmission: electric - GE IGBT traction control system, microprocessor-controlled inverters, six nose-suspended AC traction motors
Weight, tonnes: 190
Power rating, hp (kW): 4,400 (3,284)
Design speed, mph (km/h): 74 (119)
Additional features: multiple working, dynamic braking

OTHER COUNTRIES OPERATED

The GE AC4400CW is also widely used by US railroads, with more than 2,200 examples built.

TYPE DL-535A/DL535B DIESEL LOCOMOTIVE

Transandino Railway/Peru Rail (FCT) DL-535A/DL535B

Alco and MLW have been major suppliers of motive power to Peru since the late 1950s, and Class DL 535 in a variety of versions continued to be produced in batches until 1976, Types DL-535A, DL-535B, and DL-535D. The locomotive type featured here is operated by the 914 mm gauge formerly state-owned South Eastern Railway that is now run by a consortium led by Sea Containers.

SPECIAL FEATURES

The employment of Class DL-535A is widespread across Peru, but the class is now in general decline following the arrival of more modern types, including off-the-shelf General Motors GT-26CWs which have around three times the power. Most have been converted to narrow gauge from standard.

SPECIFICATION

Builder: MLW
Date introduced: 1967
Track gauge, ft/ins (mm): 3ft 0 in (914)
Axle arrangement: Co-Co
Power unit type: Alco 251
Transmission: Electric
Weight, tonnes: 70
Power rating, hp (kW): 1,200 (895)
Design speed, mph (km/h): 50 (80)

TYPE C18-7I DIESEL LOCOMOTIVE

Ferrocarrilies del Estado (AFE) Class C18-7i

Uruguay's state railway administration, AFE, ordered ten C18-7i locomotives from General Electric with a view to increasing train weights and lengths over the country's standard gauge network.

SPECIFICATION

At the time of the 'C18s' arrival, timber traffic was expected to increase substantially between Montevideo, Rivera and Blanquillo and up to 50 per cent increase in train weights was envisaged. The locomotives are also used on AFE's few passenger services alongside a number of 825 hp Alsthom-built diesel electrics.

SPECIFICATION

Number series: 2001-2010
Total built: 10
Builder: General Electric, Canada
Date introduced: 1993
Track gauge, ft/ins (mm): 4 ft 8.5 in (1,435)
Axle arrangement: Co-Co
Power unit type: GE 8-7FDL
Transmission: Electric, Six GE-752 DC traction motors
Weight, tonnes: 102
Power rating, hp (kW): 2,025 (1,500)
Design speed, mph (km/h): 75 (120)
Additional features: Multiple working

Terminology

Terminology

Abbreviations are used throughout this book for manufacturers and equipment suppliers. The worldwide business is a constantly evolving one, and many companies are no longer active, having either gone out of existence, amalgamated, or been absorbed by larger organisations. Name changes are also a frequent occurrence.

These are some of the best known names:

A E GOODWIN
Australian licensee for Alco locomotive production, no longer active.

ABB
German-Swedish rolling stock manufacturer created from a merger of ASEA and Brown Boveri, becoming Adtranz and subsequently Bombardier Transportation.

ABB SCANDIA
Formerly Scandia Randers, Danish-based rolling stock manufacturer, becoming part of ABB.

ABB YORK
Former BR, later BREL rolling stock manufacturer, now closed.

ACEC
Belgian traction equipment manufacturer, now part of Alstom.

ADTRANZ
Trading name of DaimlerChrysler Rail Systems, German-based rolling stock manufacturer created by acquisitions and mergers of companies including ABB and AEG; subsequently acquired by Bombardier Transportation.

AEG
German traction equipment manufacturer, became part of Adtranz.

W ALEXANDER
Former British bus builder, limited rolling stock manufacturer, no longer active.

ALLAN
Netherlands rolling stock manufacturer, no longer active.

ALCO
US-headquartered locomotive and diesel engine manufacturer, no longer active.

ALSTHOM
French rolling stock manufacturer, became GEC Alsthom and then Alstom.

ALSTOM LHB
German rolling stock manufacturer Linke-Hofmann-Busch, subsequently acquired by Alstom.

ALSTOM
French-headquartered rolling stock manufacturer, with plants in several countries.

ANF
French rolling stock manufacturer, now part of Bombardier Transportation.

ANSALDO
Italian rolling stock manufacturer, merged with Breda to become Ansaldobreda.

ANSALDOBREDA
Italian rolling stock manufacturer.

ASEA
Swedish traction equipment manufacturer, subsequently part of Adtranz, now part of Bombardier Transportation.

BALDWIN

US locomotive manufacturer, no longer active.

ANDREW BARCLAY

British rolling stock manufacturer

BHEL

Indian locomotive manufacturer.

BN (LA BRUGEOISE ET NIVELLES)

Belgian rolling stock manufacturer, now part of Bombardier Transportation.

BR DONCASTER

British Rail rolling stock manufacturing and repair plant, now part of Bombardier Transportation.

BOMBARDIER TRANSPORTATION

Canadian-headquartered rolling stock manufacturer with plants in several countries.

BREDA

Italian rolling stock manufacturer, merged with Ansaldo to become Ansaldobreda.

BREL CREWE

Former British Rail rolling stock manufacturing and repair plant, now part of Bombardier Transportation.

BREL DERBY

Former British Rail rolling stock manufacturing and repair plant, no longer active.

BRISSONNEAU ET LOTZ

French locomotive manufacturer, no longer active.

BROWN BOVERI

German-Swiss traction equipment manufacturer, subsequently part of ABB.

BRUSH TRACTION

British rolling stock manufacturer.

BRYANSK

Soviet locomotive builder.

BUDD

US rolling stock manufacturer, no longer active.

CAF

Spanish rolling stock manufacturer.

CASARALTA

Italian rolling stock manufacturer, no longer active.

CASERTANE

Italian rolling stock manufacturer, no longer active.

CATERPILLAR

US diesel engine manufacturer.

CEM

French traction equipment manufacturer, no longer active.

CKD

Czechoslovak then Czech rolling stock and diesel engine manufacturer, part now forming CKD Vagónka, subsequently part-acquired by Siemens.

CKD VAGÓNKA

Czech rolling stock manufacturer.

CLW

Indian locomotive builder.

CLYDE ENGINEERING

Australian rolling stock manufacturer, licensee for General Motors, subsequently Walkers, now Evans Deakin Industries/EDI Rail.

COMENG

Australian rolling stock manufacturer.

CONSORZIO TREVI

Consortium formed by Fiat Ferroviaria (now Alstom), Ansaldo and Breda (the two last-mentioned now Ansaldobreda) and Firema to supply the Italian ETR500 high-speed trainsets.

CRAVENS

British rolling stock manufacturer, no longer active.

Terminology

CUMMINS

British diesel engine manufacturer.

DAEWOO HEAVY INDUSTRIES

Korean rolling stock manufacturer, subsequently part of Koros, now part of Rotem.

DAIMLER-BENZ

German diesel engine manufacturer, subsequently absorbed by MTU.

DALIAN

Chinese rolling stock and diesel engine manufacturer.

DATONG

Chinese rolling stock manufacturer.

DE DIETRICH

French rolling stock manufacturer, now part of Alstom.

DEUTZ

German rolling stock manufacturer, no longer active.

DLW

Indian locomotive manufacturer.

DUEWAG

German rolling stock manufacturer, subsequently acquired by Siemens.

DWA

East German then German rolling stock manufacturer, subsequently acquired by Bombardier Transportation.

EDI RAIL/EVANS DEAKIN INDUSTRIES

Australian rolling stock manufacturer.

ELECTROPUTERE

Romanian rolling stock manufacturer.

ENGLISH ELECTRIC

British rolling stock and diesel engine manufacturer, subsequently part of GEC, then GEC Alsthom.

FABLOK

Polish locomotive manufacturer, no longer active.

FFA

Swiss rolling stock manufacturer, no longer active.

FIAT FERROVIARIA

Italian rolling stock manufacturer, subsequently acquired by Alstom.

FIREMA

Italian rolling stock manufacturer.

GANZ-JENDRASSIK

Hungarian diesel engine manufacturer, no longer active.

GANZ-MÁVAG

Hungarian rolling stock manufacturer, subsequently Ganz-Hunslet.

GEC ALSTHOM

Anglo-French rolling stock manufacturer formed by a merger of GEC Traction and Alsthom, subsequently renamed Alstom.

GENERAL ELECTRIC (GE)

US locomotive and diesel engine manufacturer.

GENERAL MOTORS, CANADA

GM's locomotive and diesel engine manufacturing facility in London, Ontario, Canada.

GENERAL MOTORS, EMD

GM's locomotive and diesel engine manufacturing facility in La Grange, Illinois, USA.

GONINAN

Australian rolling stock manufacturer, licensee for GE in Australia, now United Goninan.

HÄGGLUNDS

Swedish rolling stock manufacturer, no longer active.

HCP

Polish rolling stock and diesel engine manufacturer, no longer active.

HELLENIC SHIPYARDS

Greek rolling stock manufacturer.

HENSCHEL

German locomotive manufacturer, subsequently Thyssen-Henschel, subsequently Adtranz.

HITACHI

Japanese rolling stock manufacturer.

HYUNDAI

Korean rolling stock manufacturer, subsequently part of Koros, now part of Rotem.

IKK CONSORTIUM

Consortium formed by Itochu, Kawasaki and Kinki Sharyo to fulfil KCRC (Hong Kong, China) contract.

JENBACHER WERKE

Austrian rolling stock and diesel engine manufacturer, no longer active.

JUNG

German rolling stock manufacturer, no longer active.

KAWASAKI

Japanese rolling stock manufacturer.

KHARKOV

Soviet then Ukrainian rolling stock and traction equipment manufacturer.

KHD-DEUTZ

German diesel engine manufacturer, no longer active.

KIM JONG TAE PLANT

North Korean rolling stock manufacturing facility.

KINKI SHARYO

Japanese rolling stock manufacturer.

KOLOMNA

Soviet then Russian locomotive and diesel engine manufacturer.

KOMATSU

Japanese diesel engine manufacturer.

KRAUSS-MAFFEI

German locomotive manufacturer, subsequently acquired by Siemens.

KRUPP

German locomotive manufacturer, no longer active.

LEW

East German then German rolling stock manufacturer, subsequently acquired by Adtranz.

LEYLAND

Former British bus builder, limited rolling stock manufacturer, no longer active.

LHB

See Alstom LHB.

LIAZ

Czechoslovak then Czech diesel engine manufacturer.

LUGANSK

Soviet then Ukrainian locomotive manufacturer, also known as Voroshilovgrad.

MACOSA

Spanish rolling stock manufacturer, licensee for GM and Mitsubishi, subsequently acquired by Alstom.

MAN

German rolling stock manufacturer, no longer active.

MAN

German diesel engine manufacturer, now MAN B&W Diesel.

MASCHINENFABRIK KIEL (MAK)

German locomotive manufacturer, now Vossloh Locomotives.

MBB

German rolling stock manufacturer, no longer active.

METRO CAMMELL

British rolling stock manufacturer, subsequently part of GEC Traction, now Alstom.

MGO

French diesel engine manufacturer, subsequently SACM-MGO, no longer active.

MIRRLEES

British diesel engine manufacturer, now MAN B&W Diesel.

MITSUBISHI

Japanese rolling stock manufacturer.

MLW

Canadian locomotive manufacturer, Alco licensee, subsequently acquired by Bombardier, no longer active.

MSV STUDÉNKA

Czech rolling stock manufacturer, subsequently acquired by CKD Vagónka.

MTE

French traction equipment manufacturer, subsequently part of Alsthom.

MTU

German diesel engine manufacturer.

NAPIER

British diesel engine manufacturer, no longer active.

NIPPON SHARYO

Japanese rolling stock manufacturer.

NOHAB

Swedish rolling stock manufacturer, one-time licensee for GM, no longer active.

NOVOCHERKASSK

Soviet then Russian locomotive manufacturer.

OM

Italian rolling stock manufacturer, no longer active.

ORENSTEIN & KOPPEL

German locomotive manufacturer, no longer active.

PAFAWAG

Polish locomotive manufacturer, now part of Bombardier Transportation.

PAXMAN

British diesel engine manufacturer, now MAN B&W Diesel.

PERKINS

British diesel engine manufacturer.

PIELSTICK

French diesel engine manufacturer, now SEMT Pielstick.

PISTOIESI

Italian rolling stock manufacturer, no longer active.

QISHUYAN

Chinese rolling stock and diesel engine manufacturer.

RADE KONCAR

Yugoslav then Croatian rolling stock manufacturer.

REGGIANE

Italian rolling stock manufacturer, no longer active.

RIVA (RVR)

Soviet then Latvian rolling stock manufacturer.

ROBERT STEPHENSON & HAWTHORN

British rolling stock manufacturer, no longer active.

ROHR INDUSTRIES

US rolling stock manufacturer, no longer active.

SACM

French diesel engine manufacturer, subsequently SACM-MGO.

SCHINDLER

Swiss rolling stock manufacturer, subsequently part of Bombardier Transportation.

SCHNEIDER/SCHNEIDER-JEUMONT

French traction equipment manufacturer, no longer active.

SEMT PIELSTICK

See Pielstick.

SFAC

French rolling stock manufacturer, no longer active.

SGP

Austrian rolling stock and diesel engine manufacturer, subsequently acquired by Siemens.

SIEMENS

German-headquartered rolling stock manufacturer with plants in several countries.

SIFANG

Chinese rolling stock manufacturer.

SIG

Swiss rolling stock manufacturer, subsequently acquired by Fiat Ferroviaria.

SKODA

Czechoslovak then Czech rolling stock manufacturer.

SLM

Swiss rolling stock manufacturer, partly surviving as Winpro.

SMZ DUBNICA

Czechoslovak rolling stock manufacturer, no longer active.

SOFER

Italian rolling stock manufacturer, no longer active.

SOREFAME

Portuguese rolling stock manufacturer, subsequently part of Adtranz.

STADLER

Swiss rolling stock manufacturer.

STEZ

Joint-venture rolling stock manufacturer formed by Siemens and Zhuzhou, China.

STUDÉNKA

See MSV Studénka.

SULZER

Swiss diesel engine manufacturer, no longer active.

SWEDLOC

Swedish locomotive manufacturing consortium, no longer active.

Terminology

TALBOT
German rolling stock manufacturer, now part of Bombardier.

TALGO
Spanish rolling stock manufacturer.

TANGSHAN
Chinese rolling stock manufacturer.

THUNES
Norwegian rolling stock manufacturer, no longer active.

THYSSEN-HENSCHEL
See Henschel.

TIBB
Italian traction equipment manufacturer, subsequently part of Adtranz.

TOKYU CAR
Japanese rolling stock manufacturer.

TOSHIBA
Japanese rolling stock manufacturer.

TÜLOMSAS
Turkish rolling stock manufacturer.

UERDINGEN
German rolling stock manufacturer, subsequently acquired by Siemens.

UNION CARRIAGE & WAGON
South African rolling stock manufacturer.

VALMET
Finnish rolling stock manufacturer, no longer active.

VEVEY
Swiss rolling stock manufacturer, subsequently acquired by Bombardier Transportation.

VOLVO
Swedish diesel engine manufacturer.

VOROSHILOVGRAD
Soviet then Ukrainian locomotive manufacturer, also known as Lugansk.

WAGGON-UNION
German rolling stock manufacturer, no longer active.

WALKERS
Australian rolling stock manufacturer, now Evans Deakin Industries/EDI Rail.

WÄRTSILÄ
Finnish diesel engine manufacturer.

WERKSPOOR
Netherlands rolling stock manufacturer, no longer active.

ZHUZHOU
Chinese rolling stock manufacturer.

ZIYANG
Chinese rolling stock manufacturer.

Photographic Credits

The authors and publishers thank the following photographers and organisations for their contributions of images to this book. Their pictures appear on the page numbers shown.

Alcan Mass Transportation Systems: 378

ALSTOM Transport: 21, 133, 212, 220, 246, 278 (lower)

Ansaldobreda: 280, 281, 299

Felipe Arando: 351

Apurva Bahadur: 68

John C Baker: 194, 203, 204, 211, 213, 232, 373, 374, 404

Edward Barnes: 27, 102, 180, 282, 295, 450

Marcel Benoit: 480

Paul Bigland: 109, 110

John Bollans: 128, 129

Bombardier Transportation: 25, 103, 222, 252, 298, 318, 361, 377

Colin Boocock: 24, 35, 36, 37, 38, 40, 42, 50, 51, 52, 55, 58, 63, 64, 79, 106, 107, 122, 195, 200, 205, 243, 253, 256, 257, 264, 268, 273, 279, 285, 290, 294, 300, 301, 303, 316, 320, 321, 322, 324, 347, 359, 362, 368, 406, 444, 453

D Burns: 124

China Northern Locomotive and Rolling Stock Industry (Group): 82, 104, 111

Damian M Clement: 100, 251

CLW: 69, 71, 72, 73, 74

Murdoch Currie: 277

Alex Dasi-Sutton: 289, 292

DLW: 75, 78

Bruce Evans: 54, 61, 114, 115, 116, 117, 118, 121

Angel Ferrer: 458

Thomas E Fischer: 99

Flåm's Photoservice: 296

Ian Francis: 56

FreightLink: 126

Dave Gallie: 156

Aharon Gazit: 83, 196 (lower), 389

GE Transportation: 103, 478

Robin J Gibbons: 59, 62

Norman Griffiths: 43, 48, 166, 226, 239, 259 (lower), 283, 363, 479

Ernst van Gulden: 333, 379

K K Gupta: 70, 76

Andrzej Harassek: 304, 305, 307, 309

Ken Harris: 158, 159, 161, 163, 164, 165,
    201, 202, 230, 233 (upper), 244, 267,
    297, 371 (both), 392, 394, 395, 396,
    397, 398, 399, 402, 403, 407, 408, 409,
    410, 411, 412

David Haydock: 120, 175, 197, 269, 323,
    355, 365, 369

Mel Holley: 381

P J Horton: 319, 340, 341

Howard Johnston: 119, 160, 169, 170, 171,
    172 (2), 173, 176, 204 (lower), 207,
    208, 209, 210, 214, 215, 216, 219, 223,
    231 (upper), 234, 237, 238, 262, 263,
    265, 266, 275, 286, 302, 306, 308, 311,
    312, 314, 315, 317, 356, 366, 380, 382,
    383, 384, 387 (lower), 388, 390, 391
    (both), 393, 366, 370, 385, 400, 401,
    405

Ben Jones: 168, 177, 206, 217, 218, 221

Ferenc Joó: 260

JR Freight: 98

Piotr Kazimierowski: 310

KCRC: 66

Artemis Klonos: 255

Flávio Francesconi Lage: 462, 463, 464, 465,
    466, 467, 468, 469, 471

Peter Lais: 460

Michal Málek: 185, 190, 192, 193

Colin J Marsden: 415, 425, 426, 428, 441,
    443

Andrew Marshall: 376

MTRC: 67

Ralph Oakes-Garnett: 77, 151

Wilhelm Pflug: 112

Bryan Philpott: 344, 348, 349, 350, 352,
    353

Neil Pulling: 198, 224, 225, 227, 228, 235,
    240, 241, 242, 274, 343, 345, 346, 358

RAI: 80

Tim Rogers: 421

Larry Russell: 461

Robert Sandusky: 416, 418, 419

SBB: 364

João Bosco Setti: 470

Siemens Transportation Systems: 65, 105,
    162, 229, 245

Tony Sissons: 414, 417, 420, 421 (upper),
    422, 423, 424, 427, 430, 432, 434, 435,
    436, 437, 438, 439, 440, 442

Milan Srámek: 178, 179, 184, 186, 187
    (lower), 188, 189, 191, 245 (upper),
    326, 338, 339, 446

SRO: 108

Robin Stewart-Smith: 375

Stanislaw J Szewczak: 259 (upper)

Daniel Thomas: 473, 474

Sandy Thompson: 167

Tokyu Car: 89

Wolfram Veith: 84, 85, 87, 90, 94, 95, 96,
    97, 130, 131, 247, 313

Marcel Vleugels: 20, 22, 26: 33, 34, 44, 45,
    47, 53, 57, 93, 123, 258, 476

Quintus Vosman: 28, 29, 30, 31, 32: 81, 174,
    233 (lower), 248, 250, 270, 271, 272,
    276, 278 (upper), 287, 288, 291, 293,
    342, 360, 387 (upper)

David C Warner: 357, 445, 449, 451, 452,
    454

Brian Webber: 132, 134, 135, 136, 137, 138, 140, 142, 145, 146, 147, 148, 149, 150, 152, 153, 154, 155, 372, 431
Michael Wild: 183, 196 (upper), 231 (lower), 236, 284, 325, 327, 328, 329, 330, 331, 334, 335, 336, 337, 367
Andrew Wiltshire: 386
Stefan Wölfli: 475
Philip Wormald: 23, 46, 60, 199, 254, 447
Zheleznodorozhnoe Delo/Ivan Khil'ko: 332

Additional research by Mel Holley
and Ben Jones.